# Bridging the Gaps in Our Efforts to Combat Human Trafficking

This book brings together a rich international and cross-sectional collection of articles that examine the current knowledge on gaps in the research realm or intervention development as they relate to our effort to combat human trafficking/modern-day slavery. The anthology includes chapters from established scholars, practitioners, and persons with lived experience.

Modern-day slavery or human trafficking has attracted much attention from around the world in the past few decades and engendered significant growth in counter-trafficking interventions as well as empirical research on related prevalence estimation and program evaluation. However, significant gaps remain in our knowledge on how to address the crime. Understanding these gaps is essential in informing research, policy, and general response protocols. This anthology represents a rich international collection of contributions (both academic and non-academic) that offer a comprehensive overview of the most up-to-date gaps in our response protocols. The articles also offer recommendations that, if acknowledged, could help to impact the prevalence of human trafficking at a local and international level.

This book was originally published as a special issue of the *Journal of Human Trafficking.*

**John Winterdyk** has published over 40 books and dozens of peer-reviewed articles. He has (co)guest edited six special journal issues and co-edited three trafficking-related books. He is currently working on several human trafficking–related projects, a Special Issue on trafficking, and a new human trafficking–related book.

**Sheldon Zhang** has been active in research on transnational human trafficking and organized crime for more than two decades. His current research projects span from Africa, Asia, to Latin America. He has authored/co-authored 14 books and edited volumes, and more than 150 scholarly journal articles, book chapters, and technical reports.

# Bridging the Gaps in Our Efforts to Combat Human Trafficking

***Edited by***
**John Winterdyk and Sheldon Zhang**

Routledge
Taylor & Francis Group
LONDON AND NEW YORK

First published 2026
by Routledge
4 Park Square, Milton Park, Abingdon, Oxon OX14 4RN

and by Routledge
605 Third Avenue, New York, NY 10158

*Routledge is an imprint of the Taylor & Francis Group, an informa business*



*British Library Cataloguing in Publication Data*
A catalogue record for this book is available from the British Library

ISBN13: 978-1-041-08278-1 (hbk)
ISBN13: 978-1-041-08279-8 (pbk)
ISBN13: 978-1-003-64465-1 (ebk)

DOI: 10.4324/9781003644651

Typeset in Minion Pro
by Newgen Publishing UK

**Publisher's Note**
The publisher accepts responsibility for any inconsistencies that may have arisen during the conversion of this book from journal articles to book chapters, namely the inclusion of journal terminology.

# Contents

# Citation Information

The chapters in this book were originally published in the *Journal of Human Trafficking*, volume 10, issue 2 (2024). When citing this material, please use the original page numbering for each article, as follows:

**Introduction**

John Winterdyk and Sheldon Zhang
*Journal of Human Trafficking*, volume 10, issue 2 (2024), pp. 231

**Foreword**

Sheldon Zhang and John Winterdyk
*Journal of Human Trafficking*, volume 10, issue 2 (2024), pp. 232–237

**Chapter 1**

*Disrupting Human Trafficking in Canada: A Case Study in the Gaps of Meeting the UN Trafficking Protocols*
John Winterdyk (ret.) and Alexandra Ford
*Journal of Human Trafficking*, volume 10, issue 2 (2024), pp. 238–252

**Chapter 2**

*Does Anyone Care? — The Prevalence of Forced Labor Among Kenyan Migrant Workers and the Glaring Need for Better Labor Conditions in GCC Countries*
Sheldon Zhang, Nell Compernolle, Kyle Vincent, Sarah Lord, and Kareem Kysia
*Journal of Human Trafficking*, volume 10, issue 2 (2024), pp. 253–270

**Chapter 3**

*The Half-Built Road: Exploring the Impediments to Justice for Victims of Labor Trafficking*
Chase Childress, Amy Farrell, Amelia Wagner, Shawn Bhimani, and Kayse Lee Maass
*Journal of Human Trafficking*, volume 10, issue 2 (2024), pp. 271–288

**Chapter 4**

*Critical Gaps in Human Trafficking Research: A Reflection on Six Years of Learning Through the Program to End Modern Slavery (PEMS)*
Abigail Long and Casey Branchini Risko
*Journal of Human Trafficking*, volume 10, issue 2 (2024), pp. 289–301

**Chapter 5**

*When Victims of Modern Slavery Became Offenders: The Unravelling of the UK's Modern Slavery Agenda*
David Gadd and Rose Broad
*Journal of Human Trafficking*, volume 10, issue 2 (2024), pp. 302–315

**Chapter 6**

*Toward Journalism on Human Trafficking That is Trauma-Informed, Hope-Based, and Solutions-Oriented*
Kirsten Foot
*Journal of Human Trafficking*, volume 10, issue 2 (2024), pp. 316–321

**Chapter 7**

*Forced Labour and Accountability in Supply Chains: The Role of the Private Sector*
Matt Friedman
*Journal of Human Trafficking*, volume 10, issue 2 (2024), pp. 322–329

**Chapter 8**

*Mind the Gap(s)? Evidence and UK Policymaking on Human Trafficking and Modern Slavery*
Alex Balch and Olivia Hesketh
*Journal of Human Trafficking*, volume 10, issue 2 (2024), pp. 330–338

**Chapter 9**

*Making Statistics on Human Trafficking Work*
Jan Van Dijk
*Journal of Human Trafficking*, volume 10, issue 2 (2024), pp. 339–345

**Chapter 10**

*Practitioner Reflection: Reliance on Informal and Gig Economies Leaves LGBTQ+ Populations with Fewer Economic Choices and Greater Vulnerability to Trafficking*
Mark Kavenagh, Mackenzie Stoeltje, and Meredith Dank
*Journal of Human Trafficking*, volume 10, issue 2 (2024), pp. 346–355

**Chapter 11**

*A Long Journey: Integrating Caste in Anti-Trafficking Interventions*
Tarini J. Shipurkar, Shakila Khatoon, Mayank Sinha, and Pradeep Narayanan
*Journal of Human Trafficking*, volume 10, issue 2 (2024), pp. 356–360

**Chapter 12**

*Climate Change, Forced Migration and Trafficking in Persons: Risk of Young Women in Rural Cambodia*
Puthborey Phon and Rumi Kato Price
*Journal of Human Trafficking*, volume 10, issue 2 (2024), pp. 361–367

**Chapter 13**

Primary *Prevention of Sex Trafficking: Time to Move the Needle on Demand Reduction*
Marcel van der Watt
*Journal of Human Trafficking*, volume 10, issue 2 (2024), pp. 368–373

**Chapter 14**
*Hot Soup and a Blanket Don't Mean You're Safe from Human Trafficking – Gaps in the System of Receiving and Supporting Women from Ukraine in Poland After the Russian Invasion*
Zbigniew Lasocik
*Journal of Human Trafficking*, volume 10, issue 2 (2024), pp. 374–382

**Chapter 15**
*Criminalizing Human Trafficking Has Not Made a Difference: A Law Enforcement Failure*
Yvon Dandurand
*Journal of Human Trafficking*, volume 10, issue 2 (2024), pp. 383–387

**Chapter 16**
*The Canada Declaration for a Human Trafficking and Slavery Free Canada: Justice or Just Words?*
Holly Wood
*Journal of Human Trafficking*, volume 10, issue 2 (2024), pp. 388–390

**Chapter 17**
*The Capacity of the International Criminal Court to Fight Human Trafficking*
Filip Vojta
*Journal of Human Trafficking*, volume 10, issue 2 (2024), pp. 391–402

**Chapter 18**
*How Do Local Efforts Address a Global Issue? Communities Need Good Data*
Annjanette R. Alejano-Steele, Amanda A. Finger, and Kara Napolitano
*Journal of Human Trafficking*, volume 10, issue 2 (2024), pp. 403–410

# Notes on Contributors

**Annjanette R. Alejano-Steele**, Laboratory to Combat Human Trafficking, Denver, Colorado, USA; Metropolitan State University of Denver, Denver, Colorado, USA.

**Alex Balch**, Department of Politics, University of Liverpool, Liverpool, UK; Modern Slavery and Human Rights Policy and Evidence Centre, London, UK.

**Shawn Bhimani**, D'More McKim School of Business, Northeastern University, Boston, Massachusetts, USA.

**Rose Broad**, Department of Criminology, University of Manchester, Manchester, UK.

**Chase Childress**, School of Criminology and Criminal Justice, Northeastern University, Boston, Massachusetts, USA.

**Nell Compernolle**, NORC at the University of Chicago, Chicago, USA.

**Yvon Dandurand**, School of Criminology, University of the Fraser Valley, Abbotsford, Vancouver, BC, Canada; International Centre for Criminal Law Reform, Vancouver, Canada.

**Meredith Dank**, Marron Institute, New York University, New York, USA.

**Amy Farrell**, School of Criminology and Criminal Justice, Northeastern University, Boston, Massachusetts, USA.

**Amanda A. Finger**, Laboratory to Combat Human Trafficking, Denver, Colorado, USA.

**Kirsten Foot**, iSchool, Faculty Affiliate, Center for Human Rights, University of Washington, Seattle, Washington, USA.

**Alexandra Ford**, ('The Laughing Survivor'), Kamloops, British Columbia, Canada.

**Matt Friedman**, The Mekong Club, Hong Kong, China.

**David Gadd**, Department of Criminology, University of Manchester, Manchester, UK.

**Olivia Hesketh**, Modern Slavery and Human Rights Policy and Evidence Centre, London, UK.

**Mark Kavenagh**, Evident Consulting, Bangkok, Thailand.

**Shakila Khatoon**, Praxis Institute for Participatory Practices, New Delhi, India.

**Kareem Kysia**, NORC at the University of Chicago, Chicago, USA.

**Zbigniew Lasocik**, Human Trafficking Studies Center, University of Warsaw, Warsaw, Poland.

**Abigail Long**, The United States Department of State, Office to Monitor and Combat Trafficking in Persons, Washington, D.C., USA.

**Sarah Lord**, NORC at the University of Chicago, Chicago, USA.

**Kayse Lee Maass**, College of Engineering, Northeastern University, Boston, Massachusetts, USA.

**Kara Napolitano**, Laboratory to Combat Human Trafficking, Denver, Colorado, USA.

**Pradeep Narayanan**, Praxis Institute for Participatory Practices, New Delhi, India.

**Puthborey Phon**, School of Criminology and Justice Studies, University of Massachusetts, Lowell, USA.

**Rumi Kato Price**, Department of Psychiatry, Washington University, School of Medicine, St. Louis, Missouri, USA.

**Casey Branchini Risko**, The United States Department of State, Office to Monitor and Combat Trafficking in Persons, Washington, D.C., USA.

**Tarini J. Shipurkar**, Praxis Institute for Participatory Practices, New Delhi, India.

**Mayank Sinha**, Praxis Institute for Participatory Practices, New Delhi, India.

**Mackenzie Stoeltje**, Marron Institute, New York University, New York, USA.

**Jan Van Dijk**, Department of Criminology, Tilburg University, Tilberg, the Netherlands; Netherlands Institute for the Study of Crime and Law Enforcement, Amsterdam, the Netherlands.

**Kyle Vincent**, Independent Consultant, Ottawa, Canada.

**Filip Vojta**, Department for Criminal Law and Legal Philosophy, Institute for Criminal Law and Criminology, University of Bern, Bern, Switzerland.

**Amelia Wagner**, School of Criminology and Criminal Justice, Northeastern University, Boston, Massachusetts, USA.

**Marcel van der Watt**, National Center on Sexual Exploitation, Research Institute, Washington, D.C., USA.

**John Winterdyk**, Mount Royal University, Canada.

**Holly Wood**, Researcher, Marketing, Communications and Volunteer Lead, BRAVE Education.

**Sheldon Zhang**, University of Massachusetts Lowell, Lowell, Massachusetts, USA.

# Foreword

Sheldon Zhang and John Winterdyk

Following a successful session on human trafficking at the European Society of Conference annual meeting in Malaga, Spain, in September 2022, both editors of the special issue engaged in several conversations with the presenters at the conference, which sparked the idea for this special issue. As veteran researchers and writers on trafficking in persons (TIP), we both felt, despite much progress made in the field, a sense of inadequacy and narrow-mindedness in how we perceive and respond to human trafficking. Perhaps this was because anti-trafficking research and intervention remain nascent in its development but growing in status as a social science and policy topic.

Our primary purpose was to use this special issue to discuss the (conspicuous) gaps in our current knowledge of research and intervention in anti-trafficking efforts worldwide. Our recruitment approach was straightforward, albeit somewhat conventional; we relied on our professional networks and contributors to reach those actively involved in either research or programming on anti-trafficking topics.

We intended this special issue to be broad in topical areas and inclusive in the authors' analytical approach because we do not profess to understand what and where the significant gaps lie in current efforts to combat human trafficking. As a result, we invited a diverse group of experienced researchers and practitioners to contribute to this project. More importantly, we sought voices from the global south for inclusion in this volume, e.g., India, Cambodia, Hong Kong, and South Africa. We also recognize that there are far more geographical regions and labor sectors that are not addressed in this volume. We must acknowledge that our "inclusive" endeavor was far from perfect since the timing and our proposed deadline were inconvenient for a few potential contributors, thus restricting the geographical and topical coverage. Still, we are happy with what we have accomplished, as the readers will see the two broad categories of the articles included here: (1) short and poignant articles (10 in total) representing viewpoints from front-line organizations and active researchers who speak directly to the challenges of meeting their objectives and mandates; and (2) eight full-length evidence-informed articles that engage in thorough analyses to expose specific gaps in current anti-trafficking efforts.

## Introduction to the Short Essays

Relative to other topics in the broad disciplines such as inequality, labor rights, or criminal justice, research on human trafficking is still a comparatively fledgling interdisciplinary field in which scholars of increasing diversity have become significantly more engaged in the topic and its diverse issues. While all covered under the broad umbrella of human trafficking, we attempted to include many fronts. In these short essays, we imposed word limits to encourage more scholars and practitioners to succinctly highlight gaps in current countermeasures or research endeavors that have either been ignored or rarely attended to. These short essays significantly improved our coverage of a special issue and allowed us to highlight areas where future intervention development research or research on human trafficking, in general, may evolve. As the readers will hopefully discover, the diversity of our captured gaps is impressive.

Some authors argue for specific structural inadequacies in their respective national contexts, while others bring forth particularly vulnerable populations that have received limited attention or have mainly been overlooked. A few authors point out inadequate criminal justice strategies for human trafficking and insufficient coordination between justice providers. Still, a few other authors focused on topics that only began to attract attention in recent years in this field. For example, the anti-trafficking intervention programs have recently embraced climate change as a significant cause contributing to forced migration by vulnerable populations from developing countries, thus increasing exposure to forced labor and sex trafficking situations. Phon and Rice use the trafficking situation in Cambodia to illustrate the devastating impacts of climate change and resultant natural and manmade disasters. As a Tier 3 country in the least developed part of Southeast Asia, Cambodia remains a country of source, transit, and destination of trafficking in persons (TIP). The challenges are immense, but both authors propose linking climate-induced disasters and forced migration to TIP responses, which may prove more effective than past efforts.

Further, we have included emerging topics that are also timely in the current international context. Lasocik, from the University of Warsaw in Poland, was among the first academics to raise the issue of potential human trafficking violations against the many young women and girls who fled Ukraine after the Russian invasion. Because large-scale military conflicts inevitably subject large numbers of civilians to vulnerable conditions, the war in Ukraine is no different. Millions of Ukrainians, mostly women and children, crossed into Poland with little more than the clothes on their backs. Through interviews at the refugee reception centers, the author and his colleagues discovered that few were even thinking about the potential consequence of human trafficking that might befall these refugees. Losocik argued that while hot soup and a blanket are necessary for immediate survival, Western countries must do more to protect the refugees from becoming the prime targets for human trafficking. The impact of armed conflict frequently spills over national boundaries; currently, the capacity of the International Criminal Court (ICC) to combat human trafficking activities has largely been absent despite UN Sustainable Development Goal 16. Vojta from the University of Bern points out this glaring gap by analyzing the ICC's procedural capacity to combat human trafficking and how domestic investigations and prosecutions can be elevated to the international level.

Aside from timely and emerging topics, we have also included topics that have been widely covered in other places. For example, problems in TIP data science (e.g., data collection, measurement, sampling strategy, and prevalence estimation) have received much attention over the past two decades in the TIP research community. Although it is an ongoing problem, it is essential to continue the discussion because data science, in its broadest sense, is the foundation of this emerging research field and determines the quality of our future scientific inquiries. The research community has made much progress on human trafficking in the past two decades, and scientific literature has grown significantly. Among the most significant progress in research on human trafficking is the increasing publications based on primary data collection and improvement in measurement and prevalence estimation techniques. The research community has made significant efforts to create consensus on the standard indicators on the proverbial challenge of establishing the threshold to identify our target populations. Even when primary data collection remains a luxury for many researchers, those first-hand cases collected by service providers and government agencies are also actively pursued by those equipped with advanced training in statistics in their application of the multiple-system estimation (MSE). By relying on identified human trafficking cases across more than one social service agency, researchers can estimate the population size and other profiles of their study population.

The improvement of empirical data is sorely needed by community-based agencies that seek to improve and refine their anti-trafficking efforts. For example, Alejano-Steele and colleagues at the Laboratory to Combat Human Trafficking [LCHT] in Colorado reviewed lessons learned from their agency's efforts to measure progress in Colorado. The Denver-based Laboratory to initiated its anti-trafficking efforts in 2005, the same year that federal grant monies poured into Colorado to establish coalitions to conduct law enforcement and service provider training and create protocols to support victims of human trafficking. On the global level, veteran researcher Jan Van Dijk, emeritus professor in victimology at Tilburg University, pointed out the progress made by major international organizations in bringing about multi-source datasets on trafficking victims as more credible sources of information on the true prevalence of human trafficking and argued for consolidation and comprehensive analysis for better scientific inquiry and policymaking on a global level.

Readers will find equally compelling gaps in current anti-trafficking programs and research in several other aspects. Readers will notice our emphasis on a variety of international voices. Dandurand from Canada points out that criminalizing human trafficking worldwide, starting from the UN Convention and its related protocols on trafficking in persons and migrant smuggling, has not produced adequate law enforcement response or strengthened international cooperation. This lackluster situation sharply contrasts the increased numbers of potential trafficking victims, as various studies and agency reports reported. With the new technologies, traffickers are becoming increasingly more sophisticated, posing further challenges to law enforcement agencies worldwide. Wood from BRAVE Education points out the sharp discrepancies between well-intended and lofty political and legal rhetoric and the lack of concrete enforcement. Vojta from Switzerland points out that the transnational nature of human trafficking activities should push the intervention field toward exploring the potential of the ICC. ICC can contribute to the fight against human trafficking, but its role and legal capacity have been mainly neglected in current discourses. The author offers several concrete solutions to elevate human trafficking to an international crime level and bring the ICC into the fight through effective prosecution.

## Full-Length Articles

Our full-length articles, however, mainly address systemic problems that are not necessarily unknown but have long remained understudied. Unlike the short essays, authors in this section were asked to develop a comprehensive analysis and apply conventional research paper format to present methods, data analysis and findings. While the range of a topics is somewhat limited due to the length of these articles, they nonetheless represent a series of well-developed and conceptualized analyses on the most current state of research in the TIP field.

Our emphasis on identifying and analyzing gaps in current anti-trafficking efforts made our collection of full-length analytical papers critical in their findings and discussions. Most authors called out structural and systemic obstacles in national response plans, while others pointed out the need to know the impact of the existing program. For example, Winterdyk and Ford point out that despite being a Tier 1 country, Canada needs more coordination in its counter-trafficking effort. Applying a case study method, the author drew on a wide range of examples and existing data to highlight a "quilted patchwork" that is Canada's current response to trafficking. Foot's article points out that news media hold significant promise in searching for and promoting solutions to human trafficking and bringing greater attention to TIP issues.

Zhang and colleagues from National Opinion Research Center (NORC) at the University of Chicago carried out a large-scale social survey of recently returned migrant workers in the metropolitan area of Nairobi, Kenya, and the findings confirm what many news stories in recent years reported on the abuses of Kenyan migrant workers in the Gulf Cooperation Council (GCC) countries. Findings from this study help bridge a critical gap in human trafficking research: the lack of reliable data and how best to collect it threaten the effectiveness of existing and proposed interventions in the GCC. Using rigorous estimation strategies, this team of researchers found victimization of forced labor pervasive in this population. Although abuses among migrant workers are not uncommon in wealthy nations, such high rates of forced labor violations in GCC countries are rare, if not unprecedented, in current prevalence estimation research and call for massive systemic efforts to address the situation.

In their full-length article, Childress and colleagues at Northeastern University explore the varied obstacles that undermine the prosecution of human traffickers in the U.S. criminal justice system. Taking a case study approach, the team examined the criminal legal process of five different cases, identifying barriers that derailed offender prosecution and stymied victim support. The findings were based on rich data from legal advocate case records, client interview notes, correspondence between stakeholders, court records, and stakeholder interviews.

Based on their direct observations of funded research and intervention because of their official positions, Long and Risko provide a rich account of significant gaps in current trafficking research. Using the Program to End Modern Slavery's (PEMS) platform, the authors explore the progress and current challenges in searching for and evaluating various anti-trafficking interventions. PEMS represents the latest efforts by the U.S. government to implement anti-trafficking intervention and research worldwide, focusing on what works and how to evaluate and build the knowledge base for best practices.

In response to the current focus on negative news stories, Foot uses her full-length article to argue for a new orientation in the news media, focusing on constructive solutions to the reported problems. Significant social impact may be realized through such constructive journalism. The author highlights several open-access resources designed to catalyze better journalism on human trafficking.

Balch and Hesketh from the University of Liverpool examine four critical gaps in the evidence-policy relationship on human trafficking in the UK: prioritization, epistemology, synchronization and trust. Drawing on multiple sources, the authors point to a growing consensus on improving research on human trafficking and creating appropriate conditions for a productive evidence-policy system.

Finally, Friedman's article calls for greater attention to and transparency of the supply chain, where the private sector has an essential role in our fight against modern slavery through ethical business practices. Because of the complex global supply chains and the myriad of suppliers and subcontractors, companies need to work together to self-police their products or services against potential human rights abuses and exploitative labor practices. Solutions to reduce exploitative labor practices and human rights abuses include strict supply chain management policies, transparency in their operations, and oversight through a collaborative partnership with civil society organizations. The tremendous purchasing power affords the private sector a unique and powerful position to reduce the risks of modern slavery in their operations and supply chains.

## Sensitive and Exciting New Directions

While striving for inclusivity, we are keenly aware that some of the viewpoints expressed in this collection can be controversial, and we are not naïve about or blind to the political and cultural sensitivity in the identified gaps. For example, van der Watt from the National Center on Sexual Exploitation calls for a shift of counter-sex trafficking measures toward demand reduction. The overlapping nature of prostitution and sex trafficking requires that for any effective interventions to be effective, countermeasures must hold sex buyers accountable. Van der Watt argues that current anti-sex trafficking efforts frequently ignore "the glaring role of sex buyers in ringfencing sex trafficking crimes, shrouding traffickers, and obscuring victims." Although prostitution remains illegal in most parts of the United States, there is no shortage of advocates elsewhere, particularly in the Western world, who argue that sex work, when brought into the legal marketplace and properly regulated, may help curtail sex trafficking.

In another example, many anti-trafficking efforts since the beginning of the new millennium in India have focused on sex trafficking and were funded by institutions high on Western moral principles that pursued a raid-rescue-and-rehabilitation model in programming. Instead of welcoming these externally funded programs, open resentment and hostility often emerged among the communities toward these moral-driven intervention services. After witnessing years of ineffective anti-trafficking efforts, Shipurkar and colleagues from Praxis Institute for Participatory Practices in New Delhi, India, use the Nat and Bediya communities as examples to advocate a holistic and participatory model that recognizes the complexities of caste-based discrimination, limited livelihood options and deep-rooted social norms toward sex trade. Their approach aims to foster agency and empower community members to redefine their identities and improve livelihood choices.

We are also cognizant of the multiplicity of causes for trafficking victimization and complexity in any suggested solutions. For example, Kavenagh, Stoeltje, and Dank highlighted the challenges in assisting vulnerable members of the LGBTQ+ populations and the inadequate effort to address predicaments unique to these individuals. In addition to the typical vulnerabilities at-risk populations face, such as poverty, domestic violence and abuse, homelessness, unemployment, and migration status, LGBTQ+ individuals face community and workplace stigma due to their gender identities. Their frequent reliance on insecure informal gig economies for survival further complicates efforts to develop sustainable intervention efforts. Unlike conventional "rescue and rebuilding" type programming, these authors propose solutions that focus on diversifying livelihood choices while fostering psychological safety and reducing individual-level impacts of systemic stigma and discrimination.

Finally, Gadd and Broad bring forth TIP cases where victims were also offenders. While seeking protection and defense in the courts, these victims of trafficking are increasingly being viewed with suspicion. The ensuing controversy threatens to unravel the British government's agenda on victim protection. Drawing on their research data, the authors discuss the circumstances within which victims are compelled to offend and argue that academics and activists should remain vocal about how victims of human trafficking rarely fit the stereotypes commonly afforded in the criminal justice system and point out the existing immigration regime gives few choices to these victims and remain hostile to them as a social class.

We aimed to bring these issues into open for candid conversations among researchers and practitioners. Throughout this effort, we remain non-judgmental and hope to provide a venue for broader engagement and collaboration between researchers and practitioners as we face a common challenge to reduce or eradicate human suffering. We believe in multiple venues suitable for different cultural and political contexts along with this common goal. As usual, all authors here expressed their viewpoints that do not necessarily represent their employers.

Finally, although not exhaustive, we reflect on the articles presented in this issue and offer some pragmatic questions that might help to further inspire established and emerging scholars to narrow the gaps in our efforts to combat/reduce human trafficking effectively and efficiently:

(1) How might we better identify the "other" victims of human trafficking (e.g., LGBTQ+, boys, persons with some type of physical or emotional challenge(s), minority groups, etc.)?
(2) How might we improve our efforts to support victims of trafficking (e.g., access to justice, the range of complex needs survivors/victims have, guidelines for frontline workers, ensuring "proper" support for frontline workers [e.g., social workers, law enforcement, NGOs], etc.)?
(3) How can we coordinate and manage data collection activities to enable greater comparative analysis?
(4) How can we better apply robust methodologies and develop theories to guide our understanding of human trafficking issues?
(5) How might we improve the detection, apprehension, and prosecution of human trafficking perpetrators?
(6) How might we shift the lens from being reactive to human trafficking to being more proactive?
(7) How might we improve (i.e., effectively and efficiently) bridging the gaps in the corporate partnership landscape to combat human trafficking?
(8) How might we better address the growing diversity with which modern technology (e.g., social networking) is used to recruit prospective victims or vice versa to reduce individual vulnerability?
(9) How can we better accumulate and disseminate practical tools or technology to combat human trafficking?
(10) How might we develop and deploy rigorous methods to evaluate the impact or outcomes of the massive public resources invested in anti-trafficking programs so that best practices can be accumulated through accountability and knowledge building?

Despite our efforts, we fully acknowledge that this special issue has some inherent limitations, but like all "good" movies, we anticipate/hope that this issue will inspire a sequel(s) that will begin to narrow the gaps in our current state of knowledge and efforts to combat human trafficking – in all forms.

## ORCID

Sheldon Zhang http://orcid.org/0000-0002-7983-0554

# Introduction

John Winterdyk and Sheldon Zhang

After a successful session on human trafficking at ESC (European Society of Criminology) in September (2022) and in discussion with several of the attendees, a few issues started to emerge from several conversations among the presenters that gave rise to the idea of a special issue (SI) on the gaps in current research/intervention on human trafficking for the *Journal of Human Trafficking* (JHT).

This Special Issue (SI) seeks to collect the most current knowledge on gaps in the research realm or intervention development. For example, until recently, the primary focus of intervention and prevention efforts has focused on the supply side of the equation. There needs to be more quality research on the demand side of the equation. Similarly, there are ongoing issues of reliable data (i.e., measurement) and how best to collect it; the issue of under-counting and possible system failure issues; navigating the existing "system" and its barriers; the challenges of prosecutions and convictions; and "siloing" of NGOs, among a host of other themes and issues.

The SI's focus is broad, and we do not want to prejudice the process by assuming that all the (primary) challenges are adequately understood and addressed in our efforts to combat human trafficking. Instead, as acknowledged by experts in the field, we invited a group of experienced researchers and practitioners to contribute to this collective effort. More importantly, we sought voices from the global south for inclusion in this volume, e.g., India, Cambodia, and South Africa.

To assure adequate coverage and balance against the traditional preference for academic-type research papers, we included two broad types of articles in this volume: shorter articles (around 2,500 words) from several front-line organizations and services that speak directly (from their experience) to the challenges of meeting their objectives and mandates and full-length empirically based articles to point out or address some of the gaps in "human trafficking" (HT) research.

# Disrupting Human Trafficking in Canada: A Case Study in the Gaps of Meeting the UN Trafficking Protocols

John Winterdyk and Alexandra Ford

**ABSTRACT**

The signing of the 2002 United Nations' Trafficking Protocol marked a major global shift in efforts to combat human trafficking. Based on its four pillars (4Ps) (i.e. prevention, protection, prosecution, & partnership), all signatory member States were expected (legally binding) to model their response strategies around the 4Ps, which also align with the United Nations' Sustainable Development Goals number 5 (i.e. gender equality) and 8 (i.e. decent work and economic growth). As a signatory member of the Trafficking Protocol and rated as a Tier 1 country, Canada is presented as a case study of how, despite the considerable resources and initiatives being directed to combatting human trafficking, there remain notable gaps and limitations in the country's efforts to combat human trafficking. Drawing on a wide range of examples and available data, it is suggested that Canada's effort resembles a "quilted patchwork." The article concludes with several recommendations on how Canada can address the various limitations and close the gaps across the respective pillars.

'The more I learn, the more I realize I don't know'. This is one of the memorable and commonly paraphrased quotes from Albert Einstein (1879–1955) (RelicsWorld, n.d.). This paradox applies well to our efforts to understand and combat trafficking in persons (TIP).[1] TIP, modern-day slavery, or simply human trafficking, dates to ancient times, and since the abolishment of slavery circa the mid-late 1800s,[2] we have seen numerous efforts to eradicate/disrupt the growing tide and diversity of human trafficking. As Gallagher and Surtees (2012, p. 4) describe the process, we have created an "anti-trafficking industry." Yet, the more time and effort we have spent trying to eradicate TIP, the more we see that our efforts are not producing the results anticipated.

Ever since 2000, when the United Nations' *Convention against Transnational Organized Crime* (commonly referred to as the Palermo Protocol[3] or simply the Trafficking Protocol) was conceptualized – but did not come into force until December 25, 2003- Canada began to bear witness to an ever-growing number of regional, national, and international efforts to "combat" the problem.[4]

---

[1]This article is an expansion of an earlier article by the lead author "Combatting human trafficking in Canada: How do we measure up" (2019) *Justice Report*, 34(3), 16–20.

[2]Denmark banned slavery in 1792 while Canada did so on August 1, 1834, with the Slavery Abolition Act. The last country to abolish slavery was Mauritania in 1981; however, they did not make trafficking a crime until 2007.

[3]Palermo, Italy was the location where the Convention was established. Officially, it is known as the "Protocol to Prevent, Suppress and Punish Trafficking in Persons, Especially Women and Children." Initially the Trafficking Protocol included what are referred to as the 3 Ps – prosecution, protection, and prevention. In 2004, a fourth P was introduced – participation. Although Logan (2015) argues that partnership "has been at the heart of anti-trafficking since its inception" (p. 21).

[4]Quotations are placed around the term "combat" because it reflects a pejorative and emotional response to the injustice of human trafficking and (potentially) undermines the fundamental human rights issues that underpin incidents of human trafficking and the need to use evidence-informed information/data to eliminate the crime. The persistent use of the phrase "combatting" human trafficking is seen as a gap/narrow approach to trying to eradicate this grievous crime.

As recently as 2022, it is estimated that between 20 to 30 million people (primarily women and girls) are victims of some form of human trafficking (e.g., sexual exploitation, unfree labor,[5] organ trafficking, and trafficking for forced criminal activity). Depending on which source one refers to, TIP is the second or third most profitable crime worldwide (International Labor Organization [ILO], 2014a; Interpol . . . , 2022; Economic crimes, 2023).[6] The International Labor Organization estimates that TIP generates $200 US billion in illegal profits yearly (International Labor Organization, 2014b).

As reflected in this Special Issue and numerous other sources,[7] since the ratification of the Trafficking Protocol, a plethora of research has been published trying to understand and determine how best to address the multi-faceted factors such as economic, political, social, and human rights that challenge our efforts to combat TIP (see, e.g., Roots, 2022). Although there is no reliable data on the extent of human resources and financial contribution to addressing the problem, we would appear to be losing the battle on balance.[8] For example, in the introduction to the September 2014 issue of *Anti-trafficking Review*, the authors noted, "Governments, the United Nations and private foundations are pouring millions of dollars into work to stop human trafficking, yet very little of this reaches trafficked people themselves" (Dottridge, 2014, p. 6). The article states, "there is also a concerning lack of transparency among governments, international organizations and civil society regarding funding for anti-trafficking and how it is spent" (Dottridge, 2014, p. 5) Today, there remains a notable gap in available information and data on anti-trafficking funding (see Aronowitz, 2010; Moore, 2015). The data is sporadic, unreliable, and difficult to access, highlighting a need for increased transparency and concerted efforts to standardize instruments and harmonize data collection. As the International Organization on Migration [IOM] (2015) noted, a lack of reliable data and exploited persons not self-identifying "remains one of the main obstacles in effectively preventing and combating trafficking in human beings as well as protecting and assisting victims."[9] This is reflected in the fact that according to various sources (e.g., see the annual TIP Reports), the number of people involved in TIP has been officially increasing almost every year since the Protocol came into effect. Similarly, perpetrators' prosecution rates globally remain abysmally low – less than one percent (MacNamara, 2021). Despite the collective national and international efforts, there appear to be notable procedural and practical gaps in Canada's efforts to disrupt TIP.

This article is a "case study" of a Tier 1 country,[10] Canada, and examines some of the gaps within its efforts to disrupt human trafficking following the four primary pillars of the United Nations for combatting human trafficking (i.e., prevention, protection, prosecution, & partnership) and the additional pillar of "empowerment" added in September 2019. The objective of the additional pillar is to enhance support and services to victims affected by human trafficking. Although well intended, the objective is a reactive initiative. The additional pillar would be a far

[5]Although less commonly used term, Choudry and Smith (2016) use the term in the title of their book on immigrants and immigrant workers in Canada.

[6]The 2014 ILO report indicated that HT was the second or third most profitable crime worldwide.

[7]Since 2000 there are now several dedicated journals whose primary focus is human trafficking – *Journal of Human Trafficking, Anti-Trafficking Review, Journal of Global Slavery, Journal of Slavery and Data Preservation*, among others.

[8]Under a new initiative in 2020, the Canadian National Strategy has invested over $75 CDN million in federal measures to combat human trafficking over 6 years, which includes a 2018 investment of $14.51 million for the Canadian Human Trafficking Hotline, with $2.89 million ongoing, as well as a 2019 investment of $57.22 million over five years and $10.28 million ongoing. There is no reliable data as to how much is being spent/invested at a provincial or local level. This lack of detail and transparency compound efforts to combat/disrupt human trafficking of any form effectively and efficiently.

[9]Although not directly related to expenditures to combating human trafficking, a growing number of countries have or are introducing transparency legislation to combat forced labor trafficking (see, generally, Aakvik, 2018, 2018; Greer, 2018). In addition, such organization as ICMPD (International Center for Migration Policy) and the International Organization for Migration (IOM) work to help "ensure the orderly and humane management of migration." Drawing on the models and initiatives by the ICMPD and the IOM, in 2010 the European Commission also introduced the MONTRASEC project model. Vermeulen and Paterson (2010) suggest it is a promising project/model for improving the quality and reliability of trafficking data. The Office of Trafficking in Persons has also been engaged in related initiatives for several years but there still is no uniform and standardized model being used.

[10]According to the 2023 "Trafficking in Persons Report" available at: https://www.state.gov/reports/2023-trafficking-in-persons-report/. A Tier 1 country includes countries whose governments fully meet the TVPA's minimum standards for the elimination of trafficking.

more successful and sustainable plan if it empowered vulnerable populations before experiencing exploitation.[11]

First, however, we offer a brief historical overview of TIP in Canada.

## TIP: A Historical Overview of the Canadian Situation

Given the positive perception that Canada worldwide[12] tends to hold, it may come as a surprise to some that TIP in Canada dates to the early 1600s when the French colonists facilitated the transportation of enslaved people into what is now known as Quebec (eastern Canada) (for further details see McRae & McCullough, 2023). The transportation of enslaved people, primarily for domestic work and forced labor lasted until 1834, when slavery was officially abolished. The first enslaved people in what was formerly known as Upper Canada (now Quebec) were from the Pawnee Nation (i.e., the Central Plain Indian tribe). The Pawnee lived in what is now the central United States, but the people of New France also bought and sold enslaved Black people (McRae & McCullough, 2023).[13] In fact, at the peak of the Canadian slave trade in 1793, there were an estimated 4,200 enslaved persons in New France; some 64% were Indigenous, and the others were mostly Blacks (N. L. Henry, 2018). During this period, most enslaved people were used for forced labor to support the country's economic growth.

As the momentum toward abolition evolved, many Canadian enslavers adopted the practice of indentureship. Under this system, enslavers would pay their formerly enslaved workers to continue working at wages well below what the fair market would have demanded. This practice of exploitation continued until the passing of the *Slavery Abolition Act* of 1834. Though disputably not as prevalent in Canada, the practice of indentured workers is still very much alive in other parts of the world (see Choi-Fitzpatrick, 2017; Dow, 2021).[14]

As was the scenario in many other countries, the issue of slavery essentially faded from the public eye in Canada after its abolition.[15] However, the recruitment, transportation, and exploitation of primarily women and girls for sexual exploitation continue as a clandestine activity today, as seen in the current state of human trafficking (see Conroy, 2022) and commercial sex[16] (Rotenberg, 2016) in Canada. Although not all commercial sex workers are victims of trafficking, various sources suggest that in many incidents (approx. 60%), they are trafficked and forced into prostitution. Abcarian (2016), among others, describes these forms of forced prostitution as a "modern-day slave auction."

Finally, after the United Nations ratified the Palermo Protocol in 2000, Canada and many other countries suddenly appeared to recall that "modern-day slavery" had morphed into an economically underground enterprise. Gradually, various academics and organizations began to turn their attention toward TIP and demonstrate that domestic and international trafficking in persons is very much an issue in Canada (see Perrin, 2006, 2011).[17]

---

[11]This can be done through funding and resources for mental health issues, trauma prevention education, easing financial disparities, lowering the severely inflated cost of postsecondary education, action toward reconciliation and healing with Indigenous communities and, of course, gender equality.

[12]The United Nations' Human Rights Index website offers a rich searchable data base on a range of human rights issues globally (see UNIVERSAL HUMAN RIGHTS INDEX – Human Rights Recommendations (ohchr.org).

[13]Saint John, the capital of the province of New Brunswick (eastern Canada) was incorporated by the Royal Charter in 1785. Its first mayor Gabriel G. Ludlow was not only a slave owner, but he introduced several restrictions, placed specifically on the growing Black community (N. Henry, 2021).

[14]According to the ILO (2023), in 2021 some 27.6 M (55.6% of 49.6 M enslaved persons) of all enslaved persons were being trafficked for the purpose of forced labor.

[15]However, the issue of racism and discriminatory practices toward Blacks continued well after slavery was abolished and even after the passing the *Racial Discrimination Act* in 1944.

[16]New legislation was introduced in 2014 making it a criminal offense to purchase sexual services from any person. The legislation (Bill C-36) made prostitution illegal in Canada for the first time. Prior to 2014, prostitution (i.e., a transaction that involves both the purchase and sale of sexual services) was a legal activity, even though most prostitution-related activities were illegal (Rotenberg, 2016).

[17]It is interesting to note that of the dedicated journals that focus on human trafficking, they have all emerged since 2002. The first volume of the *Journal of Human Trafficking* was published in April of 2015.

### How Does Canada Measure Up in Its Efforts to Combat TIP?

In 2006, the then-Calgary-based nonprofit organization "The Future Group" prepared a report evaluating the success of eight different countries[18] and their response to combatting human trafficking (Perrin et al., 2016). The United States received the highest score (B+), while Canada scored the lowest of the eight countries. It was the only country to receive an "F" grade. Although much has changed since 2006, we are reminded of the quote often credited to the French novelist and journalist Jean-Baptiste Alphonse Karr (1806–1890), who said, "the more things change, the more they stay the same." While the statement may be pessimistic, the state of TIP in Canada remains lackluster and resembles a patchwork quilt even after Canada ratified the Protocol in May 2002, and various steps have been taken to address the problem.[19]

### Investigation and Prosecution

Between 2010 and 2020, a Statistics Canada report noted that the number of police-reported incidents of human trafficking increased from approximately 30-odd incidents in 2010 to just over 500 reported incidents in 2020,[20] for a total of 2,977 reported incidents (Conroy, 2022). Furthermore, the 2022 annual report on HT notes that between 2015 and 2020, the number of reported cases of HT fluctuated and even declined from 546 to 515 cases between 2019 and 2020 (Global Report . . . , 2023). However, it is widely acknowledged that the "dark figure" of human trafficking cases is unknown.[21] However, virtually every report/study on estimations notes that the actual number of cases is much larger (e.g., Aronowitz, 2010; Laczko, 2002).[22] Of those cases reported to the police, stays and guilty pleas are disproportionately higher than for most other serious crimes (Conroy, 2022). When compared to over 50% of all violent crimes resulting in a guilty verdict, these results raise serious questions about the effectiveness of the justice system as well as about the challenges and limitations of the current legislation in Canada (see Kaye, 2017; Perrin, 2006; Roots, 2022).[23] The disparity also speaks to one of the significant gaps in Canada's efforts to disrupt and effectively combat TIP.[24] Using Cohen and Felson's (1979) routine activity theory (RAT), the low prosecution rates while the supply of prospective victims remains high and appears to be growing (i.e., suitable targets), there is a lack of detection, apprehension, and prosecution of the perpetrators (i.e., absence of a capable guardian), and the demand (i.e., motivated offender) remains unaddressed. In her recent book, which examines the Canadian criminal justice system's response to human trafficking, Roots (2022) discusses how, despite the plethora of legislative initiatives that have been introduced to better address human trafficking, the legal system still resembles a quilted patchwork approach (see De Shalit et al., 2021; Millar & O'Doherty, 2020).[25]

And although efforts have been underway to address this gap in Canada's efforts to combat TIP effectively, it remains a significant problem. Neither the Canadian National Action Plan to Combat

---

[18]The countries included Australia, Canada, Germany, Italy, Norway, Sweden, and the United States.

[19]Canada was among the first cohort of countries to sign the Trafficking Protocol. Sweden ratified the Protocol in 2004, the United States in 2005, and the United Kingdom in 2006. Nepal only ratified the Trafficking Protocol in 2022.

[20]A six-fold increase.

[21]According to a 2019 Northeastern University study, law enforcement only identifies 2.5% to 6% of trafficking victims (Farrell et al., 2019).

[22]This fact is also acknowledged in several of the articles in the Special Issue.

[23]In her doctoral thesis on human trafficking in Canada, Roots (2018) noted that there "is to date only three empirical Canadian studies that examine frontline anti-trafficking policing and prosecution efforts with a focus on migrant worker justice (Millar et al., 2015), on international trafficking cases (Ferguson, 2012) and on Indigenous communities (Kaye, 2017), as well as a handful of European (Lester et al., 2017; Meshkovska et al., 2016) and American studies (Farrell et al., 2015, 2016)."

[24]Drawing on the 2023 TIP Report, it shows that while the number of convictions between 2016 and 2022 increased (14,939 to 15,159), the conviction rate declined (from 9,702 to 5,577). All this despite more legislation being introduced to assist law enforcement and the justice system with prosecutions (Trafficking in Persons Report, 2023).

[25]For example, there are police precincts in Canada who have openly expressed that they refuse to enforce the federal 2014 PCEPA (Protection of Communities and Exploitation of Persons Act) due primarily to the legal ambiguity of the meaning of exploitation (see *R. v. D-Souza 2016ONSC 2749.*)

Human Trafficking nor Public Safety Canada directly references TIP as an economic crime (Wheaton et al., 2010). However, a recent report shows that sex traffickers are using hundreds of potentially illicit massage parlours across Canada (and the United States) to launder their illicit profits (Paez, 2023). According to James Cohen, the Executive Director at Transparency International Canada, the absence of a national beneficial ownership registry will allow the "money from crimes that damage our society like human trafficking, the fentanyl trade, and wildlife trafficking" to keep flowing" (Paez, 2023). This later point was reflected in a legal decision in which Justice Baltman refused the Crown's request to introduce an expert widely recognized (at the time) as one of Canada's leading experts on human trafficking. Justice Baltman claimed the expert was biased in his research and only served to further conflate the judicial system's efforts in how the system responds to sex sellers and victims of trafficking by conflating the two (Kaye, 2017; Roots, 2018). For example, sex-worker organizations have consistently impeded efforts to combat HT in Canada.[26]

The prosecution trend and rate in Canada represent a severe disparity in Canada's effort to combat TIP. It is also disconcerting when official statistics show that most victims are women and girls under the age of 25 (Conroy & Sutton, 2023). Although the low prosecution rates are not unique to Canada (e.g., see the 2023 TIP Report), the phenomenon highlights that the Canadian criminal justice system is not fulfilling its mandate (see Oxman-Martinez et al., 2005; Roots, 2023). Additionally, although there is very little data on the prosecution rates for perpetrators of human trafficking, the abysmal prosecution rates reflect a significant limitation in the cost-effectiveness and cost-efficiency of the Canadian criminal justice system's efforts to prosecute perpetrators of human trafficking.[27] This is especially concerning given that despite much of the official rhetoric of being more victim-centered (phrased as "empowerment" in the National Strategy), most efforts to combat human trafficking in Canada still prioritize the law enforcement-prosecutorial approach (see National Strategy . . . ., 2019; and footnote 10 above).

A final example of the challenges Canada's legal system faces in trying to prosecute/combat is that after nearly three years, Bill S-224 (a private member's Bill – first introduced in November 2021) to amend the Canadian Criminal Code (i.e., sections 279.01 to 279.03) to "specify what constitutes exploitation for the purpose of establishing whether a person has committed the offence of trafficking in persons", is still in review (as of August, 2023), and the various briefs ($N = 20$ plus ten private witness submissions) that have been submitted to Parliament show no uniformity in their assessment of whether the Bill would help or hinder victims of sexual exploitation even though if accepted the Bill could potentially assist the Crown in prosecuting the perpetrators by reducing the burden of proof (i.e., evidence) provided by the victim (Bill S-224, 2023). For example, the Brief submitted by the Ontario Native Women's Association (ONWA) noted that while the proposed legislation would improve Indigenous women's safety and access to justice in Ontario and Canada, the Association feels that the Bill would create "further barriers to access to justice and will not address the systemic factors that render Indigenous women in Canada at greater risk of trafficking and sexual exploitation." But, in contrast, the Brief submitted by the Ontario-based NGO "Defend Dignity" argued that the Bill would "work to assist victimized individuals in their pursuit of justice . . . by removing the burden to prove that fear was involved in the abuse . . . . (and that) Canada should remove the fear element to better align with the international definition of trafficking" (Bill S-224, 2023). The Bill "died" on July 14, 2023. The fact that the Bill was not passed, despite its numerous briefs and readings, reflects yet

[26]Notably, in Appendix C of the National Strategy it says: "the Government of Canada also met with representatives of sex-worker organizations in Ottawa to hear their views on the importance of not conflating human trafficking with consensual adult sex work and the challenges faced with current approaches to law enforcement" and mention of the federal legislation, PCEPA, is notably absent (National Strategy, 2019). More broadly speaking the term "sex worker" is a controversial term among various Canadian scholars so when not directly quoting other research we use the term "sex seller(s)" to ensure we aren't providing any weight to the "sex work is work" narrative.

[27]The overall rate of guilty pleas in Canada declined from around 60% in 2007/2008 to approximately 53% in 2016/2017 (Milandinovic, 2019) and Conroy (2022) reports that "over half (54%) of human trafficking incidents were not cleared, meaning police have not identified an accused person. This was much less common among violent incidents generally (35%)."

another gap in Canada's effort to prosecute HT cases, as it could not build consensus around an amendment that aligned with the spirit of the Un Protocol.

Nevertheless, prosecution remains one of the four key pillars of the Palermo Protocol, and little has been done to address the abysmal prosecution rates (see, e.g., Ferguson, 2012). So, while prosecution is one of the main pillars of the UN Protocol, the fact that the database for domestic laws on anti-human trafficking laws has not been updated compounds not only Canada's efforts to prosecute traffickers but also that of the global community because there has been no effort to establish a fuller legal definition of the crime. Furthermore, there has been an absence or gap in reviewing laws and legal procedures governing modern-day slavery, including forced labor trafficking (see Schwartz & Allain, 2020).[28] For example, White (2020b) notes that the "last systematic attempt to gather domestic laws on slavery was published over 50 years ago, in 1966." To this point, to date, there have been fewer than a dozen empirical Canadian studies that examine frontline anti-trafficking policing and prosecution efforts with a focus on migrant worker justice (e.g., Ferguson, 2012; Kaye, 2017; Millar et al., 2015).

## Protection

Despite some of the ongoing criticism surrounding the fairness with which Canadian public institutions such as commissions and tribunals conduct their proceedings, Canadians like to view themselves as champions of the protection of the fundamental rights of others (see Eliadis, 2014).[29] As a signatory member of the 2000 UN Trafficking Protocol, Canada is expected to uphold Articles 6 to 8 concerning protecting victims. In 2006, the former Canadian-based Future Group reported that "trafficking victims are not provided with any government-funded medical, psychological or counselling support in Canada" (p. 14) and further observed that any possible support was only available through private NGOs. For example, ACT (Action Coalition on Human Trafficking) Alberta is a provincial NGO that offers support in non-emergency situations to victims, otherwise referring victims of trafficking to 911, Crime Stoppers, or the Canadian National Hotline at 1-833-900-1010.[30] Similarly, in British Columbia (west coast of Canada), there is no proactive attempt to find victims of trafficking. As Brock (2017) notes, victims are typically only found if they escape or report their situation to authorities. A temporary residence permit (TRP) can access the services mentioned above. However, given the demographic profile of many trafficked victims in Canada, it is unlikely that many of them have a TRP and/or would know how to access any such services.[31] This represents another significant gap in the services and protection of trafficking victims who are not rescued but may require support in policy and practice. This issue was highlighted in a recent case involving the rescue of 64 Mexican farm workers who had been trafficked for the purpose of forced labor (Rodrigues, 2023). The gap in service was acknowledged by Mr. Syed Hussan, Executive Director of the Migrant Workers Alliance of Canada, who, commented that, "what we often see in situations like this is that police come in, do a big splash, call it human trafficking . . . and within a few weeks, workers are being deported" (Nasser,

[28]Based on their research, Schwartz & Allain (2020) and his team found that in 94 countries, a person cannot be prosecuted for enslaving another human being.

[29]John Peters Humphrey (1905–1995), a Canadian jurist who served for 20 years (1946–1966) as the Director of the United Nations Division of Human Rights, drafting, and championing the Universal Declaration of Human Rights.

[30]The Hotline offers 24/7 service in more than 200 languages, yet the Centre's website is only available in English and French. Given the relative percentage of trafficked victims who may have limited English or French language skills, the Hotline may not be accessible to such victims. To date, no research has tried to document the relative effectiveness of the Hotline, let alone for certain vulnerable groups-individuals. Furthermore, unlike most toll-free lines in Canada which include 800 or 888 in their prefix, the prefix for the Hotline is 833 and the number 900–1010 may not be intuitive or easy to remember. There is no evidence as to how the number was assigned to the Hotline. Again, while commendable, this is considered another gap in the service and efforts to combat TIP in Canada. There is no evidence that any discussion about using three (even 4) digit number like 911, 311, etc. as emergency numbers for survivors of human trafficking would be a more effective option than an 11-digit number. By contrast, the province of Alberta offers 911 as a call number for someone in immediate danger and 211 for general resources and support.

[31]For further details see https://www.publicsafety.gc.ca/cnt/cntrng-crm/hmn-trffckng/spprt-vctms-srvvrs-en.aspx. However, in 2007, if someone was rescued from trafficking, they can be granted a TRP under the auspices of Immigration, Refugees and Citizenship Canada.

2023). Hussan further observed, "This is a systemic issue.... Many migrants are facing these issues because they don't have permanent residence rights" (Nasser, 2023). In addition, there are currently no legal provisions where frontline workers have a "duty to report" suspected cases of adults being trafficked. Although there are legal provisions for frontline workers to report suspected cases of trafficking involving children, the requirements do not apply to adults, let alone at-risk populations (Winterdyk et al., in press).

Although somewhat dated, according to the human trafficking link of the British Columbia government (which is no longer active), there were over 40 Canadian organizations and agencies addressing human trafficking in some capacity (Human trafficking . . . ., 2014). Most organizations are NGOs, and their services vary considerably (Winterdyk & Hincks, 2023a). In 2021 Winterdyk and Hincks attempted to update the list as part of a national project. Even though a few additional services were identified, the range or discrepancy in services available varied. As noted earlier, the discrepancy in services is particularly noted in the overall national inconsistency in the enforcement of Protection of Communities and Exploited Persons Act (PCEPA) and the varied push for decriminalization. This is seen as another significant gap in ensuring the needs of survivors of human trafficking are being met.[32]

Even though the Canadian Centre to End Human Trafficking (based in the province of Ontario) exists, there is no national coordination center in the sense that all agencies and organizations use or list their hotline. Furthermore, there is no clear evidence that the Center's directory, beyond listing services (almost exclusively for victims of sexual violence and exploitation), plays an active role in combatting human trafficking. This is even though the Center uses an application process when applying to be included in the directory.[33] However, some provincial NGOs[34] engage (to varying extents) in interagency collaboration. They sometimes include federal agencies such as the Royal Canadian Mounted Police (RCMP), the Canada Border Service Agency, Immigration and Citizenship Canada, and the Canadian Council for Refugees. Again, while commendable, the siloing of regional efforts to combat human trafficking is seen as a significant limitation in Canada's efforts to be effective and efficient in its efforts to disrupt a crime that knows no regional or provincial, let alone (inter) national borders.

Since 2006, some notable initiatives have been implemented to combat TIP in Canada. In 2012, through its Victim Fund, the federal government allocated $4 M over eight years to support NGOs in their efforts to support victims of trafficking (primarily focused on victims of sexual exploitation). Then, in 2016, the federal government allocated $16.7 CDN million in funding over four years to create Family Information Liaison Units nationwide. Some funds are intended to support victims from marginalized areas and Indigenous women and girls, yet there was no transparent allocation of funds to support victims of forced labor, the LGBTQ2S+ or other at-risk populations in Canada.

Also, in 2016, a consortium of Ontario partners pooled $72 M to invest over four years to support the creation of a Provincial Anti-human Trafficking Coordination Office housed under the provincial Ministry of Children, Community and Social Services. The Office's first Director was Ms. Jennifer Richardson, who has lived experience as a survivor of human trafficking and worked for over two decades combatting human trafficking in the province of Manitoba before assuming the role (Ontario Names . . . , 2016). The office offers a wide range of services for youth, women, girls, and marginalized groups, but none of the listed service programs (over 40) are (specifically) dedicated to supporting survivors of forced labor or addressing the issue of demand for service. It is the most concerted effort in Canada to combat human trafficking within any province or territory. In 2017, the Ontario government, through its Anti-Human Trafficking Community Supports and Indigenous-led

[32]In 2023 the Alberta NGO ACT started conducting the first study on sexual exploitation and forced labor with the objective of developing standardized guidelines for front line workers in both areas of human trafficking. The projects are scheduled to be completed in Spring 2024 (see, generally, https://www.actalberta.org/what-we-do/research-community-action).

[33]See https://www.canadianhumantraffickinghotline.ca/referral-directory/

[34]For example, NIMC (Not In My City in Alberta) and the Ontario anti-human trafficking strategy led by the Ministry of Children, Community and Social Services.

Initiatives Funds, allocated \$7 M to help human trafficking survivors find housing in Ontario (How 7M will help . . . , 2017). Nevertheless, as admirable as the Centre to End Human Trafficking and Provincial Coordination Office is, they work at cross-purposes as they both offer similar services and compete for similar funding.

Finally, in 2022, the provincial government of Alberta earmarked \$20.8 to be distributed over four years to implement the nine-point action plan from a task force on human trafficking (Drinkwatter, 2022).[35] Part of the funds will be used to establish an office to combat trafficking and a center of excellence for research and data collection. Included in the 9-point action plan was a call to increase efforts to educate and create awareness around the plight of human trafficking, lobby the federal government to strengthen penalties against human traffickers by bringing Bill C-452 into force, and to name and shame traffickers by publishing the names of businesses found to have knowingly facilitated human trafficking. However, as of December 2023, only two action plan points have been completed, and the remaining were still described as "work underway."[36] Also notably absent from the nine-point action plan is any mention of PCEPA, Canada's federal law.

Despite these efforts, the various national and provincial efforts still do not provide the protective measures that address the unique needs of trafficking victims across the spectrum of victims (e.g., sexual exploitation, forced labor, organ trafficking, domestic servitude, etc.). For example, Indigenous women and girls remain one of the most targeted and over-represented groups trafficked (Kaye, 2017; Schwientek, 2023) despite the various initiatives designed to protect this vulnerable group. Furthermore, as noted in the 2018 TIP Report, Canada has failed to provide any comprehensive data on the type of services victims are provided, and/or which are available nationwide or – with the rare regional exception – any information on the type and nature of emergency housing explicitly allocated for trafficking victims of any type. Finally, to date, there are still no mechanisms in place to protect victims of trafficking during an investigation. For example, no (direct) reference to such initiatives is in the 2023 TIP Report or the UN's Global Report in 2023. However, in 2023, the Alberta organization ACT (Action Coalition on Human Trafficking), with federal funding assistance, started two research projects in which they will develop guidelines to assist frontline workers. One of the projects focuses on victims of sexual exploitation, and the other on victims/survivors of forced labor exploitation (ACT, 2023).[37]

## Prevention

This section focuses on the pillar of preventing trafficking in Canada. As posted on the website "Canadian National Strategy To Combat Human Trafficking 2019–2024" (2019), Canada's approach has been guided by the United Nations Convention against Transnational Organized Crime and its supplementing Protocol to Prevent, Suppress and Punish Trafficking in Persons, Especially Women and Children. As noted earlier, the national strategy has been organized around the four broad pillars (4Ps) used by the United Nations, and in 2019 introduced a fifth pillar – empowerment.

The national strategy is supported by an investment of \$75 million Canadian over six years, and in 2019, an additional infusion of "\$57.22 million over five years, and \$10.28 million ongoing, to implement an enhanced suite of initiatives that will strengthen Canada's response and fill critical gaps" (National Strategy..., 2019, p. 6). Specifically, the national strategy refers to enhancing the "need for increased supports and services to protect and rehabilitate victims and survivors and the promotion of culturally-sensitive approaches" (i.e., protection); to increase awareness so as to "better understand the signs of this crime that can occur in their communities and improve the ability of government officials and frontline staff in key sectors to identify, detect and protect victims and

[35] In March 2023, the budget was increased to \$22.8 million but at the time any progress on the initiative "was unclear" (Black, 2023).
[36] For a complete description of the 9-point action plan and the status of the Task Force's mandate see https://www.alberta.ca/human-trafficking-action-plan.aspx
[37] The lead author is Team Lead of the research phase of the two projects.

survivors" (National Strategy..., 2019, p. 7). In addition, the National Strategy claimed that these actions will increase intelligence and data collection capacity, stimulate the private sector and with international partners, and boost law enforcement, among other initiatives that will "strengthen Canada's response and fill critical gaps" (National Strategy..., 2019, p. 5). Furthermore, the National Strategy expressed the need to "advance gender equality and provide support to marginalized and vulnerable groups, including Indigenous women and girls" (i.e., protection). Ironically, none of the main priorities listed prevention as an essential priority of the National Strategy, but the website defines prevention as "Increasing awareness and building capacity to prevent human trafficking in Canada and abroad." However, the only prevention initiative mentioned is a program in Ontario Peace, Actualization, Community, and Transformation (PACT),[38] which received funding from Public Service Canada (PSC) in 2015 – before the National Strategy was even introduced. The description notes that PACT received PSC funding to "increase awareness among youth of human trafficking." The PACT Project Northern Outreach reached 705 Anishinabek community members from North Shore and Manitoulin Island (National Strategy . . . , 2019).

Despite the description on their website, there appears to be a notable gap in implementing and actualizing prevention efforts under the national strategy. While a praiseworthy initiative, the PACT project only reached a remote area of the province and a small number of community members. Yet, it is noted that the National Strategy does include four essential prevention-oriented activities. They include:

(1) **Establishing a national case-management standard** for organizations (i.e., community service groups and victim services) with a special focus on vulnerable groups, such as Indigenous women and girls, at-risk youth, and migrants to ensure victims have access to services that address their specific needs and assist them in their recovery and healing.
(2) **Developing multi-sectoral training tools** that are culturally relevant and gender-responsive for frontline service providers and targeted groups from various sectors (i.e., hospitality, transportation) to increase awareness of the indicators and signs of human trafficking and enable employees to effectively identify victims.
(3) **Enhancing capacity under the Victims of Trafficking in Persons program** to better detect suspected human trafficking cases through the immigration system.
(4) **Assessing existing immigration processes** to evaluate the different impacts of gender-based violence throughout the immigration enforcement continuum to ensure that sufficient protection is in place for victims in contact with border officials (National Strategy . . . , 2019).

As of July 2023, there is no evidence that any of the four prevention activities is receiving any (significant) funding (see Depatie-Pelletier et al., 2022).[39] But in 2022, the Federal Government did earmark "$22.4 million for organizations working to prevent and address human trafficking and support at-risk populations and survivors" (Government of Canada, 2020). The call for proposals resulted in 63 organizations receiving funding for related initiatives.

## Partnership

In recent years, various initiatives across the country have demonstrated an attempt at national and regional levels to promote partnerships to combat human trafficking. For example, in 2012, the federal government launched the National Action Plan to Combat Human Trafficking (the "Action Plan") to help bridge the gaps in the existing response mechanisms as well as improve awareness of the plight of TIP in Canada (and internationally). Yet, as of 2024, Canada still does not have any reliable statistics on victims of trafficking, be it for sexual exploitation or forced labor trafficking, or any of the emerging forms of trafficking (e.g., organ,

[38]See https://www.pact-ottawa.org/
[39]The article appears in the Special Issue "Vulnerability and the Legal Protection of Migrants: A Critical Look at the Canadian Context" and includes several other articles that address the plight vulnerable workers and a lack of prevention and protection measures.

domestic servitude, forced or unwanted arranged marriages, etc.) (Millar et al., 2015). Despite its clandestine nature and the hidden economies in which trafficked victims are forced to work, it has long been noted that accurate statistics on the extent and nature of the problem are elusive (see Aronowitz, 2010). And while some (less than 5% of the 175 states that have undertaken legally binding obligations to criminalize human trafficking) countries still do not have trafficking legislation (e.g., China, Madagascar, Iran, Belarus, etc.) (White, 2020b), Canada is not among them. In Canada, there are six offenses in the Criminal Code which specifically pertain to human trafficking (sections 279.01 thru 279.03(2)). In terms of "partnership," Canada is a signatory member to several key international treaties that oblige the government to take steps to combat human trafficking, but they are not binding.[40]

In 2016, as mentioned earlier, the province of Ontario launched a collaborative initiative to combat TIP. The effort involved bringing together a host of provincial NGOs to help better address the complexity of human trafficking and the diverse needs of its victims/survivors. In the same year, the Ontario government launched an awareness campaign on domestic sex-trafficking of Indigenous people, while the government's Statue of Women Canada launched several campaigns to address issues such as gender-based violence (see It's Not Just: . . . , 2022). Although no source was provided, one of the members of the Ontario Human Trafficking Led Joint Force Strategy recently commented that "individuals who come from extremely vulnerable populations are more likely to be trafficked, and it is estimated that approximately 50% of the trafficked women and girls in Canada are Indigenous" (Russell, 2023). However, these and several other schemes work mainly in isolation and focus almost exclusively on sexual exploitation and none of the "newer" forms of trafficking, such as forced labor and trafficking of minority and marginalized groups. The last points were reflected in the 2018 TIP Report while addressing the partnership issue in Canada. The report noted that "the range, quality, and timely delivery of trafficking-specific services varied nationwide" (Trafficking in Persons Report, 2018, p. 130).

The most recent partnership effort to emerge in Canada was spearheaded by the Canadian chapter of the Rotary Action Group Against Slavery (RAGAS).[41] Partnering with organizations such as International Justice Mission (IJM) Canada, The Mekong Club, Rotary Canada and #NotInMyCity, and Shell Canada, a two-day conference (April 2–3, 2023) was held at the Canadian Human Rights Museum in Winnipeg, Manitoba. The conference included a host of local, national, and international experts and several survivors as keynote speakers. The title of the conference was *Beyond Zero: The Canadian Declaration against Human Trafficking*. The conference's objective was to have the Canadian government become the first "government in the world to pledge zero tolerance toward human trafficking and forced labor slavery" (Beyond Zero . . . , 2023). Although another commendable initiative, one might question the value of declaring that it is not a statement of the law nor legally binding (see Wood, 2024). Should the declaration succeed, it will be challenging to secure national support and may set unrealistic expectations (see, for example, the Universal Declaration on Human Rights of 1948[42] or the more recent Great Barrington Declaration; also see Wood in this Special Issue).[43] Nevertheless, the seven-page declaration aims to have Canada be "the first government in the world to pledge zero tolerance toward human trafficking and forced labor slavery." However, the concept of "zero tolerance" against speeding, drug abuse, bullying in schools, gang violence, or any other crime/vice is simplistic and uni-directional and fails to (fully) appreciate the complexity of

[40]The four main international treaties to which Canada is a signatory member of include 1) UN Convention against Transnational Organized Crime and its Protocol to Prevent, Suppress and Punish Trafficking in Persons, especially women and children, 2) The Optional Protocol to the Convention on the Rights of the Child (CRC) on the Sale of Children, Child Prostitution, and Child Pornography, 3) ILO Convention 182 concerning the Prohibition and Immediate Action for the Elimination of the Worst Forms of Child Labor, and 4) Rome Statute of the International Criminal Court.

[41]For more details on the work that RAGAS engages in see https://ragas.online/ RAGAS includes such partners as UPS, The Salvation Army, Delta Airlines, Mekong Club, and others.

[42]See Fraser (2008) for a detailed analysis of the promise and limitation of the Declaration.

[43]The Great Barrington Declaration was an initiative introduced and signed by the citizens of Great Barrington, Massachusetts and supposed to be based on scientific-evidence to combat COVID-19. White (2020a) describes five main flaws with the declaration which can be applied to the "Beyond Zero" declaration which based on a partnership.

human trafficking and its related factors and issues. This complexity is underscored by the varying levels of enforcement across the nation. The significant differences in the enforcement of this area of law were noted in the government's official review of PCEPA, published in 2022, as potentially concerning (Standing Committee . . . , 2022, p. 45).

In addition, the declaration risks creating false hope and false expectation that the victims of human trafficking will receive any better support and services than they already are – which, as discussed in the article, is not the case (see Winterdyk & Hincks, 2023a).[44] Again, while well-meaning, the intention demonstrates a broader gap in Canada's ability to build meaningful partnerships to combat human trafficking.

## Summary and Conclusion

This article used Canada as a case study to show that despite being ranked a Tier 1 country in the annual Trafficking in Persons Report for several years, there are still notable gaps in its efforts to combat human trafficking and its efforts to align with Sustainable Development Goals 5 and 8. Using the four pillars of the United Nations protocol and the fifth initiative (i.e., empowerment) introduced by the National Strategy to Combat Human Trafficking, an assessment of Canada's performance across the five pillars was presented. However, given the gravity of the social, economic, and human rights, and the harm/trauma that many victims of trafficking experience, Canada (as with most countries globally) does what it can to eradicate the damage of human trafficking. To this end, since being one of the first countries to sign the Palermo Protocol in 2002, Canada has undertaken a wide range of initiatives, invested considerable sums of money, and saw the establishment of numerous local, regional, and federal projects and programs to combat/disrupt human trafficking. Yet, as discussed in this article, notable gaps and limitations remain. This is most clear in the fact that despite the efforts made, the blight of TIP is growing. Conviction rates remain low and many organizations continue to operate as silos and are underfunded. In addition, data collection is not consistent or reliable, and yet initiatives and declarations which reflect the disconnect between evidence -based science and policy or legislative reform, are being proposed. Though necessary, it must be understood that a focus on survivor care will not disrupt the crime of trafficking. Despite one of Canada's main pillars being "prevention," there remains a significant disconnect around the public understanding of trafficking, which is directly connected to victims' lack of identification and self-identification. Canada's efforts reflect a patchwork quilt where efforts between the provinces and territories are still not coordinated; competing organizations are replicating efforts within the provinces/territories and with those of the federal government.[45] Concerning prevention efforts, they rely primarily on creating more awareness that, given the rising numbers, are ineffective.

Again, it is noted that since 2002, Canada has made a concerted effort to combat human trafficking on several levels, but the return on investment (i.e., cost-benefit analysis) has not produced the results that would be anticipated. For the country to narrow or close this gap, it will likely require a paradigm shift. First, to build sustainable capacity to disrupt human trafficking, organizations and agencies should consider a 5$^{th}$P – Participation. While partnerships represent an opportunity to involve different perspectives and skill sets to combat trafficking and support its victims, forming partnerships is not enough. Participation require active and equitable participation of all partners. Just as researchers and decision-makers are increasingly listening to the voices of survivors, so must all partners participate in informing whatever response is being advocated. This includes holding the government

[44]Although beyond the scope of this article, there are several notable gaps in the Declaration which suggest further consultation may be appropriate. For example, under "We know that in Canada" it is stated that "Perpetrators use various forms of social media as human trafficking recruiting tools . . . " There is a complete absence of acknowledging the growing role of augmented intelligence and other technologies which are rapidly becoming more normative in the recruiting process of prospective victims and there is mention of how to improve prosecution rates.

[45]For example, when preparing this article, there were several Bills before the government to amend the current legislation to address the gaps in TIP legislation.

of Canada accountable for their still unfulfilled commitment to establish a national survivor-led advisory committee, which is critical to ensuring that survivors are not being re-exploited but also setting the tone/requirements for all NGOs and organizations across the nation. The lack of follow-through disenfranchises survivors and sets a negative tone for all other partnering NGOs regarding the necessity of survivor-led involvement. All survivor involvement must include fair compensation.

Secondly, it is recommended that the paradigm shift also involves more significant attention to the issue of addressing demand concerning trafficking. Most of the efforts in Canada focus on victim support and related "supply" issues, which are primarily reactive. As witnessed in other regions of the world, giving greater attention to the issue of demand is a primary prevention and proactive way to combat//disrupt TIP.[46] Until we can stop the demand, there will continue to be an endless "product" supply. In the preamble to PCEPA it says that "it is important to continue to denounce and prohibit the purchase of sexual services because it creates a demand for prostitution," and although some attention is being given to the demand issue in Canada (see, e.g., Van der Watt, 2023; Winterdyk & Hincks, 2023b), the gap remains quite cavernous.[47] To effectively address the demand issue, action needs to turn away from the victims and toward the sex buyers. This includes shifting the focus from preventing the exploitation of vulnerable populations to changing the pervasive belief that purchasing human beings for sexual servitude is acceptable. This paradigm shift removes the onus from the victims needing to self-identify as a victim of trafficking or from law enforcement to discern the proper level of agency the victim does (or does not) possess. The result is a foundational understanding that all human beings are equally deserving of dignity and freedom from exploitation and the objectification of humans, and the commodification of sexual activity is socially harmful.

Finally, the pillar of empowerment is crucial but misdirected. People are not trafficked because they do not understand that exploitation is harmful – they are trafficked because they are in need. Whether those needs are basic, like safety, food or shelter, or more complex, like belonging or self-actualization, the offer presented by the trafficker and/or buyer suggests they can fulfill that need. Let's look to empower all populations with the ability and access to resources to fulfill their needs so that they are no longer vulnerable to the false promises of traffickers and the risks of harm from selling sexual services.

The plight of TIP is not likely to be eliminated in the near or immediate future, but if we are prepared to examine the gaps objectively and critically in our current efforts and embrace the need for an informed approach that is grounded in evidence and theory, then we might begin to truly impact this scourge which has been a blight on humanity for far too long.

## Disclosure Statement

No potential conflict of interest was reported by the author(s).

## Funding

This work was supported by the none [none].

## ORCID

John Winterdyk (ret.) http://orcid.org/0000-0002-6224-4399
Alexandra Ford http://orcid.org/0000-0000-0000-0000

[46]Refer to Article 9(5) of the Trafficking Protocol that mandates that signatories strengthen legislative and other measures such as "educational, social or cultural measures" that seek to "discourage the demand that fosters all forms of exploitation of persons, especially women and children, that leads to trafficking"

[47]For example, there is no reference to addressing the issue of demand in the newly proposed Zero Tolerance Declaration.

## References

2018 Trafficking in Persons Report. (2018). US Department of State. Retrieved from https://www.state.gov/reports/2018-trafficking-in-persons-report/

2023 Trafficking in Persons Report. (2023). US Department of State. Retrieved from https://www.state.gov/wp-content/uploads/2023/06/Trafficking-in-Persons-Report-2023.pdf

Aakvik, A. (2018). Seeing through transparency: Preventing human trafficking and forced labor through corporate accountability. The Freedom Fund. https://freedomfund.org/blog/seeing-through-transparency-preventing-human-trafficking-and-forced-labor-through-corporate-accountability/

Abcarian, R. (2016, January 29). How prostitution is 'modern-day slavery,' and what law enforcement is doing to stop it. *The Los Angeles Times*. https://www.latimes.com/local/abcarian/la-me-0129-abcarian-sex-traffic-20160129-column.html

ACT. (2023). What we do: Research + reports. https://act-alberta.webflow.io/what-we-do/research-community-action

Aronowitz, A. (2010). *Human trafficking, human misery: The global trade in human beings*. Bloomsbury Academic.

Beyond Net Zero – The Canada Declaration. (2023). https://notinmycity.ca/beyond-net-zero-the-canada-declaration/

Bill S-224). (2023, June 21). BILL S-224: An act to amend the Criminal Code (trafficking in persons). House of Commons Canada. https://www.ourcommons.ca/Committees/en/JUST/StudyActivity?studyActivityId=12111640

Black, M. (2023, March 03). Alberta targets human trafficking with task force budget boost. *Edmonton Journal*. https://edmontonjournal.com/news/politics/alberta-targets-human-trafficking-with-budget-boost-for-alert

Brock, M. (2017). This is what modern day slave-auction looks like. http://hopeforthesold.com/this-is-what-amodern-day-slave.auctionlooks-like

Choi-Fitzpatrick, A. (2017). *What slaveholders think*. Columbia Un. Press.

Choudry, A., & Smith, A. A. (2016). *Unfree labor? Struggles of migrant and Immigrant Workers in Canada*. PM Press.

Cohen, L., & Felson, M. (1979). Social change and crime rate trends: A routine activity approach. *American Sociological Review, 44*(4), 588–608. https://doi.org/10.2307/2094589

Conroy, S. (2022, December 06). Trafficking in persons in Canada, 2021. Statistics Canada. https://www150.statcan.gc.ca/n1/pub/85-005-x/2022001/article/00001-eng.htm

Conroy, S., & Sutton, D. (2023, June 9). Trafficking in persons in Canada 2022. *Statistics Canada, 85*(2), 3–23. https://www150.statcan.gc.ca/n1/en/pub/85-002-x/2022001/article/00010-eng.pdf?st=yk3eYRtH

Depatie-Pelletier, E., Deegan, H., & Berze, K. (2022). Band-aid on a bullet wound—Canada's open work permit for vulnerable workers policy. *Laws, 11*(3), 36. (Open access)Retrieved from. https://doi.org/10.3390/laws11030036

De Shalit, A., Roots, K., & Van Der Muelen, E. (2021). Knowledge mobilization by provincial politicians: The united front against trafficking in Ontario Canada. *Journal of Human Trafficking, 9*(4). https://doi.org/10.1080/23322705.2021.193470

Dottridge, M. (2014). Editorial: How is the money to combat human trafficking spent?. *Anti-Trafficking Review, 3*, 3–14.

Dow, L. (2021, May 25). Indentured Indian workers and anti-colonial resistance in the British empire. *The Gale Review*. https://review.gale.com/2021/05/25/indentured-workers-and-anti-colonial-resistance-in-the-british-empire/

Drinkwatter, R. (2022, October 03). Alberta announces $20.8 million in funding to fight human trafficking. CBC News. https://www.cbc.ca/news/canada/edmonton/alberta-human-trafficking-funding-announcement-1.6603930

Economic crimes. (2023). European Union Agency for criminal justice cooperation. https://www.eurojust.europa.eu/crime-types-and-cases/crime-types/economic-crimes

Eliadis, P. (2014). *Speaking out on human rights: Debating Canada's human rights system*. McGill-Queens University Press.

Farrell, A., Dank, M., de Vries, I., Kafafian, M., Hughes, A., & Lockwood, S. (2019). Failing victims? Challenges of the police response to human trafficking. *Criminology & Public Policy, 18*. https://doi.org/10.1111/1745-9133.12456

Ferguson, J. A. (2012). *International Human Trafficking in Canada: Why so Few Prosecutions?* PhD Thesis. The University of British Columbia. Faculty of Graduate Studies (Law).

Fraser, N. (2008, September 21). Dignity and hope: Too much to ask for? *The Guardian*. https://www.theguardian.com/world/2008/sep/21/humanrights

Gallagher, A., & Surtees, R. (2012). Measuring the success of counter-trafficking interventions in the criminal justice sector: Who decides—and how? *Anti-Trafficking Review, 1*(1), 10–30. https://doi.org/10.14197/atr.201211

Global report on trafficking in persons 2022. (2023). United Nations. https://www.unodc.org/documents/data-and-analysis/glotip/2022/GLOTiP_2022_web.pdf

Government of Canada. (2020). Government of Canada invests in 63 organizations to prevent human trafficking and to support survivors. Retrieved from https://www.canada.ca/en/women-gender-equality/news/2020/12/government-of-canada-invests-in-63-organizations-to-prevent-human-trafficking-and-to-support-survivors.html

Greer, B. (2018). Opaque transparency: Why California's supply chain transparency act is unenforceable. In J. Jones & J. Winterdyk (Eds.), *Human trafficking: Challenges and opportunities for the 21st Century, Ch. 3*, (pp. 42–64). Lambert Academic Pub.

Henry, N. (2021). Racial Segregation of Black People in Canada. *The Canadian Encyclopedia*. https://www.thecanadianencyclopedia.ca/en/article/racial-segregation-of-black-people-in-canada

Henry, N. L. (2018, September 07). "Black enslavement in Canada." The Canadian Encyclopedia © 2019. Historica Canada. https://www.thecanadianencyclopedia.ca/en/article/black-enslavement

How 7M will help human trafficking victims survivors find housing in Ontario. (2017, December 21). CBC News. https://www.cbc.ca/news/canada/windsor/how-7m-help-human-trafficking-find-housing-1.4461149

Human Trafficking - National List of Organizations. Government of British Columbia. https://www2.gov.bc.ca/gov/content/justice/criminal-justice/victims-of-crime/human-trafficking/human-trafficking-training/resources/national-organizations

International Labor Organization (2014a, May). ILO says forced labor generates annual profits of US$ 150 billion. ILO. https://www.ilo.org/global/about-the-ilo/newsroom/news/WCMS_243201/lang–en/index.htm

International Labor Organization. (2014b). *Profits and Poverty: The Economics of Forced Labor.* http://www.ilo.org/global/publications/ilo-bookstore/order-online/books/WCMS_243391/lang–en/index.htm

International Labor Organization. Forced labor, modern slavery and human trafficking. (2023). https://www.ilo.org/global/topics/forced-labor/lang–en/index.htm

International Organization for Migrants. (2015). Guidelines for the collection of data on trafficking in human beings, including comparable indicators. IOM. https://publications.iom.int/books/guidelines-collection-data-trafficking-human-beings-including-comparable-indicators

INTERPOL global crime trend summary report. (Oct. 20220. (2022). INTERPOL. Retrieved from file:///C:/Users/drjaw/Downloads/Global%20Crime%20Trend%20Summary%20Report%20EN.pdf

It's Not Just: National campaign raises youth awareness about gender-based violence. (2022, Dec. 1). Government of Canada: Women and gender equality Canada. https://www.canada.ca/en/women-gender-equality/news/2022/11/its-not-just-national-campaign-raises-youth-awareness-about-gender-based-violence.html

Kaye, J. (2017). *Responding to human trafficking: Dispossession, colonial violence, and resistance among indigenous and racialized women.* University of Toronto Press.

Laczko, F. (2002). Human trafficking: The need for Better Data. Migration Policy Institute. https://www.migrationpolicy.org/article/human-trafficking-need-better-data/

Lester, J., Pates, R., & Dolemeyer, A. (2017). The emotional leviathan – how Street-Level Bureaucrats govern human trafficking victims. *Digithum, 19*, 19–36.

Logan, M. P. (2015). Traits of transformative anti-trafficking partnerships. *Journal of Human Trafficking, 1*(1), 21–38. https://doi.org/10.1080/23322705.2015.1008883

MacNamara, H. (2021). Trafficking around the World: 2021 trafficking in persons report. National Center for Sexual Exploitation. Retrieved from https://endsexualexploitation.org/articles/2021-trafficking-in-persons-report/

McRae, M., & McCullough, S. (2023). The story of black slavery in Canadian history. The Canadian Human Rights Museum. https://humanrights.ca/story/story-black-slavery-canadian-history

Meshkovska, B., Mickovski, N., Bos, A. E. R., & Siegel, M. (2016). Trafficking of women for sexual exploitation in europe: Prosecution, trials and their impact. *Anti-Trafficking Review, 6*, 71–90.

Milandinovic, Z. (2019, January 24). Adult criminal and youth court statistics in Canada, 2016/2017. Statistics Canada. https://www150.statcan.gc.ca/n1/pub/85-002-x/2019001/article/00002-eng.htm

Millar, H., O'Doherty, T., & SWAN Vancouver Society. (2015). *The Palermo Protocol & Canada: The evolution and human rights impacts of anti-trafficking laws in Canada (2002 – 2015).* International Centre for Criminal Law Reform, University of British Columbia.

Millar, H., & O'Doherty, T. (2020, June 29). Canadian human trafficking prosecution and principles of fundamental justice: A contradiction in terms? *International Centre for Criminal Law Reform, & Criminal Justice Policy.* https://icclr.org/publications/canadian-human-trafficking-prosecutions-and-principles-of-fundamental-justice-a-contradiction-in-terms/

Moore, A. E. (2015, January 27). Special report: Money and lies in anti-human trafficking NGOs. Truthout. https://truthout.org/articles/special-report-money-and-lies-in-anti-human-trafficking-ngos/

Nasser, S. (Mar 03, 2023). A single foreign worker blew the lid off a massive international trafficking ring north of Toronto, police say. CBC NEWS. Retrieved from https://www.cbc.ca/news/canada/toronto/migrant-workers-rescued-york-toronto-1.6767167

National Strategy to Combat Human Trafficking, 2019–2024. (2019). Public Safety Canada. Retrieved 2022, from https://www.publicsafety.gc.ca/cnt/rsrcs/pblctns/2019-ntnl-strtgy-hmnn-trffc/index-en.aspx

Ontario Names Director of Anti-Human Trafficking Office. (2016, November 10). https://news.ontario.ca/en/release/42617/ontario-names-director-of-anti-human-trafficking-office

Oxman-Martinez, J. Hanley, J. & Gomez, F.(2005). Canadian policy on human trafficking: A four year analysis. *'International Migration', 43*(3), 7–29.

Paez, B. (2023, March 10). Sex traffickers are using shell companies to launder illicit profits. *The Globe and Mail.* https://www.theglobeandmail.com/business/article-human-trafficking-shell-companies-money-laundering/

Perrin, B. (2006). *Falling short of the mark: An international study on the treatment of human trafficking.* The Future Group.

Perrin, B. (2011). *Invisible chains: Canada's Underground World of Human Trafficking.* Penguin Books.

Perrin, B., Audas, R., & Péloquin-Ladany, S. (2016). The case for a justice system report card. Macdonald-Laurier Institute.

RelicsWorld. (n.d.). Retrieved from https://www.relicsworld.com/albert-einstein/the-more-i-learn-the-more-i-realize-i-dont-know-author-albert-einstein

Rodrigues, G. (2023, March 03). 'Deplorable living conditions': 64 Mexicans rescued from Ontario human trafficking ring. *Global News*. https://globalnews.ca/news/9525649/mexican-nationals-rescued-ontario-human-trafficking-ring/

Roots, K. (2018). *The Human Trafficking Matrix: Law, Policy and Anti-Trafficking Practices in the Canadian Criminal Justice System*. Doctoral dissertation, Dept. of Socio-Legal Studies, York University,

Roots, K. (2022). *The domestication of human trafficking: Law, policing, and prosecution in Canada*. University of Toronto Press.

Roots, K. (2023). Research methods in socio-legal studies: Experiences with research in Ontario's criminal justice system. In M. Alam, P. Dwyer, K. Roots, & J. Williams (Eds.), *Socio-legal Imaginations: A field in development*. UBC Press. Vancouver. B.C.

Rotenberg, C. (2016). *Prostitution offences in Canada: Statistical trends*. Statistics Canada.

Russell, R. (2023, February 23). Human trafficking report released by joint forces. *Myalgomamanitoulinnews*. Retrieved from https://www.myalgomamanitoulinnow.com/53743/featured/human-trafficking-report-released-by-joint-forces/

*R. v. D-Souza 2016ONSC 2749.*

Schwartz, K., & Allain, J. (2020, Feb 13). Slavery is not a crime in almost half the countries of the world. *Phys.org*. https://phys.org/news/2020-02-slavery-crime-countriesworld.html

Schwientek, S. (2023, March 24). Lack of data on human trafficking makes it hard to fight, says status of women committee. *CBC News*. https://www.cbc.ca/news/indigenous/status-of-women-committee-human-trafficking-1.6789260

Standing Committee on Justice and Human Rights. (2022, June22). JUST committee report 4 – preventing harm in the Canadian Sex Industry: A review of the *protection of communities and exploited persons act*. Retrieved from https://ourcommons.ca/DocumentViewer/en/44-1/JUST/report-4/

Van der Watt, M. (2023). Discouraging the demand that fosters sex trafficking: Collaboration through augmented intelligence. *Societies*, *13*(4), 4. https://doi.org/10.3390/soc13040094

Vermeulen, G., & Paterson, N. (2010). The measurement of human trafficking, sexually exploited & missing children in the European Union. The MONTRASEC Model – the Great Leap Forward? https://www.researchgate.net/publication/267374972_The_Measurement_Of_Human_Trafficking_Sexually_Exploited_Missing_Children_In_The_European_Union_The_MONTRASEC_Model_-_The_Great_Leap_Forward

Wheaton, E. M., Schauer, E. J., & Galli, T. V. (2010). Economics of human trafficking. *International Migration*, *48*(4), 114–141. PMID: 20645472. https://doi.org/10.1111/j.1468-2435.2009.00592.x

White, S. (2020a, November 02). 5 failings of the Great Barrington Declaration's dangerous plan for COVID-19 natural herd immunity. *The Conversation*. https://theconversation.com/5-failings-of-the-great-barrington-declarations-dangerous-plan-for-covid-19-natural-herd-immunity-148975

White, S. (2020b). Slavery is not a crime in almost half the countries of the world – new research. The Conversation. https://theconversation.com/slavery-is-not-a-crime-in-almost-half-the-countries-of-the-world-new-research-115596

Winterdyk, J. (2019). Combating human trafficking in Canada: How do we measure up?. *Justice Report*, *34*(3), 16–20.

Winterdyk, J., & Hincks, C. (2023a). *Support and assistance to survivors of human trafficking in Alberta*. International Centre for Criminal Law Reform.

Winterdyk, J., & Hincks, C. (2023b). *Understanding the demand in human trafficking for the Purpose of Sexual Exploitation: A Canadian overview*. Ottawa: Public Service Canada.

Winterdyk, J., Hincks, C., & Tuner, C. (in press). 'Duty to report': Victims of human trafficking falling through the gaps. *Justice Report*.

Wood, H. (2024 - in press). The Canada Declaration for a Human Trafficking and Salvery Free Canada: Justice or Just Words? 'J. of Human Trafficking.

# Does Anyone Care? — The Prevalence of Forced Labor Among Kenyan Migrant Workers and the Glaring Need for Better Labor Conditions in GCC Countries

Sheldon Zhang, Nell Compernolle, Kyle Vincent, Sarah Lord, and Kareem Kysia

**ABSTRACT**
Much media coverage in recent years has identified the abuses of migrant workers in the Gulf Cooperation Council (GCC) countries (e.g. Bahrain, Kuwait, Oman, Qatar, United Arab Emirates [UAE], and Saudi Arabia), an increasingly popular migrant destination for Kenyan workers. Due to their unique geo-political and economic profiles, these countries with widespread human rights violations have remained non-responsive primarily to pressure from the international community. Importantly, these factors mask another critical gap in human trafficking research: the lack of reliable data and how best to collect it threatens the effectiveness of existing and proposed interventions in the GCC. To address this gap, this team sought to measure the prevalence of forced labor among recently returned Kenyan migrant workers from GCC countries currently residing in the Nairobi Metro area. Using rigorous estimation strategies in our data collection and analysis, we found that forced labor was pervasive among this population. Practically every Kenyan migrant worker who worked in GCC countries during the studied period could be considered a victim of forced labor. Most striking was the consistency in the high rates of violations across all measures, regardless of which set of indicators we applied in our analysis. Although abuses among migrant workers are not uncommon in wealthy nations, such high rates of forced labor violations in GCC countries are truly rare, if not unprecedented in current prevalence estimation research, and call for massive systemic efforts to address the situation.

## Background

Low-skilled migration from East Africa to the Gulf Cooperation Council (GCC) countries (e.g., Bahrain, Kuwait, Oman, Qatar, United Arab Emirates [UAE], and Saudi Arabia) has increased in recent years, with data suggesting that the Kenyan migrant population is one of the fastest-growing unskilled labor migrant populations in the region (Malit & Youha, 2016a). Despite this growth, precise estimates of Kenyan migrants in the GCC vary widely (Naufal & Genc, 2012). Data from national ministries and embassies estimate approximately 100,000 Kenyans work in GCC countries, while other estimates indicate there may be up to 300,000 (Alexander, 2015; Malit & Youha, 2016b). It is also likely that such estimates are severely underestimated, as only those who leave formally and report to embassies tend to be reported. Due to high unemployment and a growing youth population, Kenyans will likely continue to seek relatively high-paying jobs in the GCC (Atong et al., 2018; Kenya National Bureaus of Statistics [KNBS], 2021).

Despite the higher wages, Kenyan workers in the region are often poor, do not speak host country languages, and lack in-country solid government and social support networks. As a result, they are vulnerable to becoming victims of forced labor and physical, verbal, and sexual abuse. In recent years, the Government of Kenya has sought to address these challenges through legislation around labor migration to GCC countries. Due to the abusive and fraudulent practices of agencies with which migrants often work within Nairobi or Mombasa to secure employment abroad (Chatzis et al., 2015), the government has also emphasized regulating formal recruitment channels (KNBS, 2021; Malit & Youha, 2016a). Despite these efforts, Kenyan migrants are still subjected to deceptive recruitment practices, forfeiture of identity documents, and abusive working conditions.

The fact that the GCC remains a hot spot for trafficking violations is partly due to the slow progress in implementing anti-trafficking efforts by sending and receiving countries in GCC countries. Notably, Kenyan diplomatic missions in Gulf countries often lack an official labor and welfare office, a safe shelter house, and other initiatives (Malit & Youha, 2016b; Mutai, 2015). Yet destination countries' emigration policies exacerbate the absence of Kenyan interventions. Although legally abolished in Bahrain and Qatar,[1] most foreign employment in the GCC continue to adhere to the *kafala* sponsorship program in practice, which essentially gives employers complete discretion over migrants' legal and mobility status in the country (Aljazeera, 2020). Moreover, a country's labor laws govern migrants in the private sector (e.g., construction), whereas domestic workers are excluded from these provisions (Malit & Naufal, 2016). No GCC government has ratified major ILO (International Labor Organization) conventions, including the ILO Convention 189 on Domestic Workers (Fernandez, 2014; ILO, 2023; Malit & Youha, 2016b, p. 11).

This slow progress reflects the GCC's essential non-response to pressure from the international community to address the region's human rights violations. Yet the region's unique geo-political and economic profile masks another critical limitation. Although abuse of Kenyan workers in Gulf countries is well-documented, prevalence estimates of this population and that of Kenyan migrants in the region remain ambiguous. In order to identify effective channels for supporting prospective and current migrants and returnees, improved prevalence estimations of this hard-to-reach population are required (Dottridge, 2017).

With funding from the U.S. Department of State's Office to Monitor and Combat Trafficking in Persons (TIP Office), the Global Fund to End Modern Slavery (GFEMS) commissioned the National Opinion Research Center (NORC) at the University of Chicago, with which this research team is affiliated, to estimate the prevalence of forced labor among Kenyan migrants in the GCC. We used innovative sampling and sophisticated analytic techniques to build on existing prevalence estimations and expand data on labor conditions in GCC countries. To ensure estimation precision within the budgetary constraint, we focused on recently returned migrants currently residing in one of the five counties in the Nairobi Metro area. The goal was to produce precise estimates of forced labor in a well-defined population. Below, we describe our innovative research methods, present our findings, and discuss data-driven recommendations to address forced labor in the GCC more effectively.

## Research Methods

Our approach for obtaining estimates is based on a link-tracing sampling and class of inference procedures developed for such designs. The rationale for applying this method was that our target population – labor migrants who experienced forced labor in the GCC – are not evenly distributed and accessible in any population, thus making conventional probability-based sampling strategies difficult in field logistics or ineffective in estimation. In other words, forced labor victims may cluster in certain geographic locations which may not be visible to the research team *ex ante* and/or would be costly to map on a sufficient scale to achieve a conventional sampling frame. Moreover, probability-based sampling will likely miss hidden individuals in the population and thus produce estimates of

[1]Bahrain and Qatar introduced new labor regulations in 2009 and 2016, respectively.

trafficking far below what network-based sampling strategies will produce. This includes those based on respondent-driven sampling (RDS) and the network scale-up method (NSUM) or non-network-based strategies, such as mark-recapture.

When recruiting hidden or irregularly distributed populations, two sampling strategies are frequently used to produce prevalence estimates – RDS and mark-recapture (or capture-recapture). Both strategies have been widely used in different contexts but have inherent problems. For example, RDS-based inference typically relies on unverifiable assumptions that impose heterophily constraints on the network structure. Moreover, RDS assumes that even with a relatively small set of initial sample seeds, the target population is well-networked enough to obtain a census with enough sample waves. Mark-recapture methods typically rely on self-selection of individuals, and estimation requires that a mathematical model can be fitted to the pattern of captures across lists/samples of captured individuals to extrapolate and arrive at an estimate of the population size.

The type of link-tracing used in this study is called the Vincent Link-Tracing Sampling (VLTS) (Vincent & Thompson, 2017), which combines the strengths of RDS and mark-recapture to provide an efficient way to estimate the size and characteristics of a hidden population. A more detailed operational description of the VLTS method can be found in Zhang and Vincent (2021).

In summary: 1) link-tracing occurs in the same fashion as RDS but does not place any sampling constraints on the individuals, and therefore the network sample is not restricted to forming a tree-like structure; 2) the design seeks "overlaps" between networks through multiple observations (i.e., redemption of more than one referral coupon) of individuals, giving rise to a more comprehensive and accurate representation of the population network; and 3) overlaps in respondents' networks can be treated as mark-recaptures for population size estimation. As such, link-tracing was successfully tested in several empirical studies and could produce estimates of high-risk populations cost-effectively and on a broad scale (see Vincent et al., 2021, 2021).

For point and variance estimation of population quantities, we rely on sampling weights generated by an innovative and newly developed procedure introduced by Thompson (2020). The design-based procedure does not rely on a network model for inference, classic RDS assumptions, or corresponding diagnostic checks. The procedure entails selecting subsamples of the observed network sample based on a relatively small amount of reseeding and tracing links/branches to reach a predetermined subsample size of observed individuals. Sampling weights are inversely proportional to the number of times individuals are resampled through the algorithm. This resampling procedure has been shown to address and mitigate the bias in point estimators commonly encountered with RDS and other network sampling designs (Thompson, 2020).

### *Sample Size Calculations*

The research team gained access to the latest census data (2019) from the Kenyan National Bureau of Statistics (KNBS). The data contained information on emigrant counts and their demographic information (e.g., age, sex, education level, destination countries, professional training, year of departure, the reason for departure, and whether they sent remittances). These data were further disaggregated by county, sub-county, division, location, and sub-location. The study team used these data to provide county-specific migrant population parameters and determine the number of seeds per county. Based on their census data, the goal was to allocate a budgeted total of 300 initial seeds proportional to the emigrant population size across the five counties in the Nairobi Metro area. This was a statistically optimal approach since it ensured a final sample that is as reflective as possible regarding geographic composition and would lead to as efficient estimators as possible. Our inference procedure relied on Vincent and Thompson (2017), which uses Rao-Blackwellized estimators to improve precision over preliminary counterparts. We calculated that $N = 1{,}000$ was required to reach a desired level of precision based on the Lincoln-Petersen estimator (Chapman, 1951) and used the expressions and calculations outlined in Robson and Regier (1964) to infer a suitable sample size.

### *Population Size Calculations*

A design-based approach was preferred for populations that are suspected of having high levels of clustering since elaborate network models do not have to be posited and tested for fit to the sample data (see Frank & Snijders, 1994). The estimator is akin to the two-sample mark-recapture estimator (Chapman, 1951) where $n_0$ is the size of the first sample, $l + r$ is the size of the second sample, and $r$ is the number of recaptures in the second sample. Population size was estimated using the R programming language (R Core Team, 2016). This includes sample size calculations and calculations of sample weights. Our data collection procedure permits for estimation of the population size based on a simple yet statistically efficient, mark-recapture type of design-based estimator derived by Frank and Snijders (1994); a design-based approach is preferred for populations that are suspected of having high levels of clustering since elaborate network models do not have to be posited and tested for fit to the sample data (Vincent & Thompson, 2017).

### *Measurement*

#### *Survey Instrument*

The survey instrument for this study used an indicator-based approach. We sought to align our key indicators of human trafficking following the legal framework established by the Trafficking Victims Protection Act (TVPA) and the ILO (2012). Our instrument contained items commonly found in prevalence studies but with different configurations. The instrument underwent several rounds of reviews with the help of our field team in Kenya, internal tests by the research staff, and cognitive tests with target population members to ensure clarity and local appropriateness. The main domains of the survey instrument included: (1) demographic characteristics (e.g., age, gender, ethnicity, and family composition); (2) debt situation due to migration decisions (e.g., debt amount, borrowing sources); (3) measures of job experiences at workplace (e.g., types of jobs, overtime, payment terms); and (4) various forms of employer-perpetrated abuses, including violence, restriction of physical/communicative freedom, and exploitative practices. Although none of these measurement items is unique, we applied two specific configurations to measure forced labor:

1. **The Scale of Harm**. Prior research has used this method to establish the threshold of defining labor trafficking or forced labor and operationalize a conceptual spectrum upon which the complexity of human trafficking violations can be managed (Zhang, 2012; Zhang et al., 2014). These categories include starting with the most severe as per their order listed below:

(1) Enacted or threatened infringement of physical integrity, i.e., physical or sexual violence against a migrant worker or their family.
(2) Enacted or threatened restriction of personal freedom, including physical movement and/or communication,
(3) Abusive and coercive employment practices compel migrant workers to do something they do not want to; and
(4) Any deceptive contracts, unfair or unsafe work arrangement, or lack of food and shelter.

2. **The ILO's Duo-Axle Indicators**. The ILO indicators use many of the same items on abusive labor practices described above. However, the ILO definition of forced labor varies in one major aspect: it applies a duo-axle qualification approach— (1) labor *involuntarily* extracted, while (2) under *the menace of penalty*. To qualify for "forced labor," a potential victim much experience at least one indicator from both axles.

### Data Collection

Our sampling design required that the field team work closely with community contacts and agencies and approach sampled counties with a predetermined number of seeds per county as our entry points to access the hidden networked population. Rigorous staff training and close supervision were in place during data collection. The recruitment targeted individuals in the survey catchment area who met the following inclusion criteria:

- Currently reside in one of the five counties in Nairobi Metro (i.e., Nairobi City, Kiambu, Kajiado, Machakos, and Murang'a),
- Are at least 18 years of age, and
- Have returned from working in one of the GCC countries within the last 18 months.

These seeds would then nominate individuals from within their networks belonging to the target population. This process involved respondents at the end of the forced labor assessment survey providing up to seven nominations from their network who meet the criteria. From this list, the enumerators followed a predetermined procedure to randomly select three nominated individuals to recruit for the next wave of interviews. The seed then was asked to approach and recruit these three nominations into the study, each given a coupon with incentives noted. The coupon included a unique identifier, study information, and a QR code. The QR code minimized gaming and ensured accurate network tracing. Those recruited after the seeds were considered Wave 1. This nomination/recruitment procedure repeated from Wave 1 to Wave 2. The recruitment activities would stop.

Importantly, these nominations had to fit the inclusion criteria for seeds noted above, as well as additional criteria specific to the two waves:

- They were not recruited into the study by a family member, and
- If they had already participated in the study, they were not recruited by the same individual.

These additional criteria ensured that the achieved sample was as diverse and representative of the underlying target population as possible. Although the county-specific location mattered for seeds, it did not for the waves; referrals for the next wave of interviews only needed to currently reside in one of the five study counties in Nairobi Metro. So, for example, seeds in Kajiado did not need to recruit participants who also currently reside in Kajiado.

### Target vs. Actual Sample

The study team fulfilled the required number and location of seeds for a total sample size of $N = 1{,}020$. Data collection began in January 2021 and ended in April 2021. Table 1 presents the target and actual location of initial seeds and the total interviews conducted by county in the Nairobi Metro area. The field and NORC teams conducted weekly status checks on the interviews. These checks provided regular overviews of the location and demographic information (e.g., gender, destination country) of seeds and waves that had participated in the study.

**Table 1.** Initial and Actual Seed and Wave Parameters.

| County | Total Emigrant Population Size Based on 2019 Census Data | Target Seed Count | Actual Seed Count | Total Interviews Conducted |
|---|---|---|---|---|
| Machakos | 10,323 | 48 | 53 | 132 |
| Murang'a | 7,551 | 34 | 35 | 120 |
| Kiambu | 42,985 | 80 | 78 | 281 |
| Kajiado | 9,838 | 38 | 40 | 135 |
| Nairobi City | 70,278 | 100 | 101 | 352 |
| *Total* | *140,975* | *300* | *307* | *1,020* |

## Analysis and Findings

Using a mark-recapture type of design-based estimator derived by Frank and Snijders (1994), like the two-sample mark-recapture estimator (Chapman, 1951), we estimate the population of resident migrant Kenyans who recently returned from GCC countries to be 5,209. Applying the jackknife procedure proposed by Frank and Snijders (1994), we estimate the 95% confidence intervals to vary between 2,992 and 7,427.

### *Demographic Characteristics*

Table 2 presents the demographic characteristics of the sample (N = 1020). There were slightly more women (53.43%) than men (46.57%), which was consistent with the fact that many Kenyans are employed as domestic workers in GCC countries, a profession mostly geared toward women. More than 95% of the sample were 40 years or younger, with similar distributions between 21 and 30 years (46.75%) and between 31 and 40 (49.01%). Kiswahili was the main language spoken at home, accounting for about two-thirds of the sample (64.80%). More than half the sample were married (57.6%); however, one in four (25.71%) were never married. Most of the respondents had children (81.96%). Compared to the census data on emigrant population in general, migrant workers to GCC countries consisted of slightly more women and primarily between the ages of 20s and 40s, which were consistent with the labor migration pattern.

Most respondents belonged to various branches of Christianity, accounting for 91% of the sample. Non-denominational Christians comprised the largest group (39%), followed by Protestants (19%), Catholics (16%), Evangelicals (11%), and other Christian (6%). Muslims only made up 5% of the sample. Ethnically, Kikuyu were the largest group in our sample (44%), followed by Kamba (17%), Luhya (12%), Luo (12%), and other ethnicities. Regarding education, study respondents were generally well-educated. Those who completed college degrees accounted for 45% of the sample, followed by people who completed secondary education (36%), college incompletes (8%), secondary incompletes

**Table 2.** Sample Demographics.

| | Total Sample | | Nairobi Metro | | | | | | | | | |
|---|---|---|---|---|---|---|---|---|---|---|---|---|
| | | | Nairobi | | Kiambu | | Muranga | | Kajiado | | Machakos | |
| | N** | % Sample* | Seed | Total | Seed | Total | Seed | Total | Seed | Total | Seed | Total |
| Sex | | | | | | | | | | | | |
| Male | 475 | 46.57 | 47 | 170 | 38 | 122 | 20 | 50 | 22 | 70 | 26 | 63 |
| Female | 545 | 53.43 | 54 | 182 | 40 | 159 | 15 | 70 | 18 | 65 | 27 | 69 |
| Age | | | | | | | | | | | | |
| 21–30 | 474 | 46.75 | 58 | 183 | 38 | 115 | 14 | 65 | 20 | 59 | 20 | 52 |
| 31–40 | 497 | 49.01 | 37 | 155 | 37 | 156 | 17 | 47 | 20 | 67 | 31 | 72 |
| 41–50 | 43 | 4.24 | 5 | 13 | 2 | 8 | 4 | 8 | 0 | 9 | 2 | 5 |
| Language spoken | | | | | | | | | | | | |
| Kiswahili | 661 | 64.80 | 81 | 268 | 51 | 145 | 23 | 56 | 32 | 96 | 37 | 96 |
| English | 17 | 1.67 | 4 | 9 | 0 | 1 | 2 | 2 | 3 | 3 | 0 | 2 |
| Other | 342 | 33.53 | 16 | 75 | 27 | 135 | 10 | 62 | 5 | 36 | 16 | 34 |
| Marital status | | | | | | | | | | | | |
| Never married | 262 | 25.71 | 40 | 101 | 20 | 57 | 8 | 43 | 11 | 33 | 14 | 28 |
| Married | 588 | 57.70 | 43 | 196 | 42 | 168 | 21 | 52 | 25 | 75 | 27 | 70 |
| Divorced/widowed/separated | 169 | 16.58 | 17 | 54 | 16 | 56 | 6 | 25 | 0 | 0 | 2 | 4 |
| Number of children | | | | | | | | | | | | |
| 0 children | 184 | 18.04 | 28 | 66 | 17 | 45 | 7 | 31 | 10 | 26 | 12 | 16 |
| 1–2 children | 523 | 51.27 | 51 | 179 | 34 | 143 | 19 | 64 | 18 | 70 | 21 | 67 |
| 3+ children | 313 | 30.69 | 22 | 107 | 27 | 93 | 9 | 25 | 12 | 39 | 20 | 49 |

*Sample statistics reflect the percentage of those identified as positive of the indicator based on the total sample size (N = 1,020); ** Number of respondents identified as positive by the indicator.

(6%). Those with only primary education only made up 4% of the sample. Education among migrant workers to GCC countries closely reflects the emigrant population in general.

### *Migration and Work in GCC Countries*

Kenyan migrants worked in all six GCC countries. Qatar was the top destination for employment among our respondents (28%), followed by UAE (23%), Saudi Arabia (21%), Kuwait (10%), Oman, and Bahrain (both 9%). Regarding job types, domestic work represented the largest share of all reported employment (44%), followed by hospitality (20%), construction (10%), driving (9%), and manufacturing (3%).

Most (nearly 92%) migrated on valid work visas to their destination countries, followed by a small number of tourist visas (6.03%) and student visas (1.21%), as shown in Table 3. Very few respondents lived and worked in GCC countries without visas or in undocumented conditions. Various strategies were used to secure jobs in GCC countries. Nearly half of the respondents went through formal channels, including government-registered recruitment agencies (43.63%), or government-registered (posted) overseas jobs (5.20%). The rest went through various informal channels, including recruitment agencies not registered with the government (16.37%), personal connections in GCC countries (14.90%), friends already in GCC countries (14.31%), family members already in GCC countries (3.53%), or even self-initiation (1.57%).

**Table 3.** Employment Characteristics.

| | N** | %* |
|---|---|---|
| Visa Type | | |
| Student | 12 | 1.21 |
| Working | 915 | 91.96 |
| Tourist | 60 | 6.03 |
| I was working without a visa | 3 | 0.30 |
| Other | 5 | 0.50 |
| How job was obtained | | |
| Family member already in GCC country | 36 | 3.53 |
| Friend already in GCC country | 146 | 14.31 |
| Government registered official job | 53 | 5.20 |
| Recruitment agency (not registered) | 167 | 16.37 |
| Recruitment agency (registered or unsure) | 445 | 43.63 |
| Individual with connections to job | 152 | 14.90 |
| I found it myself | 16 | 1.57 |
| Other | 5 | 0.49 |
| Fee/loan to secure job | | |
| Paid a fee to secure job | 588 | 57.87 |
| Took out a loan | 420 | 41.18 |
| Source of loan taken | | |
| Employer | 2 | 0.48 |
| Recruiter | 12 | 2.86 |
| Friend/family member | 319 | 75.95 |
| Bank | 56 | 13.33 |
| Other | 31 | 7.38 |
| Fee paid to secure a job in Kenyan Shilling (KES) | | |
| Mean | 58,229.96 | |
| Standard Deviation | 30,699.72 | |
| Range | 2,000.00 | 300,000.00 |
| Loan amount Kenyan Shilling (KES) | | |
| Mean | 66,423.81 | |
| Standard Deviation | 49,850.95 | |
| Range | 4,500.00 | 480,000.00 |

*Sample statistics reflect the percentage of those identified as positive by the indicator based on the total sample size (N = 1,020); ** Number of respondents identified as positive by the indicator.

More than half of the sample (57.87%) paid a fee to secure employment in GCC countries; 41.18% of respondents had to take out a loan to pay for the fee. As for the sources of loans, friends and family members represented the largest lending source, accounting for 75.95% of those who took out a loan, followed by banks (13.33%). In general, it was rare for respondents to borrow money directly from the recruiter (just 2.86%) or the employer (0.48% or 2 respondents). The average cost of fees paid to secure a job in GCC countries amounted to 58,229.96 Kenyan Shilling (KES, about $531 USD), with a standard deviation of 30,699.72 (about $278 USD) and ranged from a low of 2,000 KES (about $18 USD) to 300,000 KES (about $2,714 USD), suggesting wide variation in personal circumstances. Last, we found that the average amount of loans taken out by migrants was higher (66,423.81 KES or about $606 USD) than the average amount of fee paid to obtain a job in the GCC (58,229.96 KES), with a standard deviation of 49,850.95 and a range from 4,500 KES (about $41 USD) to 480,000 KES (about $4,349 USD).

### Forced Labor Violations

#### Actual or Threat of Physical/Sexual Violence

As shown in Table 4, we found widespread violent victimization among Kenyan migrant workers in GCC countries. Nearly two out of three (65.20%) respondents reported having experienced threatened or actual physical/sexual violence at the hands of their employers. More than one in four migrant workers (29.80%) dared not leave their job before their contracts ended for fear of physical violence. We estimate the rate of physical violence as consequence of quitting one's job before the end of their contract to be 28.90% in general, with confidence intervals between 24.26% and 33.53%. In addition, one in four had experienced physical or sexual violence at the hands of their employers, who made them do things they did not want to do. We estimate that the rate of physical violence in the Kenyan migrant workers in GCC countries in general was 28.71%, with confidence intervals between 23.95% and 33.47%. Adding threats of violence to the equation, the violation rate was even higher. Far fewer reported enacted or threatened violence against a migrant worker's family, at 2.25% for the sample and 1.63% for the general migrant worker population in GCC countries, with 95% CI between 0.49% and 2.76%.

#### Restriction of Freedom in Movement/communication

Nearly all respondents (97.45%) experienced some form of restriction of freedom in movement or communication, as presented in Table 5. Most common (89.61% of the sample) were reports that employers withheld their identification documents to make them do something they did not want to do. The rate of withholding workers' identification documents was estimated to be 88.04% in general among the migrant worker population in GCC countries,

**Table 4.** Violation of Physical Integrity.

| | | | | 95% Conf. Intervals | |
|---|---|---|---|---|---|
| Question | N* | %** | Population Estimation | Lower | Upper |
| Employer threatened or enacted physical or sexual violence on you to make you do something you did not want to do. | 624 | 61.18 | 61.98 | 56.92 | 67.05 |
| Violence will occur to migrant workers if they dare to leave his/her job before the contract is finished. | 304 | 29.80 | 28.90 | 24.26 | 33.53 |
| Employer enacted physical or sexual violence on you to make you do something you did not want. | 263 | 25.78 | 28.71 | 23.95 | 33.47 |
| Employer harmed your family to make you do something you did not want\or threatened to do. | 23 | 2.25 | 1.63 | 0.49 | 2.76 |
| *Any of the above* | *665* | *65.20* | *64.65* | *59.63* | *69.67* |

*Number of respondents identified as positive by the indicator; **Sample statistics reflect the percentage of those identified as positive of the indicator based on the total sample size (N = 1,020).

**Table 5.** Restriction of Freedom in Movement/Communication.

| Question | N* | %** | Population Estimation | 95% Conf. Intervals | |
|---|---|---|---|---|---|
| | | | | Lower | Upper |
| Employer ever withheld your identity documents or threatened to do so to make you do something you did not want to do. | 914 | 89.61 | 88.04 | 84.42 | 91.67 |
| Employer or recruiter held your identification documents, such as your passport or ID card. | 910 | 89.22 | 87.56 | 83.91 | 91.21 |
| After your shift is over, employer does not allow you to move around freely in the community. | 801 | 78.53 | 78.18 | 73.71 | 82.65 |
| (If the respondent lives in employer-provided housing) not allowed to live somewhere else and keep their current job if one decided not to live in employer-provided housing. | 709 | 69.51 | 70.65 | 65.99 | 75.31 |
| Loss of freedom of movement or communication or being stranded if one quits before the contract is finished. | 694 | 68.04 | 67.98 | 63.25 | 72.71 |
| Employer isolated, confined, or surveilled you or threatened to do so. | 477 | 46.76 | 50.96 | 45.81 | 56.11 |
| *Any of the above* | *994* | *97.45* | *97.00* | *94.99* | *99.01* |

*Number of respondents identified as positive by the indicator; **Sample statistics reflect the percentage of those identified as positive of the indicator based on the total sample size (N = 1,020).

with confidence intervals between 84.42% and 91.67%. Most respondents (78.53%) could not move around freely in their community even after their workday. The rate adjusted for the Kenyan migrant worker population in GCC countries was estimated to be 78.18%, with confidence intervals between 73.71% and 82.65%. Nearly three-fourths of our sample (69.51%) were not allowed to live elsewhere besides employer-provided housing, regardless of their preference. The loss of freedom to choose one's living quarters was estimated to be 70.65% among Kenyan migrant worker population in GCC countries in general, with confidence intervals between 65.99% and 75.31%.

Similarly, two-thirds (68.04%) of the sample reported that their employers would take away their freedom of movement and/or communication or leave them stranded in faraway places should they dare to quit before the contract expired. The rate for the Kenyan migrant population in GCC countries was estimated to be 67.98%, with confidence intervals between 63.25% and 72.71%. Finally, close to half of the sample (46.76%) reported that their employers used or threatened to use isolation, confinement, and surveillance to compel them to do things they did not want to do. We estimate this rate to be 50.96% among Kenyan migrant workers in GCC countries, with confidence intervals between 45.81% and 56.11%.

### *Abusive and Coercive Employment Practices*

Table 6 shows the victimization rates of abusive or grossly exploitative labor practices employers use to coerce their employees to do things they did not want to. Nearly all respondents (96.76%) reported having experienced at least one of the abuses listed. The most common form of coercive practice was to inflict (or threaten to inflict) significant financial, legal, and reputational costs on workers should anyone quit before their contract was finished (79.80% of the sample). The rate of these victimizations was estimated to be 79.20% among Kenyan migrant workers in GCC countries in general, with confidence intervals between 75.08% and 83.33%.

The next most common form of coercion used by employers to compel workers to do something they did not want to be withholding due wages, including overtime pay, or threatening to do so; 62.35% of our sample reported having experienced such abuses. The population victimization rate of such abuses was estimated to be 64.28% among the Kenyan migrant workers in GCC countries, with confidence intervals between 59.30% and 69.26%. Another commonly applied tactic was to denounce (or threaten to do so) migrant workers to the authorities, with 58.24% of the sample having experienced these abuses at work. We estimate the population victimization rate for these abuses to be 61.79%, with confidence intervals between 56.78% and 66.80%.

**Table 6.** Abusive and Coercive Employment Practices.

| Question | N* | %** | Population Estimation | 95% Conf. Intervals Lower | Upper |
|---|---|---|---|---|---|
| Significant financial/legal/reputational consequences if one quits before his/her contract is finished. | 814 | 79.80 | 79.20 | 75.08 | 83.33 |
| Employer unfairly withheld due wages, including overtime wages, or threatened to do so to make you do something you did not want to do. | 636 | 62.35 | 64.28 | 59.30 | 69.26 |
| Employer denounced you to the authorities to make you do something or threatened to do so. | 594 | 58.24 | 61.79 | 56.78 | 66.80 |
| Employer convinced other employers in your area to boycott hiring you or your family, or threatened to do so to make you do something you did not want to do. | 409 | 40.10 | 39.89 | 34.91 | 44.88 |
| Employer manipulated the amount of debt you owed, or threatened to do so to make you do something you did not want to do | 328 | 32.16 | 33.21 | 28.33 | 38.09 |
| Forced to work for no pay or for reduced pay to repay a loan to your employer or recruitment agency. | 206 | 20.20 | 19.21 | 15.20 | 23.21 |
| Not been paid or not been allowed to keep the money you earned. | 188 | 18.43 | 16.22 | 12.63 | 19.81 |
| *Any of the above* | *987* | *96.76* | *95.90* | *93.55* | *98.26* |

*Number of respondents identified as positive by the indicator; **Sample statistics reflect the percentage of those identified as positive of the indicator based on the total sample size (N = 1,020).

Tarnishing one's reputation or threatening to do so was also used frequently by employers to control Kenyan migrant workers, with 40.10% of the sample reporting that their employers either convinced other employers in their area to boycott hiring them or their family members or threatened to do so to compel them to do something they did not want to. We estimate that 39.89% of the Kenyan migrant workers in GCC countries encountered this type of abuse, with confidence intervals between 34.91% and 44.88%.

One-fifth of Kenyan migrant workers (20.20%) were forced to work for no pay or for reduced pay to repay a loan to their employer or recruitment agency. This practice was estimated to affect 19.21% of all Kenyan overseas migrant workers in GCC countries, with confidence intervals between 15.20% and 23.21%. The least frequent form of abuse was not being paid or not being allowed to keep the money one earned, with 18.43% having experienced this form of abuse. We estimate the rate of this abuse in the general Kenyan migrant worker population to be 16.22%, with confidence intervals between 12.63% and 19.81%.

### *Deceptive/Unfair/Unsafe Work Environments*

Table 7 presents the victimization experiences of various unfair or deceptive labor practices or unsafe work environments. Because of the varied range of abuses captured in our scale, nearly all respondents, 98.43% of the sample, reported having experienced at least one of the listed abuses. The most reported was deceptive recruitment tactics, where 97.84% of the sample claimed to have been deceived when they showed up at the worksite. We estimated deceptive recruitment tactics to be pervasive, affecting 96.88% of the Kenyan migrant workers who took jobs in GCC countries, with confidence intervals between 94.79% and 98.97%.

More than half of the respondents (58.33%) reported that their employers threatened to worsen their working conditions to make them do something they did not want to. We estimate this abusive employment practice was affecting 63.48% of the Kenyan migrant workers in the GCC countries in general, with confidence intervals between 58.55% and 68.42%. Another coercive tactic frequently used by employers was threatening to dismiss migrant workers to get them to do something they did not want to, as reported by 54.51% of the sample. We estimate that 57.30% of the general migrant worker population in the GCC countries experienced such a labor practice, with confidence intervals between 52.18% and 62.41%.

**Table 7.** Deceptive/Unfair/Unsafe Work Environment.

| Question | N* | %** | Population Estimation | 95% Conf. Intervals Lower | Upper |
|---|---|---|---|---|---|
| Some aspect of the job situations (duties, wages, hours, overtime pay, housing, or location) was worse than was promised by the recruiter. | 998 | 97.84 | 96.88 | 94.79 | 98.97 |
| Employer threatened to make your working conditions worse to make you do something you did not want. | 595 | 58.33 | 63.48 | 58.55 | 68.42 |
| Employer dismissed you or threatened to dismiss you to force you to do something outside your understood scope of work. | 556 | 54.51 | 57.30 | 52.18 | 62.41 |
| Employer deprived you of sleep to make you do something you did not want. | 539 | 52.84 | 53.87 | 48.72 | 59.02 |
| No extra pay for working overtime less than the normal rate. | 511 | 50.10 | 49.90 | 44.75 | 55.06 |
| Employer made you work extra hours as punishment. | 441 | 43.24 | 49.67 | 44.51 | 54.83 |
| Employer excluded you from future employment or overtime opportunities to make you do something you did not want to or threatened to do. | 427 | 41.86 | 44.47 | 39.35 | 49.58 |
| Employer imposed excessive taxes or fees on you to make you do something you did not want to, or threatened to do so. | 418 | 40.98 | 41.58 | 36.52 | 46.64 |
| Employer deprived you of food or water to make you do something you did not want. | 403 | 39.51 | 41.04 | 35.98 | 46.10 |
| (For respondents living in employer-provided housing) not permitted to live elsewhere; worse living conditions; too many people sleep in the room you sleep in; unsafe housing; no space to store personal belongings. | 346 | 33.92 | 33.59 | 28.76 | 38.42 |
| *Any of the above* | *1004* | *98.43* | *97.56* | *95.71* | *99.41* |

*Number of respondents identified as positive by the indicator; **Sample statistics reflect the percentage of those identified as positive of the indicator based on the total sample size (N = 1,020)..

Depriving migrant workers of food, water, or sleep, to compel them to do something they did not want to do was also reported at fairly regular rates. More than half of the sample (52.84%) reported having been sleep-deprived by their employers, and 39.51% had been deprived of food and water.

Although working overtime was frequently sought after by migrant workers to earn extra income, 50.10% of our sample reported working overtime either for no pay or less than their standard rate. We estimate the rate for this type of exploitative labor practice affected about 49.90% of the Kenyan migrant worker population in general, with confidence intervals between 44.75% and 55.06%. Furthermore, 41.86% of the sample reported that their employers made them work extra hours as punishment, which we estimate such an employment practice occurred at a rate of 49.67% among the general Kenyan migrant worker population in GCC countries, with confidence intervals between 44.51% and 54.83%. We also found that 41.86% of the sample reported that their employers deliberately excluded (or threatened to do so) future employment or overtime opportunities as a tactic to make migrant workers do something they did not want to do. We estimate that this practice occurred to 44.47% of the general Kenyan migrant worker population, with confidence intervals between 39.35% and 49.58%.

We also found that employers imposed excessive taxes or fees on 40.98% of the respondents (or threatened to do so) to make them do something they did not want to do; the rate of this practice in the general Kenyan migrant worker population was estimated to be 41.58%, with confidence intervals between 36.52% and 46.64%. Finally, more than a third of the sample (33.92%) were not permitted to live in places other than employer-provided housing and endured worse living conditions than promised, such as unsafe housing, sharing a room with too many people, or having no space to store personal belongings. We estimate that 33.59% of the general Kenyan migrant workers experienced such poor living conditions while working in GCC countries, with confidence intervals between 28.76% and 38.42%.

**Table 8.** Summary of Key Forced Labor Indicators.

| Indicator | N* | %** | Population Estimation | 95% Conf. Intervals Lower | Upper |
|---|---|---|---|---|---|
| **Scale of Harm (% positive)** | | | | | |
| 1. Violation of physical integrity | 665 | 65.20 | 64.65 | 59.63 | 69.67 |
| 2. Restriction of freedom | 994 | 97.45 | 97.00 | 94.99 | 99.01 |
| 3. Abusive/Coercive Employment Practices | 987 | 96.76 | 95.90 | 93.55 | 98.26 |
| 4. Deceptive/unfair/unsafe work environment | 1004 | 98.43 | 97.56 | 95.71 | 99.41 |
| *All of the Above (Complete Harm Spectrum)* | *663* | *65.00* | *64.14* | *59.12* | *69.20* |
| **ILO Forced Labor Indicators (% positive)** | | | | | |
| 1. Menace of penalty | 995 | 97.55 | 96.13 | 93.77 | 98.49 |
| 2. Involuntariness | 1007 | 98.73 | 98.24 | 96.65 | 99.82 |
| *ILO FL (1 menace + 1 involuntariness)* | *995* | *97.55* | *96.13* | *93.77* | *98.49* |

Number of respondents identified as positive by the indicator; **Sample statistics reflect the percentage of those identified as positive of the indicator based on the total sample size (N = 1,020)..

## *Prevalence of Human Trafficking Victimization*

In Table 8, we summarize the different dimensions of forced labor indicators. We collapse them into the 4-category scale of harm (top-most rows) and map them onto the ILO forced labor indicators (bottom-most). On the 4-category scale of harm, our study found that 65.20% of our respondents reported having experienced at least one of the most severe measures—*physical violence*; the population rate was estimated to be 64.65% with confidence intervals between 59.63% and 69.67%. On *restriction of freedom*, 97.45% of the respondents reported having encountered at least one of the listed violations; the population rate was estimated to be 97.00%, with confidence intervals between 94.99% and 99.01%. On *abusive/coercive employment practices*, we found that 96.76% of the respondents experienced abusive or coercive employment practices by their employers to do things they did not want to do; the population rate was estimated to be 95.90%, with confidence intervals between 93.55% and 98.26%. On *deceptive/unfair/unsafe work environment*, nearly all respondents (98.43%) reported having experienced at least one of the listed violations; we estimated the population victimization rate to be 97.56% with confidence intervals between 95.71% and 99.41%.

Considering the varied dimensional rates of trafficking violations, we calculated the proportion of respondents who experienced at least one type of violation across all four categories. We found that 65% of our sample experienced at least one forced labor violation in all four categories, and the population victimization rate was estimated to be 6,4.14% with confidence intervals between 59.12% and 69.20%.

Using the ILO indicators, we found that 97.55% of our respondents reported having experienced at least one item on the *menace of penalty* measures. We estimate the population violation rates to be 96.13%, with confidence intervals between 93.77% and 98.49%. On measures of *involuntariness*, we found that 98.73% of the respondents in our sample experienced at least one of the listed violations. We estimate the violation rate in the migrant labor population to be 98.24%, with confidence intervals between 96.65% and 99.82%. When both the *menace of penalty* and *involuntariness* were combined to qualify for the ILO definition of forced labor, we found that 995 out of our sample, or 97.55%, would qualify as potential victims. We estimated the rate of forced labor under the ILO definition to be 96.13% among the migrant workers in the Nairobi Metro area, with confidence intervals between 93.77% and 98.49%.

## Conclusions and Recommendations

This study sought to produce precise estimates of a well-defined target population in order to identify more effective and data-driven recommendations to address well-documented challenges related to forced labor in the GCC. Using innovative sampling and sophisticated analytic techniques, we assessed forced labor experiences among recently returned migrants living in Nairobi Metro during the study period ($N = 1{,}020$). We assessed forced labor using an indicator approach that both aligned with ILO practice and enabled us to place violations along a continuum of abuses (i.e., our scale of harm).

In general, results indicate high rates of violations across all measures, whether by the ILO indicators or our scale of harm. Using our scale of harm, we found that 98.73% of the sample or 1,007 out of the total 1,020 respondents reported having experienced at least one of the listed violations. We estimate the victimization rate among the Kenyan migrant labor population in GCC countries to be 98.24% with confidence intervals between 96.65% and 99.82%. In other words, practically every migrant worker in Kenya who ever worked in GCC countries during our survey period experienced some form of forced labor abuses. The findings based on the ILO forced labor indicators (a combination of the menace of penalty and involuntariness violations) were similar: 97.55% of our sample or 995 out of 1,020 respondents, reported having experienced both types of violations at least once during their last stay in GCC countries. We estimate the rate of violation based on ILO indicators to be 96.13%, with confidence intervals between 93.77% and 98.49%. In short, findings using either the scale of harm or the ILO indicators revealed essentially the same patterns of violations.

These improved estimates address a critical gap in existing human trafficking research: the lack of reliable data and how best to collect them. Low-wage migrant workers in the GCC are a hidden population; they are hard to reach, and therefore, little is known about how much this group experiences forced labor violations. Most existing research is, therefore, largely anecdotal or based on smaller sample sizes that fail to capture a population's diverse experiences. The innovative techniques described here contribute to a burgeoning body of research, improving data on forced labor among vulnerable populations. Moreover, our study revealed that such a high prevalence of forced labor – across all measures – underscores the urgency with which these conditions need to be addressed and critical gaps in interventions that future work should prioritize.

### *Counter Explanations*

It is perhaps prudent to explore alternative interpretations. After all, findings from this study appear to have shown a rate of forced labor far higher than most, if not all, other published prevalence estimation studies we are aware of. Several possible factors may contribute to these unusual findings.

First, our instrument may be too sensitive, thus detecting more violations than occurred or picking up too many false "positives." While instrument sensitivity may be a problem and additional studies are needed for validation purposes, the instrument contains conventional measures and has been shared in identical or similar formats by researchers in the field. In other words, our instrument reflects the most standard or status quo measurement of forced labor/labor trafficking. However, such a conventional instrument may be precisely the problem because these existing measures have been designed and applied in situations of far less severe labor rights violations. In this context, the detected forced labor violations went off the scale on our "conventional" instrument.

Second, GCC countries may be an anomaly. Some of the labor practices, common or culturally accepted in these countries, may be considered a clear sign of restriction of freedom. For instance, as reported earlier, we found that most employers in GCC countries withheld workers' identity papers, thus preventing workers from moving around freely. Whether it is intended for safekeeping or as a blatant measure of preventing workers from violating agreed-upon work contracts, such a practice would automatically qualify as an indicator of loss of freedom in any labor trafficking study. It could also be that employers in GCC countries may be particularly aware of the legal restrictions or immigration control for migrant laborers and thus become adept at taking advantage of their vulnerable situations.

While we offer these possible counter explanations, the high levels of consistency in the reported rates of violations only increase points to improved validity in our interpretation because our point estimates and 95% confidence interval values appeared to cluster closely.

The meticulous planning in our sampling procedure and our field team's close supervision and quality control gave us further confidence in the interpretations of these findings. While more studies are needed to validate or replicate our findings, these uncovered labor abuses should call for intensified action by concerned government agencies and international organizations to improve and protect workers' rights and provide a safe and dignified work environment for these Kenyan migrant laborers.

### *Gaps Where Migrant Workers' Conditions Can Be Improved*

The lack of robust prevalence estimation of forced labor or labor trafficking in GCC countries may have prevented human rights organizations from holding concerned government agencies accountable. Although more empirical studies are needed to validate these findings, results in this study nevertheless point out significant gaps where the Kenyan and GCC governments could act, and migrants themselves can reduce the chances of being victimized. Some of these actions may involve careful screening by the government agencies in all involved counties and avoidance by the migrant workers of specific trafficking-prone labor sectors or employers. Others may require committed government involvement in awareness-raising, screening of employers, and pre-departure training and education for prospective migrant workers. The following presents the gaps where efforts and policy changes are needed to improve migrant workers' conditions in GCC countries.

#### *Legal Obligation to Employers*

With such high rates of trafficking victimization among the Kenyan migrant workers, we believe that the most fundamental change that will bring about the most significant effect in reducing forced labor is to un-tie/sever the legal obligations a worker has toward his/her employer, i.e., abolishing the *kafala* system. The *kafala* system, a legal mechanism widely practiced in the GCC countries that binds millions of migrant workers to their employers who sponsor their employment, has long been rife with labor abuses and exploitation. Migrant laborers ought to have, at a minimum, the freedom to escape an abusive work environment and/or be free to seek alternative work. Changes in the guest worker program can be modified to increase the freedom of employment and movement for migrant workers. It should be noted that Saudi Arabia and Qatar recently initiated reforms to allow foreign workers to leave the country without employers' permission or change jobs by transferring the sponsorship from one employer to another (Aljazeera, 2020). It remains unclear what and when measurable differences will result from these changes in law in GCC countries in improving workers' rights.

#### *Lack of Rights Awareness Among Migrant Workers and Employers*

The high rate of forced labor violations prompted the question of whether the concept of labor trafficking or forced labor remains foreign to employers and workers and society in general. Our data and field interactions with respondents appeared to suggest that fundamental human rights to dignified working conditions were not well recognized either by the employers in GCC countries or migrant workers themselves. A gap of awareness was apparent, thus calling for interventions to teach migrant workers and employers to understand the basic parameters of proper working conditions and fundamental human rights. As more migrant workers from Kenya become familiarized with these internationally recognized employment rights and benefits, collective awareness will lead to collective action.

#### *Gaps in Government Initiatives*

We recognize that governments like Kenya are constrained due to geopolitics and economic imbalances, and other non-state actors in the Gulf region may not be allowed to partner with external anti-trafficking organizations (see Malit, 2018; Malit & Tsourapas, 2021), but we also believe it is time for the international community to increase pressure on the GCC countries to better protect their migrant labor force. Significant policy changes are needed to widen the coverage of government-sponsored welfare benefits because of the continued demand by significant construction and manufacturing sectors for stable workforce supplies in these countries.

### Gaps in Government Inspections and Liability Insurance

To reduce or prevent employer abuses, particularly in small family-operated businesses, governments in GCC countries should establish dedicated agencies to conduct scheduled and unscheduled inspections to ensure proper working conditions and fair treatment of employees. More importantly, these agencies must have legal authority to impose significant penalties to produce meaningful deterrence effects among current and prospective employers. One potential regulatory scheme is establishing liability insurance to which recruitment agencies and employers are asked to contribute. Financial compensations can be paid out from this insurance program or deducted from the bond for any verified cases of forced labor violations. However, the bond can be returned to the employer and recruitment agency if migrant workers report no labor violations during their contract period.

### Gaps in Lack of Shelters and Services for Migrant Workers in GCC Countries

Suppose that many Kenyan migrant workers heading to GCC countries will likely encounter forced labor situations. In that case, pre-departure training of services and rescue venues in the host countries is paramount. Adequate wealth exists in GCC countries to establish or make available workers' protection services to rescue or provide emergency shelter and other services to workers seeking to exit their abusive work environment. Such services need to be made known to all migrant workers as part of the departure preparation and job training. It falls on the responsibility of the Kenyan government to develop and collect information about service providers (e.g., addresses of providers or shelters, types of services, and contact information) in each of the GCC countries. Methods and appropriate processes are not difficult to develop, such as in the form of information cards or labor attaches in the GCC embassies, so that all migrant workers can quickly access these services. As part of potential interventions, the Kenyan government should consider expanding its overseas posts for labor attaches who are responsible for safeguarding migrant workers and monitoring and intervening in cases of severe violations. Deterrence effects can be achieved through diplomatic interventions on behalf of migrant workers for rights violations.

### Gaps in National Plans for Intervention and Monitoring

The widespread employment-based abuse also calls for widespread intervention. Considering the political and cultural realities of the GCC countries, intervention efforts are perhaps easier to implement inside Kenya. As mentioned, government agencies and international organizations have a target-rich environment to devise and test various intervention programs to prepare and train GCC-bound migrant workers. A bold national plan and carefully planned monitoring mechanism are needed to ameliorate the current abhorrent employment conditions for Kenyan migrant workers.

## Study Limitations

Although our findings are compelling, some limitations may challenge interpreting our study findings. Moreover, future research on forced labor prevalence estimation should be aware of these limitations and take necessary steps to address them, where possible.

### Survey Period Limitation

Our findings only reflect the experiences of migrants who recently returned from the GCC (e.g., approximately 18 or fewer months before data collection). Because labor contracts typically last 2–3 years, one cannot extrapolate these findings beyond the period as things may have changed in time since.

#### *Excluded Migrants*

Our study, by design, excluded the most severe cases of forced labor, in which individuals may not get to safely return home due to threats from their employer or even illness or death while abroad. This includes domestic workers, who are reported to be more isolated than other types of workers and who experience harsh treatment. Only those who were able to return from GCC countries, and remained in the Nairobi Metro area, were captured in our sampling. Further, our sampling may have missed those migrant workers who had more positive or lucrative experiences and were less affected by the pandemic, thus able and willing to stay overseas longer.

#### *Impact of COVID-19 Pandemic*

The pandemic affected employment practices across all labor sectors, and its impact will be felt for years to come. Because the timeframe within which these respondents worked in GCC countries preceded the pandemic, findings from this study may be susceptible to challenges for their relevancy and policy implications for the post-pandemic era. Significant changes occur across most, if not all, labor sectors that may have profound implications on how migrant workers will be recruited and treated by employers in GCC countries or elsewhere after the pandemic. Our formative assessment during the project preparation phase found evidence of a greater risk of abuse in some sectors of the GCC economies. These changes in employment practices are still taking place, and past labor practices may or may not continue into the post-pandemic era. By design, our study was intended to measure the status quo, which would then guide intervention planning. With the unprecedented interruption of the pandemic, we cannot tell if any of what we have found still applies to the overseas migrant workers from Kenya.

***Discriminating COVID-19 Policies in Determining Migrant Movement Across Borders.*** At the start of the pandemic, countries worldwide forced businesses and worksites to close, including the construction sector, and imposed internal and international travel bans. As a result, millions of migrant workers in the GCC were quarantined in low-quality camps with no indication of when they would be allowed to return to their jobs or homes. In other cases, such as with undocumented Ethiopian workers in the United Arab Emirates and Saudi Arabia, migrant workers were abruptly deported (Getachew, 2020; Sheriff & Khan, 2020). As a result, the target population of interest – recently returned migrants from the GCC – for the months in which our data were collected may not be representative of the target population of interest under normal circumstances.

## Disclosure statement

No potential conflict of interest was reported by the author(s).

## Funding

This study was funded by a grant from the Global Fund to End Modern Slavery (GFEM) to NORC at University of Chicago.

## ORCID

Sheldon Zhang http://orcid.org/0000-0002-7983-0554

## Disclaimer

This study was funded by the United States Department of State through the Global Fund to End Modern Slavery (GFEMS). The opinions, findings and conclusions stated herein are solely those of the authors and do not necessarily reflect those of the United States Department of State.

## Ethical approval

This study was approved by the Institutional Review Board (IRB) at NORC and an equivalent body in Kenya. All U.S.-based research staff-maintained update-to-date ethics training certification from the National Institutes of Health (NIH) or Collaborative Institutional Training Initiative (CITI). Our field staff were extensively trained in research ethics, including confidentiality, informed consent procedures, and the IRB-approved field procedures.

## References

Alexander, A. (2015). *Trafficking of adults for forced labour in Kenya: Gender, intersectionality and policy.* [Master's Thesis]. Aalborg University and Awareness against Human Trafficking Kenya. https://haartkenya.org/wp-content/uploads/2018/11/Alexander-2015.pdf

Aljazeera. (2020). Saudi Arabia to remove key restrictions on foreign workers. *News Report on November 4, 2020.* Retrieved September 26, 2021, from https://www.aljazeera.com/economy/2020/11/4/saudi-arabia-plans-to-remove-key-restrictions-on-foreign-workers.

Atong, K., Mayah, E., & Odigie, A. (2018). *Africa labor migration to the GCC states: The case of Ghana, Kenya, Nigeria, and Uganda.* African Regional Organization of the International Trade Union Confederation (ITUC-Africa).

Chapman, D. (1951). Some properties of the hypergeometric distribution with applications to zoological sample census. *University of California Publications in Statistics, 1*(7), 131–160. https://babel.hathitrust.org/cgi/pt?id=wu.89045844248&seq=3.

Chatzis, I., Albert, S., Kepes, Q., Hunter, P., Delgado, D., Wagner, L., & Salmane, A. (2015). *The role of recruitment fees and abusive and fraudulent practices of recruitment agencies in trafficking in persons.* UNODC.

Dottridge, M. (2017). Global trafficking prevalence data distorts efforts to stop patterns of human trafficking. *Anti-Trafficking Review, 8*(8), 161–164. https://doi.org/10.14197/atr.201217812

Fernandez, B. (2014). Essential yet invisible: Migrant domestic workers in the GCC. *An Explanatory Note GLMM No. 4/2014.*

Frank, O., & Snijders, T. (1994). Estimating the size of hidden populations using snowball sampling. *Journal of Official Statistics, 10*(1), 53–67.

Getachew, S. (2020). *Ethiopian workers are being expelled from Saudi Arabia and UAE on coronavirus suspicions.* Quartz. https://qz.com/africa/1837457/ethiopians-expelled-from-saudi-arabia-uae-for-covid-19

International Labor Organization. (2012). *Hard to see, harder to count: Survey guidelines to estimate forced labor of adults and children.* Interntaional Labor Organization. https://www.ilo.org/global/topics/forced-labour/publications/WCMS_182096/lang-en/index.htm

International Labor Organization. (2023). *Ratifications of C189 – Domestic workers convention, 2011 (no. 189).* https://www.ilo.org/dyn/normlex/en/f?p=NORMLEXPUB:11300:0:NO:P11300_INSTRUMENT_ID:2551460

Kenya National Bureaus of Statistics. (2021). *Economic Survey 2021.* Retrieved June 26, 2023, from https://www.knbs.or.ke/wp-content/uploads/2021/09/Economic-Survey-2021.pdf.

Malit, F. (2018). Frontlines of global migration: Philippine state's bureaucrats role in migration diplomacy and workers' welfare in the gulf countries. In P. Fargues & N. M. Shah (Eds.), *Migration to the gulf: Policies in sending and receiving countries* (pp. 199–220). Gulf Research Center Cambridge, University of Cambridge. https://gulfmigration.grc.net/media/pubs/book/grm2017book_chapter/Volume%20-%20Migration%20to%20Gulf%20-%20Chapter%2010.pdf

Malit, F., & Naufal, G. (2016). Asymmetric information under the kafala sponsorship system: Impacts on foreign domestic workers' income and employment status in the GCC countries. *International Migration, 54*(5), 76–90. https://doi.org/10.1111/imig.12269

Malit, F., & Tsourapas, G. (2021). Migration diplomacy in the Gulf – non-state actors, cross-border mobility, and the United Arab Emirates. *Journal of Ethnic and Migration Studies, 47*(11), 2556–2577. https://doi.org/10.1080/1369183X.2021.1878875

Malit, F., & Youha, A. (2016a). Kenyan migration to the Gulf countries: Balancing economic interests and worker protection. *Migration Information Source.* Retrieved June 26, 2023 from (PDF) Kenyan Migration to the Gulf Countries: Balancing Economic Interests and Workers' Protection (Migration Policy Institute 2016) (researchgate.net)

Malit, F., & Youha, A. (2016b). *Labor protection in the Gulf countries: A comparative analysis of Kenyan governmental dilemmas in Saudi Arabia and the United Arab Emirates.* (ILR Collection Working Paper No. 181) Cornell University. https://digitalcommons.ilr.cornell.edu/workingpapers/181/

Mutai, E. (2015, December 15). MPs plan safe haven for Kenyan workers in Saudi. *Business Daily Africa*. Retrieved June 26, 2023, from https://www.businessdailyafrica.com/MPs-plan-safe-haven-for-Kenyan-workers-in-Saudi/-/539546/2995322/-/yiemf/-/index.html.

Naufal, G., & Genc, I. (2012). *Expats and the labor force: The story of the gulf cooperation council countries*. Palgrave Macmillan.

R Core Team. (2016). *R: A language and environment for statistical computing*. R Foundation for Statistical Computing. https://www.R-project.org/

Robson, D. S., & Regier, H. (1964). Sample Size in Petersen Mark–Recapture Experiments. *Transactions of the American Fisheries Society*, *93*(3), 215–226. https://doi.org/10.1577/1548-8659(1964)93[215:SSIPME]2.0.CO;2

Sheriff, N., & Khan, Z. (2020). Covid-19 relief efforts are ignoring the people who need it most. *Quartz*. https://qz.com/1836995/how-covid-19-is-affecting-low-wage-workers

Thompson, S. (2020). New estimates for network sampling. arXiv preprint 2002.01350. https://arxiv.org/pdf/2002.01350.pdf.

Vincent, K., Dank, M., Jackson, O., Zhang, S. X., & Liu, W. (2021). Estimating young women working in Kathmandu's adult entertainment sector: A hybrid application of respondent driven sampling and venue site sampling. *Journal of Human Trafficking*, 1–16. https://doi.org/10.1080/23322705.2021.2007461

Vincent, K., & Thompson, S. (2017). Estimating population size with link-tracing sampling. *Journal of the American Statistical Association*, *112*(519), 1286–1295. https://doi.org/10.1080/01621459.2016.1212712

Vincent, K., Zhang, S. X., & Dank, M. (2021). Searching for sex trafficking victims: Using a novel link-tracing method among commercial sex workers in Muzaffarpur, India. *Crime & Delinquency*, *67*(13–14), 2254–2277. https://doi.org/10.1177/0011128719890265

Zhang, S. X. (2012). Measuring labor trafficking: A research note. *Crime, Law, and Social Change*, *58*(4), 469–482. https://doi.org/10.1007/s10611-012-9393-y

Zhang, S. X., Spiller, M. W., Finch, B. C., & Yang, Q. (2014). Estimating labor trafficking among unauthorized migrant workers in San Diego. *ANNALS of American Academy of Political and Social Science*, *653*(1), 65–86. https://doi.org/10.1177/0002716213519237

Zhang, S. X., & Vincent, K. (2021). Respondent driven sampling/link tracing sampling. In L. G. Bermudez, D. Okech, & M. Prakash (Eds.), *Prevalence estimation—methods brief* (pp. 11–13). GFEMS/Norad. https://humantraffickingsearch.org/resource/prevalence-estimation-methods-brief/

OPEN ACCESS

# The Half-Built Road: Exploring the Impediments to Justice for Victims of Labor Trafficking

Chase Childress, Amy Farrell, Amelia Wagner, Shawn Bhimani, and Kayse Lee Maass

**ABSTRACT**

The exploitation of people in forced labor is a significant human rights violation and a threat to community safety. Despite enhanced efforts to identify and prosecute labor trafficking perpetrators in the U.S. relatively few traffickers have been held accountable. Legal advocates and providers increasingly pursue civil litigation, immigration relief, and other roads to meet victims' needs and achieve justice. Less understood are the specific legal, structural, and cultural barriers that make the road to justice through the criminal legal system difficult for victims of labor trafficking. Utilizing a comparative case study approach, we examine the life course of five labor trafficking cases through crucial decision points in the criminal legal process. Cases were selected to provide a range of legal system pathways. Data for each case includes legal advocate case records, client interview notes, correspondence between stakeholders, court records, and stakeholder interviews. Through comparative analysis techniques, we identify barriers that derail offender accountability and stymie victim support. The findings provide guidance to improve offender accountability and suggest alternative roads to justice centering on the needs of victims. Identifying barriers in implementing anti-trafficking laws promotes more just, peaceful, and inclusive societies in furtherance of UN Sustainability Goal 16.

## Introduction

In the United States, forced labor and labor trafficking have been primarily addressed through a criminal justice approach. Though abusive working conditions are often the result of economic structures, cultural norms, immigration restrictions, and discrimination, the U.S. government has primarily defined human trafficking as a crime and security problem (Farrell & Fahy, 2009) and has located authority for stopping such abuses with police and prosecutors. Driven mainly by a deterrent approach, law enforcement delivers public messages that traffickers are dangerous and should be punished, often publicizing enforcement actions to identify traffickers. As is so often the case in the U.S., the carceral state is held up as the swift solution to historically complex social problems (Hagan, 2012; Beckett & Sasson, 2004).

In landmark legislation known as the 2000 Victims of Trafficking and Violence Protection Act (TVPA), the U.S. Congress defined labor trafficking as a collection of exploitative practices that had previously been processed under a handful of other statutes dating back to the 1930s and 40s (Bang, 2013). Defining labor trafficking as "the recruitment, harboring, transportation, provision, or obtaining of a person for labor or services, through the use of force, fraud, or coercion," the

TVPA was the first law to target sex and labor trafficking directly. Though labor exploitation is not new, the TVPA signaled a novel approach, bringing the tools of criminal law to bear directly on a persistent and complex social and economic problem. States have subsequently adopted their own laws criminalizing human trafficking, most including provisions criminalizing labor trafficking (Farrell et al., 2016). Since the passage of the TVPA, criminal justice agencies have received a significant share of the U.S. anti-trafficking funding; however, few labor trafficking perpetrators have been prosecuted or punished (Attorney General's Trafficking in Persons Report, 2022).

Further, victimology scholars have long argued that crime victims do not report victimization because justice system responses commonly do not meet their needs and wishes and may contribute to revictimization. Specifically, fear of perpetrators and police, the length of criminal justice processes, and the low likelihood of perpetrator accountability all undermine victim trust in the justice system as a remedy for the harms of victimization (Hart & Rennison, 2003; Wolf et al., 2003; Xie et al., 2006). Survivors of human trafficking also report concerns about the adequacy of the justice system to deliver something representing "justice" and to meet basic needs (Farrell et al., 2019; Love et al., 2018). Not surprisingly, labor trafficking victims rarely self-report to the police, even though law enforcement primarily relies on victims to disclose their abuse to uncover cases (Farrell et al., 2014). The complexity, length, and uncertainty around receiving support services also dissuade trafficking victims from seeking official help (Okech et al., 2012).

As a result, relatively few labor trafficking cases traverse the criminal legal process, and we understand little about how labor trafficking cases move through the justice system. In addition to understanding where and how labor trafficking cases are derailed in the criminal justice process, legal advocates and service providers underscore the need to understand how labor trafficking victims navigate criminal legal processes to meet their needs to prevent future victimization (Owens et al., 2014), and to identify and reduce barriers to justice.

### *The Limits of Prosecution for Offender Accountability & Provision of Victim Services*

Existing research has begun to explore the causes of low numbers of human trafficking prosecutions in the U.S. (e.g., Bang, 2013; Farrell et al., 2019); however, empirical research on labor trafficking remains in its infancy, and few studies have examined the life course of criminal labor trafficking cases (Aronowitz, 2019; Cockbain & Brayley-Morris, 2018; Zhang, 2012). Our inquiry is guided by literature on interpersonal crimes such as sexual assault, intimate partner violence, and sex trafficking, as these crimes and official responses to them share critical similarities with labor trafficking. First, the official response to the behaviors underlying these crimes has shifted over time as legislation redefined longstanding and complex social issues as crime problems (Cox et al., 2022; Goodmark, 2018; Farrell et al., 2014). Second, because of how interpersonal crimes have been defined, identification depends to some extent on culturally informed interpretations of context-specific victim and offender behavior (e.g., what behaviors constitute consent or coercion). Third, despite the adoption of laws, incidents of sexual assault, intimate partner violence, and human trafficking are severely underreported, and cases that do enter the justice system suffer from high attrition rates (Huhtanen, 2022; Fernández-Fontelo et al., 2019; Farrell et al., 2014).

Low levels of prosecution for labor trafficking crimes may be partly explained by the substantial uncertainty faced by justice system actors in the early phases of investigation – even before any formal charges are filed. Research into the early stages of investigation of sexual assault, intimate partner violence, and sex trafficking has revealed that both police and prosecutors attempt to reduce uncertainty in the criminal process by evaluating cases with a "downstream orientation" in which they try to forecast how the case will be evaluated by other criminal justice actors such as judges and juries (Spohn et al., 2001). In the labor trafficking context, uncertainty is likely exceptionally high because of (1) the relative newness of the TVPA and (2) the profile of labor trafficking offenders, many of whom wield political, economic, and social capital. Justice system norms and processes activated by this uncertainty lead to few labor trafficking prosecutions.

Unfamiliarity with the legal definition and interpretation of the TVPA among law enforcement, lack of robust legal precedent under the TVPA, and the absence of coordinating mechanisms heighten the uncertainty of labor trafficking cases. Though more than two decades have passed since the TVPA became law, the lack of substantial precedent about labor trafficking cases means that prosecutors and law enforcement continue to struggle with several challenges in interpreting and applying human trafficking laws, including a lack of awareness of jurisdiction over human trafficking, uncertainty about the proof required to show a violation of the statute, and whether criminal provisions of the statute apply to specific individuals and entities involved in trafficking (Farrell et al., 2019; Farrell et al., 2014; Farrell et al., 2010; Newton et al., 2008). When little clarity or consensus exists among courtroom actors about the requirements to establish a standard under the law, prosecutors may decline to pursue charges (Farrell et al., 2016).

Power disparities between victims and offenders in the U.S. also make labor trafficking prosecutions risky. Labor trafficking victims are frequently recruited from marginalized, impoverished populations and lured into trafficking situations by promises of money, stable housing, or lucrative jobs (Barno & Lynch, 2021). In the U.S., undocumented and foreign-born workers are overrepresented among labor trafficking victims, meaning that labor trafficking is frequently perpetrated against individuals of marginalized populations with historically negative relationships with justice systems (Farrell et al., 2019; Farrell et al., 2014; Buckley, 2008). In contrast, offenders tend to have access to significant social, economic, and political power. Not only are offenders exceptionally skilled at preying on victim vulnerabilities during the recruitment and exploitation process, but immigration status differences between victims and offenders, as well as affiliation with criminal networks, also increase the power of offenders relative to victims (Barno & Lynch, 2021; Owens et al., 2014). Using these network connections, labor traffickers can also coerce victim compliance by calling on variously affiliated contacts to credibly threaten victims' friends or family (Barno & Lynch, 2021; Owens et al., 2014).

Justice actors use institutionalized case processing strategies (Frohmann, 1991) that draw on cultural stereotypes about race, class, and gender to reduce uncertainty in prosecution (Farrell et al., 2010; Barrick et al., 2014; Farrell et al., 2015). As victim willingness to cooperate and victim credibility are two critical factors in deciding whether to move a case forward for prosecution, negative valuation of victim credibility can end a case before charges are even issued (Albonetti, 1986; Frohmann, 1997). During investigations, law enforcement may exercise discretion in ways that systematically exclude certain types of victims and offenders from being identified (Barno & Lynch, 2021), and victims face well-documented institutional barriers to aiding investigations and accessing services, including racial bias, lack of cultural competency, language barriers, and concerns over immigration status (Messing et al., 2015). From there, prosecutors make strategic decisions at the initial stages of the criminal legal process to avoid uncertainty and maximize their chances of winning at trial (Barno & Lynch, 2021; Cox et al., 2022).

## Current Study

The present study employs a comparative case study approach to explore how labor trafficking cases progress through the criminal legal system. Because scholarship on factors that may influence the process and outcome of labor trafficking criminal cases is underdeveloped, we employ an exploratory approach, using qualitative data acquired through a partnership with a U.S. victim services organization to develop an initial understanding of this phenomenon. A comparative cross-case approach allows us to identify common themes about the processing of labor trafficking cases through the justice system and barriers to successful prosecution and, ultimately, victim justice. Using data from provider interviews, case records, client interview notes, and official records, we explore (1) the life course of five labor trafficking cases through crucial decision points in the criminal legal process, from identification of victims through case adjudication – focusing mainly on *when* in the legal process labor trafficking cases get derailed, and (2) the legal, structural, and cultural challenges that help explain *why* the criminal legal system is insufficient to hold offenders accountable, meet victim needs, and deliver justice.

## Data and Methodology

Five labor trafficking cases were purposefully selected to provide a range of legal system pathways, including cases where offenders were convicted, cases where prosecution was declined but civil damages were awarded, and cases that did not progress beyond law enforcement interviews. Data for each case includes legal advocate case records, client interview notes, correspondence between crucial stakeholders, court records, and stakeholder interviews.

### *Case Information*

Table 1 briefly details the five studied cases. All five cases involved foreign national victims, three of whom worked in agricultural and domestic labor situations. Only one case was prosecuted, which resulted in a federal conviction. Three cases involved civil litigation, and multiple victims received T-Visas or immigration relief.

### *Data Collection and Availability*

The sources for this study consisted of 22 interviews, 27 legal documents, and 19 media articles that provided details on labor trafficking situations and investigations.[1] In 14 interviews, four legal advocates provided representation on the five studied cases. We conducted an additional eight interviews with law enforcement, service providers, and advocates who had information or experience with one or more of the studied cases. For each case, we collected and coded information on the case facts from the criminal indictment, sentencing documentation, hearing information, civil litigation documents, and other associated documents that outline the elements of the labor trafficking crimes as identified through Thomson Reuters Westlaw Edge, LexisNexis, and PACER. We also obtained case notes from the legal advocacy agency representing the five studied cases. Table 2 summarizes the number of interviews, news articles, and legal files collected for each case.

### *Data Analysis*

Documents (e.g., interview transcripts and text-based legal and media documents) were de-identified and imported to NVivo 12 for analysis. An axial coding technique revealed codes developed inductively through open coding. Multiple coders coded interviews, case notes, legal documents, and media articles. Then, coders held coding conferences and used comparison queries to establish agreement on final nodes and identify emergent themes. These themes were then presented and reviewed by the partner organization for external validation prior to creating a standard codebook.

Throughout this coding process, coders created analytic memos to help capture barriers to prosecution. Each barrier identified was also coded according to the criminal justice phase in which it occurred. The team divided the criminal legal process into eleven phases, including 1) investigation, 2) charging, 3) initial hearing/arraignment, 4) discovery, 5) plea bargaining, 6) preliminary hearing, 7) pre-trial motions, 8) trial, 9) post-trial motions, 10) sentencing, and 11) appeal (Offices of the U.S. Attorneys, n.d.). NVivo queries further explored unique codes and code redundancy and overlap to identify common barriers across each phases. This analysis produced a consolidated list of common barriers to indictment. Then, a final coder recoded the original set of barriers to prosecution using the consolidated list. The resulting data were then analyzed using detailed reports, hierarchy charts, matrix queries, and node examination. We coded 335 references to prosecution roadblocks across 14 common barriers. Table 3 lists the 14 barriers and the number of times each barrier was referenced within each case.

[1] Media publications were identified by performing multiple searches on Google's search engine using keywords associated with the case (including case name, as well as the names of businesses, worksites, and individuals identified as victims, defendants, or other prominent actors). This process was repeated at several points throughout the study period to ensure that the most recent reporting on the case was reflected in the collected data.

**Table 1.** Brief Details on Each Case.

| | Case #1 | Case #2 | Case #3 | Case #4 | Case #5 |
|---|---|---|---|---|---|
| Victim(s) | Haitian and Mexican workers | East Asian and North African workers | Haitian and Mexican workers, mainly minors | South American workers | African workers |
| Number Trafficker(s) | 3 | 4 | 3 | 1 | 1 |
| Industry | Agriculture | Agriculture, domestic service | Food vending | Performance | Agriculture, domestic service |
| Criminal Case Outcome | A federal indictment was issued against two of the traffickers; one pleaded guilty to illegal harboring and was sentenced to a term of imprisonment | Prosecutors issued a criminal indictment charging 3 traffickers with visa fraud; one defendant was arrested | The federal prosecutor did file charges but quickly dismissed them | The criminal case was dropped due to prosecutorial discretion | There was never an arrest or any formal filing of charges; authorities viewed the case as a domestic violence issue |
| Victim Outcome | Some victims returned to trafficker locations, several were re-trafficked by the same network, some received continued presence and T-visas | Victims received housing through a personal connection of a lawyer with the legal advocacy organization, and one victim received law enforcement parole | Some victims received T-visas; most victims returned to their home countries | Some victims received continued presence and got work authorization through the FBI Victim Support Specialist | The trafficker was forced to pay all the victim's legal fees |
| Civil Charges | The legal advocacy organization also won a civil judgment on behalf of the victims; however, to date, no money has been collected | | A class action lawsuit was filed against Trafficker 1's company; this lawsuit was settled out of court for an undisclosed amount | Civil and administrative complaints were also filed and remain pending | |

Matrix coding queries of the barriers across the cases revealed that the number of references to barriers varied, partly due to the type and number of legal documents associated with the case, and the various phases at which the cases terminated. For example, formal court documents such as indictments and complaints contained limited information on prosecution barriers, while informal legal documents such as T-Visa applications and internal advocate notes contained rich detail on barriers to indictment. Our interviews with legal advocates identified most barriers, indicating the importance of information attained through direct engagement with legal aid service providers.

### *Process Maps*

To visually align our results with the phases of the criminal justice process, we developed process maps to indicate the points where each of the studied labor trafficking cases stalled, were abandoned, or ultimately concluded. The process maps show the pathways each case followed. Based on the coding, barriers were identified inductively and inserted in the process maps at specific stages to summarize the findings of the cross-case analysis. Multiple barriers can appear at each stage of the criminal legal process. Barriers can also repeat across a case's path, and notes along the pathway describe significant

**Table 2.** Sources of Information for Each Studied Case.

| | Interviews | News Articles | Legal Files | Total |
|---|---|---|---|---|
| Case #1 | 4 | 4 | 8 | 16 |
| Case #2 | 3 | 7 | 2 | 12 |
| Case #3 | 2 | 3 | 9 | 14 |
| Case #4 | 2 | 0 | 5 | 7 |
| Case #5 | 3 | 5 | 3 | 11 |
| Total | 14 | 19 | 27 | 60 |

**Table 3.** Barriers across cases.

| Barriers | Case 1 | Case 2 | Case 3 | Case 4 | Case 5 | Total |
|---|---|---|---|---|---|---|
| **Legal/conceptual** | | | | | | |
| Complicated legal structures | 2 | 3 | 0 | 11 | 14 | **30** |
| Lack of clarity about standards to bring case | 3 | 0 | 0 | 0 | 0 | **3** |
| Victim intimidation by trafficker or fear of trafficker | 19 | 4 | 2 | 42 | 10 | **77** |
| **Institutional** | | | | | | |
| Victims not seeking help from law enforcement | 2 | 1 | 0 | 3 | 8 | **14** |
| Victims not wanting to participate in investigations | 8 | 4 | 0 | 6 | 3 | **21** |
| Disruption of influential people, economic interests | 12 | 5 | 3 | 6 | 2 | **28** |
| Lack of legal advocates or public defenders | 1 | 0 | 2 | 0 | 4 | **7** |
| Lack of trained law enforcement | 10 | 1 | 0 | 4 | 8 | **23** |
| Lack of specialized trained prosecutors | 1 | 2 | 3 | 4 | 0 | **10** |
| **Cultural** | | | | | | |
| Myths or biases about labor trafficking | 4 | 4 | 0 | 3 | 7 | **18** |
| Cultural norms and perceptions of victim credibility | 8 | 10 | 2 | 12 | 9 | **41** |
| Role conflict, lack of cohesion and clarity | 14 | 7 | 4 | 1 | 4 | **30** |
| Choosing easiest or most certain strategy | 9 | 9 | 2 | 1 | 1 | **22** |
| Difficulty finding or securing a person to arrest | 3 | 5 | 2 | 0 | 1 | **11** |
| **Total** | **96** | **55** | **20** | **93** | **71** | **335** |

path changes. The process map of Case 1 found in Figure 1 below is shaded to indicate the source of a barriers identification (e.g., interview or court document).

## Findings

### *When Did Barriers Occur on the Road to Justice?*

The criminal justice process can be seen as a series of phases beginning with the investigation and ending with the release of a convicted offender from correctional supervision. Though formal rules guide many decisions along this path, criminal justice actors command significant discretion in moving cases forward to the next phase in the criminal process (Lafave, 1970). Depicting the criminal legal process as a series of consecutive phases, we mapped the life course of each of the five cases in our sample. In three of five cases, a prosecutor filed charges (in one case, the charges were filed and dropped), or an indictment was issued. Of those cases, only one resulted in a conviction, however, that conviction was not for labor trafficking; instead, the offender was convicted and incarcerated for conspiracy to hire illegal aliens. The remaining four cases ended before adjudication during either the investigation or charging phase.

Utilizing a case process mapping technique, we identified barriers occurring in six of the eleven stages of our criminal justice process (investigation, charging, initial hearing/arraignment, pretrial motions, trial, and sentencing). Sixty-six percent (66%) of the coded barriers occurred in the investigation phase, while 27% of the barriers occurred in charging phase. *Victim intimidation by trafficker or fear of trafficker* was the most common barrier identified in the investigation phase (occurring 77 times across the five studied cases), followed by *cultural norms* (41 times), lack *of cohesion and clarity of roles* (30 times), *complicated legal structures* (30 times), and *disruption of powerful people, economic interests* (28 times). *Choosing the easiest or most certain strategy* (14 times) was the most common barrier coded in the charging phase. The remaining 7% of barriers were spread out across multiple phases.

To demonstrate how the 14 identified barriers impact labor trafficking case processing, we walk through the barriers identified in the process mapping for Case 1, using a visualization of the case process map illustrated in Figure 1 (for additional details in the five cases, see Appendix A). Case 1 is an agricultural labor trafficking case involving labor contractors and multiple victims and defendants. Despite the ultimate prosecution of three perpetrators, numerous barriers made the criminal legal process difficult. In the investigation phase, *victim intimidation by the trafficker or victim fear of the trafficker* was a significant barrier. During the investigation and charging, *role conflict, lack of cohesion and clarity, lack of understanding of the cultural norms of victims*, and *justice system perceptions of victim credibility* each weakened the case. Prosecutors ultimately declined to charge under the TVPA and instead charged the lead defendant with illegal harboring, which does not require victim testimony or proof of force, fraud, or coercion. The following sections explore how the barriers, occurring alone or in combination with others, impacted labor trafficking case pathways across all five studied cases.

### *How Did Barriers Divert the Road to Justice?*

We found that numerous barriers endemic to the criminal legal system blocked the road to justice for victims of labor trafficking. We categorize these barriers into legal, institutional, and cultural barriers. **Legal** barriers are challenges within the legal landscape of labor trafficking and other areas of the law that result in misunderstanding the crime. **Institutional** barriers refer to inter- and intra-agency policies, goals, and routines that delay or derail investigations resulting from uncoordinated federal, state, and local responses. **Cultural** barriers include law enforcement's unfamiliarity with victims' cultures and reliance on stereotypes about victims in identifying trafficking cases (Farrell et al., 2019). In addition to appearing at different stages in each studied case, barriers frequently appeared in combination. Confirming the importance of decisions made early in the criminal legal process on the ultimate outcomes (Barno & Lynch, 2021), we argue that the barriers to prosecution render the criminal legal system an inefficient, insufficient, and sometimes hazardous road to justice for victims.

#### *Legal Barriers*

During the investigation stage, a *lack of clarity* among justice officials about the legal standards necessary to bring the case, notably without clear evidence of force, is complicated by deliberate efforts by traffickers to weaponize the *complicated legal structures* found in labor trafficking situations. Without legally authoritative guidance on applying trafficking statutes, law enforcement can mistake legal ties for complicity. All cases except Case 3 involved legal arrangements that strengthened the legal entanglement between the victim and trafficker.

Trafficking offenders frequently create legal ties by trapping victims in a cycle of debt (Cases 1, 2, 3, and 4) based on fraudulent contracts, by deceiving victims into letting their visas expire (Case 4), by using or fraudulently claiming familial relationships (Case 4 and Case 5), or by manipulating the visa application process of victims and their relatives (Case 5). Though these ties were created during the commission of the crime, their impact could be observed across multiple phases of case processing. For example, in Case 4, the trafficker forced a victim to sign purported "immigration paperwork" before arriving in the U.S. The victim later learned that the document was a contract stating essentially that if he ever worked for any other employer while in the U.S., he would owed the trafficker $8,000. As seen in Case 4, legal ties created by the trafficker prolonged victim vulnerability by causing victims to live with the trafficker even as the case transitioned from investigation to charging.

In Case 5, legal and documentary ties that enabled exploitation also caused law enforcement to misinterpret the context in which the alleged harm occurred and to misidentify the behavior of both trafficker and victim. Ultimately, because the trafficker and victim were legally married, law enforcement fell back on patterned ways of interpreting a domestic incident, drawing on stereotypes and

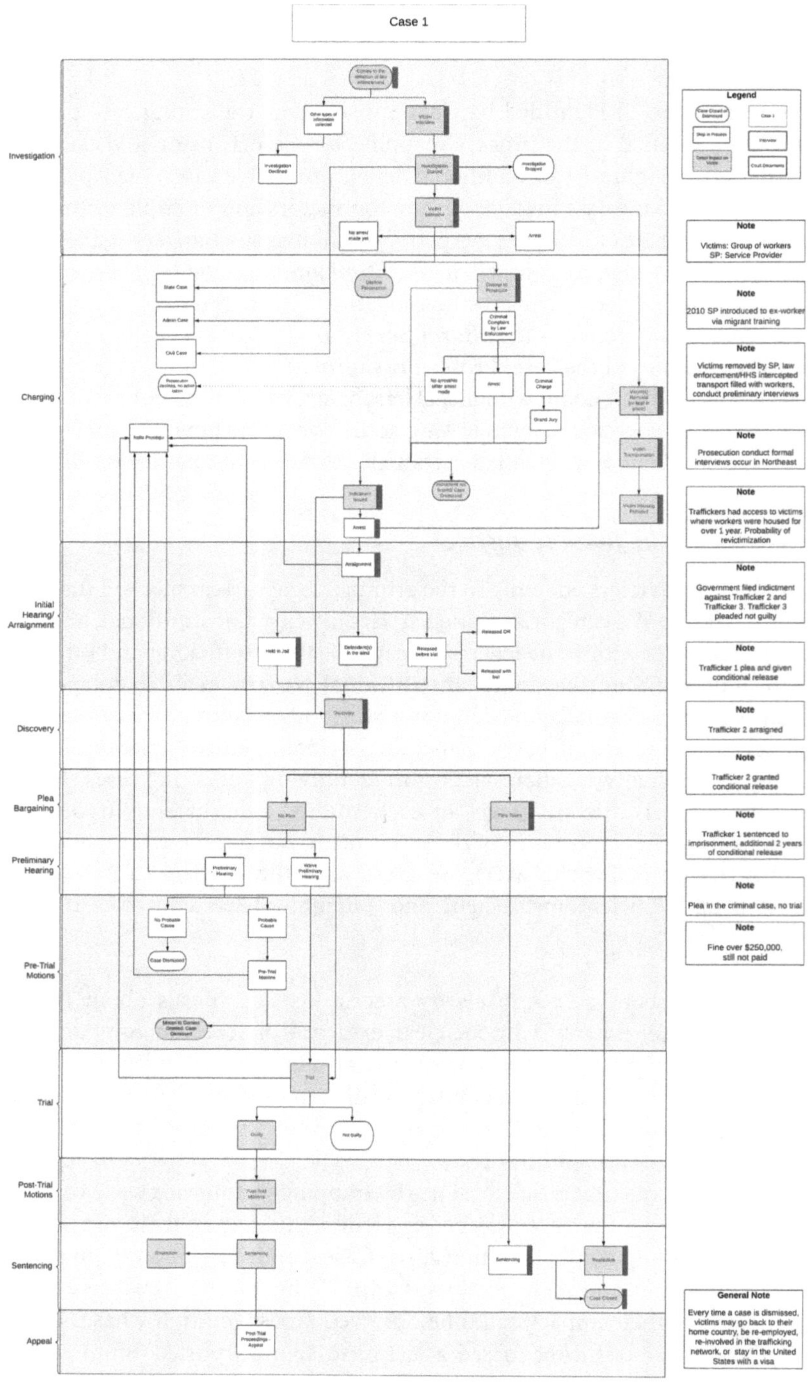


**Figure 1.** Case 1 Criminal Justice Process Map.

assumptions often cited in the domestic violence context. In discussing this case, a legal advocate recounted the difficulties the victim had in leaving the trafficking situation and separating herself from her trafficker:

> The way that our culture, our society, views marriage skewed the lens [with which] law enforcement looked at this case . . . [police] would say . . . "Well, she left. She went to [home country]. She came back. She did this twice." So, it was like very much their whole . . . [idea] that they're not chained to the wall . . . Why would she come back if it was that bad? They just don't understand the psychology of it. (Case 5, Interview 3)

Legal ties between victims and traffickers continued to complicate the victim's efforts to seek justice across multiple legal avenues in Case 5 because the trafficker remained the legal guardian of the victim's relatives. Dealing with ongoing legal issues retraumatized the victim and reduced the victim's ability to contribute effectively to the investigation. Labor traffickers, who often enjoy a greater understanding of the American legal system than victims, can strategically create or weaponize *complicated legal structures* within immigration law, family law, contract law, and other legal areas, making it more challenging to distinguish voluntary participation in crime from coercion in the early stages of a case.

*Victim intimidation by trafficker or victim fear of trafficker* refers to the limits of real protection afforded to labor trafficking victims through the criminal justice system. In our sample, traditional justice responses were inadequate to keep victims safe, as law enforcement only became involved after victims reported abuse and could not discern whether isolated behaviors were part of broader patterns of exploitation. In Case 4, though a victim successfully contacted the police for help, the reactionary nature of the police response failed to discover the exploitative context in which the offending behavior occurred. As recounted by the victim:

> Even though I could not speak English much at all, I did my best to explain to [the police] that [the trafficker] was trying to keep me at her house and not let me go home[] and that she had my passport and would not give it back. I thank God because somehow the officer understood and believed me and called [the trafficker] and told her to return my passport. A little while later, [the trafficker's] daughter brought my passport to the police station . . . I did not understand labor trafficking; I did not know what it was, that it could happen to me, or how to report it. (Case 4, T-Visa Application)

Here, the local officer identified one strategy of control used by the trafficker (withholding the passport); however, they did not follow up to identify the trafficking situation.

When arrests did result from the criminal investigation, the risk of victimization continued for many victims in our studied cases. In Cases 1, 2, and 4, victims remained at or near the exploitation site after investigations began due to fear of retaliation by traffickers or their associates against victims or family members in the U.S. or overseas. In Case 3, failure to follow through with a criminal prosecution meant that several perpetrators were not held accountable even though civil settlements resulted; arguably, the most culpable offender exited the case early, avoided hostile public relations by early settlement, and continued conducting business after the case ended. Moreover, failure to follow through on prosecution after victims have agreed to participate in the investigation – often at serious risk of harm to themselves and their families – causes distrust and frustration with law enforcement, heightening victim vulnerability to re-trafficking. Describing the impact of the failure to prosecute a labor trafficking suspect, one legal advocate highlighted the importance of offender accountability to their clients:

> [W]e always manage expectations . . . [We tell clients that there is a] very small chance that [prosecutors] will take this case . . . [but clients will] say a lot of times [that], "We want there to be some sort of accountability." It's not like I want money, it's that I want them to go to jail or I want them to stop doing this. So, when we give them this like broad picture of like . . . all the remedies under these different avenues. A lot of them are interested in criminal prosecution, more so than anything else, more so than money . . . And I think that they were really disappointed because I think they internalized that to mean that nobody cared. (Case 4, Interview 2)

Victims in our studied cases did not immediately understand the harms that had occurred to them as labor trafficking. Once they understood the definition of trafficking and connected their experiences to the crime, it was hard to accept that offenders would not be held accountable.

### *Institutional Barriers*

We identified numerous institutional barriers, indicating the challenges victims must navigate in obtaining relief through official channels. Barriers that fell into the institutional thematic category included *role conflict, lack of cohesion, lack of clarity, lack of trained law enforcement, lack of trained prosecutors*, and *disruption of influential people, interests, or economy*. As seen in the Case 1 process map, institutional barriers include challenges caused by the lack of coordinating mechanisms among the processes, agencies, and entities available to identify and sanction offenders and aid victims of labor trafficking. In part, the number of different actors and agencies potentially involved in a labor trafficking investigation results from numerous legislative efforts to respond to exploitation in the U.S., and victims of labor trafficking can theoretically pursue both state and federal administrative, civil, and criminal avenues.

When victims connected with the legal service organization, client advocates worked to meet victim needs and explain the variety of legal avenues for justice. Our data supports the need for a variety of remedies, as victims reported multiple needs and goals following exit from the immediate trafficking situation, including safe housing, protection for victims and their families in the U.S. and in their home countries, trauma-informed medical and psychological services, legal representation, and financial support. Though multiple avenues for relief are appropriate, institutional factors frequently impede their practical use. Victims initially sought help from local law enforcement, but we found that mechanisms for accountability were hampered by the social, economic, and political power of offenders, discussed more fully in the cultural barriers section below. When victims accessed federal processes with the aid of legal advocates, a lack of official coordinating mechanisms threatened to derail cases early in the justice process because of the institutional separation between administrative, civil, and criminal investigations.

When victims turned to federal law enforcement for justice, *role conflict, lack of cohesion, and lack of clarity* combined during the investigation phase to delay the justice process and discourage victim participation, heightening victim vulnerability to further harm in the immediate aftermath of escape (Owens et al., 2014). Namely, victims were called on to persevere in assisting law enforcement despite needing to fight competing interpretations of the exploitative situation across multiple agencies and to navigate through the inadequate training and insufficient skillsets among agency personnel (including lack of training on trauma-informed interviewing techniques and inadequate translation services).

Failure to coordinate among agencies allowed siloed and conflicting interpretations to develop and resulted in confusing and contradictory case outcomes. In our data, this looked like law enforcement treating victims as suspects unworthy of respect or assistance, despite the presence of evidence indicating victimization experiences. Recalling an unexpected interview of his clients by ICE (U.S. Immigration and Customs Enforcement), one legal advocate recounted that:

> ... it felt like an interrogation. The agents were disrespectful and humiliating toward him. At one point, for example, when they looked at [victim's] passport, an agent laughed and made some crude comments in English. One of the other agents said that he thought the victim understood some English, so he should stop. The victim told them that he wasn't going to talk with them further because he felt they were "muy groseros" (very rude) with him. The victim also told them that he couldn't understand the Spanish translation very well and his English wasn't very good, so he didn't want to say something that was inaccurate because of the lack of understanding between them or lack of clarity in the questions. The victim was feeling really upset about the whole situation. He and another victim talked about just closing up the whole thing; it's taking too long; they have their families to support. (Case 1, Factual Narrative)

Poor treatment by law enforcement not only distracts from the investigation into exploitative labor conditions but actively hinders prosecution by alienating victims who would otherwise be willing to testify and prolonging (and potentially worsening) victims' financial straits.

Specifically, inconsistency and conflict among agency standards, routines, and goals led to differing interpretations and strategies for responding to a single case. The problem is particularly acute around the granting of continued presence to victims, as agencies have differing standards for its provision. In Case 2, one legal advocate stated:

> There was a game of hot potato that happened with the continued presence where I have this theory that most anyone with like Department of State, FBI, federal law enforcement or investigators, they're either scared of it, or I think there's like an unwritten, and all this is speculation, or there's like an unwritten we're not gonna do this, we're just gonna dangle the carrot, because it gets us what we need. And then after we get what we need, it's kind of their problem. So, we would, we were asking for [continued presence] . . . It was promised. And then it was like, yeah, we don't . . . really do that. This other office does it. And so that ended up being probably a month and a half of me calling them on a regular basis and just being the biggest pain in the *** as possible. . .If it's not your office, what office does it? Who does it? What's the number? . . . I was super frustrated. (Case 2, Interview 1)

When anti-trafficking teams do not have formal legal coordinating mechanisms and legal advocates are placed in a mediating roles, the advocates are forced to rely on personal contacts, as well as informal and, at times, inconsistent processes for information sharing and investigation.

The result is that legal advocates and their clients – victims of labor trafficking who often continue to suffer from financial and legal hardship, abuse, and trauma as agency investigations are ongoing – must perform the additional work of navigating competing interpretations of the exploitative situation with and among different agencies. This dynamic lengthens investigations, prevents information sharing, and delays effective intervention into the trafficking scheme, prolonging victimization experiences and increasing risk of retaliation by traffickers. Over the course of engaging with first state and then federal criminal justice processes, victims became cynical, frustrated, or otherwise unconvinced that this path could assist with their goals.

*Lack of capacity to build legal cases* also delayed accountability for offenders and the provision of services to victims. Specifically, the lack of sufficient translation services was explicitly mentioned in two cases as an impediment to investigatory and legal processes (Case 1 and Case 5). This capacity gap is more than a matter of convenience: the inability to explain the details of an exploitation experience can exacerbate cultural stereotypes held by law enforcement that led to the miscategorization of crime and misidentification of victims and offenders. When the police fail to identify factors that would promote prosecution (e.g., presence of a minor, multiple victims, use of weapons), legal advocates use alternative strategies to make the case attractive to prosecutors, who are beholden to strong economic interests in the community. Here, legal advocates described political influences on the exercise of prosecutorial discretion to bring charges, observed in three out of five cases.

> I also explained to [the victim] that . . . I'm sorry that this is the way our system works here, that it sounds like I'm, you know, pitching something to them, but I really am because there's so many different cases you have to try and find creative ways to get them interested in your case . . . With some of these prosecutors that they're like, boom, like what's the story here? What would be the headline, like, do I want to be involved in this case? . . . You can feel that vibe in the room. So I wasn't I wasn't explaining it necessarily like that to her, but I was saying . . . [we have to] somehow present this case to them in away that's going to make them want to punish [the trafficker] . . . At the same time, it's 100% their discretion to take the case and they could just say no. (Case 5, Interview 2)

*Disruption of influential people, interests, or economy* refers to hesitance on the part of justice officials to intervene when individuals or entities suspected of labor trafficking have powerful economic, political, or social connections. These connections become barriers to prosecution in the labor trafficking context as criminal justice actors weigh the fear of adverse political/career/legitimacy outcomes in the decision to investigate and/or charge. We found that initial interactions with local law enforcement were ineffective in all cases, either because of traffickers' power and influence, including existing relationships with law enforcement, or law enforcement's failure to understand the context in which the behavior occurred. In Case 1, the power of the growers who benefitted from the trafficking halted investigations before they began; in fact, instances in which local police were called to the property became staged displays of the trafficker's power to discourage worker dissent or escape. The power of growers was exacerbated by a law enforcement culture that values legitimacy and risk avoidance. In Case 5, the victim turned to the media for help because her trafficker's connection to and influence over local police impeded the investigation (Case 5, News).

At the charging phase, prosecutors consider the political fallout of charging particular offenders in ways that tend to allow politically and economically powerful offenders to escape prosecution; indeed, the same laws that contribute to the legal uncertainty around the charging of labor trafficking may protect these economic interests (e.g., corporate forms, joint employment law). For example, the criminal investigation in Case 2 came to a grinding halt when U.S. criminal justice agencies clashed with the politically sensitive diplomatic status of one of the traffickers. In Cases 1 and 3, companies that likely knew about and benefitted from trafficking were able to escape criminal and civil sanctions:

> ... you know that there were a lot of powerful people in that case, a lot of powerful people. They're dealing with a powerful industry, which is the same as Case 3 ... The governor would have been implicated in it, the guest worker program would have been implicated in it, there's a lot of implications ... If you decide to someone charge with trafficking ... , now you have to inevitably bring other laws. (Case 1, Interview 1)

But even outside of explicitly political influences on the decision whether to charge, the nature of labor trafficking (in which perpetrators tend to hold substantially more political, economic, and social status than victims) and the nature of prosecution (which is affected by these political, economic, and social factors) tends to result in offenders escaping accountability.

### *Cultural Barriers*

Barriers to prosecution in the cultural category included *choosing the most straightforward or most certain strategy*, *cultural norms and perceptions of victim credibility*, and *myths or biases about what labor trafficking looks like*. Cultural barriers are those circumstances in which culturally informed beliefs among criminal justice actors interact with unfamiliarity with the culture of populations vulnerable to labor trafficking to activate institutional responses to uncertainty. The effects of this confluence of barriers are especially acute when assessing victim and witness credibility. Because credible witness testimony is believed to be critical to obtaining a conviction at trial, difficulties recognizing victimization experiences have a negative impact on the probability of a case moving forward. Our study suggests that cultural norms or beliefs found among both criminal justice actors and victims coincide with reducing the likelihood that labor trafficking investigations move forward to trial for several reasons.

Because the definition of labor trafficking requires force, fraud, or coercion, victim testimony is often necessary to provide clear evidence of these elements. Absent other evidence, prosecutors depend on victim testimony to prove trafficking and encourage survivor participation sometimes as a mechanism to obtain the resources and immigration permissions to meet basic needs (e.g., work authorization, health care, housing) (Roby et al., 2008).

The tendency to *choose the most straightforward or most certain strategy* in pursuing a criminal case shaped criminal justice response to labor trafficking situations from the outset, as criminal justice actors engaged in early, downstream-oriented analyses that aimed to predict the probability of success at trial. First, as the need for credible witness testimony is especially high when there is no clear evidence of force, the belief that a victim will make a poor witness at trial reduces the likelihood that the criminal justice process will progress. As one legal advocate recounted, even though the investigation of Case 2 had established at least some elements of trafficking:

> [T]here was no physical violence, there really was only sort of psychological abuse ... [and] emotional abuse[, but] it wasn't like bruising on your body ... [And] because of[the victims'] forgiving nature, it was sort of like, 'We're not going to win this case'.(Case 2, Interview 2)

Then, when prosecuting actors believe that victim testimony is unavailable, untrustworthy, or unbelievable, charges like alien harboring or smuggling are more likely to issue during the investigation phase because these charges are less onerous to prove and less reliant on victim testimony. Therefore, charging offenses other than labor trafficking is a strategy to reduce the uncertainty associated with proving a trafficking offense to an imagined American jury. Moreover, as observed in other contexts, this hypothetical jury shares a common cultural background that views certain victim behaviors and circumstances as more or less trustworthy or deserving of protection and relief. It is by evaluating victim behavior against this cultural background that prejudicial beliefs along race, class, and gender lines can systematically derail cases involving the most vulnerable victims from the justice process.

*Cultural norms and perceptions of victim credibility* frequently coincided with both legal and institutional barriers, including *victim intimidation by traffickers and fear of traffickers, lack of trained law enforcement* and *myths and biases about what labor trafficking looks like.* As criminal justice actors tend to hold more positive evaluations of victim credibility when recall of alleged sexual assaults is consistent over time (Frohmann, 1991) and to expect that trafficking victims respond in culturally recognizable ways to victimization (Musto, 2016), legal advocates cited common symptoms of trauma, cultural differences in trauma response, and lack of training among criminal justice actors as key contributors to the high attrition rate of cases in our sample, particularly at the investigation phase. A legal advocate explained that the victim in Case 5 would apologize and correct herself or correct facts during investigation interviews. While police interpreted these statements as evidence of her "changing her story," the legal advocate tried to educate them about the fact that such patterns are standard among trauma survivors. In Case 4, law enforcement was reluctant to refer the case for prosecution because they perceived the victim's reaction to the perpetrator as inappropriate. As the legal advocate explained:

> [The victim is] just a very like happy go lucky happy human, not much can [] bring him down . . . [W]hen they were interviewing him and especially when the prosecutor was interviewing him . . . I think they got a sense of this, and it wasn't helpful for him, unfortunately . . . We would prep him before these interviews, especially when [he needed to discuss how] she would do horrendous things to him. He would laugh, he would smile . . . he would kind of look up and then, hit his leg like, "Oh, she's so nuts." And I would explain to him that I think that there's going to be some cultural disconnect . . . with the way that he is [] sharing his experience with [the trafficker] because for whatever reason in America the survivor or the victim is portrayed as, like, very traumatized, sad, crying . . . will never recover. And he did not present in that way, and he explained to me that in his culture, he's like, "Well, maybe it will be helpful for the . . . agents to know that in my culture . . . when we would have something horrible happen . . . we would celebrate. We have a party [when] someone dies. There's a horrible accident, someone loses a baby, and we have a party, and that's to stay in the moment and it's to lift our spirits." (Case 4, Interview 1)

Cultural factors thus also funnel cases involving immigrant populations out of the justice system.

The barrier *myths or biases about what labor trafficking looks like* refer to the justice actor's expectation that victims adhere to a particular behavior profile reminiscent of the iconic victim of human trafficking. Among the prosecutorial strategies documented by Frohmann (1991) in her study of sexual assault case rejections are to question post-incident victim behaviors; decisions to continue the relationship with the alleged offender after the fact is considered particularly suspect, despite the prevalence of revictimization experiences. In our sample, explicit evidence of re-trafficking experiences was present in Cases 3 and 4, and victims' return to the same or similarly exploitative work environments led law enforcement and other actors to negatively evaluate their credibility as witnesses and the likelihood of success at trial. But even without evidence of re-trafficking, under a law enforcement culture in which credible victims are perfectly innocent and always willing to assist in criminal investigations, victims' survival strategies are construed as evidence of complicity in the crime – evidence that the victims were "in on it." Delays in reporting due to fear of retaliation by the trafficker (Case 4), inconsistent factual statements commonly related to traumatic victimization experiences (Cases 2, 3, and 4), and decisions to trust the trafficker in ways that law enforcement struggles to understand (all cases) also resulted in negative evaluations of victim credibility.

In addition to drawing on images of the "iconic victim" as young, white, innocent, and eager to help the police, our data suggest that law enforcement extends *myths or biases about what labor trafficking looks like* to draw on "iconic offender" frames in deciding how to intervene in cases. Criminal justice actors tend to believe that labor trafficking offenders share demographic characteristics and are more willing to move forward with prosecutions when offenders are male, nonwhite, and foreign (non-American). In explaining why Case 1 might have been charged as an illegal harboring case, rather than as trafficking when there had been evidence of force used to control victims, one legal advocate reflected that:

> Brown people are criminals who are presenting false documents and it's hurting some poor person with identity theft . . . you know the narrative[] . . . there's some racism. You know it's like it's cool when the trafficker is Brown, but once you start really, really realizing that [the Employer] isn't and then no, no, that changes the narrative . . . It changes the statistics, you know, it changes everything . . . [If] the trafficker is Mexican, then it's all good. I mean, it's still they're "bad hombres" over there. (Case 1, Interview 2)

As the advocate observes, a corollary to the tendency to identify Black and Brown suspects more readily as violators of labor trafficking or other criminal laws is that other, potentially more culpable defendants (e.g., growers and corporate actors) continue to operate unfettered by law enforcement intervention. This profile includes assumptions that labor traffickers are male, an assumption that was complicated in Case 4 when the trafficker was a woman: FBI communications indicate the prosecutors were not interested in charging an older woman without clear evidence of physical abuse. That traffickers are thought to reflect a particular profile that is male, nonwhite, and foreign was echoed across all study sources and multiple cases, indicating that the assumption is widespread among criminal justice actors and the public.

Together, the identified barriers diverted the path of labor trafficking cases across various stages of the criminal process. The road to justice for victims was fraught with challenges, and ultimately, none of the five cases studied received the idealized version of justice where offenders are held accountable, and victims are protected from future harm.

## Discussion

Prosecution has been declared a cornerstone of anti-trafficking efforts domestically and abroad (Brunovskis & Skilbrei, 2016). Our data suggests that barriers to prosecution tend to concentrate at the early stages of the criminal justice process, explaining why so few labor trafficking cases have gone forward to charging and conviction. In all, our findings concerning *when* barriers occur on the road to justice suggest that reforms concentrated on improving law enforcement training in activities concentrated in the investigation and charging stage could make the road to justice more accessible for victims. Our findings indicate that the creation and implementation of formal coordinating mechanisms, such as task forces and interagency agreements, are needed to organize and coordinate effective trafficking interventions effectively. Additionally, criminal justice agencies should work to remedy identified resource capacity gaps by providing training in common labor trafficking-specific coercion and control strategies, trauma and victimization experiences, and additional translation services.

However, such reforms would do little to counter the insufficiency of the traditional criminal justice processes to protect victims and others from further abuses. Our analysis supports previous findings indicating that prosecutors' political goals and desire for career success shape their perception of and strategy toward interpersonal crimes (Albonetti, 1986), and that local, as well as international, political factors can impede the criminal justice process in ways that systematically fail to identify and sanction particular kinds of offenders. Ultimately, the labor trafficking context may provide another example of the function of the justice system as a political legitimacy tactic, where elites wield criminal law for political advantage and governance strategy – but do little to meaningfully respond to the crime problem (Hagan, 2012). In our sample, criminal processes primarily served to alienate and disappoint victims, many of whom were blocked from accessing theoretically available relief. Given the numerous barriers reported in this study, we argue that labor trafficking victims may be better served along avenues outside the criminal justice system. So, are there alternative roads?

Civil avenues for relief may provide a viable option, as victims enjoy greater autonomy through this process than criminal prosecution. However, there are several limitations to this road. First, victims typically must disclose their identities to pursue civil remedies, and without adequate law enforcement aid, fear of traffickers may continue to chill litigation. Second, litigation against repeat players such as corporations may require resources beyond the capacity of public legal services organizations (Dryhurst, 2013). Third, the award of monetary damages does not necessarily mean a cessation of exploitation or financial relief; moreover, awards must be collected, and, as our data reflect, victims do not always receive money awarded in judgments.

Broader regulatory and policy change is another potentially viable avenue. It is critical to examine the life course of labor trafficking cases because they represent a unique domain where business structures and networks are central to facilitating abuses, obscuring harm, and shielding traffickers from accountability (Childress et al., 2023). De Vries (2019) highlights the numerous connections between illicit trafficking networks and legitimate industries, even as the crime framing of these problems ignores the role of the capitalist economy in producing harm. Exploitative behaviors in the labor sector are closely linked with common market factors and business processes, intimately connected to the broader regulatory environment that isolated law enforcement intervention is unequipped to remedy (Barrick et al., 2014). Recognizing the connection between exploitative business practices and labor trafficking victimizations means also acknowledging the role of broader economic, labor and immigration policy in contributing to harm. Our findings indicate that, on many levels, changing the nature of how we protect, and respect U.S. workers is critical to reducing the harms of labor trafficking.

### *Future Study, Limitations, and Research Learnings*

The opportunity to interview victim service providers yielded surprising insights into how cases might travel through the criminal justice process and, more importantly, how they will be impeded from moving forward. The identified barriers and their respective process maps were presented to and reviewed by the partner organization for feedback (e.g., node naming conventions, clarifications on pathways, and discussion of any missing details) prior to finalization. Engagement with the partner organization through interviews and data collection resulted in significance findings about the limitations of criminal justice system pathways in achieving justice for victims or meeting their needs. Though a potential limitation of our analysis is that barriers were primarily identified through provider interviews, future research should strive to include partner organizations and survivors' voices, as these provided rich sources of data. Additionally, because labor trafficking victims also pursue civil avenues for relief, future research should examine barriers to administering civil remedies.

A limitation to be overcome by future work is that these five cases might not be representative of all labor trafficking victims, as our sample is comprised of those involving victims who sought some remedy. However, our data is valuable because several victims articulated a desire to work with law enforcement but ran into barriers along that specific path. Though labor trafficking literature emphasizes the difficulty in detecting labor trafficking because of the disinclination of victims to come forward, our data suggest that the road to criminal justice was not a road traversable for victims of labor trafficking. If a road is meant to deliver people to their destination, we find that the criminal legal process is only half-built to facilitate such movement. As a result, it may be more productive to consider alternative routes to justice outside the criminal justice system.

## Acknowledgments

This material is based upon work supported by the 2021 Northeastern University TIER 1: Seed Grant/Proof of Concept Program. We are grateful for the assistance of Alexis Yohros, Jesenia Robles, and Kate Rich, who assisted in gathering data, coding, and visualizing the labor trafficking disruptions.

## Disclosure Statement

No potential conflict of interest was reported by the author(s).

## Funding

This work was supported by the Northeastern University.

## ORCID

Chase Childress http://orcid.org/0000-0001-7227-1609

## References

Albonetti, C. A. (1986). Criminality, prosecutorial screening, and uncertainty: Toward a theory of discretionary decision making in felony case processing. *Criminology*, *24*(4), 623–644. https://doi.org/10.1111/j.1745-9125.1986.tb01505.x

Aronowitz, A. A. (2019). Regulating business involvement in labor exploitation and human trafficking. *Journal of Labor and Society*, *22*(1), 145–164. https://doi.org/10.1111/wusa.12372

Attorney general's trafficking in persons report. (2022). https://www.justice.gov/Human trafficking/attorney-generals-trafficking-persons-report

Bang, N. J. (2013). Unmasking the charade of the global supply contract: A novel theory of corporate liability in human trafficking and forced labor cases. *Houston Journal of International Law*, *35*(2), 255–322. https://justis.vlex.com/#vid/635605313

Barno, M., & Lynch, M. (2021). Selecting charges. In R. F. Wright, K. L. Levine, & R. M. Gold (Eds.), *The oxford handbook of prosecutors and prosecution* (pp. 35–58). Oxford University Press. https://doi.org/10.1093/oxfordhb/9780190905422.001.0001

Barrick, K., Lattimore, P. K., Pitts, W. J., & Zhang, S. X. (2014). When farmworkers and advocates see trafficking but law enforcement does not: Challenges in identifying labor trafficking in North Carolina. *Crime, Law and Social Change*, *61*(2), 205–214. https://doi.org/10.1007/s10611-013-9509-z

Beckett, K., & Sasson, T. (2004). *The politics of injustice: Crime and punishment in America*. SAGE Publications, Inc. https://doi.org/10.4135/9781452229614

Brunovskis, A., & Skilbrei, M.-L. (2016). Two birds with one stone? Implications of conditional assistance in victim protection and prosecution of traffickers. *Anti-Trafficking Review*, *6*, 13. https://doi.org/10.14197/atr.20121662

Buckley, C. (2008). Forced Labor in the United States: A contemporary problem in need of a contemporary solution. *Human Rights and Human Welfare*, *8*(1), 116–117.

Childress, C., Farrell, A., Bhimani, S., & Maass, K. L. (2023). Disrupting labor trafficking in the agricultural sector: Looking at opportunities beyond law enforcement interventions. *Victims & Offenders*, *18*(3), 473–511. https://doi.org/10.1080/15564886.2022.2133036

Cockbain, E., & Brayley-Morris, H. (2018). Human trafficking and labour exploitation in the casual construction industry. *Policing: A Journal of Policy and Practice*, *12*(2), 129–149. https://doi.org/10.1093/police/pax032

Cox, J., Daquin, J. C., & Neal, T. M. S. (2022). Discretionary prosecutorial decision-making: gender, sexual orientation, and bias in intimate partner violence. *Criminal Justice and Behavior*, *49*(11), 1699–1719. https://doi.org/10.1177/00938548221106498

De Vries, I. (2019). Connected to crime: An exploration of the nesting of labour trafficking and exploitation in legitimate markets. *The British Journal of Criminology*, *59*(1), 209–230. https://doi.org/10.1093/bjc/azy019

Dryhurst, K. (2013). Liability up the supply chain: Corporate accountability for labor trafficking. *New York University Journal of International Law & Politics*, *45*(2), 641–676.

Farrell, A., Dank, M., Vries, I., Kafafian, M., Hughes, A., & Lockwood, S. (2019). Failing victims? Challenges of the police response to human trafficking. *Criminology & Public Policy*, *18*(3), 649–673. https://doi.org/10.1111/1745-9133.12456

Farrell, A., DeLateur, M. J., Owens, C., & Fahy, S. (2016). The prosecution of state-level human trafficking cases in the United States. *Anti-Trafficking Review*, *6*(6), 48–70. https://doi.org/10.14197/atr.20121664

Farrell, A., & Fahy, S. (2009). The problem of human trafficking in the U.S.: Public frames and policy responses. *Journal of Criminal Justice, 37*(6), 617–626.

Farrell, A., McDevitt, J., Pfeffer, R., Fahy, S., Owens, C., Dank, M., & Adams, W. (2012). *Identifying challenges to improve the investigation and prosecution of state and local human trafficking cases.*

Farrell, A., Owens, C., & McDevitt, J. (2014). New laws but few cases: Understanding the challenges to the investigation and prosecution of human trafficking cases. *Crime, Law and Social Change, 61*(2), 139–168. https://doi.org/10.1007/s10611-013-9442-1

Farrell, A., & Pfeffer, R. (2014). Policing human trafficking: Cultural blinders and organizational barriers. *The ANNALS of the American Academy of Political and Social Science, 653*(1), 46–64. https://doi.org/10.1177/0002716213515835

Farrell, A., Pfeffer, R., & Bright, K. (2015). Police perceptions of human trafficking. *Journal of Crime & Justice, 38*(3), 315–333. https://doi.org/10.1080/0735648X.2014.995412

Fernández-Fontelo, A., Cabaña, A., Joe, H., Puig, P., & Moriña, D. (2019). Untangling serially dependent underreported count data for gender-based violence. *Statistics in Medicine, 38*(22), 4404–4422. https://doi.org/10.1002/sim.8306

Frohmann, L. (1991). Discrediting victims' allegations of sexual assault: Prosecutorial accounts of case rejections. *Social Problems (Berkeley, Calif.), 38*(2), 213–226. https://doi.org/10.1525/sp.1991.38.2.03a00070

Goodmark, L. (2018). Decriminalizing domestic violence: A balanced policy *approach to intimate partner violence* (1st ed., pp. 1—11). University of California Press.

Hagan, J. (2012). *Who are the criminals? : The politics of crime policy from the age of Roosevelt to the age of Reagan.* Princeton University Press.

Hart, T. C., & Rennison, C. M. (2003). Reporting crime to the police, 1992-2000. U.S. Dept. of Justice, Office of Justice Programs.

Huhtanen, H. (2022). *Gender bias in sexual assault response and investigation* (part 1). End violence against women international. https://evawintl.org/wp-content/uploads/TB-Gender-Bias-1-4-Combined-1.pdf

Lafave, W. (1970). The prosecutor's discretion in the United States. *The American Journal of Comparative Law, 18*(3), 532–548. https://doi.org/10.2307/839344

Love, H., Hussemann, J., Yu, L., McCoy, E. & Owens, C. (2018). Comparing Narratives of Justice. https://www.urban.org/sites/default/files/publication/97346/comparing_narratives_of_justice_0.pdf

Messing, J. T., Ward-Lasher, A., Thaller, J., & Bagwell-Gray, M. E. (2015). The state of intimate partner violence intervention: Progress and continuing challenges. *Social Work, 60*(4), 305–313. https://doi.org/10.1093/sw/swv027

Musto, J. (2016). Control and protect: Collaboration, carceral protection, and domestic sex *trafficking in the United States.* University of California Press.

Newton, P. J., Mulcahy, T. M. & Martin, S. E. (2008). Finding victims of human trafficking. https://doi.org/10.1037/e540892008-001

Offices of the United States Attorneys. (2016, January 15). Steps in the federal criminal process. Justice.gov. https://www.justice.gov/usao/justice-101/steps-federal-criminal-process

Okech, D., Morreau, W., & Benson, K. (2012). Human trafficking: Improving victim identification and service provision. *International Social Work, 55*(4), 488–503.

Owens, C., Dank, M., Breaux, J., Bañuelos, I., Farrell, A., Pfeffer, R., Bright, K., Heitsmith, R., & McDevitt, J. (2014). *Understanding the organization, operation, and victimization process of labor trafficking in the United States.* Urban Institute.

Roby, J. L., Turley, J., & Cloward, J. G. (2008). U.S. Response to human trafficking: Is it enough? *Journal of Immigrant & Refugee Studies, 6*(4), 508–525. https://doi.org/10.1080/15362940802480241

Spohn, C., Beichner, D., & Davis-Frenzel, E. (2001). Prosecutorial justifications for sexual assault case rejection: Guarding the "gateway to justice. *Social Problems, 48*(2), 206–235. https://doi.org/10.1525/sp.2001.48.2.206

Wolf, M. E., Ly, U., Hobart, M. A., & Kernic, M. A. (2003). Barriers to seeking police help for intimate partner violence. *Journal of Family Violence, 18*(2), 121–129. https://doi.org/10.1023/A:1022893231951

Xie, M., Pogarsky, G., Lynch, J. P., & McDowall, D. (2006). Prior police contact and subsequent victim reporting: Results from the NCVS. *Justice Quarterly, 23*(4), 481–501. https://doi.org/10.1080/07418820600985339

Zhang, S. X. (2012). Measuring labor trafficking: A research note. *Crime, Law and Social Change, 58*(4), 469–482. https://doi.org/10.1007/s10611-012-9393-y

## Appendix A

Case 1 involved traffickers who recruited primarily undocumented Mexican workers, including minors, to perform agricultural work on various farms. Traffickers maintained control over victims by a combination of surveillance and threats. Our legal organization partner learned of potential trafficking from an ex-worker who attended a trafficking training session. After involving law enforcement at the rescue victim's request, a lengthy criminal investigation ensued, and additional potential victims were identified. Victims received varied services: some victims were located in the housing for the entirety of the investigation, while others returned to areas where traffickers had access to victims, and several were re-trafficked by the same network. Some victims received continued presence and T-visas. A federal indictment was issued against two of the traffickers; ultimately, one pleaded guilty to illegal harboring and was sentenced to imprisonment. The legal advocacy organization also won a civil judgment on behalf of victims; however, to date, no money has been collected.

In Case 2, traffickers fraudulently procured visas for approximately 15 to 20 predominately East Asian and North African victims over the course of multiple years. Though the visa applications stated that victims would be employed as administrative or technical staff, victims were employed as the traffickers' personal drivers, domestic helpers, farmhands, and assistants at their residences and farms. The case came to the attention of the legal advocacy organization when a victim phoned their office from a supermarket. After involving law enforcement at the victim's request, the FBI collected information using search warrants and interviews. The prosecutor eventually issued a criminal indictment charging three individuals with visa fraud. One defendant was arrested, while others remained at large. Victims received housing through a personal connection of a lawyer with the legal advocacy organization, and one victim received law enforcement parole. The legal organization reported significant and unusual difficulties obtaining continued presence or deferred action relative to their experience in similar situations.

In Case 3, traffickers used recruiters in several areas to lure Mexican victims to the United States and fraudulently obtain H-2B visas. Victims were transported via railroad and were responsible for unloading, setting up, and breaking down large-scale entertainment events; they also worked during railroad transit as concession workers. After removal from the immediate trafficking situation, some victims received T-visas; however, most victims in need of work returned to their home countries. The legal advocacy organization filed a civil class action based on the TVPA, FLSA, RICO, ATCA, and other state law claims. Shortly after, the prosecutor filed a criminal complaint. A defendant was arrested, but the case was quickly dismissed on a motion from the prosecutor, apparently after reaching a deal with the defendant that if he paid workers' back wages, he would be released. The legal advocacy organization also settled a civil suit with the company and one of the traffickers.

Case 4 involved two periods of exploitation in which victims were re-trafficked by the same entertainment company. Initially, multiple workers were recruited for an entertainment company and traveled from their home country in South America to the United States on P-1 visas. In this first period, only some victims were exploited. The second time the victims arrived, their documents were confiscated, and they were forced to sleep in the trafficker's home and pay rent to her. During this time, one of the victims escaped from the trafficker's home and ultimately reported the incident to the FBI. A federal investigation led by the FBI identified the situation as trafficking. Though some victims initially remained with the trafficker, eventually, the victims were removed and provided with housing. During this investigation, some victims received continued presence and work authorization through referral to an FBI Victim Support Specialist known for his training in obtaining continued presence. However, the criminal case was dropped due to prosecutorial discretion, and individuals who had been granted continued presence under that investigation lost it. Civil and administrative complaints were also filed and remain pending.

In Case 5, one victim was sold to, and forced to marry, a wealthy male trafficker who brought her from her home country to the United States. For nearly two decades, the victim and several family members were all forced to work on the trafficker's "family farm." The victim escaped by obtaining a divorce and a restraining order against the trafficker. Though the victim attempted to report her experiences to several local and federal authorities and contacted multiple lawyers and agencies, she faced significant difficulty obtaining help. There was never an arrest or any formal filing of charges. Authorities viewed the case as a domestic violence issue rather than a trafficking case.

# Critical Gaps in Human Trafficking Research: A Reflection on Six Years of Learning Through the Program to End Modern Slavery (PEMS)

Abigail Long and Casey Branchini Risko

**ABSTRACT**
After over 20 years of anti-trafficking programming, the field remains reliant on promising practices rather than evidence-based ones. This article identifies eight key gaps in human trafficking research and shares the Program to End Modern Slavery's approach to addressing them. It aims to inform future strategies to build the evidence base on "what works" and "what doesn't" and identify model interventions. The gaps demonstrate the immense progress made so far; however, further research and evaluation is needed to better understand *how* and *why* a particular intervention works so it can be adapted and implemented at scale.

## Introduction

While the Protocol to Prevent, Suppress and Punish Trafficking in Persons, Especially Women and Children (hereafter referred to as *The Palermo Protocol*) was adopted by the U.N. General Assembly and opened for signature in 2000 and entered into force in 2003, international efforts to address the root causes and exploitation that amounts to human trafficking started much earlier. Anti-trafficking programs and policies are rooted in international agreements and powerful social movements, such as the fight for democracy, civil rights, and women's empowerment, which do not directly address human trafficking but can decrease risk among those that benefit, directly or indirectly, from such programs. Civil rights, for instance, gave new rights to previously disadvantaged populations that reduced their risk and vulnerability to potential exploitation in human trafficking. These inter-related fields started long before the Palermo Protocol was even negotiated and, thus, have had a significant head-start in developing monitoring, evaluation, and research programs to determine "what works" in terms of programming and policy. In recent years, those studying human trafficking have collaborated with others studying public health, education, migration, gender-based violence, poverty alleviation, etc., to identify lessons learned and evidence-based programs and policies that can be adapted for use in the human trafficking space.

Research in human trafficking is advancing rapidly to identify promising programs and policies; however, it must still overcome built-in challenges related to resourcing these efforts and challenges inherent to measuring the complex social phenomenon of trafficking in persons. Other fields of study do not regularly track data on human trafficking cases, and thus, the anti-trafficking field has missed critical opportunities to enhance knowledge about what makes an effective program or policy. This is not to say that we have no idea what works in anti-trafficking programs; we have limited evidence that some activities within prevention, protection, and prosecution programming seem to or benefit the target audience and what might cause an adverse reaction. For example, well-conducted awareness-raising programs can lead to behavior change. Providing quality social services to victims and those at-risk of trafficking frequently leads to improvements in their situations. We also know that some anti-trafficking training for law enforcement is better than no training. However, we are still left without the necessary details and mechanisms to maximize the effectiveness of the limited foreign assistance and other funds allocated to combating trafficking in persons. This is compounded by the lack of coherent, comprehensive, and systematic guidance for conducting research and evaluating anti-trafficking efforts. The field could also benefit from more vital coordination amongst donors, governments, and implementers, who frequently operate in silos and cannot share data to maximize learning.

To address these gaps, the Office to Monitor and Combat in Trafficking in Persons (hereafter the TIP Office) at the U.S. Department of State (hereafter referred to as the State Department), building off the tremendous progress made by others, has developed foreign assistance funding programs that fastidiously measure critical outcomes, set standards for data reporting and program design, foster collaboration among research teams, and encourage rigorous research that conclusively shows what programs and policies most effectively reduce the prevalence of human trafficking. Most research funded by the TIP Office is considered action research, as it is directed primarily toward the specific objective or aim of informing or influencing anti-trafficking policy and programming. We define research, the most critical term for this article, as original investigation undertaken to gain knowledge and understanding.

Research and evaluation are distinct from programming and policy. For this article, programming refers to contracts or grants awarded to organizations that implement activities in foreign countries with a specific goal, such as promoting the human rights of marginalized communities or reducing inter-communal violence. Policies are government-funded or organized systems, principles, or mechanisms that indirectly or directly impact their intended beneficiaries. This article explains how the research and evaluation gaps we have identified impact programs and policies. More than 70% of funding through the Program to End Modern Slavery (PEMS) supports programmatic efforts. Approximately 20% support action research efforts that inform programming and assist the TIP Office and its grantees in identifying programming priorities and designs, gauging programming impact, and identifying risk factors of human trafficking. The remainder of the funding supports regular monitoring and evaluation efforts, including data collection, analysis, and adaptive management principles.

Although each serves a unique purpose, research and evaluation are highly interconnected and share many similarities, particularly regarding the types of methods they use. Program evaluation is a systematic method for collecting, analyzing, and using information to answer basic questions about an ongoing or completed program or intervention model. There are multiple types of evaluations (e.g., formative, process, summative, outcome, and impact), and the methods need to be tailored to the purpose of the evaluation. An evaluation can use qualitative or quantitative data or a combination, and the methods used are often like research and monitoring. Feedback from affected stakeholders and beneficiaries (actual and potential), specifically human trafficking survivors, is critical for monitoring, evaluation, and research, primarily when used to inform the design of an anti-trafficking intervention or policy. Evaluation measures and assesses implementation progress to help improve performance and achieve results. Unlike research, evaluation cannot exist without a program or policy. Research is often viewed as a first step in the intervention development process, whereas evaluation can sometimes begin after an intervention. Research is critical to informing the design of an intervention and ensuring it is responsive to the needs of the target population. Both research and evaluation are essential in determining the most innovative use of the limited funding in the anti-trafficking field.

We will now explain the role of the TIP Office in foreign assistance programming, further discuss what we see as the primary gaps in research and evaluation in the context of human trafficking and highlight some of the programs our office has supported to address them.

## Background on the TIP Office

The TIP Office was established following the Trafficking Victims Protection Act (TVPA) of 2000. The TIP Office began issuing grants in 2001 and has since awarded more than $490 million in grants and contracts to approximately 175 international and nongovernmental organizations, academic institutions, and some private companies worldwide. Over the years, the anti-trafficking movement has professionalized its grantmaking significantly, following trends in domestic and international government foreign assistance programs and social justice movements worldwide. As one of the largest funders of anti-trafficking programs globally, the U.S. Government, including the TIP Office, has used its influence to develop strategies and decisions that impact not just potential award recipients, but the anti-trafficking field writ large, including partner governments, victims, survivors, and those at-risk of human trafficking. The TIP Office has introduced and implemented cutting-edge programs and research that comply with legal and administrative requirements and fill the gaps in our knowledge of human trafficking. One of these programs is PEMS.

The U.S. legislation establishing PEMS was enacted in 2017 and created an ambitious foreign assistance program that was intended to be transformational and innovative, establishing rigorous monitoring and evaluation requirements to determine whether foreign assistance resources genuinely led to a reduction in the prevalence of human trafficking. Since Congress authorized the PEMS program, the TIP Office has allocated $25 million each year, making it the most extensive foreign assistance program within the TIP Office (U.S. Department of State, n.d.). The PEMS program has identified several research gaps that are critical to the advancement of the anti-trafficking field.

## Critical Gaps in Human Trafficking Research and How PEMS is Addressing or Trying to Address Them

### *Lack of Standardized Victim and Survivor Measurement Protocols*

The lack of international agreement on systematically estimating the victim population was the first and most significant hurdle for PEMS to overcome. Foreign assistance grants that fund research, monitoring, and evaluation must rely on widely-accepted methods to ensure the results are credible and foster support for changes in anti-trafficking programs or policies. Suppose it is easy to poke holes in the chosen methods. In that case, it will make it possible for governments or civil society partners to justify any refusal to make improvements and disregard the findings.

Consequently, the Prevalence Reduction Innovation Forum (PRIF) was created by PEMS in 2020 to serve as a testing ground for the most common methods to measure the number of victims of human trafficking. The goal was to establish an evidence base beyond repute that would give authority to the research that adhered to those findings. Through an open and competitive funding process, six research teams were selected to measure the victim population in seven distinct settings worldwide using at least two different prevalence measurement methodologies. The goal was to implement the research with the same hypothesis, at roughly the same time, with the exact sampling specifications, thereby systematically comparing the methods against a common methodology. This marks the first time that sufficiently similar human trafficking prevalence measurements have been conducted to enable a meta-analysis (*forthcoming*). In fact, to the best of our knowledge, this is the first pre-identified meta-analysis on the measurement of victims and survivors in a social science discipline. It will allow State Department program managers and policymakers to determine empirically which methods return the lowest standard of error and analyze which contextual elements lead to the greatest measurement success. A byproduct of the meta-analysis will be a framework where future studies can contribute their data, update the results, and maintain and strengthen the research integrity and rigor standard. This framework has already enabled another research study that started later, funded by the U.S. Department of Health and Human Services (HHS) and implemented by RTI International, to contribute to the meta-analysis simply by following the guidelines.[1]

[1]For more information regarding the meta-analysis, please visit https://macartan.github.io/hidden_populations/.

Bringing together researchers from various academic disciplines and geographic areas also helped to catalyze and uplift the anti-trafficking research community. Coordinating research and strengthening the evidence-base requires significant efforts to build community among researchers. The anti-trafficking research environment is ordinarily highly competitive, so the PRIF leadership had to encourage scientific innovation where teams were required to share data, change their methods to increase commonality, work together to solve problems and learn from failures and mistakes. In a departure from the usual competitive funding world, a premise of the PRIF is that "failing" would not mean losing out on future grants; this was a scientific exercise which included uncovering what does not work to identify what does. The meta-analysis is only as powerful as the number of studies contributing to it, so the PRIF needed to see the maximum number of studies succeed. That is more likely to happen if an open environment allows for acknowledgment and learning from failures to benefit others. Data collection for nearly all seven PRIF-funded prevalence studies has been completed, and findings will be shared by the TIP Office by the end of the year.

One of the biggest challenges to advancing the field until this point was the lack of dedicated funding for such work. Researchers would often be required to conduct studies on limited budgets and unrealistic timeframes. When conducting field-based research, unexpected events and delays can push timelines or introduce unexpected costs. The PRIF represented a significant investment in victim-centered, anti-trafficking research, providing reasonable flexibility for researchers to complete their objectives and connect their work to programming outcomes. The PRIF is also attempting to provide a more comprehensive and systematic understanding of trafficking methods to use for programming and policy purposes; however, there remains more work to be done.

As a next step, the TIP Office is funding the International Labour Organization (ILO) in coordination with the International Organization for Migration (IOM), the United Nations Office on Drugs and Crime (UNODC), and the University of Georgia (UGA), to develop a shared understanding of human trafficking victim and survivor measurement across several different international standards. This project aims to develop operational definitions, tools, methodologies, and uniform guidance for measuring trafficking in persons, forced labor, and trafficking for forced labor. The legal framework for this work consists of the Palermo Protocol, the TVPA, and the International Forced Labour Convention, 1930 (No. 29) and "trafficking in persons for the purpose of forced labor," which is a separate fourth definition rooted in the Palermo Protocol and the ILO convention No. 29. While the Palermo Protocol and the TVPA set clear legal definitions of trafficking in persons, there has been no clear consensus on how and to what extent the definitions overlap or differ, nor how they relate to existing guidance on forced labor measurement and what implications this has on the measurement of trafficking in persons. This project aims to operationalize these legal definitions for statistical research and identify and validate a set of common indicators and tools to measure trafficking in persons according to the most prominent international agreements, further enabling joint analysis and comparison from a single data set. The guidance will clarify longstanding confusion in the international community and allow the field to move forward efficiently without duplicating expensive surveys.

Once complete, the authors will encourage all implementers of TIP Office foreign assistance projects or programs to use the common indicators developed by the ILO and the meta-analysis. This will not bring the field into alignment on all aspects of programmatic data (e.g., what outcomes should be used to measure the effectiveness of an anti-trafficking awareness campaign, the validity of a victim screening tool, etc.), but it will facilitate greater coordination on the study of human trafficking prevalence and some of the most critical proxy indicators. We also hope researchers will continue using it outside of PEMS (Price et al., 2022).

### *Multiple and Rigorous Research and Evaluation Methods*

Complex interventions, such as those developed to address human trafficking, typically involve multiple components or levels of intervention whose effectiveness usually cannot be fully understood using a single research method. This can make it difficult to isolate the effects of the intervention from other factors. Rigorous and multiple methods can help account for these complexities and ensure that the findings are valid and reliable. Methods may include qualitative (e.g., social mapping, participatory action research, in-depth interviews) and quantitative methods (e.g., household surveys). Using multiple methods can provide a more comprehensive understanding of the intervention, its implementation, and its impact, as well as help to triangulate findings and address potential biases. By capturing different aspects of the intervention and its effects, the findings are more likely to be generalized to different contexts and populations. Although greater focus has been on applying a mixed-methods approach when studying a phenomenon as complex as human trafficking, there is still a need for improvement. In recent years, PEMS has moved away from funding projects that rely on a single method (e.g., quantitative survey) in favor of those that apply a combination of qualitative and quantitative approaches, mainly when the purpose is to inform the design of anti-trafficking interventions and policies. To engage survivors, researchers must also employ survivor-centered, trauma-informed approaches to build trust and develop relationships that facilitate increased engagement in the research process and, ultimately the intervention over time. For example, multiple rigorous research methods, including participatory action research, were identified as a priority for the first time in PEMS' most recent Notice of Funding Opportunity (NOFO).

Due to the cost and scale, longitudinal study is one of the most challenging research and evaluation methods. These studies involve following subjects over a long time, sometimes decades, and continuously monitoring key outcomes. Although understanding the long-term impact of anti-trafficking programs on survivors is paramount, much progress still needs to be made. In October 2022, for example, The Global Knowledge Partnership on Migration and Development (KNOMAD), a global hub of knowledge and policy expertise on migration and development, issued a methodology for a longitudinal study on reintegration outcomes for migrants who have returned to their countries of origin (Malakooti & Zwick, 2022). A similar methodology needs to be developed for trafficking victims, as it would fill a critical knowledge gap by allowing for the standardized monitoring of return and reintegration across seemingly diverse contexts. Investing time and resources can reap dividends for donors, implementers, and governments in designing and implementing long-term policies and programs that can stand the test of time. In turn, this would facilitate a better understanding of the longer-term outcomes of anti-trafficking interventions – information critical to informing return and reintegration programs and policies. Safe and ethical modes of contact that use common standard technology platforms, such as WhatsApp, could be explored. Evaluations typically do not follow victims and survivors for more than six months, and we know little about their situations in the long term. Another challenge is a lack of understanding and consensus around "successful reintegration." Research also needs to identify a set of criteria that can be adapted and used to assess reintegration success in each context and consider how this information can support future programs.

### *Standardizing Measurement and Indicators*

One of the most critical steps in identifying successful programs and policies is ensuring comparability, which can be challenging due to the lack of program design and implementation standards and the diversity of the field. The PEMS implementing partners represent a wide variety of organizational types. Basic structures range from three to five people who may work from home to massive international organizations with thousands of staff members in hundreds of offices worldwide. Implementing partners' motivations are similarly diverse. Some implementing partners are singularly focused on ending human trafficking, while others are focused on economic inequality or social justice. For the latter type of organization, any effect their previous programs have had on ending human trafficking may have been a secondary benefit or outcome that the organization has not typically measured but is doing now for PEMS. This leads to actors that are unlikely to communicate with each other and often utilize different measurement standards on different indicators. Experimental and quasi-experimental studies are the norm in fields like economics and criminology, and many indicators are standardized and quantitative (e.g., recidivism, time incarcerated, income, business profit, rate of debt, etc.). Some organizations take a more qualitative research, monitoring, and evaluation approach and focus on victim case studies or stories. These organizations are less likely to measure the same quantitative indicators as related fields, such as economics and criminology.

There are also differences within program types. For instance, organizations that are implementing only prevention programming are likely to have different modalities and may not agree on what defines success. To some organizations, prevention programming focuses on providing people with safer job alternatives that lessen the need to accept risky job offers and move to foreign countries. Young women might be targeted, and the dangers of sex trafficking should be explained to them to affect behavior change and refuse those opportunities. To other organizations, prevention programming might mean an awareness campaign at ports of entry that aims to increase the likelihood of people calling and reporting suspicious behavior. When no experimental research method is used to assess which programs reduced the rate of trafficking victimization in the treatment and the control groups of each program, it is impossible to discover which programs actually "worked."

Another complicating factor is that while human trafficking does not require movement, many violations of this crime occur within another national jurisdiction from where the victims or the perpetrators are located. This means that even if there is political will, it may not be possible to pursue criminal or civil charges in the national jurisdiction where some or all the crime occurred if the victim or the perpetrator is not in the country, may have been there illegally or does not feel safe participating in the criminal justice process. In many jurisdictions, it is possible to conduct prosecutions without the victim present or where the victim can testify via videoconference. However, the victim or perpetrator's lack of presence can be considered a negative factor when prosecutors decide whether to pursue charges. In some jurisdictions, the case must otherwise be very strong for the prosecution team to decide to move forward. These are several reasons why developing measures of success for prosecution programming is particularly complex. For example, do we define success based on the number of successful convictions? In many cases, the victim sincerely desires to return home and not pursue criminal or civil charges (Wechsler, 2019). This has been apparent in several PEMS-funded projects, including in Kenya and Uganda, which adopt a trauma-informed approach and victim-centered investigations. Another challenge is that depending on a country's anti-trafficking legal framework, the objectives and activities that make up a prosecution project might need to be completely different. For example, compared to countries with only recently adopted anti-trafficking laws, those with more well-established laws might have had access for several years to advanced forensic equipment for use in investigations and would be less likely to need training support to use them effectively. Countries with newer anti-trafficking laws might need extensive training support to help law enforcement process forensic evidence and potentially without any equipment available to them.

### *Research Design That Enables Causal Identification*

Building on the points above, the PEMS Team has been working hard to create a sea change in monitoring and evaluation. Most TIP Office monitoring and evaluation efforts focused on outputs, and few used rigorous research methods, such as experimental or quasi-experimental studies, that could identify causal factors. They relied on observational methods practical in the anthropological sense to understand the dynamics of human trafficking or the victims' experiences. However, they are rarely sufficient to tease out causal mechanisms that can remove victims from trafficking situations or prevent the crime from occurring in the first place. The TIP Office recognized the value of using a program design that enables comparison of the population that receives the foreign assistance intervention with one that was similar but did not receive the intervention (aka the control) to determine which programs and policies lead to a significant change in the victim population.

An important component was structuring PEMS grants with more than a "before" and "after" measurement methodology. Even with the most rigorous victim measurement protocols, a before and after measurement could not correctly tell whether foreign assistance programs contributed to increased or decreased victims. Randomized treatment and control groups coupled with before and after measurements should be a pivotal tool to help detect if programs made a difference. The Global Fund to End Modern Slavery set up randomized treatment and control groups using a quasi-experimental method in Uganda that allowed them to identify key findings related to the programmatic success of an attitude and behavior change campaign on child sex trafficking (Global Fund to End Modern Slavery [GFEMS], 2023). PEMS encouraged this methodology in recent NOFOs and officially funded it with programs in Bangladesh, Pakistan, Southern Africa, and Brazil's coffee industry for the first time.

PEMS also funded the Human Trafficking Research Initiative (HTRI) at Innovations for Poverty Action, whose purpose is to increase the quantity of rigorous research studies that allow us to determine causal mechanisms, such as through experimental methods, i.e., randomized controlled trials (RCTs) or quasi-experimental methods. HTRI provides competitive funding for research on the interventions, systems, settings, and conditions that will enable sustainable change in the fight against trafficking. HTRI has funded several large-scale studies on the efforts to prevent trafficking, prosecute crimes, and protect victims of trafficking. They also funded several pilot grants to set the stage for future randomized control trials (RCTs). Although RCTs are complex to implement and challenging to get funded, pilot grants can help test RCTs before funding is committed and make necessary connections for the success of the research. Another key goal of the project is to clarify ethical concerns that might prevent some groups from using RCTs. These efforts should increase the availability of evidence in the human trafficking field and the number of high-level academic journal articles from various fields on human trafficking and enable funders and governments to use the results to affect and design evidence-based programs and policies in the future.

### *Lack of Minimum standards[2] Of Care for Anti-Trafficking Service Providers*

The development of universal service standards of care for anti-trafficking service providers will not only ensure consistent quality of care and reduce potential harms to trafficking victims and survivors but will also provide an international basis for comparison of key assistance and protection measures across anti-trafficking programs. The standards would consist of a minimum package of services to victims and survivors even in the most resource-constrained settings, such as in the aftermath of a natural disaster or conflict. The standards would cover a range of direct services, including case management, shelter and housing, legal, mental, and physical health, economic empowerment, and more.

The *Minimum Standards for the Prevention and Response to Gender-Based Violence (GBV) in Emergencies* introduced by the United Nations Population Fund (UNFPA) is perhaps the most well-known and relevant example of a universally accepted minimum standards of care for service providers (United Nations Population Fund [UNFPA], 2019). These standards have been used to inform GBV prevention and response strategies for nearly 10 years. Similar standards for anti-trafficking services providers would also need to be grounded in research and developed through an international process that seeks support from as many countries as possible; once developed, the standards would need to be adopted globally.

Like the *Minimum Standards for the Prevention and Response to GBV in Emergencies* introduced by UNFPA, standards developed for victims of trafficking would also cover protection as it relates to victims' engagement with officials in the criminal justice system. This may also involve, for example, the creation of assessment tools and checklists that help to ensure that the victim is not re-traumatized through their involvement with the criminal

[2]Please note that these minimum standards are different from the congressionally mandated "Minimum Standards for the Elimination of Severe Forms of Trafficking in Persons" established under the Trafficking Victims Protection Act that are used by the U.S. Department of State to assess governments' efforts in the annual Trafficking in Persons Report.

justice system. An assessment tool may include questions, such as: 1) Can court proceedings occur on camera (in private) for human trafficking cases (i.e., the presiding judge clears the courtroom or hears the testimony in chambers)? Who decides?; 2) What is the capacity (vehicles, fuel, staff, etc.) or limitations in instituting procedures for victim and/or witness transport, care, and protection?; or 3) What is the typical time frame for prosecution from date of charges filed to the date of acquittal or conviction? Does the statute require a specific time frame, and if so, what is it?, etc.

The more validated standards of care that exist at any administrative level globally, the easier the process will be for developing international minimum standards of care for victims. Developing such standards would also help to address ethical concerns around withholding services from individuals enrolled in the "control" arm of RCT of an anti-trafficking intervention; it would be required to use the international minimum standards of care for the control population, which would guarantee a basic level of services and ensure that no participants in an RCT ever have services withheld. While the PEMS team is not currently implementing such an effort to develop a universally accepted minimum standard of care for the protection of victims, the team has supported the development of Standards of Care in Uganda and notes that standards of care already exist in the United Kingdom (GFEMS, 2021; Independent Anti-Slavery Commissioner, 2018; U.S. Department of State, 2022b).

### *Intervention Development Research (IDR)*

As previously described, current research does not provide clear, evidence-driven direction on "what works" to prevent or respond to human trafficking. The anti-trafficking field still looks to "promising" rather than "evidence-based" practices. The current evidence base does not offer sufficiently robust findings on the effectiveness of anti-trafficking interventions, nor does it detect the interventions' interactions within the local context and more prominent systemic factors at play. The complexity of human trafficking requires a nuanced understanding of the various social, economic, and policy factors at multiple levels and requires us to unpack the "black box" that exists between intervention Y and outcome X. There is an urgent need to develop more robust evidence that applies a whole-of-systems approach based on deep, contextual knowledge and engagement with local actors.

A growing field of research on complex social interventions examines traditional pharmaceutical and medical research methods for guidance, which typically requires a significant amount of discovery and development (i.e., research and development or R&D) and pre-clinical research before going to a clinical trial. Although the R&D stage takes a significant investment of time and money, it is arguably the most important as it allows researchers to identify what formulas or clinical procedures will fix the problem with the fewest dangers or side effects. It is the foundation of any clinical trial – a due diligence step – that must be carried out to avoid wasting resources and causing harm to the population the intervention or drug seeks to help. When combating human trafficking, this R&D step is essentially absent, as evidenced by the trivial amount of time and money invested in research focused on intervention development.

Intervention development research (IDR) is a tool that can help address this gap. IDR involves developing interventions that consider the broader systems and identify the elements that can change. IDR will provide the TIP Office and the anti-trafficking field an opportunity to deepen our understanding of the environments we seek to change and strengthen local capacity to create enduring impact. IDR also requires the pilot testing of interventions to determine whether they will likely work before implementing them at scale and/or proceeding to a full-scale evaluation. The PEMS team devoted its 2023 Notice of Funding Opportunity (NOFO) to funding IDR projects. In addition, over the last few years, PEMS emphasized the importance of causal identification in intervention design by funding an increased number of programs that include elements of IDR, including co-creation and systems thinking, which will be described later.

### *Systems Thinking Approach to Harm Reduction*

As alluded to throughout this text, human trafficking is a complex social phenomenon that should be viewed along a spectrum of severity that is highly context-dependent. Unfortunately, human trafficking is often viewed as a black-or-white issue: an individual is either exploited or not when it must be examined using a systems lens, which is also a core component of IDR. The anti-trafficking field must also acknowledge that human trafficking exists along a continuum. An intervention may not necessarily eliminate it but could reduce the harm associated with the crime sufficiently so that while the individual might still be in a situation of exploitation, it would be far less severe. They would no longer officially be considered a victim of trafficking according to the *Palermo Protocol.* This approach requires us to look slightly differently at measurement, focusing not only on the prevalence of human trafficking but also its associated harms. For example, for the first time, the 2022 NOFO issued by PEMS allowed applicants to measure the prevalence of human trafficking and/or "proxy indicators" of the crime (U.S. Department of State, 2022a). Change takes time and a reduction in overall trafficking prevalence may not be seen over a one- or three-year intervention period. However, that does not mean that an intervention did not reduce the level of exploitation experienced by the intended beneficiaries.

One example could be an anti-trafficking intervention specifically aimed at improving working conditions, a vital component of the human trafficking system. Following the intervention, beneficiaries may report fewer cases of workplace violence, better access to personal protective equipment, etc., but they may still work excessive hours. However, if the economic system leads to unequal profit distribution, the increased income from the extra hours may be critical to their livelihoods. Limiting the number of hours, they can work is one indicator of trafficking; this may be removing their ability to ensure their household's basic needs are met. PEMS is grappling with issues like this and working to identify ways to better measure the complex nature of trafficking and achievable and desirable outcomes.

Systems thinking can also help better identify a beneficiary's assets that were not clear beforehand. There is a tendency for research to apply a deficit-based approach when studying human trafficking. Although it is essential to study the factors that increase one's risk of human trafficking, it is equally important to also study factors that reduce one's risk. The field must move toward applying an assets-based approach in research and programming. We should be asking, "What can we build on?" (i.e., asset- or strengths-based approach) rather than only "What needs fixing?" (i.e., deficit-based approach). More attention must be paid to identifying factors amenable to an intervention to complement efforts focused on the more significant structural issues, such as poverty, lack of education, etc. PEMS is trying to address this issue by funding and evaluating preventive interventions focusing on reducing risk and building and enhancing protective factors.

### *Co-Creation/Co-Production*

Co-production of knowledge and action has been promoted as a valuable approach for bringing about the transformational change needed for accelerating progress toward sustainable development outcomes; however, to date, it has not received enough attention within the anti-trafficking space (Bourne et al., 2023). Co-production is "processes that iteratively bring together diverse groups and their ways of knowing and acting to create new knowledge and practices to transform societal outcomes" (Wyborn et al., 2019, p. 322). It allows us to reframe complex issues, such as human trafficking, more effectively and produce actionable knowledge that can inform the design of programs. Co-creation must be emphasized from the very beginning of both research and intervention design. Research questions, for example, are often predetermined by policy priorities, academic interests, etc., without discussing them with the individuals tasked with using the information (e.g., law enforcement, service providers, etc.). The importance of co-creation is important in designing research and interventions that are relevant to those impacted (directly or indirectly) by human trafficking, but also for ensuring buy-in and, ultimately, the sustainability of interventions. The TIP Office encourages co-creation by its grantees and in its most recent PEMS NOFO, as co-creation is a core principle of IDR.

Co-creation brings together organizations and individuals, including members of the target population, to identify solutions to human trafficking challenges and foster local ownership. Thus, key stakeholders, including change agents, potential beneficiaries of an intervention, and human trafficking survivors, should play a central role in identifying the problem to be addressed, developing intervention(s) to address it, and determining how success is measured. This is where it can get tricky because, as we all know, we also need to be able to standardize measurements in some way and develop interventions that can be adapted and, ultimately, scaled up in similar contexts. In looking ahead, measurement standards that stress the importance of adaptation must be developed. This may take the form of a core set of indicators, for example, that must be standardized (regardless of the setting) with an additional sub-set of indicators that can be tailored to a specific operating context. Careful attention must also be paid to the utility of the knowledge generated and ensure that the deliverables are tailored to specific stakeholders/groups and do not consist solely of peer-reviewed publications and policy briefs. Co-creation also plays a key role in ensuring deliverables are relevant to those using them (e.g., community members, policymakers, etc.). Knowledge can be highly contextual, and researchers must acknowledge that deliverables, such as reports, must be shared with the communities where the research takes place and tailored for use by stakeholder groups of varying capacities, including members of the target population.

### *Build Upon Existing Knowledge and Integrating with Other Sectors and Disciplines*

As mentioned, human trafficking does not exist in a silo, nor should efforts to address or measure it (e.g., policies, programs, etc.). Practitioners, policymakers, and researchers must make a concerted effort to build upon the evidence base in related fields, such as those studying gender-based violence, mental health, poverty reduction, etc., rather than reinventing the wheel.

Although progress has been made recently, adapting research and evaluation methods from other disciplines should be expanded to the human trafficking field. When possible, researchers should adapt and/or expand upon scientifically rigorous frameworks and theories from other disciplines (e.g., epidemiology, behavioral science, & demography) applicable to human trafficking. The methods or theories do not have to have been used before in anti-trafficking research to help us understand the scenario, inform the design and piloting of the intervention model, and establish evidence on its potential for adaptations for other settings and/or scale-up. Every social science field has its strengths and provided that the processes are clear, and there is evidence that the research will provide insight into the context in which the intervention operates (e.g., social, environmental, and economic), each method, even if not having previously focused on anti-trafficking, should be considered.

The field must also make a more concerted attempt to integrate the study of human trafficking into ongoing efforts in other fields, identifying intervention leverage points or existing mechanisms both in terms of programming and measurement. For example, one approach could involve integrating a human trafficking screening tool into the ongoing training of community health workers or piloting an anti-trafficking module in nationwide child violence surveys. Implementing either or both of these strategies will enhance our understanding of the issue's prevalence within a specific geographic area and enable us to identify trends over time. Adaptation is also relevant when considering intervention strategies. Before designing an intervention from scratch, implementers should thoroughly review the evidence to identify evidence-based interventions used in similar contents (e.g., child labor, rural settings, etc.). Rather than duplicating efforts, such interventions could be adapted among trafficking victims. For example, recent research suggests that, in Cambodia and elsewhere, assistance to men and boys focuses on return and basic emergency needs (e.g., transportation and brief shelter stays) rather than long-term re-integration (Aberdein & Zimmerman, 2015; Nodzenski et al., 2020; Surtees, 2013). Men and boys represent a neglected group that is not being reached by existing services, particularly regarding mental health. As discussed earlier, IDR could be used to adapt evidence-based psychosocial interventions for survivors of gender-based violence for use among male trafficking survivors in Cambodia and beyond. In addition to focusing on IDR, PEMS has also encouraged the collaboration of researchers from various disciplines, including public health, criminology, epidemiology, etc. through the PRIF and other initiatives.

Future efforts to address evidence-to-action gaps in the anti-trafficking space should be accompanied by dedicated funding to create a standardized framework for generating and documenting knowledge that can be strengthened and adapted over time. One step in filling this gap is to address the lack of systematic reviews, defined by the Cochrane Collaborative as an "attempt to identify, appraise and synthesize all the empirical evidence that meets pre-specified eligibility criteria to answer a specific research question" (Cochrane Library, n.d..). Unlike the pre-identified meta-analysis, as discussed earlier, these can be done *ex-post facto*, but require enough similar studies to draw generalizable conclusions. They also require significant time and resources. Like what Innovations for Poverty Action (IPA) has done to inform its PEMS-funded research and learning agenda, "rapid" or "brief reviews of evidence are another way to ensure a learning framework in human trafficking begins to emerge and can be used to facilitate the use of evidence in decisions around programming and policies (IPA, 2023). Although there is no single definition of a rapid review, they typically involve examining empirical evidence that is limited in timeframe (less than six months) and/or in scope (Abrami et al., 2010). Methodological "shortcuts" can also be used to shorten the timeframe (e.g., searching fewer databases, limited use of gray literature, relying on existing systematic reviews, etc.) (Abrami et al., 2010; Ganann et al., 2010; Hartling et al., 2015). The TIP Office occupies a unique position as one of the largest donors of anti-trafficking programming and research, which allows access to a large amount of monitoring data and evaluation reports. Although progress has been made, there is an urgent need to synthesize learnings and findings across our various projects and share them with the broader anti-trafficking field.

## Discussion and Conclusions

We acknowledge that this article does not identify all the gaps in research in the human trafficking space. However, it is a starting point from which we can build in coordination with the broader anti-trafficking field globally, including human trafficking survivors. As we address these gaps, we must address the resource-constrained environment in which this field functions. It is essential to recognize and leverage overlaps of human trafficking with other fields and not rely on trafficking-specific funding alone to address the problem. In addition, addressing some of the above mentioned research gaps can ensure the best use of the limited funds. Understanding evidence gaps can also help governments and donors better set funding priorities.

We know these research gaps cannot be addressed overnight, but one step in that direction can be bringing donors, implementers, researchers, human trafficking survivors, and other members of the target population together on equal footing, acknowledging the importance of expertise and experience to discuss these gaps and decide on actionable steps forward. This can help us ensure a unified research agenda that results in information/knowledge that will ultimately lead to sustainable change. In facing the perennial challenge of resistance to the need for research, it is critical to be clear on how research directly enhances the development of effective programs grounded in evidence and potentially grounded in evidence that can be adapted and scaled up. There is an ethical imperative to address human trafficking most cost-effectively. Donors cannot continue to allocate funding to programs that may or may not work or, even worse, result in adverse consequences. Targeted funding for action-oriented research and monitoring and evaluation is ultimately the most cost-effective, as it provides information on what is worthwhile to fund – or not – to reduce the prevalence of human trafficking sustainably.

## Disclosure Statement

No potential conflict of interest was reported by the author(s).

## Disclaimer

The contents are those of the authors and do not necessarily represent the official views of, nor an endorsement, by the Department of State or U.S. Government.

## References

Aberdein, C., & Zimmerman, C. (2015). Access to mental health and psychosocial services in Cambodia by survivors of trafficking and exploitation: A qualitative study. *International Journal of Mental Health Systems*, *9*(1), 1–13. https://doi.org/10.1186/s13033-015-0008-8

Abrami, P. C., Borokhovski, E., Bernard, R. M., Wade, C. A., Tamim, R., Persson, T., Bethel, E. C., Hanz, K., & Surkes, M. A. (2010). Issues in conducting and disseminating brief reviews of evidence. *Evidence & Policy*, *6*(3), 371–389. https://doi.org/10.1332/174426410X524866

Bourne, M., Magaju, C., Neely, C., Peterson, N., Lamanna, C., Chesterman, S., & Vågen, T. G. (2023). Enhancing co-production of knowledge: Visualisation and engagement approaches for evidence-based decision making within the Kenya agroforestry strategy. *Environmental Science & Policy*, *140*, 152–162. https://doi.org/10.1016/j.envsci.2022.11.021

Cochrane Library. (n.d.). *Cochrane Database of Systematic Reviews (CDSR)*. https://www.cochranelibrary.com/cdsr/about-cdsr.

Ganann, R., Ciliska, D., & Thomas, H. (2010). Expediting systematic reviews: Methods and implications of rapid reviews. *Implementation Science*, *5*(1), 1–10. https://doi.org/10.1186/1748-5908-5-56

Global Fund to End Modern Slavery (GFEMS). (2021, March 22). *GFEMS Partners with Hope for Justice to Improve Survivor Care in Uganda*. https://gfems.org/uncategorized/gfems-partners-with-hope-for-justice-to-improve-survivor-care-in-uganda/.

Global Fund to End Modern Slavery (GFEMS). (2023, 01 March). *Assessing change regarding the sexual exploitation of children in Napak District, Uganda*. https://gfems.org/reports/assessing-change-regarding-the-sexual-exploitation-of-children-in-napak-district-uganda/.

Hartling, L., Guise, J. M., Kato, E., Anderson, J., Aronson, N., Belinson, S., Berliner, E., Dryden, D., Featherstone, R., Foisy, M., Mitchell, M., Motu'apuaka, M., Noorani, H., Paynter, R., Robinson, K. A., Schoelles, K., Umscheid, C. A., & Whitlock, E. (2015). EPC Methods: An Exploration of Methods and Context for the Production of Rapid Reviews. *Research White Paper. (Prepared by the Scientific Resource Center under Contract No. 290-2012-00004-C.) AHRQ Publication No. 15-EHC008-EF*. Rockville, MD: Agency for Healthcare Research and Quality. https://www.effectivehealthcare.ahrq.gov/reports/final.cfm

Independent Anti-Slavery Commissioner. (2018, October). *The Slavery and Trafficking Survivor Care Standards*. https://www.antislaverycommissioner.co.uk/media/1235/slavery-and-trafficking-survivor-care-standards.pdf.

Innovations for Poverty Action (IPA). (2023). *Research and Learning Agenda | Human Trafficking Research Initiative*. https://poverty-action.org/research-and-learning-agenda-human-trafficking-research-initiative.

Malakooti, A., & Zwick, H. (2022). *A methodology for a longitudinal study on reintegration outcomes for returnees*. https://www.knomad.org/sites/default/files/2022-10/knomad_paper_45_return_migration_methodology_a_malakooti_and_h_s_zwick_october_2022.pdf

Nodzenski, M., Kiss, L., Pocock, N. S., Stoeckl, H., Zimmerman, C., & Buller, A. M. (2020). Post-trafficking stressors: The influence of hopes, fears and expectations on the mental health of young trafficking survivors in the greater Mekong sub-region. *Child Abuse & Neglect*, *100*, 104067. https://doi.org/10.1016/j.chiabu.2019.104067

Price, R. K., Bender, A. K., Milazzo, F. H., Rich, E. G., Roman, N. V., Zhang, S. X., & Koegler, E. L. (2022). Prevalence estimates of trafficking in persons using statistical definitions: A cross-sectional high-risk community survey in Cape Town, South Africa. *British Medical Journal Open*, *12*(12), e063617. https://doi.org/10.1136/bmjopen-2022-063617

Surtees, R. (2013). *After trafficking: Experiences and challenges in the (re) integration of trafficked persons in the greater Mekong sub-region*. UNIAP/NEXUS Institute.

United Nations Population Fund (UNFPA). (2019, November 01). The inter-agency minimum standards for gender-based violence in emergencies programming. https://www.unfpa.org/minimum-standards.

U.S. Department of State. (2022a, March 03). *TIP Office Funding Opportunity Common Questions and Answers (PEMS)*. https://www.state.gov/tip-office-funding-opportunity-common-questions-and-answers-pems/.

U.S. Department of State. (2022b, August). *TIP Office Project Descriptions.* https://www.state.gov/program-to-end-modern-slavery//.
U.S. Department of State. (n.d.). *Program to End Modern Slavery: Office to Monitor and Combat Trafficking in Persons.* https://www.state.gov/program-to-end-modern-slavery/.
Wechsler, R. J. (2019). Deliberating at a crossroads: Sex trafficking victims' decisions about participating in the criminal justice process. *Fordham Int'l LJ*, *43*, 1033.
Wyborn, C., Datta, A., Montana, J., Ryan, M., Leith, P., Chaffin, B., Miller, C., & Van Kerkhoff, L. (2019). Co-producing sustainability: Reordering the governance of science, policy, and practice. *Annual Review of Environment and Resources*, *44*(1), 319–346. https://doi.org/10.1146/annurev-environ-101718-033103

OPEN ACCESS

# When Victims of Modern Slavery Became Offenders: The Unravelling of the UK's Modern Slavery Agenda

David Gadd and Rose Broad

**ABSTRACT**

While victims of trafficking who commit crimes have a defense in law in England and Wales, this has not been without controversy in the courts and is increasingly threatened in practice as British government ministers heap suspicion on those formally seeking recognition as victims of modern slavery. In the first part of this article, we review recent criminal cases decided by the Court of Appeal in England and Wales to explore why it is that some victims of trafficking break the law. These cases reveal the impossible choices that constitute the nexus of circumstances that lead victims to offend. In the second part of this article, we examine the cases of three people convicted of modern slavery and allied immigration crimes that are excluded from the statutory defense in English and Welsh law to show how morally comprehensible the commission of serious crimes can be in the aftermath of exploitation, destitution and trauma. We conclude by urging academics and activists in the modern slavery field to be vocal about how few victims fit their stereotypes and to help articulate the irreconcilably difficult choices that explain why some break the law in immigration contexts that are overtly hostile toward them.

## Introduction

While efforts to count the number of people worldwide trapped in "slavery," or conditions like it, have mobilized many national governments to tackle trafficking in people, the idealization of victimhood accompanying this quantification has not been without consequence. Nowhere is this more apparent than in the UK, where what was once pitched as a "world-leading" modern slavery agenda that other nation states should emulate has been deployed by ministers to heap suspicion on the many thousands of potential victims whom earlier administrations promised to "rescue" and "protect" (Craig et al., 2019).

In this article, we chart the emergence of this new demonizing discourse about modern slavery victims, exposing its roots in "hostile" immigration policies as well as misunderstandings of section 45 of the Modern Slavery Act 2015[1] (the Modern Slavery Act): a legislative provision that was designed to protect victims whose offending derives from being exploited. Having reviewed how senior Conservatives in the UK have recast victims of modern slavery as suspects, we then explore how the parameters of the section 45 defense have been clarified in cases heard by the Court of Appeal of England and Wales. Its rulings reveal not that justice is easily gamed but just how unforgiving the law in practice has become to those who commit criminal or immigration offenses in the aftermath of acute exploitation. In the penultimate section of this article, we introduce case study material from interviews we conducted with three research participants in our Economic and Social Research

[1]The Modern Slavery Act (https://www.legislation.gov.uk/ukpga/2015/30/contents/enacted) applied only to the jurisdiction of England and Wales, which is our focus in this article. The Human Trafficking and Exploitation (Scotland) Act 2015 did not include a statutory defense.

Council (ESRC)-funded study (ES/R004471/1) of people convicted of modern slavery offenses. The three case studies reveal how complex the "nexuses" of circumstances are that lead many victims of crimes involving fraud, deception, coercion, and exploitation to commit other offenses, including those that are routinely presented to the public as "serious" and "organized crimes", such as people smuggling and modern slavery. These case studies also reveal how few protections there are in practice for victims of exploitation who do offend and, hence, how misleading it is to claim that many are "taking advantage" of British "tolerance" or loopholes in the law.

## Gaming the System?

Over the last decade, the UK government's policy on modern slavery appears to have gone full circle. In 2013, the Home Secretary, Theresa May (2013), announced to the Conservative Party Conference that she was going to tackle the "appalling crime … known as human trafficking", by calling "it what it is – modern slavery," an "evil in our midst," and bringing forward a Modern Slavery Bill that would "give the authorities the powers they need to investigate, prosecute and lock up the slave drivers" who exploit the "thousands of people in Britain … bought and sold as commodities" with "little chance of escape." By way of contrast, in 2022, Suella Braverman addressed the 2022 Conservative Party Conference by promising to confront "the hard truth" that our modern slavery laws, together with the Conservative's "proud history of offering sanctuary to those in need," are "being abused … by people smugglers and criminals pedalling false promises". Launching what subsequently became dubbed the 'Rwanda policy' - an attempt to deter would-be migrants from crossing the North Sea in small boats - Braverman had told a televised press briefing how she'd 'love to have a front page of *The Telegraph* newspaper with a plane taking off to Rwanda. That is my dream. It's my obsession'.[2] Braverman (2022) consolidated the point in her conference speech by asserting that many asylum seekers are actually "convicted paedophiles and rapists trying to game the system" by presenting as "modern slaves:"

> We've seen a 450% increase in modern slavery claims since 2014. Today, the largest group of small boat migrants are from Albania – a safe country. Many of them claim to be trafficked as modern slaves. That's despite them having paid thousands of pounds to come here or having willingly taken a dangerous journey across the Channel. The truth is that many of them are not modern slaves, and their claims of being trafficked are lies. Moreover, it's not just illegal migrants. Since entering the Home Office, I have seen egregious examples of convicted paedophiles and rapists trying to game the system, making last-minute claims of modern slavery to block their removal from our country. Some have even gone on to commit further crimes in the interim. In one case, we convicted a sex offender from South Africa who spent a year in prison. He was about to be deported from the UK – and lo and behold, he claimed modern slavery. Our removal was stalled, and he went on to commit a further rape.

Then the Home Secretary extended the argument made repeatedly by her predecessor Priti Patel, who brought forward the 2022 Borders and Nationality Act on the unsubstantiated premise that "major increases in child rapists, people who threaten national security and failed asylum seekers" are "clogging up the modern slavery system" (Home Office and Patel, 2021). Braverman (2022) promised to resolve the logjam by withdrawing the UK from the European Court of Human Rights jurisdiction:

> UK policy on illegal migration should not be derailed by abuse of our modern slavery laws, Labour's Human Rights Act, or orders of the Strasbourg Court … [W]e cannot allow this abuse of our system to continue … we will redouble our efforts to go after them … The Labour Party will try to stop this … I won't give up on the British people … Now is the time … to put the will of the hard-working patriotic majority at the heart of all we do … It's time to tackle the small boats – no ifs, no buts.

Her most conspicuous claims about how easy it is for convicted foreign national sex offenders to secure release from prison – seemingly without the input of the Parole Board or oversight from the police

[2]The policy was deemed unlawful by the UK's Supreme on 15th November 2023, which noted that there were 'substantial grounds for believing that asylum seekers would face a real risk of ill-treatment by reason of refoulement to their country of origin if they were removed to Rwanda'. *(R (AAA (Syria) and others) v Secretary of State for the Home Department (UNHCR intervening)* [2023] UKSC 42). This prompted Braverman's successor, James Cleverly, to bring forward the Safety of Rwanda (Asylum and Immigration) Bill in January 2024 to require 'every decision-maker' in the UK to 'conclusively treat the Republic of Rwanda as a safe country'.

or National Probation Service – notwithstanding, the overall tenor of Braverman's speech was remarkably like the one May had delivered nine years prior. May (2013) also equated the values of "hard-working," "law-abiding" "British people" with those of the Conservative Party. May had also constructed immigration as an insult to British tolerance and a gateway exploited by criminals threatening the nation's security. Both Home Secretaries attributed this threat to people smugglers and traffickers: the two groups conflated in ways that conceal the differences between paying to migrate across borders that are closed to them and being coerced into exploitation (Gadd & Broad, 2018). Both Home Secretaries depicted the Conservative party as the only party able to restore the "law and order" needed to fend off this international security threat, May (2013) also postulating that Labour "deliberately let immigration get out of control . . . passed the Human Rights Act and put the law on the side of criminals."

## Offending Victims

The critical difference between the two speeches, however, was that May (unlike Braverman) delineated a subgroup of exploited migrants toward whom the public should be sympathetic – very vulnerable women and children forced or duped into "work in the sex industry" - from the broader populace of those deemed "illegal immigrants" and asylum seekers the Conservative government cultivated hostility toward. Braverman, conversely, raised suspicion about the motives of anyone and everyone reporting modern slavery victimization, implying that many of those who claim to be exploited are foreign national offenders seeking to avoid deportation. This cast all those claiming to be potential victims of modern slavery as a suspect population, leaving little room for the idealization of a vulnerable subset of victims that had initially been used to rally a coalition of interest groups to support the Modern Slavery Bill a decade prior (O'Connell Davidson, 2015).

This shift in emphasis in Conservative rhetoric prompted various commentators from within the anti-slavery sector to challenge the government on its betrayal of victims and those working to safeguard them. Dame Sara Thornton, the former Independent Anti-Slavery Commissioner, explained that the number of referrals to the National Referral Mechanism (NRF) had risen in recent years, not because the system is being abused, but because the Home Office, police and immigration authorities became better at identifying victims (Dearden, 2022). Likewise, Elysia McCaffrey, the chief executive of the Gangmasters and Labour Abuse Authority (GLAA), responded to Braverman by explaining that the GLAA had not seen anyone "gaming" the modern slavery system for immigration purposes (Dugan, 2022). Instead, cuts to their own – already vastly understaffed (Kenway, 2021) – service had rendered it impossible for the GLAA to investigate all but a tiny minority of reports of exploitation in UK supply chains. Subsequently, the NGO, *After Exploitation*, coordinated a formal complaint to the Office of Statistics Regulation on behalf of 23 NGOs, alleging that Home Secretaries Braverman and Patel had knowingly deployed "misleading" statistics to secure sensationalist newspaper headlines. At the same time, the British government had unjustifiably withheld the data requested in both Houses of Parliament, as well as via Freedom of Information requests, needed to evaluate the veracity of its claims-making (Esslemont, 2022) and policymakers were unable to point to any specific evidence when asked about this by the Director General for Regulation (Humpherson, 2022).

Indeed, Braverman's speech misrepresented her department's role, not only regarding its duty of care toward victims of modern slavery but also the processing of asylum claims, managing immigration detention, and controlling crime more generally. It is the Home Office that oversees the NRM, border control and immigration enforcement, as well as large parts of the criminal justice system. As the Migrants Right's Network highlighted, annual reports from these various agencies revealed that 90% of those forcibly held in immigration detention and referred to the NRM are subsequently confirmed to be victims of trafficking (Qureshi et al., 2022). NRM referrals are made by officially recognized first responders, predominantly police officers, social workers, immigration enforcement, and border control officers, leaving little scope for baseless applications. "Positive conclusive grounds decisions" officially validate applicants' claims to be victims of modern slavery and are issued by either the Single Competent Authority (SCA) or the Immigration Enforcement Competent Authority, both of which are part of the

Home Office. However, these do not guarantee any right to remain in the UK. While 87% of adult and 90% of child applicants to the NRM received positive grounds decisions in 2022, on average, only 7% of those confirmed as victims of trafficking from overseas were granted leave to remain in the UK (Home Office, 2023; Taylor, 2022).

## Compulsion and the Section 45 Defence

What few of the government's critics were willing to explain publicly, however, is that some victims of modern slavery do break criminal and immigration laws as they attempt to navigate the near-impossible choices displacement, destitution, and desperation confront them with (Hodkinson et al., 2021; Schwarz & Williams-Woods, 2022). To some degree, the Modern Slavery Act anticipated this, taking inspiration from European legal frameworks addressing the needs of exploitation victims who had little choice but to engage in crime (Muraszkiewicz, 2019). As a signatory to Article 26 of the (2005) Council of Europe Convention on Action Against Trafficking in Human Beings, for example, the UK committed to do the following: provide for the possibility of not imposing penalties on victims for their involvement in unlawful activities to the extent that they have been compelled to do so.

The UK remains legally committed to Article 8 of Directive 2011/36 issued by the European Parliament (2011) on "Preventing and Combating Trafficking in Human Beings and Protecting its Victims". This requires states to:

> take the necessary measures to ensure that competent national authorities are entitled not to prosecute or impose penalties on victims of trafficking in human beings for their involvement in criminal activities ... as a direct consequence of being subjected to any of the acts referred to in Article 2. [which defines "Offences concerning trafficking in human beings"]

Section 45 of the Modern Slavery Act represented a somewhat perfunctory attempt by the UK to comply with the 2005 Convention and Directive 2011/26. By contrast, both European provisions aim to prevent punishment rather than introducing a defense once proceedings have been established. Contrary to the inferences made in Braverman's (2022) Conservative Party Conference speech, adults and children have no defense under section 45 of the Modern Slavery Act for most serious crimes. Robbery, manslaughter, murder, sexual offenses, acts of terrorism, and possession of firearms, alongside many other offenses against the person – including threats to kill and wounding with intent to cause grievous bodily harm and abandoning children – were explicitly excluded from the section 45 defense, as was the immigration offense of assisting unlawful immigration (Muraszkiewicz, 2019). The breadth of these offenses betrays the commitment to protecting survivors since some of them are committed by victims of trafficking who consider themselves as having few other choices in the context of their entrapment. Other offenses can, however, be excused if the following criteria in s.45(1) are met:

> (a) the person is aged 18 or over when the person does the act which constitutes the offence,
> (b) the person does that act because the person is compelled to do it,
> (c) the compulsion is attributable to slavery or relevant exploitation, and
> (d) a reasonable person in the same situation as the person and having the person's relevant characteristics would have no realistic alternative to doing that act.

If the accused is under the age of 18, the element of compulsion is not relevant. In these cases, under s.45(4) the person is not guilty if:

> (a) the person does that act as a direct consequence of the person being, or having been, a victim of slavery or a victim of relevant exploitation, and
> (b) a reasonable person in the same situation as the person and having the person's relevant characteristics would do that act.

Neither "compulsion" nor the absence of a "reasonable alternative" is adequately defined in section 45 of the Modern Slavery Act. Deciphering what these terms mean has thus fallen mainly to the Court of

**Table 1.** Number of Appeals Heard by the Court of Appeal of the Section 45 Defense. Source: Lexis+ UK.

| Year | Number of appeals heard by the Court of Appeal of the Section 45 defence for slavery or trafficking victims who commit an offence |
|---|---|
| 2016 | 0 |
| 2017 | 1 |
| 2018 | 2 |
| 2019 | 3 |
| 2020 | 3 |
| 2021 | 3 |
| 2022 | 6 |

Appeal, which, since 2017, has heard a small but growing number of cases where the section 45 defense has not been adequately applied at earlier stages (see Table 1). Definitions of key terms in the section 45 defense have thus developed piecemeal across official documents and case law, as the Court of Appeal has attempted to achieve clarification and consistency through reference to broader aspects of jurisprudence and international law.

In the Principles and Guidelines for Human Rights and Human Trafficking set out by the United Nations High Commissioner for Human Rights, the "trafficked persons shall not be detained, charged or prosecuted" for unlawful activities that were a "direct consequence" of their victimization (Office of the High Commissioner of Human Rights [OHCHR], 2002, p. 1). The Organisation for Crime and Security in Europe's (OSCE) Office of the Special Representative and Co-ordinator for Combatting Trafficking in Human Beings Policy and Legislative advocates for "an interpretation of compulsion based on the consequences of the victim's situation as a trafficked person" (Knight, 2023, p. 197; Organization for Security and Cooperation across Europe [OSCE], 2013). Building on this, the International Labour Organisation (ILO) expanded the meaning to include offenses which victims "have been compelled to commit as a direct consequence" of their victimization (ILO, 2014, Article 4). "A defendant needs to prove a nexus between their offending and their status as a VoT [victim of trafficking]" (Knight, 2023, p. 192).[3] Knight (2023) argues that despite the broad view of "compulsion" by the Organization for Security and Co-operation (OSCE) and International Labour Organization (ILO), the term has been defined too narrowly and inconsistently in England and Wales. Its courts need, therefore, to take a more "expansive view" defined as "the direct consequence of the victim's situation as a trafficked person" (Knight, 2023, p. 193). Not doing so, Knight maintains, is inconsistent with the UK's obligations under international law and fails to protect trafficked victims effectively.

Previous rulings of the Court of Appeal have exposed how difficult it is for defendants to evidence a "nexus" between trafficking victimization and their offending and hence how hard it is for many to exercise their rights under international law (PEC, 2022). Many victims of trafficking suffer severe forms of mental health issues in the aftermath of years of complex trauma and stress, and few have the resources needed to mount complex legal defenses (Evans et al., 2022). Within the lower courts, establishing what "a reasonable person" with the same "relevant characteristics" would consider as having "no realistic alternative" (as per the section 45 defense) has also proved challenging. What might it be reasonable for someone told they will be deported if they report their years of sexual or criminal exploitation and physical abuse to do if they have no money of their own and no faith that there is any help, professional or otherwise, available to them? How "reasonable" can one be in the aftermath of extreme and prolonged trauma? Furthermore, how might one persuade a jury with little-to-no experience of what it is like to suffer destitution, live in servitude, or fear deportation that one has been so?

[3]The U.K. Court of Appeal (Criminal Division) held that the non-punishment provision section 45 of the Modern Slavery Act 2015 placed the evidential burden on the defendant who is claiming that their experience of modern slavery victimization compelled them to break the law. It stated that "it is for a defendant to raise the evidential burden that she has been subjected to trafficking, slavery or servitude." However, once raised the "burden of proof" falls to the prosecution to disprove such a claim to the criminal standard," i.e., "beyond a reasonable doubt." It requires objective evidence of compulsion that is directly and causally related to the trafficking (Heys, 2023, p. 462).

The Court of Appeal's rulings in this regard have typically articulated a preference to assess reasonableness more in terms of whether there is an *immediate* connection between being trafficked and committing an offense than a willingness to grapple with the impossible choices made by destitute people who have endured a lifetime of trauma. For example, in 2020, an appeal was refused in the case of *R. v A*[4] an 18-year-old Afghan man who had pleaded guilty to burglary charges. The defendant came to the UK aged 11 after the murder of his father and had subsequently become involved in a criminal gang while in the care of the British state. Though he was recognized by the NRM as a victim of trafficking when he was 16, the Court of Appeal took the view that the defendant's vulnerabilities were insufficient to prove that the "aggravated burglary was committed as a consequence of the dominant force of compulsion from his traffickers."[5]

In a subsequent case (*R. v BYA*[6]), the Court of Appeal reconsidered the case of a defendant convicted in November 2009 of being in "possession of a false identity document with intent" contrary to the Identity Cards Act 2006 s.25(1). The defendant had pleaded guilty to the charge but managed to resist deportation in 2011 because she had a legitimate asylum case, having been smuggled from Ghana to the Netherlands to escape female genital mutilation. The defendant was sexually exploited in the Netherlands only to be re-trafficked, first to Spain and then to the UK, where she was forced into prostitution. The Court of Appeal accepted that the defendant had been:

> trafficked . . . and . . . re-trafficked . . . sexually exploited and subjected to sexual abuse (including daily rapes) over a lengthy period, having fled her family home because of the threat of female genital mutilation . . . . The effect of these experiences upon her must have been to cause significant trauma. . . [S]he knew nobody save for her traffickers, to whom she was in debt bondage. She spoke no English . . . felt isolated and alone . . . was obviously vulnerable [and] knew nobody in the UK to whom she could turn for help.[7]

The Court of Appeal quashed the defendant's conviction in 2022, 13 years after it had been secured, on the basis that *due process had not been followed*, both with respect to identifying her as a victim of trafficking and whether it was in the public interest to prosecute her:

> the speed with which she was processed, interviewed by police and then prosecuted following her arrest gives rise to the inference that there was . . . inadequate consideration . . . [of] indicators of human exploitation and/or trafficking . . . when she was introduced into the criminal justice system . . . Accordingly, we consider it open to this court to consider the public interest question without trespassing on territory already appropriately considered by the prosecuting authority.[8]

The Court of Appeal accepted that there "was a strong nexus of compulsion to flee her traffickers", which included the victim's desire to reunite with her son in the Netherlands. However, it also noted that this was "not a paradigm case in the sense that the compulsion the applicant was under did not lead directly to the offending."[9] In other words, the court did not deem it proven that a woman who had been trapped in sexual exploitation in three European countries, raped, and physically abused over many years – someone who simply could not find safety anywhere in the world – had no other reasonable alternative but to seek out false travel documents. Its position was primarily that the Crown should consider on a case-by-case basis whether the public interest is served by prosecuting those who offend in such circumstances.

The former Independent Anti-Slavery Commissioner's review of how the section 45 defense was working suggests that such considerations need to begin much earlier in the criminal justice process, noting how police officers often fail to consider "from the outset of an investigation whether a suspect could be a victim of trafficking and whether the statutory defence may apply" (IASC, 2020, p. 7). The

**Court of Appeal Judgments**
[4][2020] EWCA Crim 1408.
[5][2020] EWCA Crim 1408 [69].
[6][2022] EWCA Crim 1326.
[7][2022] EWCA Crim 1326 [48].
[8][2022] EWCA Crim 1326 [55].
[9][2022] EWCA Crim 1326 [51].

review found that when the defense was raised early in investigations, cases were sometimes dropped, either by the police or the Crown Prosecution Service (CPS), without a proper investigation or the being case fully prepared because some criminal justice professionals assume incorrectly "that past exploitation provides immunity from prosecution." However, this is "not the case and ironically could make the young person even more vulnerable to further exploitation as their exploiters view them as having a 'get out of jail free card'" (IASC, 2020, p, 20). This misguided presumption has been made in cases involving young people, predominantly British men, involved in so-called "county lines" drug-dealing. In these county lines cases, the section 45 defense can be mobilized when defendants explain their own "possession with intent to supply" offenses as a "direct consequence of their exploitation" or intimidation by more senior figures within criminal gangs (Ahluwalia, 2018).

There is, however, little evidence to support the view that such a defense is readily accepted in the UK. There is evidence to suggest that law enforcement is often less-than-supportive of suspects who claim to be victims of trafficking (IASC, 2020), and legal precedents that reveal that the courts can deem a conclusive grounds decision from the Single Competent Authority (SCA) insufficient to evidence that one is a victim of trafficking. In the case of *R. v Brecani*,[10] in 2020, a 17-year-old Albanian national convicted of conspiracy to supply cocaine faced trial before the SCA accepted that there were "conclusive" grounds to consider the defendant a victim of modern slavery. The original trial judge had rejected an application by the defense to submit the conclusive grounds decision as expert evidence. The Court of Appeal upheld this decision, noting that:

> It is not sufficient to assume that because administrators are likely to gain experience in the type of decision-making they routinely undertake that, simply by virtue of that fact, they can be treated as experts in criminal proceedings.[11]

The Court of Appeal noted that the reasoning of the SCA had not been documented in a form that is accessible to the courts, that its decision-making processes do not meet the standard of proof – beyond a reasonable doubt – required by juries, and that in this instance the conclusive grounds decision had been made prior to new digital evidence coming to light to the effect that the defendant had "an entirely different history from that accepted" by the SCA caseworker. The defendant's phone record revealed a history of:

> independent trips ... across northern France prior to entering the United Kingdom and thereafter travelling freely within this country. The digital record was devoid of any suggestion of trafficking, including by way of relevant contact with the individuals who were suggested to have recruited and exploited the appellant, and instead it tends to demonstrate a happy and carefree life on his part. He maintained seemingly cheerful contact with his family and booked the services of escorts for himself and a friend ... Given none of this vital material was reviewed by [the SCA Caseworker], we regret to conclude that his opinion was rendered valueless.[12]

While some legal commentators read the precedent set by this decision as undermining the viability of the section 45 defense (Munro Kerr, 2021) – defendants who have been trafficked unable thereafter to rely on conclusive grounds decisions as supporting evidence – the Brecani judgment also re-iterated the UK's obligations under article 4 of the European Convention on Human Rights to protect victims and for its criminal justice system to "investigate situations of potential trafficking"[13] (Topolski, 2021). In turn, the circumstances in which prosecutors may disagree with a positive conclusive grounds decision were clarified (Knight, 2023). In *VCL and AN v UK*,[14] in 2021, the European Court of Human Rights (ECtHR) found the UK to have violated both Article 4 and Article 6 of the Convention for the Protection of Human Rights and Fundamental Freedoms when conclusive grounds identification as a trafficked victim (a child) was questioned (Youth Justice Legal Centre, 2021).

[10][2021] EWCA Crim 731.
[11][2021] EWCA Crim 731 [54].
[12][2021] EWCA Crim 731 [74].
[13][2021] EWCA Crim 731 [64].
**European Court of Human Rights Judgments.**
[14][ECtHR] 16th February 2021, V.C.L. AND A.N. v. THE UNITED KINGDOM, Applications nos. 77587/12 and 74,603/12

Further protections for victims were reestablished in 2022 in the Court of Appeal's decisions to stay proceedings in cases where the defendant had been identified as a victim of trafficking, *R v AAD, AAD and AAI*[iv]. These rulings established it as an 'abuse of process' when the Crown Prosecution Service fails to follow is own guidelines regarding the non-punishment of victims of trafficking (Gregory, 2022). How consistently this will happen in subsequent cases remains to be seen. Victim-blaming, criminalization and deportation are all adverse consequences that greet foreign national victims of trafficking in the context of the UK's hostile immigration policy (Gearon, 2019; Rodríguez-López, 2020) and the resulting calls to "quit" the European Convention on Human Rights the politics around this have yielded (Forrest, 2022). As criminologists, this suggests to us that a much fuller deconstruction of what lawyers call the "nexus of compulsion" is urgently required. It cannot be just that the tough choices that lead many victims of exploitation to offend have no defense in law, especially when many of these choices are enmeshed by the UK's social and immigration policies. The case analyses that follows is offered in this spirit.

## Methodology

Between 2016 and 2021, the authors conducted primary research in the UK with 30 people who had been convicted of modern slavery and associated immigration or drug-related offenses (Broad & Gadd, 2023). Participants were recruited primarily through HM Prison and Probation Service, with the consenting process initiated by probation officers responsible for managing those still serving sentences. The interviews were audio recorded and conducted using the Free Association Narrative Interview Method (Hollway & Jefferson, 2000). All but two participants were interviewed twice (of the remaining two, one was interviewed once and the other three times). Participants were invited to tell their life stories in the first interview, and the interviewer used narrative-focused questions and active reflection to encourage them to complete their stories. The authors then reviewed transcripts of the first interviews to identify areas where there was a lack of detail, unexplained changes of tone, or inconsistencies. These were then further probed in the second interview. The authors then reviewed and analyzed both transcripts to generate case studies to capture the stories' complexities, including any contradictory elements.

For this article, we revisited the 30 case studies to identify those where connections between experiences of victimization, exploitation and engagement in criminal behavior were described as crucial features of the life histories of our participants. Half of the sample ($n = 15$) met this criterion, though a more significant number could have been included had we incorporated those who had experienced domestic or sexual abuse or neglect as children ($n = 6$) or who were born into families that were routinely engaged in criminal enterprises ($n = 4$). The 15 cases where there appeared to be connections between experiences of victimization or exploitation and engagement in criminal behavior that constituted modern slavery could be further codified into three subgroups (see Table 2):

(i) Victims of exploitation who were either adults who were (arguably) "compelled to commit" a criminal act, or children, at the time, who began offending as "a direct consequence of their exploitation." Three participants appeared to meet the criteria for the section 45 defense. A further one would have done so had their offenses not been so severe as to be exempt from the defense ($n = 4$).
(ii) Those who were victims of other (non-exploitation) offenses who, though not compelled, were cajoled or manipulated into offending due to an enduring vulnerability ($n = 8$)
(iii) Those previously subject to exploitation that had ceased when they began offending ($n = 3$).

In the following section, one case is selected from each of these categories to exemplify how exploitation, coercion and vulnerability contributed to modern slavery offending. We present

**Table 2.** An Overview of the 15 Participants with Details of Exploitation Perpetrated and Victimization Experienced.

| Name | Age | Sex | Nationality /Ethnicity | Exploitation Perpetrated | Victimization-Offending Nexus |
|---|---|---|---|---|---|
| *Group 1: Victims of exploitation who were either adults compelled to commit a criminal act or children at the time who began offending as a direct consequence of their exploitation.* | | | | | |
| Susan | 20s | Female | British (White British) | Trafficking for Child Sexual Exploitation | Sexually abused by co-accused. Previously sexually exploited while substance dependent. |
| Nina | 40s | Female | Slovakian | Sexual exploitation | Domestic abuse by boyfriend and co-accused, sex trafficker |
| Vicky | 20s | Female | British (White British) | Forced County Lines Drug Dealing | Groomed by uncle into drug dealing |
| Rasheed | 30s | Male | Pakistani | Forced Marriage Rape | Victim of labor exploitation, including a history of indentured labor in Pakistan and hired into exploitive labor in the UK while living where worked, and at risk of deportation because working illegally on a tourist visa. |
| *Group 2: Those who were victims of other (non-exploitation) offences who, though not compelled, were cajoled or manipulated into offending due to an enduring vulnerability.* | | | | | |
| Aron | 20s | Male | Albanian | Facilitating Illegal immigration | Threatened with a gun before fleeing to become a migrant with false papers. |
| Alessandro | 40s | Male | Albanian | Facilitating illegal immigration | Fell into debt borrowing money for brother's operation. Suffers PTSD, having been a young soldier |
| Thierry | 40s | Male | British (Black British) | Facilitating Illegal immigration | Tricked into giving a lift across the UK border to an undocumented migrant. |
| Raja | 50s | Male | British (Asian) | Making False Documents Labour exploitation | Defrauded by business partners into applying for work permits for migrant workers whose qualifications were falsified. |
| Andrei | 30s | Male | Romanian | Sexual Exploitation Keeping a Brothel | Substance dependency led to engagement in working to produce marketing for sex workers to finance substance use and treatment. |
| Anton | 30s | Male | Romanian | Sexual Exploitation | Became drug dependent, then encouraged by the dealer to undertake further driving jobs for sex workers. |
| Estelle | 30s | Female | Portuguese (African Portuguese) | Sham marriage | Was cajoled into accruing gambling debts and obligations to the man who helped children come to the UK. |
| Linda | 40s | Female | Zimbabwean | Sexual exploitation | Debts and substance dependency coincided with facilitating the sexual exploitation of her daughter to men she had become obligated to. |
| *Group 3: Those previously subject to exploitation that had ceased at the time of the offence.* | | | | | |
| Naz | 40s | Male | British (British Asian) | Sexual Exploitation | Exploited as an underpaid worker in the takeaway industry, socially isolated, becomes engaged in the sexual exploitation of young women who rely on him for food and somewhere to stay, |
| Idris | 60s | Male | Nigerian | Sexual Exploitation | Child soldier who became a drug trafficker, hiring vulnerable people to carry illicit substances across international borders. |
| Grace | 40s | Female | Kenyan | Sexual Exploitation | Victim of domestic servitude who becomes implicated in profiting from the sexual exploitation of other women. |

these cases to reveal the different forms taken by the nexus of relationships between criminal victimization and crimes of exploitation. We argue that when adequately explained, this nexus of relationships can render the perpetration of "serious and organized" forms of trafficking and immigration crime morally comprehensible.

## Case Studies

### *Vicky*

Vicky was a British national serving a seven-year sentence for conspiracy to supply class A drugs (heroin) in the context of county lines drug dealing. Vicky's mother had died when she was aged 10, and she had become estranged from her abusive dad. Aged 13 and still consumed by grief, Vicky was permanently excluded from school, having "set the toilets on fire". She left school with no qualifications and, at 16 moved into a flat with her brother James, then aged 18, "far away from family and friends". Her Uncle Steve used to "ring" James and "ask if he ... needed anything". When it "got to the point where" James and Vicky "couldn't pay the rent" – partly because James "was feeding his girlfriend's [drug] habit" – Steve offered them money. Neither James nor Vicky wanted to "go down that path," but Steve kept saying "you need it," which became his way of recruiting his niece and nephew into a county lines drug supply chain that endured for eight years.

James initially made "thirty grand a week" selling the drugs locally, while Vicky resisted, worrying that her "mum wouldn't have been happy." But after James offered her £100 a day, Vicki agreed to support James in running the drug supply, wrapping small packets of heroin. When Vicky was 23, she was arrested for intent to supply, bailed, and banned from the town where she had been dealing. Vicky and James were then charged with conspiring to supply drugs for over eight years alongside seven men – all friends of James', two of whom alleged that James and Vicky were "forcing them" to move the "supply" and threatening to "beat" them up if they did not. One of the co-accused friends said he'd "never got paid, he'd lost everything ... lost his kids, he's lost his house". In return, the two friends were given very short prison sentences, while James and Vicky took the rap for their uncle, who was never charged.

### *Alessandro*

Alessandro was an Albanian man in his late forties, serving a three-year sentence for conspiring to facilitate the illegal entry of 11 Albanian men and women into the UK, including bringing people "for slavery." At 18, Alessandro had been conscripted into the Albanian army before joining the Kosovan Liberation Army. There, he became an escort for Albanians attempting to flee to Kosovo. This involved him carrying dismembered children and soldiers across the mountains and "helping" them escape the ethnic cleansing that was pervasive at this time.

When the war formally ended in the 1990s, Alessandro became a decorated war hero, but the threats to his life persisted. He fled on foot to the UK, where he was detained in an immigration centre. This detention was remembered positively, as immigration officials had tried to "help" Alessandro with "everything" and directed him to an asylum hearing, where he was recognized as a refugee on the first day. Alessandro then married and found a job as a laborer in the construction industry, but the trauma he had experienced during the war limited his ability to work. He became depressed and suffered nightmares about "friends ... being killed in the war." He worried for the wives and children of the war dead left in "poverty" and starving while others became rich and powerful members of the political elite. These worries escalated when his brother suddenly became ill and asked Alessandro to help him find the money needed to pay for heart surgery from a private clinic, as no public health care was available to him in Albania.

Alessandro turned to a man – Denard – whom he knew from the building sites and who was acquainted with his brother back in their village. Denard lent Alessandro £2000 but made it clear Alessandro needed to repay the money immediately in case his brother did not survive. Knowing that Alessandro was "off work," Denard asked Alessandro to do him a "favor" and go with a younger man who spoke no English by taxi to collect a "bag of clothes" from the back of a lorry parked 50 miles away. While denying he knew there were Albanian migrants in the back of this lorry, Alessandro explained that he was trying to "help people", "men" "with no work" "to cross border" and "make some money", as others had once helped him when he was a young refugee. Arresting him at the scene, the police discovered both men and women in the lorry's cargo, one of whom claimed to have been "kidnapped". Now in prison, Alessandro feared he would be deported, as the Home Office had begun to question whether he was Kosovan as opposed to Albanian, the village from where he originated having been contested territory. While in prison, Alessandro missed his wife, who was terminally ill and was thus unable to travel hundreds of miles from their home to visit him. He expressed no ill-will toward Denard, who continued to deny knowing there would be migrants stowed away on the lorry.

### *Grace*

Grace was a Kenyan woman in her 40s, serving a custodial sentence of over ten years for trafficking for sexual exploitation. When Grace was 13 and living in Kenya, her mother moved to a nearby town to escape Grace's abusive and 'alcoholic' father. Grace was left alone to look after her sisters for five years, "cooking, cleaning, going to the farm to look for food" whilst attending school. When Grace resisted taking on these responsibilities, her mother returned to "beat" her "so badly."

At 22, Grace traveled from Kenya to Ireland "looking for a better life ... to help a family" care for their children. Grace's family saw this as an opportunity – telling her "Don't forget us, help us, support us". Grace nevertheless became entrapped in domestic servitude for three months. The couple paid for her flights to Ireland, where Grace was told she would go to college in exchange for "looking after the ... children". However, the college enrollment never materialized. Instead, the couple mistreated Grace, refused to pay her, and "confiscated" her passport.

Grace turned to a friend, Amanda, who suggested she could escape her predicament by working as a receptionist in a brothel where she might make "five thousand a month" and would also live. Without better options, Grace "had no choice" and earned enough to send money home to her family - £50 notes sent in envelopes – though she never disclosed to her mother how she came by them. Cajoled out of the receptionist role and into providing sexual services, Grace endured the work for a year before teaming up with a British man she had met there who invited her to run a brothel in partnership with him. Grace recruited some of her coworkers and advertised their services online, making enough money to buy a property. When Amanda tried to exact revenge on Grace by notifying the couple who had exploited her as a domestic worker, Grace became fearful she would be deported. To protect herself, she entered a marriage to a man 20 years her senior who paid £4000 to the Irish couple to retrieve her passport. Though Grace established a "legitimate business ... a hair and beauty salon", the brothel work proved too lucrative to close. She saved half a million pounds distributed between five different bank accounts before she was arrested for tax evasion, "lost everything" and was prosecuted for profiting from the sexual exploitation of others. At first, she was acquitted "because all the girls said they worked for themselves." However, a re-trial secured her conviction when a woman who had worked at the brothel "for a few days" claimed Grace had forced her to have "sex for money."

## Discussion

We began this article by highlighting how Conservative discourse about modern slavery has shifted from a rescue narrative addressed to "ideal" victims – those who are "innocent" of any wrongdoing who become trapped by modern slavers – to one that demonizes fraudulent claimants in the modern slavery system who are trying to avoid deportation despite having committed serious crimes. We explained that there is little evidence of such abuse of the modern slavery system in the UK, which, in any case, provides few rights to survivors and is slow to recognize their claims. We also explained how the statutory defense against criminal culpability enshrined in section 45 of the 2015 Modern Slavery Act offers only the slimmest protections against criminalization for those victims of modern slavery who are charged with various forms of criminality, including immigration offenses that were previously treated as civil infractions.

While the anti-slavery sector has become increasingly critical of the British government for reneging on its commitments to survivors, we argue that it is no less important to recognize that many victims become involved in offending. This is because much trafficking for the purposes of exploitation involves implicating victims in immigration-related or criminal law violations that render them highly reluctant to seek protection from the police. The entrapment that constitutes modern slavery typically arises because victims believe they have no recourse to law and that contacting the police will compound their plights in some ways (Schwarz & Williams-Woods, 2022). This was self-evident in the cases of both Grace and Vicky, which were described above. Though Vicky's involvement in county lines drug dealing began when she was still a child, struggling with grief, and groomed by an uncle who exploited her financial precarity, she was prosecuted as an adult. The section 45 defense was not mounted in her case, though it should have been considered not only because she was a minor when she began offending but also because she secured no educational qualifications and should have been considered legally within the state's care until she was 21.

Grace, by contrast, escaped being trapped in domestic servitude by going to work in a brothel, later overcoming her exploitation, setting up her own sex work business and repurchasing her passport – though this also involved entering a marriage of convenience. Though now an adult, her journey into exploitation began when her parents abandoned her, leaving her to raise her younger siblings in Kenya. Sociologically, the connections between her exploitation and offending appeared self-evident, though Grace would have no defense in law because it would be impossible to demonstrate that she was "compelled" to open a brothel four years after being held in domestic servitude. The nexus between her victimization and offending was not immediate and straightforward. Likewise, Alessandro's involvement in smuggling, though fleeting, could be traced back to his traumatization as a teenage soldier, the guilt he felt for those left behind after the Balkans war, and the role this played in him accruing a debt to a man who who lent him money for his brother's operation back in Albania. Alessandro would have had no defense under section 45 – he was not compelled to collect the passengers from the lorry, and he both denied and rationalized doing so. But it was not difficult to appreciate why he felt obligated to help those he regarded as fellow "refugees," nor how this sense of obligation rendered him persuadable to returning a favor to the man who had paid for the life-saving surgery his brother needed. Arguably, in all three cases there was reason to consider if the the non-punishment principles should have prevailed and to ask whether justice was actually served by processing people who had been multiply victimized and exploited predominantly as 'modern slavery offenders'.

## Conclusion

Anticipating such contingencies in criminal law is perhaps an impossible challenge. There are no easy amendments that can be made to the section 45 defense that can anticipate how, over the process of decades, exploited, vulnerable and traumatized people – from the UK as well as from the many crunch points of globalization – will become involved in supporting others to make illegal journeys, sell their own and other's bodies, or trade in illicit substances to escape their destitution or come to terms with terrible and terrifying pasts. Indeed, the UK Government is seeking, through the Illegal Immigration Act 2023, to further diminish the protections afforded to victims of modern slavery who have entered the UK through irregular routes. What we must, therefore, do as academics and activists in the field of modern slavery is be much more vocal in public debate about how few victims fit the stereotypes of either dangerous foreign national offenders or ideal and helpless victims (Burland, 2019). We can also ask whether it is genuinely in the public interest to subject those who have been abused and exploited much more than they have been abusive and exploitative to very long prison sentences that further estrange them from family members worldwide who are typically economically dependent on them. This will entail being far clearer in public debate about the complex nexus of relationships – spread across generations and continents – that global counts of modern slavery victims allude to. It will also mean countering the narrative that the UK alone can somehow lead the world in beating modern slavery while simultaneously closing its eyes and ears to the acute inequalities and insecurities that generate so much of the immigration its political leaders are keen to deem "illegal".

## Acknowledgments

The authors acknowledge the support of the Economic and Social Research Council (ES/R004471/1) in funding the study for which the interview material presented in this article was collected. They are also grateful to Sarah Devaney, Stephen Knight, Rudolph Spurling and Phillipa Roberts for their critical feedback on earlier drafts of this paper.

## Disclosure statement

No potential conflict of interest was reported by the authors.

## Funding

This work was supported by the Economic and Social Research Council.

## ORCID

David Gadd http://orcid.org/0000-0002-0362-7648
Rose Broad http://orcid.org/0000-0001-9197-9901

## References

Ahluwalia, P. (2018). 'The predicament of county lines and section 45 modern slavery act 2015' *Criminal Bar Quarterly December 2018*, https://www.criminalbar.com/wp-content/uploads/2018/12/CBA_Winter_2018.pdf [Last accessed 22/02/23]

Braverman, S. (2022). 'Speech to conservative party Conference'04/10/22, https://www.ukpol.co.uk/suella-braverman-2022-speech-to-conservative-party-conference/ [Last accessed 22/02/23]

Broad, R., & Gadd, D. (2023). *Demystifying modern slavery*. Routledge.

Burland, P. (2019). Still punishing the wrong people: The criminalisation of potential trafficked cannabis gardeners. In eds. G. Craig, A. Balch, H. Lewis, & L. Waite. *The modern slavery agenda* (pp. 167–186). Bristol University Press.

Council of Europe. (2005). *Convention on action against trafficking in human beings*. 16/5/2005. https://rm.coe.int/168008371d

Craig, G., Balch, A., Lewis, H., & Waite, L. (2019). Editorial introduction: The modern slavery agenda: Policy, politics and practice. In G. Craig, A. Balch, H. Lewis, & L. Waite (Eds.), *The modern slavery agenda: Policy, politics and practice* (pp. 1–28). Policy Press.

Dearden, L. (2022). 'Suella Braverman's modern slavery 'abuse' claims questioned by former watchdog', *The Independent 05/10/22*https://www.independent.co.uk/news/uk/politics/suella-braverman-modern-slavery-abuse-b2195548.html [Last accessed 22/02/23]

Dugan, E. (2022). 'Watchdog disputes Braverman's claim modern slavery laws being 'gamed', *The Guardian*, 09/10/22. https://www.theguardian.com/uk-news/2022/oct/09/watchdog-disputes-bravermans-claim-migrants-gaming-slavery-laws [Last accessed 22/02/23]

Esslemont, M. (2022). 'Modern slavery data: Joint sector letter' 26/10/22, https://afterexploitation.files.wordpress.com/2022/10/osr-letter-modern-slavery-data-final-1.pdf [Last accessed 22/02/23]

European Parliament. (2011). 'Directive 2011/36/Eu of the European parliament and of the council of 5 April 2011 on preventing and combating trafficking in human beings and protecting its victims, and replacing council framework decision 2002/629/JHA' *Official Journal of the European Union* 15 411 https://eur-lex.europa.eu/LexUriServ/LexUriServ.do?uri=OJ:L:2011:101:0001:0011:en:PDF

Evans, H., Sadhwani, S., Singh, N., Robjant, K., & Katona, C. (2022). Prevalence of complex post-traumatic stress disorder in survivors of human trafficking and modern slavery: A systematic review. *The European Journal of Psychiatry*, *36*(2), 94–105. https://doi.org/10.1016/j.ejpsy.2022.01.005

Forrest, A. (2022). 'Suella Braverman sparks new government row after calling for UK to quit ECHR'. The Independent, 05/10/2022 available at https://www.independent.co.uk/news/uk/politics/suella-braverman-european-convention-human-rights-b2195809.html last accessed 16/03/23.

Gadd, D., & Broad, R. (2018). Troubling recognitions in British responses to modern slavery. *The British Journal of Criminology*, *58*(6), 1440–1461. https://doi.org/10.1093/bjc/azx082

Gearon, A. (2019). Child trafficking: Young people's experiences of front-line services in England. *The British Journal of Criminology*, *59*(2), 481–500. https://doi.org/10.1093/bjc/azy042

Gregory, C. (2022). The modern slavery defence. *The Cambridge Law Journal*, *81*(3), 470–473. https://doi.org/10.1017/S0008197322000770

Heys, A.(2023). The UK's Statutory Defence for Victims of Modern Slavery and its narrow understanding of victimhood. *The Journal of Criminal Law*, *87*(4), 237–251. https://doi.org/10.1177/00220183231179181

Hodkinson, S. N., Lewis, H., Waite, L., & Dwyer, P. (2021). Fighting or fuelling forced labour? The modern slavery act 2015, irregular migrants and the vulnerabilising role of the UK's hostile environment. *Critical Social Policy*, *41*(1), 68–90. https://doi.org/10.1177/0261018320904311

Hollway, W., & Jefferson, T. (2000). *Doing qualitative research differently*. Sage.

Home Office. (2023). *Modern Slavery: National Referral Mechanism and Duty to Notify Statistics UK, End of Year Summary 2022*, Published 2 March 2023, https://www.gov.uk/government/statistics/modern-slavery-national-referral-mechanism-and-duty-to-notify-statistics-uk-end-of-year-summary-2022/modern-slavery-national-referral-mechanism-and-duty-to-notify-statistics-uk-end-of-year-summary-2022 {Last accessed 27/03/23]

Home Office & Patel, P. (2021). 'Press release: Alarming rise of abuse within modern slavery system' 20/03/21https://www.gov.uk/government/ne.ws/alarming-rise-of-abuse-within-modern-slavery-system [20/03/21]

Human trafficking and exploitation (Scotland) Act. (2015). https://www.legislation.gov.uk/asp/2015/12/contents/enacted

Humpherson, E. (2022). *Open Letter – Ed Humperson to Jennifer Rubin: Use of National Referral Mechanism Statistics*, https://osr.statisticsauthority.gov.uk/correspondence/ed-humpherson-to-jennifer-rubin-use-of-national-referral-mechanism-statistics/ [Last accessed 27/03/23]

IASC. (2020). *The Modern Slavery Act 2015 Statutory Defence: A Call for Evidence*, Independent Anti-Slavery Commissioner. http://www.antislaverycommissioner.co.uk/media/1478/the-modern-slavery-act-2015-statutory-defence-call-for-evidence.pdf [Last accessed 22/02/23]

ILO. (2014). *P029 protocol of 2014 to the forced labour convention, 1930*. International Labour Organization.

Kenway, E. (2021). *The truth about modern slavery*. Pluto Press.

Knight, S. (2023). The trafficking defence in criminal law: Nexus and compulsion. *The Journal of Criminal Law*, *87*(3), 192–206. https://doi.org/10.1177/00220183231151920

May, T. (2013). '2013 speech to conservative party conference', 30/09/13 https://www.ukpol.co.uk/theresa-may-2013-speech-to-conservative-party-conference/ [Last accessed 22/02/23]

Munro Kerr, M. (2021). 'Modern slavery after DS and Brecani – What Does a Conclusive Grounds Decision Mean for a Criminal Case?' https://www.onepumpcourt.co.uk/news/modern-slavery-after-ds-and-brecani-what-does-a-conclusive-grounds-decision-mean-for-a-criminal-case/#:~:text=Section%2045%20of%20the%20Modern,victim%20of%20slavery%20or%20trafficking [Last accessed 22/02/23]

Muraszkiewicz, J. (2019). Protecting victims of human trafficking from liability: An evaluation of section 45 of the Modern Slavery Act. *The Journal of Criminal Law*, *83*(5), 394–405. https://doi.org/10.1177/0022018319857497

O'Connell Davidson, J. (2015). *The margins of freedom: Modern slavery*. Palgrave.

Office of the High Commissioner of Human Rights (OHCHR). (2002). Recommended principles and guidelines on human rights and human trafficking available https://www.ohchr.org/sites/default/files/Documents/Publications/Traffickingen.pdf [Last accessed 27/03/23].

Office of the Special Representative and Co-ordinator for Combating Trafficking in Human Beings (OSCE). (2013). *Organization for security and cooperation across Europe*. https://www.osce.org/files/f/documents/6/6/101002.pdf [Last accessed 17/01/24].

PEC. (2022). 'Evidence Review of Section 45 of the Modern Slavery Act: Background and Context' *Policy and Evidence Centre April 2022* https://modernslaverypec.org/assets/downloads/Section-45-full-review.pdf

Qureshi, F., Achi, A., Makhlouf, P., Granada, L., & Ahmed, N. (2022). 'Letter to the Home Secretary: Protecting the rights of modern slavery victims'. https://migrantsrights.org.uk/wp-content/uploads/2022/11/Joint-Letter-on-Exploitation-of-Migrant-Workers.pdf.

Rodríguez-López, S. (2020). Telling Victims from Criminals: Human Trafficking for the Purposes of Criminal Exploitation. In J. Winterdyk & J. Jones(Eds.), *The Palgrave International Handbook of Human Trafficking* (pp. 303-318). Cham: Palgrave Macmillan. https://doi.org/10.1007/978-3-319-63058-8_17

Safety of Rwanda (Asylum and Immigration). 2023. https://bills.parliament.uk/publications/53802/documents/4312

Schwarz, K., & Williams-Woods, A. (2022). Protection and support for survivors of modern slavery in the UK: Assessing current provision and what we need to change. *Journal of Poverty & Social Justice*, *30*(2), 98–119 . https://doi.org/10.1332/175982721X16418164636200

Taylor, (2022). 'Revealed: Just 7% of trafficking victims given leave to remain in UK' *The Guardian*, 04/01/22, https://www.theguardian.com/uk-news/2022/jan/04/trafficking-victims-leave-to-remain-uk-data [Last accessed 22/02/23]

Topolski, C. (2021). 'R v Brecani - the end of s.45 modern slavery defences?' *Crucible Law Insights*, 27th May 2021, https://crucible.law/insights/r-v-brecani-the-end-of-s45-modern-slavery-defences [Last accessed 22/02/23]

Youth Justice Legal Centre. (2021). 'V.C.L and A.N v the United Kingdom: A positive step forward for victims of Modern day Slavery'. Youth Justice Legal Centre: London available at https://yjlc.uk/resources/legal-updates/vcl-and-v-united-kingdom-positive-step-forward-victims-modern-day-slavery last accessed 16/03/23

OPEN ACCESS

# Toward Journalism on Human Trafficking That is Trauma-Informed, Hope-Based, and Solutions-Oriented

Kirsten Foot

**ABSTRACT**

Developments in related practices termed solutions journalism or constructive journalism and scholarship on those journalistic practices hold significant promise for improving journalism on human trafficking but have yet to be engaged robustly by either journalists or scholars of journalism on human trafficking (HT). This commentary article reviews recent scholarship on constructive journalism considering patterns in media framing of human trafficking that have been established over the last two decades through studies of HT journalism. It highlights several open-access resources designed to catalyze better journalism on human trafficking that could be utilized fruitfully to improve journalism education and expand research on human trafficking journalism.

The power of journalists and other media producers to shape public opinion, social movements, and policy on societal issues is well-established by scholarship from political communication and media studies (Benford & Snow, 2000; McCombs & Shaw, 1972; Wanta, 1997). How media reports are framed, i.e., with certain aspects of an issue foregrounded and others not, shape media users' perceptions of the issue. More specifically, media frames define problems, diagnose causal relations, produce and validate opinions (or moral judgments) on problems, and suggest remedies or solutions (Entman, 1993). Therefore, patterns in media framings of human trafficking (HT) are consequential for countering it more effectively.

Developments in a set of related practices termed solutions journalism or constructive journalism and scholarship on those journalistic practices hold significant promise for improving journalism on human trafficking but have yet to be engaged robustly by either journalists or scholars of journalism on HT (referred to hereafter as HT journalism). The two aims of this commentary article are to: 1) review recent scholarship on constructive journalism considering patterns in media framing of HT that have been established over the last two decades through studies of HT journalism, and 2) highlight several open-access resources designed to catalyze better journalism on HT that could be utilized fruitfully for both improving journalism education and expanding research on HT journalism.

Mike Dottridge (2002) appears to have published the first article in an English-language academic journal assessing extant journalism on any form of human trafficking, specifically the trafficking of children from Central and West Africa. His analysis is worth examining closely for this article. Dottridge observed:

> In numerous cases Western journalists reminded their audiences that the region where children were being enslaved was precisely the same "Slave Coast" visited by ships involved historically in the Trans-Atlantic slave trade. They seemed to be suggesting that West Africans are irredeemably attached to slavery as a way of recruiting cheap labor, although the sentiments were rarely voiced in such racist terms. Most reporters focused on the

> sectors where cruelty and exploitation were most visible – the horrendous experiences of children in transit and after arriving at their destinations. Very few visited the children's villages or towns of origin to report on the factors propelling children away. (p. 39)

After describing the investigations of human trafficking conducted by nongovernmental organizations in several Central and West African countries in the late 1990s, Dottridge noted a single journalist-led investigation and report:

> In 1998, a newspaper in Côte d'Ivoire denounced the trafficking of children from Burkina Faso and Mali into Côte d'Ivoire, and claimed that boys were being sold to work on farms for as little as US$30, producing a range of commercial crops (IVOIR'SOIR, 1998, 18, cited in Dottridge, 2002, p. 40).

He described the significant impact that news reports had on national policy in two countries this way: "The newspaper publicity led the governments of Côte d'Ivoire and Mali to set up a commission of inquiry and, in September 2000, to sign an agreement to curb the traffic" (p. 41).

While Dottridge is not a media scholar, his anecdotal observations of both the narrow and shallow problem focus of journalism on HT in the West and Central African regions during the late 1990s, and the constructive impact of broader framing and deeper journalistic investigation, were confirmed and extended by subsequent systematic studies of journalism on HT. Pajnik's (2010) analysis of news articles published in Slovene 2003–2005 found that "trafficking appears within 'frames' [labeled] 'criminalization', 'nationalization', 'victimization' and 'regularization'; together, this help to shape a specific anti-trafficking paradigm, one that depicts trafficking as a criminal issue and calls for stricter policing, saving victims and tightening borders" (p. 45). Scholars examining English news reports in various media published in multiple countries and regions of the world in the 1990s, 2000s, and 2010s had broadly consistent findings. In aggregate, they characterized the framing of HT in media reports as a crime problem, with a greater proportion of reports focused on child sex trafficking than any other type of HT (followed by the trafficking of women for sex), and with little to no attention to root causes or remedies (Austin & Farrell, 2017; Farrell & Fahey, 2009; Friedman & Johnston, 2018; Gulati, 2011; Johnston et al., 2014, 2015; Sobel, 2014; Sobel et al., 2017; Walllinger, 2010).

Johnston et al. (2014) took a deeper look at these patterns by analyzing how news reports in the U.S. defined the problem of sex trafficking throughout 2009 and whether any reports identified any remedy. They found that news coverage of trafficking was overwhelmingly framed as a crime issue and proposed no remedies. In Friedman and Johnston's (2018) introduction to a special issue of the *Journal of Human Trafficking* on media and human trafficking, their review of extant scholarship confirmed and elaborated the patterns described above but also highlighted a few notable exceptions as exemplars of what they argue should become the norm in media representations of HT. Moreover, an article in that special issue by Sanders (2018), a survivor-leader, contrasts her experience with two reporters: one whose interviewing and reporting re-traumatized her and did nothing to contribute to ending human trafficking, and another who exemplified the potential for journalism on HT to be not only trauma-informed but also constructive. Her conclusion is a powerful call for change:

> we [survivors] are more than the stories of our trafficking experiences. Journalists have a choice to tell the stories that make the greatest impact – the biggest impact will come from the truths that lead to prevention and recovery, and survivors are a vital source of those truths. (p. 88)

Sanders' experience-based call for trauma-informed and constructive journalism on HT resonates with a growing body of work by journalists and scholars of journalism alike on the importance – and ethical imperative – of changing journalistic practices around complex issues such as HT. Hopkinson and Dahmen (2021) advocate for journalists to employ:

> forms of journalistic practice – some old, some reinvigorated, some new – that hold true to journalism's professional values while implementing productive, socially responsible reporting approaches to informing the public. By productive, we mean practices that push the conversation forward, that engage and empower audiences, and that seek to create meaningful impact. By socially responsible, we mean journalism that considers society's best interests by covering the news beyond problem-based narrative, by reporting with depth and

> embracing complexity, and by emphasizing connection and collaboration with the community. To be clear, these journalistic practices are not positive news or fluff reporting intended to create feel-good pieces. They are rigorous reporting practices that can be applied in covering socially significant and unrelenting issues: climate change, immigration, homelessness, racial injustice, gun violence, human trafficking, economic disparity, and the like. (pp. 1–2)

In a study of how solutions journalism practices were implemented in local contexts, Usery (2022) found that "solutions journalism gives agency to those in underrepresented communities. It allows for storytelling that develops them as characters rather than victims or criminals. In turn, this agency promotes liberation in underrepresented communities, which can spur tangible change" (p. 14). This finding holds promise for survivors of HT, as their perspectives have been routinely excluded or marginalized in journalism on HT (Johnston et al., 2014).

The kinds of evidence on which Hopkinson and Dahmen base their normative argument for productive, socially responsible journalism are complemented by accounts of the nonprofit Solutions Journalism Network (SJN), founded in 2013, the mission of which is to "transform journalism so that all people have access to news that helps them envision and build a more equitable and sustainable world" (Solutions Journalism Network, n.d.-a). As of April, 2023, the SJN's website states, "More than 500 news organizations and 20,000 journalists worldwide have worked with us and inspired one another to integrate solutions journalism into their reporting" (Solutions Journalism Network, n.d.-a). The SJN curates a database of "rigorous reporting on responses to social problems: 14900 stories produced by 6,000 journalists and 1,900 news outlets, from 190 countries," which its staff vets, and characterizes the database as "growing every day" (Solutions Journalism Network, n.d.-b). As of April 2023, a search of the Solutions Story Tracker database for stories on "ending slavery and human trafficking" resulted in 42 reports published in English between 2013–2022 in multiple countries on multiple forms of HT – all of which included a way that slavery or HT was being countered.

Corresponding with scholarly critiques of the predominant patterns in journalism on HT and the push for constructive, solutions-oriented journalism across complex social issues, there is a growing set of open-access resources for journalists covering HT to gain knowledge and skills in employing interviewing and reporting practices that are trauma-informed, hope-based, and solutions-oriented. The earliest of these appears to have been the *Trafficking in Women Manual for Journalists*, published in English and Serbian by the nonprofit ASTRA (Anti Sex Trafficking Action, 2003). A second edition, retitled the *Human Trafficking Manual for Journalists* followed in 2008 with contributions from journalists alongside ASTRA staff (Radović et al., 2008). The purpose of the manual was explained like this:

> Adequate media reporting on this problem is very important for deconstructing prejudice and stereotypes, popular awareness raising, preventing future recruitment and improving the quality of assistance and reintegration process of persons who have managed to come out of the trafficking chain. We considered this to be in our common interest. Therefore, we hope you will find this Manual useful for your work. (p. 6)

The *Irina Project* at the University of North Carolina – Chapel Hill "monitors media representations of sex trafficking and advocates through research and engagement the accurate and responsible coverage of this complex issue" (Friedman & Johnston, n.d..).

Several open-source resources for journalists strongly articulate the importance of a solutions orientation in journalism on HT. For instance, the *Human Trafficking Toolkit* (Gastélum Félix et al., 2017) aims to "expand the conversation around human trafficking," arguing that

> successful media coverage of human trafficking can highlight the efforts being made against human trafficking, the partnerships in place working to stop the crime and the success stories of survivors, social workers, law enforcers and many other people doing tremendous work. Stories that inspire people to focus on solutions rather than problems are a powerful way to reach the public. (p. 87)

This toolkit, published by The Arab Initiative to Build National Capacities to Combat Human Trafficking in the Arab Countries with support from the UNODC Office for the Gulf Cooperation Council Region, urges journalists to include practical advice on how readers or viewers can help prevent and counter HT, point to protection resources for victims, and highlight current prevention efforts and available resources.

The *Media and Trafficking in Human Beings Guidelines* by Aidan White and the Ethical Journalism Network (2017) make an even more specific argument for solutions-oriented journalism, explaining,

> Media and journalism should play a positive role in persuading the world that trafficking can be diminished if not eradicated. Political leaders and the public at large need to read, hear and see the full story. It is an essential first step in generating the political will needed to overcome the fundamental causes of human trafficking. (p. 6)

This resource provides efficient guidance for journalists on how to craft constructive stories about HT.

The latter two resources articulate the relationship between hope and solutions-oriented journalism on HT. According to Gastélum Félix et al. (2017), "without information about solutions, audiences are left with a sense of hopelessness. The media has the potential to educate people about human trafficking and to empower them to take actions to prevent it and to protect those who have been victimized" (p. 87). White and the Ethical Journalism Network (2017) exhort journalists to

> Build hope. It's easy for the public to think of people who are victims of trafficking or in forced labor as powerless individuals who are permanently damaged. That isn't always true. Journalism that highlights human resilience and tells how people can rebuild their lives from the tragedy of modern slavery and forced labor tells a different story. (p. 17)

However, neither of these resources provides specific guidance to journalists on building hope other than focusing on solutions.

Foot et al. (2022) attempt to redress that gap via the *Toolkit for Hope-Based and Solutions-Oriented Journalism on Human Trafficking*, developed collaboratively by a multisector group of scholars, survivors, community-based advocates, and public information officers, together with journalists and producers of other types of media. The premise of this toolkit is:

> Journalism in a democracy aims to contribute constructively to society by providing audiences with information necessary to make informed decisions about their lives, communities, and government. Reporting that focuses narrowly on the problem of HT can cause harm, because the problem is only part of the story that needs to be told. Journalists can maximize positive impact by reporting more holistically on the many efforts to combat HT being advanced within and across multiple sectors, including by survivors themselves. Stories have the ability to heighten public awareness in identifying potential survivors and not criminalizing victims. Responsible reporting can influence policy development and provide a means to hold exploiters and beneficiaries of trafficking accountable. (e.g., businesses profiting from exploitation or buyers of a trafficked person).

This toolkit envisions journalism on HT as coproduced between journalists, survivors, their advocates, and public information officers in their intermediary role between survivors and journalists. Ways to go beyond being trauma-informed to also convey hope as the foundation for solutions-oriented journalism on HT are articulated in three coordinated guides explicitly addressed to each type of reader.

All the resources described above provide solid rationales for evidence-based, practical guidance toward trauma-informed, hope-based, and solutions-oriented journalism on HT. An emerging body of scholarship explores how various types of audiences respond to particular forms of constructive journalism. For example, experiments conducted by Dahmen et al. (2019) found that narrative engagement can play an important role in involving audiences in visual solutions reporting, with data showing that solutions visual reporting is more engaging on average. Additional findings included that when audiences are more engaged in the visual solutions reporting, participants report more positive outcomes for interest, self-efficacy, and behavior intentions. In another experiment-based study, Hermann and Prins (2022) found that including constructive elements of hope and inspiration and solution-based information in the news can improve emotional responses among Millennials.

## Conclusion

The need for constructive journalism on HT is clear, and people in every sector can help advance trauma-informed, hope-based, and solutions-oriented media on HT. Scholars, journalists, and anti-trafficking practitioners can employ and help disseminate open-access resources like those described above and contribute to the Solutions Journalism Network's database of constructive news reports addressing slavery and human trafficking. More research is needed to illuminate how constructive HT journalism can be crafted more effectively.

## Disclosure statement

No potential conflict of interest was reported by the author.

## ORCID

Kirsten Foot http://orcid.org/0000-0002-3080-7230

## References

ASTRA Anti Sex Trafficking Action. (2003). *Trafficking in women manual for journalists*. https://drive.google.com/file/d/1GIPRSstcrV42jX38yj6IdIBK-3SYa0ow/view

Austin, R., & Farrell, A. (2017). Human trafficking and the media in the United States. In H. N. Pontell (Ed.), *Oxford research encyclopedia of criminology and criminal justice*. Oxford University Press. https://doi.org/10.1093/acrefore/9780190264079.013.290

Benford, R. D., & Snow, D. A. (2000). Framing processes and social movements: An overview and assessment. *Annual Review of Sociology*, *26*(1), 611–639. https://doi.org/10.1146/annurev.soc.26.1.611

Dahmen, N. S., Thier, K., & Walth, B. (2019). Creating engagement with solutions visuals: Testing the effects of problem-oriented versus solution-oriented photojournalism. *Visual Communication*, *20*(2), 271–288. https://doi.org/10.1177/1470357219838601

Dottridge, M. (2002). Trafficking in children in west and central Africa. *Gender & Development*, *10*(1), 38–42. https://doi.org/10.1080/13552070215890

Entman, R. M. (1993). Framing: Toward clarification of a fractured paradigm. *Journal of Communication*, *43*(4), 51–58. https://doi.org/10.1111/j.1460-2466.1993.tb01304.x

Farrell, A., & Fahey, S. (2009). The problem of human trafficking in the U.S.: Public frames and policy responses. *Journal of Criminal Justice*, *37*(6), 617–627. https://doi.org/10.1016/j.jcrimjus.2009.09.010

Foot, K., Dhanoa, S., Dahmen, N. S., & Pembrook, D. (2022, April 24). *The Toolkit for Hope-Based and Solutions-Oriented Journalism About Human Trafficking*. Department of Communication, University of Washington. Retrieved from http://hopebased.info

Friedman, B., & Johnston, A. (2018). Editors' note: Introduction to the special issue on media and human trafficking: Negotiating meaning, representation, and change. *Journal of Human Trafficking*, *4*(1), 1–5. https://doi.org/10.1080/23322705.2017.1423442

Friedman, B., & Johnston, A. (n.d.). *What We Do*. University of North Carolina Hussman School of Journalism and Media. [2023, April 25]. Retrieved from http://www.theirinaproject.org/what-we-do.html

Gastélum Félix, S., Kozeschnik, S., & Gill, H. (2017). Human trafficking toolkit for journalists. U. N. O. O. D. A. Crime. https://www.unodc.org/documents/human-trafficking/2018/Toolkit_HT_Final_Book_Finish_2017_English_comp.pdf

Gulati, G. J. (2011). News frames and story triggers in the media's coverage of human trafficking. *Human Rights Review*, *12*(3), 363–379. https://doi.org/10.1007/s12142-010-0184-5

Hermann, L., & Prins, T. (2022). Interest matters: The effects of constructive news reporting on millennials' emotions and engagement. *Journalism*, *23*(5), 1064–1081. https://doi.org/10.1177/1464884920944741

Hopkinson, K. M., & Dahmen, N. S. (2021). *Reporting beyond the problem: From civic journalism to solutions journalism*. Peter Lang.

Johnston, A., Friedman, B., & Shafer, A. (2014). Framing the problem of sex trafficking: Whose problem? What remedy? *Feminist Media Studies*, *14*(3), 419–436. https://doi.org/10.1080/14680777.2012.740492

Johnston, A., Friedman, B., & Sobel, M. (2015). Framing an emerging issue: How U.S. Print and broadcast news media covered sex trafficking. *Journal of Human Trafficking*, *1*(3), 235–254. https://doi.org/10.1080/23322705.2014.993876

McCombs, M. E., & Shaw, D. L. (1972). The agenda-setting function of mass media. *Public Opinion Quarterly*, *36*(2), 176–187. https://doi.org/10.1086/267990

Pajnik, M. (2010). Media framing of trafficking. *International Feminist Journal of Politics*, *12*(1), 45–64. https://doi.org/10.1080/14616740903429114

Radović, I., Bogićević, J., Anđelković, M., Gligorić, M., Teodorović, M., Stojiljković, M., Milenković, N., Todorović, O. M., Otašević, O., Leković, S., Savić, S., & Vukasović, T. (2008). *Human trafficking manual for journalists*. ASTRA Anti Trafficking Action. https://drive.google.com/file/d/1u7wUl5oX85v0YaVNI_z3kyjQ-nlDdubA/view

Sanders, S. J. (2018). What will be the headlines when we die? Survivors as news stories & news sources. *Journal of Human Trafficking*, *4*(1), 86–88. https://doi.org/10.1080/23322705.2018.1423449

Sobel, M. (2014). Chronicling a crisis: Media framing of human trafficking in India, Thailand, and the USA. *Asian Journal of Communication*, *24*(4), 315–332. https://doi.org/10.1080/01292986.2014.903425

Sobel, M., Friedman, B., & Johnston, A. (2017). Sex trafficking as a news story: Evolving structure and reporting strategies. *Journal of Human Trafficking*, *5*(1), 43–59. https://doi.org/10.1080/23322705.2017.1401426

Solutions Journalism Network. (n.d.-a). *About*. [2023, April 24]. Retrieved from https://www.solutionsjournalism.org/about

Solutions Journalism Network. (n.d.-b). *Solutions Story Tracker*. [2023, April 24]. Retrieved from https://www.solutionsjournalism.org/storytracker#%23top

Usery, A. G. (2022). Solutions journalism: How its evolving definition, practice and perceived impact affects under-represented communities. *Journalism Practice*, 1–17. https://doi.org/10.1080/17512786.2022.2142836

Walllinger, C. S. (2010, October). *Media representation and human trafficking: How anti-trafficking discourse affects trafficked persons*. Second Annual Interdisciplinary Conference on Human Trafficking University of NebraskaLincoln, NE. https://digitalcommons.unl.edu/humtrafconf2/4

Wanta, W. (1997). *The public and the national agenda: How people learn about important issues*. Lawrence Erlbaum Associates.

White, A., & Ethical Journalism Network. (2017, April 27). *Media and Trafficking in Human Beings Guidelines*. International Centre for Migration Policy Development. Retrieved from https://ethicaljournalismnetwork.org/media-and-trafficking-in-human-beings-guidelines?swcfpc=1

# Forced Labour and Accountability in Supply Chains: The Role of the Private Sector

Matt Friedman

**ABSTRACT**
Modern slavery is a pervasive human rights issue that deprives individuals of their freedom and rights, often exploiting them for labor or other forms of exploitation. While governments have a vital role to play in addressing modern slavery, the private sector also has an essential role to play. Supply chains are a critical area where the private sector can take action to address modern slavery. Many industries rely on complex supply chains across multiple countries and involve numerous suppliers and subcontractors. These complex supply chains make it difficult for companies to ensure that their products or services are not tainted by modern slavery. Despite these constraints, the private sector can contribute to combating modern slavery by adopting ethical business practices that prioritize protecting human rights. This can be achieved through various means, such as implementing strict supply chain management policies, ensuring transparency in their operations, and collaborating with civil society organizations to promote responsible practices. By conducting due diligence, establishing clear contractual requirements, collaborating with other businesses and industry groups, and using their purchasing power, companies can also mitigate the risks of modern slavery in their operations and supply chains.

## Background

Modern slavery, which represents the recruitment, transport, receipt, and harboring of people for the purpose of exploiting their labor (United Nations, 2000), affects almost all parts of the world. Globally, it is estimated that there are over 50 million men, women, and children in modern-day slavery today, with more than half in Asia alone (International Labor Organization [ILO], 2022). These victims, found in factories, construction sites, and within fisheries and sex venues, are forced to work for little or no pay, deprived of their freedom, and often subjected to unimaginable suffering.

While much of the discourse on modern slavery centers on sex trafficking, the majority (64% of the victims) are associated with supply chains and the private sector, which begin with a grower or producer and end as a finished product purchased by consumers in the retail market.

For more than a decade, the international response has not come close to meeting its full potential. While individual success stories can be found, most victims are never identified. For example, the 2022 Trafficking in Persons Report (TIP Report) only accounted for 90,354 victims receiving assistance globally – approximately 0.2% of the estimated 50 million victims of trafficking (United States Department of State [USDOS], 2022). During the same period, there were fewer than 5,260 convictions. Less than one percent of the victims are identified and assisted annually. This number has remained unchanged for over 10 years.

According to the ILO, the profits generated from this illicit trade are estimated to exceed U.S. $150 billion annually (ILO, 2014). This means that every 60 seconds, this criminal industry makes more than U.S. $285,000. According to the United Nations, modern slavery generates proceeds representing the second most profitable multi-national criminal activity after drug trafficking. Despite the size of the problem, annual global donor contributions add up to only around U.S. $350 million, which represents less than one percent of total profits generated by the criminals.

Why are these numbers so low? There is a considerable gap between what we believe human trafficking to be and what we can substantiate with the number of identified victims. Modern slavery is an economic crime whose illegal profits not only impact economies and undermine civil governance, but more broadly speaking, they also violate human rights. One significant gap in our knowledge-building and intervention planning is how private sector players, i.e., those who stand to gain the most from unregulated cheap labor, may need to be monitored and held accountable for their supply chains.

## Why Should the Private Sector Care About This Topic?

Many essential goods we buy have been through a manufacturing, packaging and distribution process known as a supply chain. Supply chains begin with a manufacturer and end as a finished product consumers purchase. Modern slavery can be found at any stage within these supply chains.

As major companies attempt to compete, they are often pressured to keep their costs as low as possible. Labor represents a significant portion of product costs, so reducing these expenses can be achieved by working with manufacturing suppliers in locations where labor is cheap. In some cases, unscrupulous actors in the supply chain exploit workers to gain the highest profits in locations where labor standards are unregulated or non-existent, often without the knowledge of the brand or retailer.

Indicators of modern slavery vary but can include debt bondage, physical and sexual violence, threats against employees and their families, wage withholding, restrictions on freedom of movement, and retention of personal documents. As a result of these practices, it is possible for modern slavery to infiltrate the supply chains of many of our everyday consumer products.

On-site audits have been used to reveal signs of modern slavery in a manufacturing facility; however, supply chains frequently stretch long distances and involve multiple players, making the verification process difficult to trace, if practical at all.

To illustrate this point, a standard manufacturing process might include a range of tiers within its supply chain. Let's take a pair of running shoes as an example. In this case, one company's supply chain might have three tiers: tier one, where the shoe is assembled; tier two, where the component parts, shoelaces, rivets, textiles, and sole of the shoe are produced; and tier three, where the raw materials, including metal, cotton, wool, and rubber are acquired. Most major shoe manufacturing companies regularly audit tier-one facilities, but fewer audits, if any, are being done among the lower tiers. This is often where the most significant potential for modern slavery exists.

Another concern is the limitations of auditing that have been identified in recent years. These include inadequate training for interviewers, corruption resulting in modern slavery practices being ignored, audits that focus only on health and safety, and audits that don't include worker interviews.

## Case Examples

The first testimonial summarizes the experience many migrants face in an extreme forced labor situation.

> When I was 18 years old, I heard that there were many electronics factories in Thailand that needed unskilled workers. So, I went there. I didn't know which one had work, so I just chose one. The man who managed the factory said I could have a job. We negotiated a salary of U.S. $50 a month. For me, this was a huge amount of money. But he said I couldn't leave the factory compound. I was okay with this. I needed the money, so I agreed. After working 15 hours daily for nearly two months, I asked the employer for my pay. He smiled and laughed before saying, 'I am sorry, I forgot to mention that it costs me U.S. $54 a month to keep you here, and I am only paying you U.S. $50. So, you owe me money. Until you pay it back, you cannot leave this place.' For three years, I was not able to leave. With armed security guards, barbed wire, and CCTV cameras watching everything, I couldn't escape. None of us could. The more I worked, the more debt I owed. With so much work with nothing in return, my heart was filled with hopelessness and despair. If that fire hadn't brought the authorities, I would never have been able to leave. I lost three years of my life. Gone ... stolen from me. Something I can never get back again.
>
> *Myanmar victim – Thailand Exploitation*

The second testimonial provides another good summary of the experience many workers face in a forced labor situation.

> Before migrating to Malaysia, I was working in Nepal. Since my salary was low, I struggled. I was excited after the recruitment agent came and told me about work elsewhere. He said I could earn up to U.S. $250 per month. But he said I'd have to come up with U.S. $1,500. I told him I didn't have this money. He said no problem. I can borrow it from a money lender. After signing a contract, I went to Kathmandu, got my documents, and then was sent to Malaysia. When I got there, I was told that my debt was now U.S. $3,000. I was so surprised. I didn't understand the interest and fees. For months, I had to work to pay this back. This created a real problem for my family back in Nepal. I wanted to return home, but the debt held me in place. They also made me sign another contract in a language I didn't understand. I later found out there were clauses that cheated me. When I said I wanted to go home, they said I couldn't. I asked for my passport back. They wouldn't give it to me. They said I had to stay the full four years. I never should have accepted this job. I was worse off than when I started.
>
> *Nepalese victim – Malaysia Exploitation*

From these two profiles, one can see that several characteristics are common in modern slavery: the use of fraud or deception to trick a person into an exploitative labor situation; debt, violence, or threats to hold the person in place; document retention, contract substitution and the lack of any payment in exchange for services provided. In both cases, the workers toiled in forced labor and were unable to leave.

## Proposed Responses

When addressing this issue, private sector responses must address the "4Ps" of the United nations, including prevention, protection, prosecution, and partnerships. Each category must identify the issue, offer solutions to prevent or stop it and address the outcome among potential victims. Because many industries rely on complex supply chains that span multiple countries and involve numerous suppliers and subcontractors, it is difficult for companies to ensure that their products or services are not tainted by modern slavery. There are 10 critical ways in which major manufacturing companies can address the risk of modern slavery within their supply chains:

(1) Company leadership (board and C-suite) should receive periodic detailed briefings on the relevance and importance of due diligence processes and procedures related to modern slavery at all levels of their supply chains.
(2) A designated individual or team should be a focal point for any actions and communication related to this topic.
(3) Internal and external policies related to modern slavery should be implemented or fine-tuned. These include codes of conduct, annual compliance certifications, standard contract language, due diligence questionnaires, and supplier statements of conformity. Portions of these policies should be included in contracts with suppliers down the supply chain.
(4) Purchasing practices should be revised and tailored toward a more responsible approach. This includes studying and understanding the impact of costing, forecasting, and suppliers' workload management.
(5) Emerging transparency legislation now requires that major brands know their supply chain from top to bottom. Supply chain mapping efforts should aim at complete product traceability, from raw materials to finished goods. This helps to conduct effective risk assessments to identify potential modern slavery vulnerabilities at all levels. This exercise should engage various company employees, including legal, CSR, supply chain management, risk, and HR. Once completed, training should be offered to employees and business partners at all levels to improve their understanding of the problem.

(6) Investigative audits should be carried out among new and existing suppliers to illuminate the conditions workers face throughout the supply chain. These investigations should verify that:

- All workers have written employment contracts in a language they understand;
- Contracts have not been substituted at either source or destination;
- Contracts are compliant with local labor laws;
- Legal and industry limits on working hours are observed;
- All deductions are included in the contract within legal or industry regulations;
- Withholding of wages is not tolerated;
- There are no restrictions on freedom of movement;
- Recruitment and brokerage fees paid by workers are within legal limits established by the governments of the workers' origin. Likewise, many brands are now mandating that no workers among their suppliers have debt. If any debt does exist, the supplier is expected to pay it back to the workers in full;
- Workers retain copies of their identification documents or have unencumbered access to their documents, should they leave them with their employers to hold them for safekeeping; and
- No overcharging, or any other method, leads to worker dependence and denial of choice.

(7) Companies should ensure that grievance mechanisms, such as phone apps or third-party hotlines, are available to workers. This allows workers to provide valuable feedback about their working conditions safely.
(8) Capacity development programs should be implemented to equip suppliers with the right expertise and tools to start implementing changes within their business operations to cascade this knowledge and responsibilities down the supply chain.
(9) Manufacturing companies should join multi-stakeholder initiatives that unite workers, civil society, and governments to focus on strategic and practical methods of collectively reducing modern slavery.
(10) If modern slavery is found anywhere in a manufacturing supply chain, companies should have a plan to address the problem in an effective manner and remediate it. This should include a response that protects the workers from further harm, supports them, provides rehabilitation options and offers them access to judicial and non-judicial remedies.

## Migrant Recruitment within Manufacturing Businesses

Since many manufacturing brands rely on migrant labor to support their business, understanding how the migrant worker recruitment process works is essential to protecting a company's business and reputation. According to data from the ILO, below are some general trends for industries that use the most migrant workers globally. They include:

- Domestic work: Migrant workers, particularly women, comprise a significant portion of domestic workers globally. According to the ILO, migrant workers comprise over 70% of the domestic work sector in some countries.
- Agriculture: Agriculture is a labor-intensive industry that relies heavily on migrant workers in many countries. Migrant workers often perform low-skilled and physically demanding jobs, such as harvesting crops and planting.
- Manufacturing: Migrant workers are often employed in manufacturing industries in countries with lower labor costs. They may work in factories producing clothing, electronics, and toys.
- Construction: The construction industry also employs a significant number of migrant workers, particularly in developing countries where there is a high demand for construction workers.

- Healthcare: The healthcare industry in many countries faces a shortage of skilled workers, and migrant workers are often hired to fill these gaps. They may work as nurses, doctors, or other healthcare professionals.

Related to the use of migrant workers, forced labor occurs in many of the same sectors. According to the ILO, the following sectors have a higher risk of forced labor:

- Agriculture and fishing: Workers in agriculture and fishing may be forced into labor due to long working hours, low pay, and poor working conditions.
- Construction: The construction industry is vulnerable to forced labor due to using undocumented workers, who may be at risk of exploitation and abuse.
- Domestic work: Domestic workers, including live-in maids and caregivers, are often isolated and may be subjected to forced labor, including physical and sexual abuse.
- Manufacturing: Workers in the manufacturing industry may be at risk of forced labor, especially in low-wage countries where labor laws are weakly enforced.
- Mining: The mining industry is associated with hazardous working conditions, including exposure to toxic chemicals and physical risks. Workers may be at risk of forced labor due to debt bondage, intimidation, and threats.
- Textiles and apparel: The textile and apparel industry are associated with low wages, long working hours, and poor working conditions. Workers may be subjected to forced labor, including debt bondage and human trafficking.

It is important to note that forced labor can occur in any sector and is often associated with weak labor protections, poverty, and social exclusion (ILO, 2017).

Many people in less developed countries seek job opportunities elsewhere in hopes of a better life for themselves and their families. Those who leave with the specific intention to find employment are migrant workers. This could be within their own country or another country that is often considered more prosperous.

If a migrant is associated with people who have no intention of exploiting him, the outcome can be positive. In the best circumstances, the working conditions are good, compensation is fair, and the migrant is happy with the terms and conditions. But if a migrant encounters an employer whose intent is to exploit, he might not be able to leave the worksite, be paid, or lose control of his life.

There are several reasons why migrants are easier to exploit than non-migrants. Many do not speak the local language, don't know where to go for help or would not receive sympathy from the local authorities for their situation (Office of the United Nations High Commissioner for Human Rights [OHCHR], 2018).

For many migrants, the initiation of this exploitative process begins within their community. Labor agents approach them with a promise of a good job opportunity abroad. This can be done through a formal or informal process. Through the informal system, the migrant might receive help to cross a border to take up a job in another country for a fee. When a more formal process is used, labor brokers act as a facilitator for an employment agency. Once a person has been identified, he is introduced to the agency, and negotiations begin. At this stage, deception or false promises may be made regarding terms and conditions of employment, including the job type, length of contract, salary, and benefits.

Whether informal or formal, many migrant workers are tricked or cajoled into debt to pay excessive fees with the promise of an eventual payoff down the line. To obtain money for the fees, workers may mortgage their family's land, sell valuable possessions or find a money lender who charges excessive interest rates, which adds to mounting debt. Sometimes, the person may also be given money as an advance on his salary. Often, the terms of this payment are unclear or never explained. While many of these fees are illegal, without someone to help them through the process, migrants and their families are often cheated even before they leave their country. The actual range of fees varies from country to country but can be as high as 21 months of proposed wages.

Upon arrival in the destination country, the workers' descent into forced labor can be reinforced through a host of additional burdens, which might include:

- Physical or verbal abuse and discrimination, and their freedom of movement may be strictly curtailed;
- Having signed one contract, upon arrival, migrants are required to sign an amended contract, often in a foreign language, agreeing to deductions and lower wages;
- Excessive, unexplained, or illegal deductions may be made from workers' salaries that result in induced indebtedness;
- Wages may be withheld, delayed or unpaid;
- Identity documents, passports or other valuable personal possessions may be confiscated or withheld; and
- Workers may be unable to terminate their employment without incurring significant financial penalties.

In these cases, migrant workers quickly realize that their job is not the route out of poverty they thought it was.

## Remedies

To address the issue of modern slavery within manufacturing settings that use a high percentage of international migrant labor, the International Labor Organization, and the International Organization for Migration (OM), working closely with the private sector, have outlined practical guiding principles for businesses.

If these steps are taken, significant progress can be made to help reduce modern slavery among migrant workers. They including doing the following:

- Ensure that recruiter agreements include principles that explicitly prohibit trafficking in persons, forced labor, and child labor.
- Ensure that labor recruiters comply with all legislation on labor migration and policies related to recruiting migrant workers in the jurisdictions of origin, transit, and destination countries.
- Ensure that labor recruiters have policies to ensure their recruitment activities treat migrant workers with dignity and respect, free from harassment or coercion.
- Encourage that all manufacturing facilities recruit migrants through legal channels that do not result in the potential for debt bondage. Companies should have a clear policy related to the payment of recruitment fees and related costs.
- Ensure that labor recruiters do not require migrant workers or their family members to provide a monetary deposit or other collateral as a condition of employment.
- Ensure that suppliers and their sub-contractors treat migrant workers fairly. This can be done by having third-party auditors carefully monitor the agencies that provide contract labor, especially across borders, blacklisting those known to have used abusive practices and modern slavery.
- Ensure that all migrant workers have written contracts, in a language that they can easily understand, specifying their rights regarding payment of wages, overtime, retention of identity documents, and other issues related to preventing modern slavery. If the workers are illiterate, the contract should be read to them before signing it.
- Ensure that labor recruiters do not confiscate documents, wages, or personal belongings that are used to limit the worker's freedom of movement.

- Ensure that if modern slavery is found among migrant workers, the victims are provided support services and are not punished for immigration-related offenses during the identification procedure.
- Ensure that migrant workers have effective access to remedy, without fear of recrimination, reprisal, or dismissal. This might include internal grievance procedures of the labor recruiter or the employer.

## Conclusion

Supply chains are undeniably a critical area where the private sector can play a crucial role in addressing modern slavery. However, it is essential to acknowledge the limits and gaps in supply chain accountability when combating this heinous crime. To effectively tackle modern slavery, the traditional response using the 4P's (policing, prosecution, protection, and prevention) must be bolstered by the active involvement of the private sector.

While traditional responders, such as law enforcement agencies and NGOs, have made significant efforts to combat human trafficking, the scale and complexity of the issue necessitate a multi-stakeholder approach. Private sector organizations possess considerable resources, influence, and expertise, combined with traditional responders' efforts, can significantly enhance the fight against modern slavery.

One of the primary reasons why the private sector should be involved in eliminating modern slavery is its ability to conduct due diligence. By thoroughly examining their supply chains, companies can identify potential risks of modern slavery, including forced labor and human trafficking. Through comprehensive risk assessments and audits, private sector organizations can implement robust measures to effectively prevent and address these issues. This proactive approach, coupled with clear contractual requirements, ensures that suppliers adhere to strict standards, thus mitigating the risks of modern slavery.

Collaboration is another critical aspect that the private sector brings to the table. Businesses can collaborate with other companies, industry groups, governments, and civil society organizations. By sharing best practices, knowledge, and resources, these collaborations can develop industry-wide standards, guidelines, and initiatives that promote responsible and ethical supply chains. Such collective efforts strengthen accountability and create a more united front against modern slavery.

Furthermore, the private sector possesses significant purchasing power, which can be harnessed as a force for positive change. By leveraging their buying influence, companies can demand transparency and ethical practices from suppliers. This includes requiring suppliers to demonstrate compliance with anti-slavery regulations, human rights standards, and fair labor practices. By using their purchasing power as a tool for social responsibility, businesses can incentivize suppliers to uphold ethical practices and contribute to eliminating modern slavery.

While traditional responders play a crucial role in combating modern slavery through law enforcement, victim support, and advocacy, they often face limitations due to resource constraints and jurisdictional boundaries. Here is where the private sector can step in and complement these efforts. By integrating modern slavery prevention into their business strategies, private sector organizations can allocate dedicated resources, such as personnel and funds, to address this issue effectively. This collaboration between traditional responders and the private sector fills the gaps in accountability and amplifies the impact of anti-slavery efforts.

The active involvement of the private sector in combating human trafficking bolsters the traditional response using the 4Ps and addresses the limits and gaps related to supply chain accountability. By conducting due diligence, establishing precise contractual requirements, collaborating with other businesses and industry groups, and leveraging their purchasing power, companies can mitigate the risks of modern slavery in their operations and supply chains. Thus, the private sector has a compelling case for helping to eliminate modern slavery alongside traditional responders.

Supply chains are a critical area where the private sector can take action to address modern slavery. By conducting due diligence, establishing clear contractual requirements, collaborating with other businesses and industry groups, and using their purchasing power, companies can mitigate the risks of modern slavery in their operations and supply chains. By taking these actions, the private sector can help to create a world where modern slavery no longer exists.

## Disclosure statement

No potential conflict of interest was reported by the author(s).

## References

International Labor Organization (ILO). (2014). *Profits and poverty: The economics of forced labor*. ILO. Retrieved December 8, 2023 from https://www.ilo.org/wcmsp5/groups/public/—ed_norm/—declaration/documents/publication/wcms_243391.pdf.

International Labor Organization (ILO). (2022). *Global estimates of modern slavery: Forced labor and forced marriage*. ILO. Retrieved December 8, 2023 from https://www.ilo.org/wcmsp5/groups/public/—ed_norm/—ipec/documents/publication/wcms_854733.pdf.

International Labour Organization (ILO). (2017). *Global estimates of modern slavery: Forced labor and forced marriage*. ILO. Retrieved December 8, 2023 from https://www.ilo.org/wcmsp5/groups/public/—dgreports/—dcomm/documents/publication/wcms_575479.pdf.

Office of the United Nations High Commissioner for Human Rights (OHCHR). (2018). *Principles and Guidelines*: Supported by practical guidance, on the human rights protection of migrants in vulnerable situations. United Nations. Retrieved December 8, 2023 from https://www.ohchr.org/sites/default/files/Documents/Issues/Migration/PrinciplesAndGuidelines.pdf.

United Nations. (2000). Protocol to prevent, suppress and punish trafficking in persons especially women and children, supplementing the United Nations convention against transnational organized crime. *General Assembly resolution 55/25*. https://www.ohchr.org/en/library.

U.S. Department of State (USDOS). (2022). *Trafficking in persons report 2022*. Retrieved December 8, 2023 from https://www.state.gov/wp-content/uploads/2022/10/20221020-2022-TIP-Report.pdf.

OPEN ACCESS

# Mind the Gap(s)? Evidence and UK Policymaking on Human Trafficking and Modern Slavery

Alex Balch and Olivia Hesketh

**ABSTRACT**

This article examines four critical gaps in the evidence-policy relationship on human trafficking and modern slavery (HTMS) in the UK: prioritization, epistemology, synchronization and trust. Drawing on multiple sources, the authors outline key features of the landscape around evidence and policy in the UK, identify ways to address gaps and bring together researchers, those directly affected, and policymakers. The findings point to a growing consensus on improving research on HTMS, but a continuing need for work to provide appropriate conditions for a productive evidence-policy system. The conclusions reflect opportunities and challenges in the light of recent political moves in the UK that undermine linkages between evidence and policy.

## Introduction

There is now a substantial and growing amount of research on human trafficking and modern slavery (HTMS), despite it being a comparatively new field of inquiry. Yet there remain concerns about the effectiveness of policies (McDonald, 2014) and the quality and methodological rigor of evaluations of HTMS policies and programs, even if they may be improving (Bryant & Landman, 2020). The UK government has been repeatedly urged to improve the evidence base for its activities in this area (e.g., (Commonwealth Parliamentary Association [CPA], 2018; Independent Commission for Aid Impact [ICAI], 2020), and policy development has been described by scholars as non-rational, "running ahead of research" (Broad & Turnbull, 2019).

Focusing on the UK as a case study, the article identifies and examines four critical gaps or differences – around prioritization, epistemology, synchronization, and trust. We reflect in each case on opportunities and challenges for developing a more productive relationship between research and policy.

The role of evidence in UK policymaking on HTMS came to the fore in 2022 and 2023 concerning two pieces of legislation: the Nationality and Borders Act 2022 and the Illegal Migration Bill (introduced in March 2023). Both aimed to address the UK Government's claims that the modern slavery system is being "abused" by individuals claiming to be victims to avoid deportation and to secure their immigration status. Yet these claims have been widely criticized as "unevidenced" by civil society and described as "counter to all evidence" by scholars.[1] They pointed out that the government's research (Home Office Analysis & Insight

[1]Written Evidence by the Labour Exploitation Advisory Group (ASU0044) https://committees.parliament.uk/writtenevidence/114295/pdf/

[HOAI], 2020) concluded that deterrence does not work and worsens the risks of exploitation and forced labor.[2] The UK's statistics regulator has also raised concerns about the improper use of statistics on modern slavery by the Home Secretary (Humpherson, 2022).

Analysis of the UK's policy development in this area suggests a limited role for research and evidence, pointing to the importance of path dependency and embedded organizational interests of immigration and criminal enforcement agencies (Balch & Geddes, 2011). Some academics have criticized the policy as being driven not by evidence but by ideology, racism and misogyny (O'Connell Davidson, 2015), or following a securitized and politicized logic (Broad & Turnbull, 2019). Meanwhile, international scholarship on HTMS frequently features complaints about data availability[3] [4] and quality and conceptual confusion over definitions (Loff & Sanghera, 2004).

This sits somewhat at odds with the growing number of international initiatives and programs, often government-funded, which are specifically designed to improve the use of evidence on HTMS, e.g., the Delta 8.7 knowledge platform of Alliance 8.7,[5] the Human Trafficking Research Initiative[6] and Monitoring to Evaluation of Trafficking in Persons (METIP).[7] In the UK, those who deliver or scrutinize policy on HTMS have published their priorities for research and evidence (e.g., see Independent Anti-Slavery Commissioner [IASC] research priorities[8]), notably, the UK Annual Report on Modern Slavery 2018, produced by the UK Government and devolved administrations, which included an annex on research priorities. Academics in the UK are increasingly encouraged to pursue impact for their research through the Research Evaluation Framework (REF), by developing what are called 'impact case studies' which describe how their research has made a difference. In the 2014 REF there were 21 impact case studies submitted that mentioned "human trafficking" OR "modern slavery", and in the 2021 REF this had more than doubled to 48 cases.[9]

Why do problems of evidence usage continue to affect this area, and what can be done to address them? As part of the Modern Slavery and Human Rights Policy and Evidence Centre (MS-PEC), launched in 2019 based in the UK and dedicated to improving the evidence-policy relationship in this area, the authors are well-placed to answer these questions. The MS-PEC is a £10 m investment funded through the UK Research and Innovation (UKRI) Strategic Priorities Fund (SPF) through the Arts and Humanities Research Council with the support of the Economic and Social Research Council. As with similar centers, the MS-PEC aims to improve the use of evidence in policymaking but has some unique characteristics around collaboration, co-production, and human rights. Its Strategic Delivery Plan explained its mission as bringing together "academics, policymakers, businesses, civil society, survivors, and the public on a scale not seen before in the UK to collaborate on solving this global challenge. The Modern Slavery PEC's approach is rooted in human rights" (MS-PEC, 2021, p. 3).

The authors help lead the MS-PEC. One is the Director of Research at the MS-PEC and a professor of politics at the University of Liverpool, and the other is the Director of Policy Impact at the MS-PEC and has worked in government social research and policy advisor roles in the UK civil service. In the rest of this article, we draw on multiple sources, including relevant literature, narrative "impact case studies" on modern slavery and human trafficking from the UK's Research Evaluation Framework exercise (which took place in 2014 and 2021), a consultation on research priorities on modern slavery

---

[2]March 15, 2023: "311 migration experts sign a letter to The Times" https://channelcrossings.org/2023/03/15/311-migration-experts-sign-a-letter-to-the-times/

[3]https://www.gcomsoft.com/insights/why-a-lack-of-reliable-data-hinders-human-trafficking-prevention-programs-and-what-state-governments-can-do-about-it/

[4]https://news.stanford.edu/press-releases/2018/09/05/get-good-data-human-trafficking/

[5]https://cpr.unu.edu/research/projects/delta-8–7.html#outline

[6]5-year program implemented by Innovations for Poverty Action (IPA), funded by the Program to End Modern Slavery (PEMS), U.S. Department of State's Office to Monitor and Combat Trafficking in Persons (TIP Office).

[7]A global community of practice Monitoring, Evaluation and Learning professionals and researchers on anti-human trafficking.

[8]https://www.antislaverycommissioner.co.uk/news-insights/iasc-launch-research-priorities-briefing-paper/

[9]Total impact case studies submitted: 2014 = 6,637, 2021 = 6,361.

carried out by the MS-PEC in 2020, and our own experiences of engaging with policymakers on research, and funding and managing multiple research projects.[10]

We are interested in the evidence-policy system, the gaps and differences, why they persist, and what works to develop a more productive relationship. Sometimes, accounts of how evidence usage works can risk descending into an exchange of "slogans" between policymakers and critical scholars (Cairney, 2021). On the one side, there is the accusation that evidence is 'cherry-picked' by politicians to support dubious claims and to further a particular political approach (Thomas, 2022). While the concept of "evidence-based policymaking" (EBPM) is often criticized as betraying an overly positivist, empiricist understanding of the world, assuming research can produce reliable answers or that difficult "ethical and moral issues faced by policymakers can be reduced to questions of 'best evidence'" (Greenhalgh & Russell, 2009). We seek to develop a more constructive approach, identifying why and where the critical gaps or areas of difference are between the researcher and policymaker communities and developing new ways for these to be more effectively bridged. Before turning to this, it is helpful to provide some context on the UK's development of policies to address HTMS, because norms and practices around evidence usage in decision-making are embedded, as observed during the COVID-19 pandemic (Hadorn et al., 2022).

## Context: From Palermo to the UK's Modern Slavery Act

The HTMS policy field is relatively new, traced to an international agreement on a definition of human trafficking at Palermo in 2000 (UN, 2000). This agreement included one mention of research (Art 9: 2) and encouraged "information exchange and learning" (Art 10) but, in general, established a quite prescriptive framework for how states should address the issue, referred to as the 3 P's: prosecution, protection, and prevention. States like the UK have scope to determine their path to interpret, prioritize and integrate Palermo with existing policies. The UK's policy response, currently framed by the Modern Slavery Act (2015), sees the Palermo definition of human trafficking as one form of modern slavery, used as an umbrella term and including other types of exploitation, such as forced labor in business supply chains. There are multiple intersections and overlaps with other types of exploitation, leading to competition at the international level around appropriate terminology and policy responses (Chuang, 2014).

Implementation is also mediated via regional forms of governance. In the European context, this means additional agreements and instruments on human trafficking through the European Union (EU) and Council of Europe (CoE), both with elements of evidence and expertise. Notably, the European Convention on Action against Trafficking in human beings (ECAT)[11] included the creation of Group of Experts on Action against Trafficking in Human Beings (GRETA), an international "multidisciplinary" team that evaluates signatories every four years. The 2011 EU directive requires, among other things, the creation of national/special rapporteurs with a role that includes connecting evidence with policy, through scrutinizing policies, assessing trends, co-operating with other organizations and reporting.[12] Although the UK left the EU on 31 January 2020, it remained part of the Council of Europe and had already set up (from 2014) a similar position in the Independent Anti-Slavery Commissioner (IASC) to encourage best practice, which explicitly included the duty to "undertake or support the carrying out of research" (IASC, 2022, p. 46).[13]

In the UK, responsibility for HTMS sits with the Home Office, which has its tradition of carrying out and commissioning research, predominantly on crime and criminal justice issues. Capacity has grown significantly in the last 20 years with the growing number of researchers and analysts re-

[10] At the time of writing, the Modern Slavery PEC had funded teams comprising 89 academic team members from over 35 universities and academic institutions, 26 individuals from 17 NGOs, four private sector organizations several other governmental and international organizations, and independent parties.

[11] Adopted in 2005, came into force 2008.

[12] EU Directive 2011/36/EU "on preventing and combating trafficking in human beings and protecting its victims."

[13] This position has been vacant since April 2022.

organized under Science, Technology, Analysis, Research and Strategy (STARS) in 2020, which acts as "a strategic center that informs, drives, coheres and connects the delivery of the Home Office priorities across government and beyond."[14] Home Office Analysis and Insight, a Directorate within STARS, has more than 350 analysts.[15] Finally, it should be noted that this policy area is not only the responsibility of Westminster. The UK's devolved administrations have developed their own legislation and strategies, with some distinctions from the UK Government. For example, the Scottish Government uses the terminology "human trafficking and exploitation" in its legislation and strategy.[16]

## Evidence and UK Policy on HTMS: 4 Key Gaps

What are the critical gaps and differences around evidence and policy on HTMS in the UK? The following analysis is based primarily on three key sources: 1) a consultation into research priorities on modern slavery carried out between July and October 2020, including a short survey with 121 respondents and eight roundtables with experts and stakeholders (Balch, 2021); 2) analysis of impact case studies submitted in 2014 and 2021 to the UK's Research Evaluation Framework, where narrative examples of impact relating to research are submitted by UK academic institutions and published; and 3) internal monitoring and evaluation of the work and impact of the Modern Slavery PEC.

### *Prioritization*

There are several differences between stakeholders on the priorities for research into HTMS. This is not simply researchers versus policymakers; stakeholders in research include civil society and non-government organizations (NGOs) that play an essential role in delivering services and, perhaps most importantly, those directly affected. The consultation on research priorities by MS-PEC (Balch, 2021) identified some differences between these groups and areas of overlap and consensus. While policymakers strongly preferred research on the effectiveness of different interventions ("what works"), academics were keen to prioritize social justice and equity. NGOs (and some academics) championed equality, diversity, and inclusion (EDI) issues in research. There was, however, evidence of a consensus on prioritizing the meaningful inclusion of people with lived experience in research. In terms of different research areas, academics were more likely to say they prioritized research into "modern slavery in supply chains" and less likely to say they prioritized "preventing modern slavery" or "understanding survivor needs and enhancing victim support" when compared with non-academic respondents (Balch, 2021, p. 16).

Evidence from the 2014 and 2021 REF case studies indicates a growing body of academic work but also reveals quite specific approaches and priorities concerning impact. In both evaluations, researchers were less involved in strategic policy development and more focused on exerting influence via expert scrutiny. In 2014, there was more research helping develop support services or treatments for "at-risk" populations by relevant organizations, particularly NGOs, and research on the consequences of policy and services for groups such as sex workers, but the focus of this research was very geographically spread with relatively few projects specifically on the UK. In 2021, considerably more case studies appeared on supply chains. As of 2014, a key theme in terms of the type of impact was influenced through improving understanding/awareness of the problem itself or producing research that improves scrutiny of existing approaches because relatively fewer case studies claimed to have influenced UK governments' anti-trafficking policy development strategically. There may be several reasons for this, not least that the positive impacts of research directly helping those affected can be

[14]https://www.gov.uk/government/publications/home-office-annual-report-and-accounts-2020-to-2021
[15]A call for academics to present research findings in 2018 noted that HOA&I employs "more than 350 analysts" https://wrdtp.ac.uk/exciting-opportunity-at-the-home-office/
[16]Human Trafficking and Exploitation (Scotland) Act 2015 https://www.legislation.gov.uk/asp/2015/12/contents/enacted
Trafficking and Exploitation Strategy for Scotland 2017
https://www.gov.scot/policies/human-trafficking/trafficking-and-exploitation-strategy/

directly observable but could also indicate the importance of the other gaps highlighted here (e.g., synchronization, epistemology, trust) impacting the relationship between policymakers and researchers in this area.

In addition to consulting on research priorities across the sector, the MS-PEC has sought to navigate and bridge gaps in research priorities between those creating the "demand" for policy-oriented research and those who "supply" research. The MS-PEC regularly engages with policy officials working on modern slavery to understand their ongoing priorities for evidence. We have found that policymakers' needs for evidence often fall into two broad categories: "evergreen" or "responsive". The former refers to strategic areas of interest, such as what works and for whom in addressing HTMS, while the latter refers to more narrow and specific needs for evidence, such as how a specific policy is working in practice or the nature of a particular issue. The MS-PEC has designed various research funding and commissioning models that enable funding of a portfolio of longer-term projects that address "evergreen" policy priorities and more agile and focused projects that address "responsive" evidence gaps. The MS-PEC funds most of its research through open funding calls that set the objectives for research in consultation with policymakers and people with lived experience to increase the research projects' relevance. Throughout research projects, the MS-PEC is "hands-on" with funded research teams, supporting projects to maximize their policy impact.

### *Epistemology*

When working with researchers, practitioners, and policymakers, the different understandings of the nuances, strengths, and weaknesses of different types of knowledge and knowledge production can be quite noticeable. Differences remain over perceptions of the meaning/value of (or problems with) the terms "modern slavery" and "human trafficking," and around the causal understandings of the phenomena and linkages with other policy issues and agendas. As mentioned earlier, there is one area of growing consensus: the value of lived experience as an important type of evidence and expertise. However, more work is needed to integrate this into the evidence-policy system and establish the appropriate standards for research that meaningfully engages and includes people with lived experience to avoid it being unethical and tokenistic (Asquith et al., 2022).

Different preferences exist over methodological approaches (qualitative vs quantitative), but these link to different understandings of the strengths and weaknesses of such approaches, sampling techniques, etc. and the extent to which findings can support recommendations or courses of action. The MS-PEC has developed new ways to communicate these complexities to policymakers but also works intensively with funded research teams, encouraging them to establish clear linkages between findings and recommendations and to explain the relative strengths and limitations of methods and findings in written and verbal briefings to policymakers.

One assumption is that policymakers prefer "hard data," economic modeling, cost-benefit analysis or randomized control trial (RCT) and are skeptical of any work with a more humanities-type approach. For issues like HTMS, it may not always be possible or ethical to carry out RCTs to accurately determine the effectiveness of different interventions. These kinds of approaches to evidence may even be at odds with scholarship on social issues, where problems are usually understood to be complex, systemic, or "wicked" (Eden & Wagstaff, 2021). There is undoubtedly greater demand from policymakers for "hard" social science, and while there is a sub-set of researchers working on prevalence methodologies and quasi-experimental studies, research in this area is generally dominated by qualitative approaches. This could be for several reasons, not least because this type of research can have lower costs; the short history of research in the area also means that measures and indicators are relatively new, not standardized or still being developed, so quantitative techniques are not yet viable. Our consultation on research priorities also revealed a desire for researchers and civil society to focus on a deeper understanding of the phenomena itself and foreground the experiences of those affected and the role of context, all conducive to qualitative approaches from the arts and humanities.

Notwithstanding this, we have found policymakers open to the merits of qualitative and small-sample studies. Moreover, their interest in more and "better" data to inform decisions on HTMS is shared by other research stakeholders. It is just that this means different things to different groups – depending on what that data is, who collects and holds it, what analysis/research can be carried out with it, and for what purpose. There are well-documented challenges around the ethics of data, but also more practical obstacles to achieving the potential of data science approaches, including the difficulties of sharing data between government, non-government organizations, and research teams. Preparing data for research can be costly, and an understandably cautious approach when data relates to criminal and traumatic experiences means the barriers to sharing are high.

### *Synchronization*

One of the biggest challenges to bridge for those working on the evidence-policy system is the gap between the timing for policymakers who need research to inform decisions, and the timescales required to carry out that research, especially if it is to be done equitably, inclusively, and to involve lived experience. It is often assumed that policymakers need evidence as quickly as possible, and this is often true, but there are also the longer-term ("evergreen") priorities that are less time-bound. Ultimately, there are limits to synchronization: even apparently "responsive" and narrow demands for new research can be dynamic, for example, as politicians' priorities evolve. This is particularly evident when trying to insert evidence into the development of legislation, where Bills are frequently amended as they pass through Parliament.

The MS-PEC has designed multiple research commissioning models to ensure a balanced portfolio between agile, quick turnaround research and longer-term 12-month projects. The MS-PEC's regular engagement with policy officials has also been an opportunity to maintain an open dialogue about the schedule that policymakers are working to and build policymakers' understanding of what kinds of research on HTMS are possible within different timescales. Evidence reviews assessing existing literature can be completed more quickly than survivor-involved empirical research, which requires ethical clearance processes and recruitment of a research team. The MS-PEC has increasingly drawn on the capacity and expertise of its core team members to produce highly agile syntheses of evidence, for example, to inform Parliamentary committee inquiries or to set out the evidence base on an issue via Policy Briefs. A key challenge remains for responsive research and rapid reviews to meaningfully include or be led by those with lived experience.

### *Trust*

Developing trusted and resilient relationships between policymakers and those involved in producing research is central to addressing all the gaps and differences outlined above. The results of the MS-PEC consultation showed that the bridge-building challenge extends beyond connecting academics and officials – it highlighted the need to create a more inclusive and collaborative space to enhance the quality and potential impact of research.

Researcher (dis)engagement with the Home Office is tied up with political differences and previous experience, e.g., criminologists calling for a boycott based on how their work had been used (Walters, 2008). Conventional wisdom is that most academics ideologically oppose Home Office priorities, particularly on immigration (Van de Werfhorst, 2020). Added to this is the growing willingness of some prominent UK politicians to denigrate experts and expertise, which creates a challenging backdrop to productive engagement (Norris & Inglehart, 2019). Even more complicated is bringing together policymakers with survivors who have had negative experiences with other Home Office officials working in immigration and asylum.

The MS-PEC's core organizational values of independence and transparency[17] have established a clear position in the research-policy ecosystem, which is impartial and nonpartisan. The MS-PEC has sought to act as a convenor, bringing together different groups working to understand and address HTMS that may not typically interact and to maintain an ongoing dialogue with and between policymakers and researchers.

There are practical issues which are more easily bridged. Our experience suggests that, on the one hand, researchers are unaware of both the policy processes in the areas they are conducting research, and the level of expertise officials may have in their field. On the other hand, officials can find some academic work inaccessible and difficult to filter and identify relevant findings from the rapidly growing pool of gray literature.

Since its launch in 2019, the MS-PEC has developed different strands of ongoing engagement with stakeholders in research and policy on HTMS. In 2022, more than 80 meetings were conducted with policymakers and stakeholders and encompassed other partnership work, including the development of platforms for collaboration. The research priorities exercise led to the funding of new research on EDI and an agenda on survivor inclusion. In practice, this means putting in place processes for equitable inclusion in research production, such as requiring applicants to demonstrate commitment to partnerships and to consider meaningful ways to involve people (e.g., as peer researchers or through advisory groups). The MS-PEC has enabled this by increasing the proportion of funding available to non-academic partners and supporting research teams to begin influencing targets right from the start of the research process.

## Conclusions

There are a range of challenges and opportunities in bringing stakeholders together and improving the relationship between evidence and policy on HTMS. The evidence-policy relationship in this area is dynamic and fast-moving due to the complex and politicized nature of exploitation which is so intimately tied to structural hierarchies and inequalities. Gaps and differences thus persist across many aspects of this area, but there are signs of convergence around changing norms over "what counts" as evidence, "who counts" as an expert, and how research should be funded and carried out. This connects with a shared desire for a more ethical, equitable, and inclusive approach to research, rooted in the conviction that this is the best pathway to generating the kinds of impactful evidence to support policymakers in making better decisions.

Is it possible for a more responsive, synchronized, evidence-policy system to be built that both responds to this desire for better research but also improves how governments approach and combat HTMS? The examination of key gaps presented here suggests that some differences can be narrowed, but the objective should not be simple alignment because there is a productive tension in having greater diversity in the research field and in exposing decision-makers to new kinds of evidence and expertise. Consensus is not the point: the most potent evidence will challenge problematic assumptions about causality and disrupt systems and preferences tied to vested interests.

The risks to, and fragility of, this evidence-policy system thus becomes apparent. We saw this in the UK in 2022–2023 when a political shift suddenly and significantly widened gaps between evidence and policy on HTMS. This can appear to unravel the long-term, painstaking work to build bridges between different actors in the evidence-policy space. But it only further underlines the importance of sustaining trust and resilience in those relationships. New arguments about HTMS, however tenuous or politically inspired, require careful and rigorous scrutiny and investigation; it is through research and evidence involving those directly affected that their power with policy development can be strengthened or weakened. For entities such as the Modern Slavery and Human Rights Policy and Evidence Centre, the challenge only strengthens our resolve to develop new high-quality evidence in

[17] https://modernslaverypec.org/resources/strategy.

collaboration with those directly affected and to continue on a journey to deepen our understanding in a way that includes both researchers and policymakers.

## Disclosure statement

No potential conflict of interest was reported by the author(s).

## References

Asquith, W., Kiconco, A., & Balch, A. (2022). *A review of promising practices in the engagement of people with lived experience to address modern slavery and human trafficking*. University of Liverpool and MS- PEC.

Balch, A. (2021). *'Consultation on the modern slavery PEC's research priorities' modern slavery and human rights policy and evidence centre*. Bingham Centre, British Institute for International Comparative Law.

Balch, A., & Geddes, A. (2011). Opportunity from crisis? Organisational responses to human trafficking in the UK. *The British Journal of Politics and International Relations, 13*(1), 26–41. https://doi.org/10.1111/j.1467-856X.2010.00437.x

Broad, R., & Turnbull, N. (2019). From human trafficking to modern slavery: The development of anti-trafficking policy in the UK. *European Journal on Criminal Policy and Research, 25*(2), 119–133. https://doi.org/10.1007/s10610-018-9375-4

Bryant, K., & Landman, T. (2020). Combatting human trafficking since Palermo: What do we know about what works? *Journal of Human Trafficking, 6*(2), 119–140. https://doi.org/10.1080/23322705.2020.1690097

Cairney, P. (2021). *The politics of policy analysis*. Palgrave Pivot.

Chuang, J.(2014). Exploitation creep and the unmaking of human trafficking law. *The American Journal of International Law, 108*(4), 609–649. https://doi.org/10.5305/amerjintelaw.108.4.0609

CPA. (2018). *'Reducing modern slavery', house of commons, committee of public accounts, thirty-sixth report of session 2017–19*. https://publications.parliament.uk/pa/cm201719/cmselect/cmpubacc/886/886.pdf

Eden, L., & Wagstaff, M. F. (2021). Evidence-based policymaking and the wicked problem of SDG 5 gender equality. *Journal of International Business Policy, 4*(1), 28–57. https://doi.org/10.1057/s42214-020-00054-w

Greenhalgh, T., & Russell, J. (2009). Evidence-Based Policymaking: A Critique. *Perspectives in Biology and Medicine, 52* (2), 304–318. Project MUSE. https://doi.org/10.1353/pbm.0.0085

Hadorn, S., Sager, F., Mavrot, C., Malandrino, A., & Ege, J. (2022). Evidence-based policymaking in times of acute crisis: Comparing the use of scientific knowledge in Germany, Switzerland, and Italy. *Politische Vierteljahresschrift, 63*(2), 359–382. https://doi.org/10.1007/s11615-022-00382-x

HOAI. (2020). Sovereign borders: International asylum comparisons report (section 1: Drivers and impact on asylum migration journeys)'. *Migration and Border Analysis September 2020, Home Office Analysis and Insight*. https://freemovement.org.uk/wp-content/uploads/2022/11/Annex-A-Sovereign-Borders-International-Asylum-Comparisons-Report-Section-1-Drivers-and-impact-on-asylum-migration-journeys.pdf

Humpherson, E. (2022). *'Ed Humpherson to Jennifer Rubin: Use of National referral mechanism statistics' letter published 8 December 2022 from the director general for regulation at the office For statistics regulation* https://osr.statisticsauthority.gov.uk/correspondence/ed-humpherson-to-jennifer-rubin-use-of-national-referral-mechanism-statistics/

IASC. (2022). *'Independent anti-slavery commissioner, annual report 2021-2022', presented to parliament pursuant to section 42 (10) (b) of the modern slavery Act 2015, April 2022*. https://assets.publishing.service.gov.uk/government/uploads/system/uploads/attachment_data/file/1070482/E02718100_Un-num_Act_Independent_Anti-Slavery_Commission_Web_Accessible.pdf

ICAI. (2020). 'The UK's approach to tackling modern slavery through the aid programme', report published by the Independent Commission for aid Impact (ICAI), 14th October, https://icai.independent.gov.uk/review/the-uks-approach-to-tackling-modern-slavery-through-the-aid-programme

Loff, B., & Sanghera, J. (2004). Distortions and difficulties in data for trafficking. *Lancet, 363*(9408), 566. Health Research Premium collection. https://doi.org/10.1016/S0140-6736(04)15548-7

McDonald, W. F.(2014). Explaining the under-performance of the anti-human-trafficking campaign: Experience from the United States and europe. *Crime, Law, & Social Change, 61*, 125–138.

MS-PEC. (2021). *'Strategic delivery plan' modern slavery and human rights policy and evidence centre*. Bingham Centre, British Institute for International Comparative Law (BIICL). https://modernslaverypec.org/assets/downloads/Modern-Slavery-PEC-Strategy.pdf

Norris, P., & Inglehart, R. (2019). *Cultural backlash: Trump, Brexit, and authoritarian populism, Cambridge*. University Press.

O'Connell Davidson, J. (2015). *Modern slavery: The margins of freedom*. Palgrave Macmillan.

Thomas, G. (2022). Evidence, schmevidence: The abuse of the word "evidence" in policy discourse about education. *Educational Review, 75*(7), 1297–1312. https://doi.org/10.1080/00131911.2022.2028735

UN. (2000). 'Protocol to prevent, suppress and punish trafficking in persons especially women and children, supplementing the United Nations convention against transnational organized crime' United Nations General Assembly resolution 55/25. 15 November 2000.

Van de Werfhorst, H. G. (2020). Are universities left-wing bastions? The political orientation of professors, professionals, and managers in Europe. *The British Journal of Sociology*, *71*(1), 47–73. https://doi.org/10.1111/1468-4446.12716

Walters, R. (2008). Government crime policy and moral contamination. *Criminal Justice Matters*, *72*(1), 39–41. https://doi.org/10.1080/09627250802058565

# Making Statistics on Human Trafficking Work

Jan Van Dijk

**ABSTRACT**

An overview is given of available international statistics on victims of human trafficking from official records (UNODC and Eurostat), survey research (Walk Free) and Multiple Systems Estimation. It is argued that official figures should be seen as output indicators of law enforcement and other involved institutions rather than as indicators of prevalence. The author welcomes the Global Slavery Index of Walk Free and Multiple Systems Estimations applied to multi-source datasets on trafficking victims as more credible sources of information on true prevalence. These two data sources should be consolidated into a comprehensive analysis to enhance the overall impact of available datasets on policymaking.

## Introduction

This paper reviews the state of measuring or estimating the prevalence of human trafficking worldwide. The statistics of officially recorded victims collated by United Nations Office on Drugs and Crime (UNODC) and Eurostat will be presented and compared first, followed by the survey-based estimates of the Global Slavery Index and actual prevalence estimates based on Multiple Systems Estimation. Although each of these statistical systems has limitations and merits, their utility for academic and policy purposes would be significantly enhanced if they were consolidated and analyzed comprehensively, which is the gap in the current development of human trafficking estimation methodology.

## Official Statistics on Victims of Human Trafficking

Two particular circumstances facilitate the collection of international statistics on detected victims of trafficking. First, trafficking is a rare crime for which the United Nations adopted a broad international legal definition as part of the Palermo Protocol on Trafficking in Persons, adopted in 2000 by the United Nations and almost universally ratified since then. Second, an increasing number of countries have set up special multi-institutional arrangements for the identification of presumed victims of trafficking by both law enforcement and service providers, so-called National Referral Mechanisms (Organization for Security and Economic Cooperation in Europe [OSCE], 2004). These mechanisms allow for the collection of more comprehensive statistics on detected victims.

Since 2003 UNODC has published international statistics on officially identified victims in its Global Reports on Trafficking in Persons (GLOTIP). The latest report shows that the number of detected victims has shown a steady upward trend since 2003 but has dropped in 2020 by 11% compared to 2019. If these statistics would indeed, as the title of the report suggests, provide information on the trends in trafficking in persons, the downward swing would be interpreted as evidence that COVID measures, or sustained anti-trafficking efforts, have reduced prevalence. The report concludes that the decline in the number of identified victims could also result from reduced opportunities for effective law enforcement due to COVID measures or reduced institutional capacity to detect victims. In other words, these statistics on detected victims provide little or no useful information on trends in trafficking in persons over time.

The UN's Global Report on Trafficking in Persons presents no statistics on individual countries, but these can be derived from the underlying datasets with some difficulties. Table 1 shows the total number of victims in 2020 from a selection of the world's largest countries.

The national numbers of recorded victims show a strikingly high degree of variation. By far, the highest rates are reported by the UK and India. By comparison, the absolute numbers registered in Brazil and the USA are much lower and in Japan, China and Russia even lower still. The German rates compare poorly with those of the UK, a country with a similarly sized population in the same region. The comparatively low numbers of several of the largest countries suggest fundamental insufficiencies in their methods of identifying victims of human trafficking. Most of them, including the USA and Germany, lack nationwide identification mechanisms like those in the UK. They most likely refer to victims identified by federal law enforcement agencies. Without detailed metadata, the numbers cannot be adequately understood.

The numbers of many countries also show significant instability over time. This lack of stability over time points to changes in identification and/or recording mechanisms.[1] The conclusion that these statistics on recorded victims alone provide no helpful information on what is happening with human trafficking globally or in individual countries seems hard to escape.

Within Europe, Eurostat, the statistical arm of the European Commission, regularly reports on detected victims in the 27 Member States of the European Union. Since these countries are part of an economic and political union that has passed mandatory legislation on anti-trafficking policies, some measure of uniformity in recording detected victims is expected. The latest publication shows that the number of registered victims has since 2008 continued to fluctuate around 7,000, suggesting that the mechanisms to detect and record victims are indeed relatively stable compared to those across the world. However, rates of individual countries for 2020 and 2021 per one million inhabitants (with data from the UK conspicuously missing) show massive variations in the levels and trends over time (see Figure 1).

The Eurostat report mentions that the high rate of Luxembourg, a mini-state, in 2021 is caused by a one-off police raid on a labor exploitation ring. The variation between the other countries is hard to understand. A previous in-depth analysis of the EU data on human trafficking (van Dijk et al., 2014) showed that this variation primarily reflects differences in the recording systems of the Member States. The relatively low numbers of recorded victims reported on by Germany, for example, relate to victims

**Table 1.** Absolute Numbers of Detected Victims per Country in 2020.

| Country | *2020* |
|---|---|
| Brazil | *313(labor exploitation)* |
| China | *<5* |
| Germany | *494* |
| India | *4,709* |
| Japan | *48* |
| Russia | *290* |
| UK | *10,613* |
| USA | *704* |

Source: UNODC's GLOTIP dataset.

[1]The 2018 UNODC report provided several examples of sudden increases in the number of detected victims in a country after the introduction of new institutions or anti-trafficking policies (United Nations Office on Drugs and Crime UNODC, 2018).

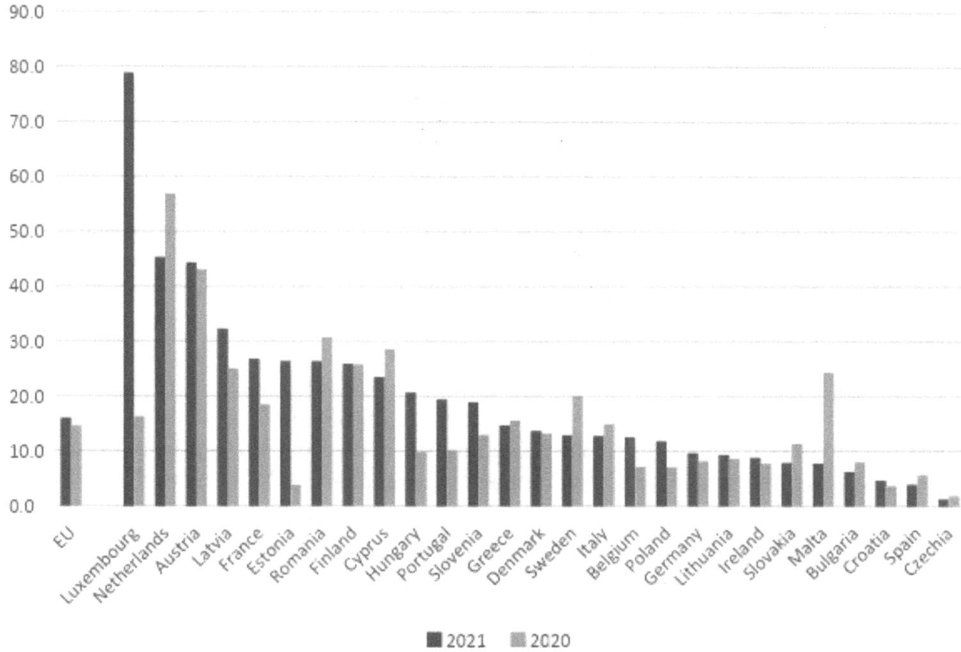


**Figure 1.** Identified victims of trafficking in persons per 1 million inhabitants in 2020 and 2021 in the EU. Source: Eurostat (2023).

recorded by the police only, excluding those recorded by NGO's. At the other extreme, the Netherlands reported on all persons showing "any sign of having been trafficked" encountered by state institutions or a wide range of dedicated NGOs. The UK similarly collects data on all persons identified as presumed victims of trafficking by "first responders" including NGOs. Apparently, the UK, or Eurostat itself, has decided not to include these comparatively high numbers (see Table 1 above for UK figures on 2020) in the Eurostat publication.

Considering the vast differences in operationalizing an identified or presumed victim, the EU statistics on detected victims are as incomparable to each other as those in the UNODC's global database. Statistics on detected victims of trafficking are only meaningful when presented together with detailed information on the legal and institutional settings of their production. In this respect, the UNODC and the Eurostat reports are flawed as meaningful statistics.

The fact that statistics on recorded victims of human trafficking say next to nothing about the prevalence of human trafficking does not mean they provide no useful information. They can be used to identify gaps between the number of identified victims and the number of successful prosecutions of traffickers (GRETA, 2015; UNODC, 2018). In many countries, especially some countries in Africa and Asia, as well as some countries in Europe, the latter gaps are so huge thus suggesting near impunity for traffickers (UNODC, 2023). They can also be used to calculate which proportions of identified victims receive assistance, residence permits or compensation.

The main point here is that official counts of detected victims should be seen not as proxy indicators of the prevalence of human trafficking but as indicators of the outputs of the institutions and NGOs involved in the fight against human trafficking. This point is underlined by the fact that the two European countries with the most identified victims, the UK and the Netherlands, feature at the top of Walk Free's performance index in anti-trafficking policies (to be discussed below). The better actions against trafficking are resourced, the more victims are detected. It would obviously be highly misleading to interpret these numbers as an indicator of high prevalence.

Since statistics on detected victims are only meaningful in their national institutional context, they should preferably be presented on a country-by-country basis detailing which institutions have been involved in their production and the resources available. If these conditions are met, they would be highly informative as indicators of the output of anti-trafficking actions and indicative of their effectiveness.

## Estimating True Prevalence Through Survey Research

A significant event in the field of trafficking statistics was the commissioning by the Australian NGO Walk Free of fully standardized surveys among representative, probabilistic samples of national populations to estimate true prevalence along the lines of the International Crime Victims Survey. The program executed in the frame of the Gallup World Poll was expanded in 2021 to surveys in no less than 68 countries, including, for the first time, several European, including Western European countries (Walk Free, 2023). In collaboration with International Labour Organization (ILO) and the latest batch, the International Organization of Migration, estimates are made of global and regional prevalence of various forms of human trafficking/modern slavery, published as the Global Estimates of Modern Slavery (Global Estimates) (International Labour Organization, Walk Free and International Organization for Migration, 2022) Through imputation and risk modeling, estimates are also made of the national rates of 170 countries.[2] In addition, the organization has designed indices for the vulnerability of countries to human trafficking and the quality of their governments responses to it (Government Responses Index). The latter index can be seen as a refined and politically independent alternative to the TIP ratings from the US State Department (transposed into a quantitative index by Young Cho, 2013).

Although the Global Slavery Index (GSI) has been criticized for its methodological shortcomings (Gallagher, 2017; DELTA 8.7, 2019), its latest edition, based on surveys in 68 countries, unquestionably provides a rough yet credible comparative measure of the true prevalence of various forms of human trafficking across the world, unaffected by legal peculiarities and varying detection or recording practices of individual countries. As with surveys on victimization by common crimes, especially violent crime, the estimated prevalence tends to be many times higher than the recorded numbers. Possibly, the rates are inflated by misperceptions of some respondents about what has happened to them in recent years or other shortcomings of survey-based estimates. At this juncture, however, the critical challenge for the GSI does not seem to lie in its methodology -which, considering the track record of ILO and Walk Free, is likely to be incrementally further improved over the years – but in its disappointedly low impact on national policymaking.[3] This is especially true in the Western world. The GSI is rarely referred to in governmental documents, and even media coverage seems disappointing and diminishing.[4] This lack of recognition in governmental circles probably hinges on issues of governance – the sponsor being a private foundation rather than an intergovernmental institution.[5]

But its underutilization might also be contingent on how the data is analyzed and presented: a mere ranking of countries according to the survey-based estimates. Its impact could probably be enhanced with analyses of how official figures and survey-based estimates can supplement each other, as previously demonstrated with official and survey-based statistics concerning common crimes (Lynch & Addington, 2006). To give just one obvious example, recent declines in many countries in the recorded numbers of detected victims, as reported by UNODC, could be usefully crosschecked against the GSI prevalence estimates to see whether they reflect changes in detection, true prevalence or both.[6] The results of such analysis might be received better by policymakers because they provide

[2]The IOM database on repatriated victims is used for the estimation of victims of trafficking for sexual exploitation.
[3]This is not to say that there is no need for extended survey research on human trafficking. Considering the concentration of victimization among hard-to-find population segments, such as illegal migrants in many western countries, bespoke surveys applying innovative sampling strategies are urgently called for (Zhang et al., 2014).
[4]Illustrative for the lack of official recognition is the absence of references to the GSI indices or the Government Responses index in the country reports of GRETA and the TIP reports of the USA State Department.
[5]Many governments consider crime rates as politically sensitive information (van Dijk, 2008). For this reason, they are reluctant to acknowledge indicators that have been produced outside their administrative control.
[6]Given the limited sizes of the samples in the Gallup World Poll (usually 1.000 per country) changes between two sweeps might not be statistically significant. The repeat of the GWP will permit combining samples from two or more years and averaging the victimization rates.

more pertinent information than the one-dimensional ranking tables of the GSI and because the "official figures" have been made part of the equation.

## MSE

In countries with functioning National Referral Mechanisms, victims of human trafficking are often identified by several governmental agencies such as the police, immigration and labor inspectorates as well as by NGOs delivering services to victims. While the possibility of the same victims being recorded by two or more organizations was initially regarded as compromising the counts of detected victims, recording the same victims on more than one list offers opportunities for estimating the actual numbers through statistical modeling. The technical terms for such modeling are Capture Recapture analysis and the more advanced version of Multiple Systems Estimation (MSE). In 2022 UNODC published a manual on the use of MSE for estimating the true prevalence of human trafficking, building on the experiences of projects in several countries, including the UK, the Netherlands, Romania, Ireland, Serbia, the USA and Australia (UNODC, 2022). An MSE-based estimate was also made using a multi-source dataset on detected trafficking victims from Spain (UNODC, 2023).

In the UK, the true volume of victims, as estimated through MSE, using data from inter alia the police, labor inspectors and NGOs, was four times higher than the number of identified victims. In the Netherlands, the number was estimated to be five times the official number. On average, the estimated numbers were found to be three or four times higher than the observed numbers. The Dutch estimates differentiate between gender, age (minor/adult), Dutch national/non-Dutch national and type of exploitation (sexual/non-sexual) of the victims. The estimations show that victims of non-sexual exploitation (forced labor) and child victims are significantly less likely to be identified than other categories. This finding by itself is of immediate relevance for policy-setting, regardless of the prevalence estimates. The Dutch estimates were recently extended up to 2020 and now cover a ten-year period (van Dijk et al., 2021). The latest results suggest that the falls in observed numbers of victims of sexual exploitation in the Netherlands since 2015 may at least partly reflect a decline in prevalence.

MSE-based estimates can be regarded as the numbers that existing National Referral Mechanisms would record if all agencies involved would maximize their identification efforts. These estimates may possibly miss the cases that remain hidden from the authorities and NGOs or fall outside their existing operational mandates.[7]

For governments, MSE is a cost-effective method to gauge the hidden numbers of human trafficking. It has the additional advantage that it takes as its starting point the government's administrative data, recorded by officially dedicated and/or publicly funded institutions working within the legal and operational infrastructure of the country. For this reason, MSE-based estimates provide pertinent feedback to policymakers on the number of victims, which could be recorded if all institutions involved in detecting and supporting victims were fully functional and optimally resourced. The knowledge that, for example, four times more child victims could potentially be reached if detection efforts were stepped up allows policymakers to set realistic, evidence-based targets for their country's anti-trafficking policies within a chosen timeframe and earmarked budget.

## Discussion

As discussed above, national rates are available regularly on the official figures regarding detected victims, arrested and convicted offenders, and survey-based estimates of true prevalence for 150 or more countries. In addition, comprehensive national indices on governmental

[7]A pertinent example from the United Kingdom are minors working as drug couriers for so-called "county lines" in different parts of the country. By now, these minors make up a significant part of identified victims of trafficking, but they have largely been missed in the MSE study that used data from 2013 since few such victims had been recorded at the time.

performance are also available. If combined, the UNODC and GSI datasets offer opportunities for promising new quantitative analyses. As mentioned, changes in the number of detected victims should be checked against changes in true prevalence. Such analyses of supplementary statistics would provide policymakers with a better understanding of the meaning of their administrative statistics. In nations or regions where official figures of identified victims show declines while prevalence has remained roughly stable or has been increasing, focused analyses should subsequently be made of output indicators such as numbers of arrests and convictions and the national scores on the Government Responses Index to diagnose failures in resourcing the implementation of the near universally ratified Palermo Protocol. Where possible, the analyses could be further deepened and refined by looking at the results of MSE's on multi-source datasets of detected victims.

The combination of available datasets will not only allow cross-checking or triangulation of estimates. Integrated datasets will also create the potential for in-depth analytical work informing academic understanding and policymaking. An obvious challenge is a better understanding of the gaps between the level estimates of the three measurement modes at issue. For example, over the past five years, the number of officially identified victims in the Netherlands has stabilized at around 1,000. The prevalence rate has been estimated at 5,000 by MSE and 10,000 by the Walk Free's latest GSI. What selection processes determine the attrition of 10,000 victimization experiences into 1,000 officially identified persons? Hypotheses on the causes of this attrition should be empirically tested in as many countries as possible, building on the knowledge gained with the design and pilot testing of general and bespoke victimization surveys over the past 50 years.

Data availability in 150 or more countries over an increasing number of years opens many other possibilities for innovative quantitative analysis. Analyses of the ratios between arrests or convictions and detected victims should, for example, be expanded to include estimated prevalence. Such analyses are likely to reveal that in most parts of the world the chances for traffickers to be detected are even more minimal than assumed, putting into question the political will to tackle human trafficking.

Consolidating data on trafficking from various sources should not be limited to quantitative analysis alone. As argued above, data on detected victims is highly idiosyncratic and must ideally be presented in their national contexts. This is, to some extent, also true for data on arrests and convictions determined as they are by national legislation and practices. For this reason, data from various sources should also be combined in national narratives, as pioneered in the latest report on the Global Slavery Index for up to fifteen countries countries (https://www.walkfree.org/global-slavery-index/country-studies/united-kingdom/). These qualitative accounts could also integrate information on national case law stored in UNODC's Case-law Database, Sherloc.3 (https://www.unodc.org/unodc/data-and-analysis/glotip.html).

Over the past twenty years, great strides have been made in collecting international statistics on human trafficking. These newly available metrics have proven to be practical tools of global and national awareness raising. In combination with GRETA (the Group of Experts on Action against Trafficking in Human Beings) or the USA State Department evaluation reports, they may occasionally have pressurized countries into action. They have not, however, provided a comprehensive cognitive framework allowing policymakers and lobbyists to set quantitative targets for further action against human trafficking. If international statistics on victims of human trafficking – ideally based on fully harmonized recording, expanded standardized survey research and a more comprehensive application of MSE – would be consolidated and analyzed comprehensively, planning and monitoring for global and national actions against human trafficking could be put on stronger evidential footing.

## Disclosure statement

No potential conflict of interest was reported by the author(s).

## References


DELTA 8.7. (2019). Symposium: modelling modern slavery risk. Available online: http://collections.unu.edu/eserv/UNU:6722/Symposium_ModellingModernSlaveryRisk_Final.pdf

Eurostat. (2023). *Trafficking in Human beings*, EUROSTAT, Statistics Explained, January 2023. Retrieved July 18, 2023, from https://ec.europa.eu/eurostat

Gallagher, A. T. (2017). What's wrong with the Global Slavery Index?, *Anti-Trafficking Review*, 8, 2017, Retrieved July 18, 2023, from. https://doi.org/10.14197/atr.20121786

GRETA. (2015). *Fourth General report*, Council of Europe. Retrieved July 18, 2023, from https://rm.coe.int/16805aa45f.

International Labour Organization, Walk Free and International Organization for Migration. (2022), Global estimates of modern slavery: Forced Labour and Forced marriage , ILO. Retrieved July 18, 2023, from https://www.ilo.org/global/topics/forced-labour/publications/WCMS_854733/lang–en/index.htm

Lynch, J., & Addington, L. (Eds.), (2006). Introduction. In *Understanding crime statistics* (pp. 3–14). Cambridge University Press.

Organization for Security and Economic Cooperation in Europe (OSCE). (2004). *Joining efforts to protect the rights of trafficked persons*. A Practical Handbook.

United Nations Office on Drugs and Crime (UNODC). (2018). *Global Report on Trafficking in Persons 2016*, UNODC. Available online: http://www.unodc.org

United Nations Office on Drugs and Crime (UNODC). (2022). *Monitoring human trafficking prevalence through multiple systems estimation, a United Nations manual for policymakers, practitioners and researchers engaging with sustainable development goal 16.2.* UNODC.

United Nations Office on Drugs and Crime (UNODC). (2023). *Global Report on Trafficking in Persons 2022*, UNODC. Available online: https://www.unodc.org/unodc/data-and-analysis/glotip.html

van Dijk, J. J. M. (2008). *The world of crime: Breaking the silence on problems of security, justice and development across the world*. Sage.

van Dijk, J. J. M., Cruyff, P., & van der Heijden, G. M. (2021). *A multiple systems estimation of presumed victims of human trafficking in the Netherlands during 2016-2019 (full text only available in Dutch, with an English summary)*. WODC.

van Dijk, J. J. M., van der Knaap, L. M., Aebi, M. F. M., & Campistol, C. (2014). *Counting what counts: Tools for the validation and utilization of EU statistics on human trafficking*. PrismaPrint.

Walk Free. (2023). *The Global Slavery Index 2023*. Retrieved July 18, 2023, from https://www.walkfree.org/global-slavery-index/downloads/

Young Cho, S. (2013). Towards a Comprehensive Index on anti-trafficking policy- an assessment of the 3P Index, GRETA-based Scorecard and EuroStat. In J. Van Dijk, M. F. A. Van der Knaap, & C. Campistol, (Eds.), *Counting what counts: Tools for the validation and utilization of EU statistics on human trafficking* (pp. 154–198). PrismaPrint.

Zhang, S. X., Spiller, M. W., Finch, B. K., & Qin, Y. (2014). Estimating labor trafficking among unauthorized migrant workers in San Diego. *The Annals of the American Academy of Political and Social Science*, *653*(1), 65–86. https://doi.org/10.1177/0002716213519237

# Practitioner Reflection: Reliance on Informal and Gig Economies Leaves LGBTQ+ Populations with Fewer Economic Choices and Greater Vulnerability to Trafficking

Mark Kavenagh, Mackenzie Stoeltje, and Meredith Dank

**ABSTRACT**

Vulnerability to human trafficking is exacerbated by poverty, familial violence and abuse, homelessness, un- and under-employment, and migration. Many of these established vulnerabilities to human trafficking are also common vulnerabilities experienced by lesbian, gay, bisexual, transgender, queer and other (LGBTQ+) populations worldwide. Further, LGBTQ+ individuals face additional risks due to community and workplace stigma. These circumstances result in disproportionate barriers to formal employment, particularly in stable jobs that pay a living wage and are insulated from economic shocks. Yet anti-trafficking efforts frequently overlook LGBTQ+ people's particular needs. LGBTQ+ people frequently rely on insecure, informal, and gig economies for their livelihoods, making them susceptible to trafficking. Yet informal work opportunities also have positives. Individuals may maintain control of their work circumstances in ways they cannot if they work in formal settings. LGBTQ+ people report being able to choose contracts and clients or move on quickly when encountering unsafe situations. It should be noted that controlling our circumstances is a key tenet of trauma-informed support. Anti-trafficking interventions frequently seek transformational change with "rescue and rebuilding" underpinning programming. The authors propose an alternative model built around i) diversifying livelihood choices, ii) fostering psychological safety and iii) addressing the individual-level impacts of systemic stigma and discrimination.

Push and pull factors have been extensively explored in the human-trafficking literature, and correlations have been established between vulnerability to trafficking and factors such as poverty (Sheu et al., 2021), familial violence (Franchino-Olsen, 2021), abuse (Koegler et al., 2022), homelessness (Hogan & Roe-Sepowitz, 2023), un- and under-employment (John, 2019), and migration (Yousaf, 2018). Many established vulnerabilities to trafficking are common to lesbian, gay, bisexual, transgender, queer and other (LGBTQ+) populations generally, particularly in Global South countries. While research on LGBTQ+ vulnerability to trafficking outside the Global North remains scant, limited existing data resemble trends seen in the developed world (Chynoweth et al., 2020; Dwyer, 2022; U.S. Department of State, 2022). For example, LGBTQ+ populations in Global South countries have been shown to experience higher rates of sexual violence than the general population (Blondeel et al., 2018; Newman et al., 2021), and face challenges in educational attainment which can impact their labor market participation (Badgett et al., 2019; Feijo et al., 2022). Documented experiences by LGBTQ+ people of community and workplace stigma (United Nations Development Programme [UNDP] and United States Agency for International Development [USAID], 2014) add further to the barriers in accessing these formal work opportunities. They also have higher rates of homelessness resulting from escaping family discrimination or violence (End Child Prostitution and Trafficking [ECPAT] International, 2021; Lutnick, 2016); one study found that over 70% of gay and lesbian homeless youth in the United States reported family rejection regarding their sexual orientation as a major factor for being homeless, especially among lower-income families (Robinson, 2018). Additionally, LGBTQ+ individuals are disproportionately vulnerable to trafficking, due in part to underreporting (Hogan & Roe-Sepowitz, 2023). In most countries, North and South, vulnerabilities to trafficking are frequently exacerbated by stigma and discrimination on the basis of LGBTQ+ status. It is important to note that no research has been conducted to date specifically on the prevalence of trafficking among LGBTQ+ populations, and having a better understanding of the prevalence is essential for developing policies and interventions to reduce the risk of human trafficking (David, 2017).

### *Over-Reliance on Informal Economies*

Frequently, LGBTQ+ individuals encounter significant barriers when accessing formal employment, particularly in stable jobs, that pay a living wage, and are protected from economic shocks (Bosley-Smith, 2023; Carpenter et al., 2022). In countries with large informal economies, like Thailand, LGBTQ+ people therefore gravitate toward informal economies with less job security and benefits, including trading sex (Suriyasarn, 2016). Over 60% of Thailand's workforce may be engaged in the informal economy in some way (Kongtip et al., 2015), which is defined by the ILO (International Labor Organization) as "all economic activities by workers and economic units that are – in law or in practice – not covered or insufficiently covered by formal arrangements" (International Labor Organization, 2024). Inclusion in the informal economy has increasingly also involved emerging "gig" economies over the past decade, such as ride-sharing, delivery and professional services, especially in the wake of the economic difficulties precipitated by COVID-19 (Mieruch & McFarlane, 2022). Work within "gig" economies often refers to short-term work completed through online or digital platforms, where providers of a service are connected to a consumer and paid directly per service rendered (Mieruch & McFarlane, 2022).

The COVID-19 pandemic led to an increase in the gig economy in many countries due to the increased demand of specialized services and delivery networks (Gupta & Gupta, 2023). However, individuals engaged in "gig" economies or informal employment have little protection from economic and social shocks, as witnessed during and in the wake of the COVID-19 pandemic (Komin et al., 2021). This reduced autonomy over their circumstances leaves them vulnerable to exploitation and the increased risk of trafficking (McAdam, 2020). Ongoing reliance on insecure livelihood options maintains vulnerability to situations of exploitation/trafficking (Janyam et al., 2020) and could even enhance susceptibility to trafficking by engendering a readiness to gamble with a continuing array of presented opportunities based on perceived payoffs.

Yet informal and gig livelihood opportunities also have some positive implications for LGBTQ+ populations. Many advocates for "gig" work mention the flexibility of the work as well as the ability for individuals to supplement their income or find alternative means of employment, especially for those who otherwise experience workplace discrimination (Johnston & Land-Kazlauskas, 2018). Individuals may be able to maintain control of their working circumstances in ways they cannot in formal work settings. For example, LGBTQ+ people may choose or decline contracts and clients or can move on quickly when encountering unsafe situations, discrimination or stigma. It should be noted that controlling our circumstances is a key tenet of trauma-informed care responses to trafficking (Centers for Disease Control and Prevention [CDC], 2020). Trauma-informed counter-trafficking approaches should initially focus on physical and psychological safety, the provision of basic needs, a non-judgmental stance, and building upon strengths and support networks (Kavenagh et al., 2023).

In this paper, the authors present elements of the existing global literature that are relevant to understanding LGBTQ+ populations' vulnerability to trafficking. In response to the identified broad gap in literature from the Global South, emphasis is placed on demonstrating how reduced autonomy over economic circumstances increases vulnerability to sex trafficking of

LGBTQ+ people in Thailand as a case example that applies global trends to local context. A reliance on informal economies is noted for LGBTQ+ individuals, which can generate risk. However, it is argued that increasing autonomy over economic circumstances within informal settings, including trading sex, can reduce vulnerability while simultaneously reinforcing some of the benefits in agency and personal safety that informal work settings can represent to LGBTQ+ people.

Counter-trafficking programming commonly promotes addressing risk factors and institutional vulnerabilities among target populations (Akanbi, 2020). Although the adoption of the UN Trafficking Protocol of 2000 increased the prevalence of counter-trafficking interventions (Alam et al., 2023), there is also currently no global standard for evaluating trafficking indicators and counter-trafficking efforts (Akanbi, 2020). Research on the efficacy of counter-trafficking efforts in various regions of Asia indicates that although steps are being taken to minimize the risk of trafficking in these areas, there are still many gaps to be addressed (Akanbi, 2020; Dwi, 2021; Tan & Segrave, 2020). Many of the counter-trafficking responses in Southeast Asia also focus more on relying on the criminal justice system rather than taking a victim-centered approach (Denney et al., 2023). The authors propose an alternative harm-minimization model that prioritizes agency for LGBTQ+ people vulnerable to sex trafficking. The proposed model i) diversifies livelihood choices, ii) fosters psychological safety, and iii) addresses the individual-level impacts of systemic stigma and discrimination while leaving autonomy for change in the hands of LGTBQ+ people.

### *Measuring LGBTQ+ Vulnerability to Trafficking*

It has been argued elsewhere that measuring trafficked populations presents challenges due to the hidden nature of the population, making identification and outreach difficult (Bryant & Landman, 2020; Farrell & De Vries, 2020; Farrell & Reichert, 2017; Zhang, 2022). Estimating prevalence is hindered by difficulties in accurately defining what constitutes trafficking activities and issues in the methodologies used to obtain accurate population estimates for a hard-to-reach population (Zhang & Larsen, 2021). Additionally, it may also be difficult to use universal indicators to achieve an unbiased estimate of trafficked populations (widely considered a "hidden population"), which are reflective of sociopolitical environments and institutional agendas regarding counter-trafficking efforts (Engle Merry, 2016). Furthermore, many trafficked individuals are hesitant to seek help due to fear of retribution, fear of the police, or past and present trauma, which limits their ability to take these measures for their own protection (Farrell & De Vries, 2020). Even when individuals do come forward, they may not always be recognized as trafficking survivors due to a lack of awareness and training for law enforcement officials and service providers (Farrell et al., 2019). These challenges limit the ability of counter-trafficking efforts to support survivors, identify risk and protective factors, and develop evidence-based interventions and policies (Schroeder et al., 2022).

The terminology used to describe human trafficking, particularly in relation to victimized individuals, has been the subject of extensive discussion. Many individuals may be highly reluctant or unable to self-identify as victims due to the shame and stigmatization associated with some of the rhetoric used to label survivors (Hoyle et al., 2011), particularly regarding sex trafficking (Camak & RNC-MNN, 2022). This reluctance further discourages individuals from self-identifying and limits prevalence estimation efforts. While self-identification sensitivities exist in all human-trafficking discourse, special care must be taken in the terminology used to describe sex trafficking and victimization for LGBTQ+ people, considering the intersection and impact of multiple minority identities. LGBTQ+ trafficking survivors may experience unique challenges in self-identifying, such as the impact of homophobia in engendering silent suffering (Chynoweth et al., 2020) or gender norm-based victim-blaming stereotypes; such stereotypes serve to invalidate lived experience and perpetuate perceptions that LGBTQ+ populations are promiscuous, actively engaged in their own exploitation or are less impacted by such experiences (Kavenagh et al., 2023). This is further compounded by challenges with providers when affirming identities and offering survivor-centered, trauma-informed care, as uninformed providers may use outdated terminology pertaining to the LGBTQ+ community or foster harmful preconceived assumptions in regard to trading sex among the community (Gerassi & Pederson, 2022).

However, the low visibility of LGBTQ+ populations in the human-trafficking research literature results from more fronts than only discouragement of self-identification. Acceptance of prevailing gender norms and the perceived privacy of certain measurement efforts affects reporting of non-heterosexual identities. Gender norms influence social behavior, status and, unfortunately, stigma. Such norms maintain power hierarchies and patriarchal structures that limit access to resources and freedoms for those outside (Connell, 2005, Darmstadt et al., 2019). In Thailand, heteronormative expectations and a rigid gender binary create well-recognized challenges for women (and in some ways for men), but these can be even more challenging for LGBTQ+ people who tend to fall outside the gender binary classification/category. These gender norms may lead individuals to underreport non-heterosexual or non-cisgender identities due to social pressures that reduce the desirability of identifying as non-heterosexual (Gates, 2011).

The language used to describe LGBTQ+ populations is also complex and dynamic, which has justifications and benefits, but also poses barriers to research, such as prevalence estimation, population identification for outreach, and policy reform. In Thailand, for example, English terminology from Global North contexts is sometimes borrowed and used within the Thai language, but these words may evolve and take on different meanings. In this context, "gay" may be used by some to describe one's gender – not man or woman, but gay. Additionally, sexual orientation and gender expression/identities are often a secondary concern in the trafficking field, and as such policies and awareness-building efforts may leave little room for diverse identities or victim experiences (Buckinx et al., 2022). This poses challenges when moving forward in counter-trafficking efforts and discourse while respecting individual identity and ensuring that different genders are not devictimized.

Limitations on prevalence estimates for LGBTQ+ populations hinder the implementation of targeted services addressing adverse health outcomes and social disparities (Meerwijk & Sevelius, 2017). Moreover, information about health risks, demographic factors, and other contextual factors affecting these populations are often understudied (Coffman et al., 2017). Because of these limitations in data collection, baseline information collected on specific vulnerabilities and disparities is often not disaggregated by sexual orientation/gender identity (Arredondo et al., 2016), which Newman et al. (2021) highlight when discussing challenges to LGBTQ+ inclusion in Thailand.

### *Diversify Livelihood Opportunities*

Despite regular mention of higher vulnerability, there is little actual research evidence outside Global North countries that explores LGBTQ+ intersections with trafficking. Research conducted in Thailand in 2021 with LBGTQ+ people engaged in trading sex, revealed that a range of clear vulnerabilities to sex trafficking were present. The research found that 16 out of 20 young respondents interviewed described having migrated to urban centers from rural locations – frequently as a result of homelessness and/or familial conflict or rejection based on their sexuality or gender identity. Almost all respondents had run away from home at least once to escape familial violence. Pathways into trading sex for these young people always resulted from struggles to identify sufficient, secure employment (ECPAT International, 2021). Another study conducted in 2019 found that gender-diverse individuals in Thailand faced employment discrimination, which restricted them from accessing alternative employment. However, once involved in trading sex, many experienced high rates of physical and sexual abuse, stigma and discrimination, and financial insecurity (Davis et al., 2019).

For many young people engaged in trading sex, the income potential far exceeds what they can earn in informal employment, and attempts to "rescue" them for a dramatically different life can be a very difficult "sell" with target populations (Ahmed & Seshu, 2012). Individuals in Thailand interviewed for a study on sex worker vulnerabilities indicated that they would be unwilling to take an alternative job paying a wage equivalent to the average income for an unskilled worker

(Davis et al., 2019). Decision points that motivate exit from trading sex may not come until later in their lives. However, by that time, fewer alternative opportunities may be available due to stigma or other challenges – such as health issues or the after effects of violence and trauma. People may feel locked in with an ever-narrowing range of alternatives by this point. Thus, the lack of access to alternative pathways restricts opportunities individuals have for exiting this work, and even after quitting, many feel compelled by economic circumstances to re-enter, instigating a quit-reentry-quit cycle (Manopaiboon et al., 2003).

While informal sector work, particularly trading sex, carries inherent risks, there are also a range of perceived benefits – particularly when considering perspectives of those with lived experiences. Informal economic contexts can offer greater rewards for entrepreneurship, and the freelance and "gig" nature of employment may be preferred by LGBTQ+ people who can exert more control over their expression and can potentially select more tolerant and accepting clients. Informal contexts, such as the tourism or entertainment industries, may also provide exposure to like-minded clientele and be a straightforward answer to avoiding discriminatory colleagues and/or conservative workplace cultures.

Therefore, it is proposed that engaging those at risk involves framing that broadens their range of economic options, creating a mix of opportunities that include both informal and formal economies and future/shock-proofing their income streams, which may be more palatable than a full exit. Corresponding skills and knowledge – such as financial literacy and future-planning – will increase understanding of the value of diverse options.

### *Foster Psychological Safety*

Trauma significantly affects our ability to undertake organized or future-oriented thinking, as the brain is instead stuck in hypervigilance and immediate survival mode. Those who have experienced trafficking will benefit from trauma-informed care approaches (Heffernan & Blythe, 2014). To move straight to imagining an alternative future without recognizing or addressing the impact of trauma may be unrealistic – you cannot imagine a future when your brain is focused on immediate survival. This is where less holistic counter-trafficking programming can fall short. "Support for victims is effective when it is victim-centered, applies a trauma – focused lens and prioritizes the sense of identity of the victim" (Bryant & Landman, 2020, 18). In general, LGBTQ+ survivors seek mental health treatment at higher rates than cisgender or heterosexual individuals but often do not remain engaged in treatment (Platt et al., 2018). One study found that over 40% of LGBTQ+ homeless youth in the United States experienced severe mental health struggles such as depressive symptoms and suicidal ideation (Robinson, 2020). Availability of mental health supports also varies substantially in the Global South settings, and access, for both financial and social stigma-related reasons, is a major barrier (Esponda et al., 2020). Peer-based support to improve treatment engagement methodology using motivational interviewing could be a way forward (Ellis et al., 2021).

### *Individual-Level Implications of Systemic Stigma and Discrimination*

Simultaneously with individual-level counter-trafficking program activities, there is a need to address and dismantle the stigma that plays a hugely confounding role in the effectiveness of interventions. Frequently, programs talk of addressing this at a systematic rather than individual level. While broad-community stigma reduction work is certainly part of the anti-trafficking equation, it is nearly impossible to see the impact of such work in short project timelines at the level of individual program participants. Many interventions are not evaluated comprehensively, with more emphasis on process evaluations that may not accurately reflect the ultimate outcome (Davy, 2016). Lip service to the impact of the ecological system is doomed to undermine even the best laid interventions.

For individuals engaged in counter-trafficking programming, direct actions with immediate individual impact are needed to overcome stigma-based barriers for them. Interventions also need affirmative actions that provide access to opportunities, or gender affirming supports (psychological and physical) for the targeted individuals to overcome stigma-resultant barriers in the here and now.

Housing discrimination also affects many LGBTQ+ individuals in the United States and impacts their ability to access safe, stable housing, especially for trans individuals (Kattari et al., 2016). Many trans individuals also experience barriers to healthcare utilization, with over 50% of trans individuals in the United States delaying medical care that is needed due to discrimination in healthcare settings and challenges accessing health insurance (Lerner & Robles, 2017). Workplace exclusion has previously been documented as a central vulnerability for LGBTQ+ populations occurring at both a social and institutional level. Examples include situations where gender may not be changed on official identity documents, which forces transgender people to remain identified by their gender assigned at birth, opening them up to frequent discrimination.

A 2014 analysis established that LGBTQ+ people in Thailand frequently found their employment impacted by stigma and discrimination related to the terms of their employment, unequal wages, discrimination during recruitment, and being denied promotions based on their sexual orientation, gender identity and/or expression (UNDP & USAID, 2014). Harassment and negative treatment by supervisors and coworkers were also described. A subsequent economic participation survey in Thailand of 2,302 LGBTQ+ and 1,200 heterosexual individuals confirmed and expanded on these findings, revealing that many LGBTQ+ participants – particularly those who were trans or third gender – indicated discrimination in many domains including employment to health insurance to renting or buying property (World Bank, 2018).

It is likely that many LGBTQ+ people in Thailand opt to avoid formal employment in favor of informal economies due to direct experiences or fear of discriminatory experience. The evidence seems to suggest that their assumptions are correct. It is probable that a significant portion of Thailand's estimated 43–54% of the informal workforce (Komin et al., 2021) is comprised of LGBTQ+ people.

## Conclusion

There is a glaring gap in data that enables understanding of LGBTQ+ populations that are vulnerable to trafficking, particularly in Global South countries. Existing data from developed countries may help inform policy and intervention programming. Similar to their heterosexual and cisgender counterparts, LGBTQ+ individuals involved in trading sex have frequently experienced high levels of familial poverty, violence in the home and homelessness (Hogan & Roe-Sepowitz, 2023). Unlike their counterparts, most encounter high rejection and discrimination based on sexual orientation and gender identity by families, communities and employers (Dank et al., 2015; ECPAT International, 2021). However, contextualization to Global South contexts should not be over-simplified as social norms, stigma and discrimination, and structural complexities will influence policy and programming for these diverse populations in country and context-specific ways.

Approaching LGBTQ+ populations engaged in trading sex from a harm reduction framework that prioritizes autonomy instead of a rescue and rehabilitation framework is critical to reducing vulnerability to sex trafficking. The three fundamental tenets of this harm reduction framework are as follows: i) providing access to a range of economic options and creating a mix of opportunities that includes both informal and formal economies and future/shock-proofing their income streams; ii) providing trauma-informed services to foster psychological safety; and iii) implementing individual-level activities to reduce systemic stigma and discrimination. Most importantly, including those with lived experience in all aspects of decision-making is crucial to ensuring continued participation and sustainable outcomes. This inclusive approach will reduce the number of LGBTQ+ individuals vulnerable to sex trafficking as a result of limited autonomy or the lack of viable alternative options.

## Disclosure statement

There are no relevant financial or non-financial competing interests to report with regard to the article.

## ORCID

Mark Kavenagh http://orcid.org/0000-0002-6051-0278

## Data availability statement

Data sharing is not applicable to this article as no new data were created or analyzed in this study.

## References

Ahmed, A., & Seshu, M. (2012). We have the right not to be 'rescued…': When anti-trafficking programmes undermine the health and well-being of sex workers. *Anti-Trafficking Review*. Available at: https://antitraffickingreview.org/index.php/atrjournal/article/view/28/48

Akanbi, A. (2020). Assessing the effectiveness of global and international cooperation in tackling human trafficking. *Journal of Global Social Sciences*, *1*(4), 75–90.

Alam, E., Molla, M. H., Islam, M. K., Rahman, M. A., & Barua, J. (2023). Non-state initiatives on enhancing counter-trafficking of Rohingya influx in cox's bazar of Bangladesh. *Frontiers in Public Health*, *11*, 1040546. https://doi.org/10.3389/fpubh.2023.1040546

Arredondo, M., Gray, C., Russell, S., Skiba, R., & Snapp, S. (2016). Documenting disparities for LGBT students: Expanding the collection and reporting of data on sexual orientation and gender identity. Retrieved from https://indrc.indiana.edu/tools-resources/pdf-disciplineseries/sogi-brief-final.pdf

Badgett, M. V. L., Waaldijk, K., & van de Meulen Rodgers, Y. (2019). The relationship between LGBT inclusion and economic development: Macro-level evidence. *World Development*, *120*, 101–114. https://doi.org/10.1016/j.worlddev.2019.03.011

Blondeel, K., de Vasconcelos, S., García-Moreno, C., Stephenson, R., Temmerman, M., & Toskin, I. (2018). Violence motivated by perception of sexual orientation and gender identity: A systematic review. *Bulletin of the World Health Organization*, *96*(1), 29–41L. https://doi.org/10.2471/BLT.17.197251

Bosley-Smith, E. R. (2023). Anticipatory economic stressors: Perceived and potential sources of economic disadvantage for LGBTQ adults. *Sociological Inquiry*, Advance online publication. https://doi.org/10.1111/soin.12533

Bryant, K., & Landman, T. (2020). Combatting human trafficking since Palermo: What do we know about what works? *Journal of Human Trafficking*, *6*(2), 119–140. https://doi.org/10.1080/23322705.2020.1690097

Buckinx, B., Hogg, C. L., & Vaughn, L. (2022). *The intersection of conflict-related sexual violence against men, boys, and LGBTQI+*. Persons and Human Trafficking. Princeton University, Liechtenstein Institute on Self-Determination.

Camak, D. J., & RNC-MNN, F. C. N. (2022). Recognizing and addressing the needs of sex trafficking victims. *Online Journal of Issues in Nursing*, *27*(2), 1–8. https://doi.org/10.3912/OJIN.Vol27No02PPT53

Carpenter, C. S., Lee, M. J., & Nettuno, L. (2022). Economic outcomes for transgender people and other gender minorities in the United States: First estimates from a nationally representative sample. *Southern Economic Journal*, *89*(2), 280–304. https://doi.org/10.1002/soej.12594

Centers for Disease Control and Prevention [CDC]. (2020, September 17). Infographic: 6 guiding principles to a trauma-informed approach. CDC, Center for Preparedness and Response. Retrieved from https://www.cdc.gov/cpr/infographics/6_principles_trauma_info.htm

Chynoweth, S. K., Buscher, D., Martin, S., & Zwi, A. B. (2020). A social ecological approach to understanding service utilization barriers among male survivors of sexual violence in three refugee settings: A qualitative exploratory study. *Conflict and Health*, *14*(1), 43. https://doi.org/10.1186/s13031-020-00288-8

Coffman, K. B., Coffman, L. C., & Ericson, K. M. M. (2017). The size of the LGBT population and the magnitude of antigay sentiment are substantially underestimated. *Management Science*, *63*(10), 3168–3186. https://doi.org/10.1287/mnsc.2016.2503

Connell, R. W. (2005). Masculinities. https://doi.org/10.4324/9781003116479

Dank, M., Yahner, J., Madden, K., Banuelos, I., Yu, L., Ritchie, A., Mora, M., & Conner, B. (2015). Surviving the streets of New York: Experiences of LGBTQ youth. In *YMSM, and YWSW engaged in survival sex* Urban Institute. Retrieved fromhttps://www.urban.org/sites/default/files/publication/42186/2000119-Surviving-the-Streets-of-New-York.pdf

Darmstadt, G., Heise, L., Gupta, G., Henry, S., Cislaghi, B., Greene, M., Hawkes, S., Hay, K., Heymann, J., Klugman, J., Levy, J., Raj, A., & Weber, A. (2019). Why now for a series on gender equality, norms and health? *The Lancet*, *393*(10189), 2374–2377. https://doi.org/10.1016/S0140-6736(19)30985-7

David, F. (2017). Building the infrastructure of anti-trafficking, part II: Why measurement matters. *Anti-Trafficking Review*, *8*(8). https://doi.org/10.14197/atr.20121789

Davis, J. D., Miles, G. M., & Quinley, J. H., III. (2019). Same same, but different: A baseline study on the vulnerabilities of transgender sex workers in the sex industry in Bangkok, Thailand. *International Journal of Sociology and Social Policy*, *39*(7/8), 550–573. https://doi.org/10.1108/IJSSP-01-2019-0022

Davy, D. (2016). Anti-human trafficking interventions: How do we know if they are working? *American Journal of Evaluation*, *37*(4), 486–504. https://doi.org/10.1177/1098214016630615

Denney, L., Alffram, H., Domingo, P., & Jesperson, S. (2023). Addressing exploitation of labour migrants in Southeast Asia: Beyond a counter-trafficking criminal justice response. In *ODI thematic brief*. ODI. https://odi.org/en/publications/addressing-exploitation-of-labour-migrants-in-southeast-asia-beyond-a-counter-traffi

Dwi, R. (2021). The effectiveness of the International Organisation for Migration (IOM) in addressing human trafficking against Indonesian migrant workers in Malaysia post-voche effectiveness of the International Organization for Migration (IOM) in addressing human trafficking against Indonesian migrant workers in Malaysia post-COVID-19. *Mediasi: Journal of International Relations*, *4*(2). https://ejournal.unida.gontor.ac.id/index.php/mediasi/article/view/10036

Dwyer, E. (2022). A very beautiful but heavy jacket: The experiences of migrant workers with diverse sexual orientation, gender identity and expression in South-East Asia. International Labor Organisation. Retrieved from: https://www.ilo.org/asia/publications/WCMS_854686/lang–en/index.htm

Ellis, A. E., Martino, S., Simiola, V., Mackintosh, M., Bellamy, C., & Cook, J. M. (2021). Study design and interventions for a peer-delivered motivational interviewing group treatment for sexual and gender minority male sexual trauma survivors. *Contemporary Clinical Trials*, *111*, 106597. https://doi.org/10.1016/j.cct.2021.106597

End Child Prostitution and Trafficking [ECPAT] International. (2021). Global initiative to explore the sexual exploitation of boys: Thailand report: Retrieved from https://ecpat.org/wp-content/uploads/2021/05/ENG-Global-Boys-Initiative-Thailand-Report_April-2021_FINAL_2.pdf

Engle Merry, S. (2016). *The seductions of quantification: Measuring human rights, gender violence, and sex trafficking*. University of Chicago Press.

Esponda, G. M., Hartman, S., Qureshi, O., Sadler, E., Cohen, A., & Kakuma, R. (2020). Barriers and facilitators of mental health programmes in primary care in low-income and middle-income countries. *The Lancet Psychiatry*, *7*(1), 78–92. https://doi.org/10.1016/S2215-0366(19)30125-7

Farrell, A., Dank, M., de Vries, I., Kafafian, M., Hughes, A., & Lockwood, S. (2019). Failing victims? Challenges of the police response to human trafficking. *Criminology & Public Policy*, *18*(3), 649–673. https://doi.org/10.1111/1745-9133.12456

Farrell, A., & De Vries, I. (2020). Measuring the nature and prevalence of human trafficking. In G. Antonopoulos & M. Groenhuijsen (Eds.), *The Palgrave international handbook of human trafficking* (pp. 147–162). Palgrave Macmillan.

Farrell, A., & Reichert, J. (2017). Using US law-enforcement data: Promise and limits in measuring human trafficking. *Journal of Human Trafficking*, *3*(1), 39–60. https://doi.org/10.1080/23322705.2017.1280324

Feijo, M., Wendt, G., Bloniewski, T., Fontanari, A., Boeira, L., & Costa, A. (2022). Improving school outcomes for transgender and gender-diverse youth: A rapid review. *Policy Insights from the Behavioral and Brain Sciences*, *9*(1), 27–34. https://doi.org/10.1177/23727322211068021

Franchino-Olsen, H. (2021). Vulnerabilities relevant for commercial sexual exploitation of children/domestic minor sex trafficking: A systematic review of risk factors. *Trauma, Violence, & Abuse*, *22*(1), 99–111. https://doi.org/10.1177/1524838018821956

Gates, G. J. (2011). How many people are lesbian, gay, bisexual, and transgender?. The Williams Institute, UCLA School of Law. https://williamsinstitute.law.ucla.edu/wp-content/uploads/Gates-How-Many-People-LGBT-Apr-2011.pdf

Gerassi, L. B., & Pederson, A. C. (2022). Social service providers' knowledge of and practice with LGBTQ+ people at risk of sex trafficking. *Social Work Research*, *46*(2), 101–114. https://doi.org/10.1093/swr/svac001

Gupta, R., & Gupta, R. (2023). Lost in the perilous boulevards of gig economy: Making of human drones. *South Asian Journal of Human Resources Management*, *10*(1), 85–106. https://doi.org/10.1177/23220937221101259

Heffernan, K., & Blythe, B. (2014). Evidence-based practice: Developing a trauma-informed lens to case management for victims of human trafficking. *Global Social Welfare*, *1*(3), 169–177. https://doi.org/10.1007/s40609-014-0007-8

Hogan, K. A., & Roe-Sepowitz, D. (2023). LGBTQ+ homeless young adults and sex trafficking vulnerability. *Journal of Human Trafficking*, *9*(1), 63–78. https://doi.org/10.1080/23322705.2020.1841985

Hoyle, C., Bosworth, M., & Dempsey, M. (2011). Labelling the victims of sex trafficking: Exploring the borderland between rhetoric and reality. *Social & Legal Studies*, *20*(3), 313–329. https://doi.org/10.1177/0964663911405394

International Labor Organisation. (2024). Definition of 'informal economy'. Website accessed on Jan 27, 2024. https://www.ilo.org/global/programes-and-projects/prospects/themes/informal-economy/lang--en/index.htm

Janyam, S., Phuengsamran, D., Pangnongyang, J., Saripra, W., Jitwattanapataya, L., Songsamphan, C., Benjarattanaporn, P., & Gopinath, D. (2020). Protecting sex workers in Thailand during the COVID-19 pandemic: Opportunities to build back better. *WHO South-East Asia Journal of Public Health* [Retrieved from], *9*(2), 100–103.

https://www.who-seajph.org/article.asp?issn=2224-3151;year=2020;volume=9;issue=2;spage=100;epage=103;aulast=Janyam;type=3

John, G. (2019). Human trafficking prevalence in Rwanda: The role played by unemployment. *American Journal of Social Sciences and Humanities, 4*(1), 163–177. https://doi.org/10.20448/801.41.163.177

Johnston, H., & Land-Kazlauskas, C. (2018). *Organizing on-demand: Representation, voice, and collective bargaining in the gig econom.* Conditions of Work and Employment Series No. 94. https://doi.org/10.13140/RG.2.2.12235.90400

Kattari, S. K., Whitfield, D. L., Walls, N. E., Langenderfer-Magruder, L., & Ramos, D. (2016). Policing gender through housing and employment discrimination: Comparison of discrimination experiences of transgender and cisgender LGBQ individuals. *Journal of the Society for Social Work and Research, 7*(3), 427–447. https://doi.org/10.1086/686920

Kavenagh, M., Hua, N., & Wekerle, C. (2023). Sexual exploitation of children: Barriers for boys in accessing social supports for victimization. *Child Abuse and Neglect, 142*(2), 106129. https://doi.org/10.1016/j.chiabu.2023.106129

Koegler, E., Howland, W., Gibbons, P., Teti, M., & Stoklosa, H. (2022). "When her visa expired, the family refused to renew it": Intersections of human trafficking and domestic violence: Qualitative document analysis of case examples from a major Midwest city. *Journal of Interpersonal Violence, 37*(7–8), NP4133–NP4159. https://doi.org/10.1177/0886260520957978

Komin, W., Thepparp, R., Subsing, B., & Engstrom, D. (2021). Covid-19 and its impact on informal sector workers: A case study of Thailand. *Asia Pacific Journal of Social Work and Development, 31*(1–2), 80–88. https://doi.org/10.1080/02185385.2020.1832564

Kongtip, P., Nankongnab, N., Chaikittiporn, C., Laohaudomchok, W., Woskie, S., & Slatin, C. (2015). Informal workers in Thailand: Occupational health and social security disparities. *New Solutions: A Journal of Environmental & Occupational Health Policy, 25*(2), 189–211. https://doi.org/10.1177/1048291115586036

Lerner, J. E., & Robles, G. (2017). Perceived barriers and facilitators to health care utilization in the United States for transgender people: A review of recent literature. *Journal of Health Care for the Poor and Underserved, 28*(1), 127–152. https://doi.org/10.1353/hpu.2017.0014

Lutnick, A. (2016). *Domestic minor sex trafficking: Beyond victims and villains.* Columbia University Press.

Manopaiboon, C., Bunnell, R. E., Kilmarx, P. H., Chaikummao, S., Limpakarnjanarat, K., Supawitkul, S., St. Louis, M. E., & Mastro, T. D. (2003). Leaving sex work: Barriers, facilitating factors and consequences for female sex workers in northern Thailand. *Aids Care-Psychological & Socio-Medical Aspects of Aids/hiv, 15*(1), 39–52. https://doi.org/10.1080/012021000039743

McAdam, M. (2020). *Vulnerability, human trafficking, and COVID-19.* ASEAN-Australia Counter Trafficking Program and Cardno.

Meerwijk, E. L., & Sevelius, J. M. (2017). Transgender population size in the United States: A meta-regression of population-based probability samples. *American Journal of Public Health, 107*(2), e1–e8. https://doi.org/10.2105/AJPH.2016.303578

Mieruch, Y., & McFarlane, D. (2022). Gig economy riders on social media in Thailand: Contested identities and emergent civil society organizations. *Voluntas: International Journal of Voluntary and Nonprofit Organizations, 34*(6), 1–11. https://doi.org/10.1007/s11266-022-00547-7

Newman, P. A., Reid, L., Tepjan, S., & Akkakanjanasupar, P. (2021). LGBT+ inclusion and human rights in Thailand: A scoping review of the literature. *BMC Public Health, 21*(1), 1816. https://doi.org/10.1186/s12889-021-11798-2

Platt, L. F., Wolf, J. K., & Scheitle, C. P. (2018). Patterns of mental health care utilization among sexual orientation minority groups. *Journal of Homosexuality, 65*(2), 135–153. https://doi.org/10.1080/00918369.2017.1311552

Robinson, B. A. (2018). Conditional families and lesbian, gay, bisexual, transgender, and queer youth homelessness: Gender, sexuality, family instability, and rejection. *Journal of Marriage and Family, 80*(2), 383–396. https://doi.org/10.1111/jomf.12466

Robinson, B. A. (2020). *Coming out to the streets: LGBTQ youth experiencing homelessness.* University of California Press.

Schroeder, E., Edgemon, T. G., Aletraris, L., Kagotho, N., Clay-Warner, J., & Okech, D. (2022). A review of prevalence estimation methods for human trafficking populations. *Public Health Reports, 137*(1_suppl), 46S–52S. https://doi.org/10.1177/00333549211044010

Sheu, J. C., Torres, M. I. M., Gordon, M. R., Nguyen, P. T., & Coverdale, J. H. (2021). Potential impact of climate change on human trafficking: A narrative review. *The Journal of Nervous and Mental Disease, 209*(5), 324–329. https://doi.org/10.1097/NMD.0000000000001312

Suriyasarn, B. (2016). Discrimination and marginalization of LGBT workers in Thailand. In C. Lombardi & B. van der Tuin (Eds.), *Sexual orientation and transgender issues in organizations: Global perspectives on LGBT workforce diversity* (pp. 183–203). Springer.

Tan, S. J., & Segrave, M. (2020). An examination of counter trafficking responses in the Asian region: Hong Kong and Singapore. In *The Palgrave International Handbook of Human Trafficking* (pp. 917–934). https://link.springer.com/referenceworkentry/10.1007/978-3-319-63058-8_57

United Nations Development Programme [UNDP] and United States Agency for International Development [USAID]. (2014). Being LGBT in Asia: Thailand country report. Retrieved from https://www.refworld.org/pdfid/54ed82784.pdf

U.S. Department of State. (2022). Trafficking in persons report. Retrieved from https://www.state.gov/reports/2022-trafficking-in-persons-report/

World Bank. (2018). Economic inclusion of LGBTI groups in Thailand. Retrieved from https://www.worldbank.org/en/country/thailand/publication/economic-inclusion-of-lgbti-groups-in-thailand

Yousaf, F. N. (2018). Forced migration, human trafficking, and human security. *Current Sociology*, *66*(2), 209–225.

Zhang, S. X. (2022). Progress and challenges in human trafficking research: Two decades after the palermo protocol. *Journal of Human Trafficking*, *8*(1), 4–12. https://doi.org/10.1080/23322705.2021.2019528

Zhang, S. X., & Larsen, J. J. (2021). Estimating the size of the human trafficking problem: MSE and other strategies. *Crime & Delinquency*, *67*(13–14), 2169–2187. https://doi.org/10.1177/00111287211029856

# A Long Journey: Integrating Caste in Anti-Trafficking Interventions

Tarini J. Shipurkar, Shakila Khatoon, Mayank Sinha, and Pradeep Narayanan

**ABSTRACT**

Recognizing the limitations of the raid-rescue-and-rehabilitation model, this article emphasizes the need for anti-trafficking interventions to follow a more holistic approach toward addressing the challenges of trafficking. Using the case study of a community-led collectivization initiative facilitated by Praxis – Institute for Participatory Practices that addressed the challenges faced by the Nat and Bediya communities, the article traces the history and current plight of the Nat and Bediya communities in North India. It notes how the broader social-cultural-historical background of these communities plays a crucial role in their vulnerability to trafficking and involvement in the sex trade. The case study emphasizes the need for community-led interventions that recognize the complexities of caste-based discrimination, limited livelihood options and deep-rooted social norms. This approach aims to foster agency, challenge stereotypes, and empower community members to redefine their identities and livelihood choices by involving community leaders.

## Background

> "It is very common for young girls, even those that are not involved in sex work to be picked up by the police here, following which we have to go bail them out and negotiate with the police. Just a few days ago, a young girl who studies in school, in class 11, was taken to the police station under the pretext of her being a sex worker"
>
> *Social Worker from the Bediya community, Madhya Pradesh, India*

As an approach to anti-trafficking, the raid-rescue-rehabilitation paradigm has often followed a moralistic and abolitionist framework, often conflating sex work and trafficking (Doezema, 2010; Miranda, 2011; Sanders & Campbell, 2014). In India, several anti-trafficking interventions have led to brothels being raided and women being "rescued" and placed in rehabilitation facilities. On many occasions, as in the example quoted above, the raid, with its violent process, has implications for sex workers and their families. Similar stories from across India highlight the impact raid-rescue-rehabilitation interventions have exacted upon the lives of sex workers, often putting them at risk and making them more vulnerable to violence (Ahmed & Seshu, 2012; Pai et al., 2018). Using the case study of the Nat and Bediya communities in India, this article emphasizes the shortcomings of conventional anti-trafficking approaches. By shedding light on the complexities of caste discrimination and entrenched social norms, the article highlights the need for adopting a community-led approach to address the challenges that Nat and Bediya communities face in combating human trafficking.

## Historical Background of the Nat and Bediya Communities

To understand the limitations of the raid-and-rescue approach, it is essential to delve into the social-cultural-historical context of these communities and examine the factors that contribute to their involvement in the sex trade. Based primarily in North India, the Nat and Bediya communities are among the 198 Denotified tribes and nearly 1,500 nomadic and semi-nomadic tribes that have experienced historical injustices in colonial and independent India. Historically, these communities were performers and entertainers, traditionally skilled in various dances, including folk and acrobatic dances. The livelihood of the members of these communities revolved around being acrobats, jugglers, rope dancers, and tattoo artists, with several past generations engaged in traditional medicine and collecting herbal plants from forest areas (Bokil, 2002; Editorial, 2008).

The Nat and Bediya communities' involvement in the sex trade can be traced back to the colonial period in India. The mobility of these populations was subject to several restrictions during this time by the British government under the Criminal Tribes Act.[1] When passed in 1871, this Act immediately deemed generations to come as "born criminals". Nearly 198 communities, mostly belong to nomadic and semi-nomadic tribes, were listed under this notification, thus granting sweeping powers to the police to control and monitor the movement of these communities. The Act allowed surveillance, and all members of these communities were compelled to register themselves at local police stations and register their attendance at regular intervals (Bokil, 2002; Dandekar 2014; Renke, 2008). This confinement of the community and the following marginalization added to the loss of any livelihood options and skill-building opportunities, forcing many of the women from the community into the sex trade. Although the Act was repealed in 1952, thereby "de-notifying" these tribes, the discriminatory law was replaced by the Habitual Offenders Act across different states in the following years. To this date, sex trade remains the key source of income for some families from these communities. As an occupation that has been practiced over generations, sex work is often considered the most accessible livelihood option for the community. Women from these communities often migrate to Mumbai, Delhi, Kolkata and even Dubai to work in dance bars and sex trade.

In this context, anti-trafficking interventions aimed at these communities have always focused solely on their identity as sex workers, not the community as a whole. In the process, it has ignored their caste identity, which has determined their life and livelihood options. An outcome of these punitive interventions is that almost all households have at least one person who has some police case against them, as shared by several community members in Morena, Madhya Pradesh. The result has been further criminalizing a community that had faced criminalization for centuries.

To move away from the raid-rescue-rehabilitation model and to focus on the complexities of caste and social norms, over the past few years, Praxis – Institute for Participatory Practices has attempted facilitating a community-led intervention with these communities. This work began with an attempt to collectivize leaders within the community.

## Case Study: Collectivizing

As the Secretariat for the National Alliance Group for the Denotified and Nomadic Tribes,[2] Praxis has been working with the Denotified and Nomadic Tribes to bring forth the voices of these historically marginalized communities. After thoroughly assessing anti-trafficking interventions, Praxis formulated a community-led intervention focused on addressing the challenges faced by the community, ranging from lack of access to education, social services, employment opportunities, and social exclusion.

As one such attempt, in the form of action research, in 2018, Praxis facilitated community-led collectivization of the Nat community in Forbesganj, Araria district, Bihar, and in Bandar Sindri, Ajmer district, Rajasthan (Praxis – Institute for Participatory Practices, 2018). An action research process was also facilitated in the destination area with girls from the Nat community in Araria studying in Patna City, Bihar. Using "higher education for girls" and "livelihood" as entry points, an attempt was made to bring together vocal community leaders who had chosen to move away from inter-generational sex work through

[1]Criminal Tribes Act, 1871 https://www.indiacode.nic.in/repealed-act/repealed_act_documents/A1871-27.pdf

[2]The National Alliance Group for Denotified and Nomadic Tribes is a network of community-based organizations, Civil Society Organizations, academic institutions and volunteers working with Nomadic and Denotified Tribes toward ensuring their Constitutional rights and entitlements.

education and hence become role models. The idea was to facilitate the agency of these community leaders to form a broader group that could engage in action research on the issue of social entitlements for the community. This approach aimed to engage so that those who choose to be out of the profession do not face obstacles from within the community or the broader social-economic-legal system outside.

The research group found that the process of collectivization was very challenging in both locations. The membership of the action research group was inconsistent, barring a few members who remained with the group throughout. The process helped identify practical challenges in collectivization in source and destination areas. In the context of the source area, especially the family, the Praxis model does not openly discourage members from getting into the sex trade. In the case of the Nat and Bediya communities, the source area could be the location of exploitation, affecting mainly those who aspire to pursue higher education and get into occupations other than the sex trade.

A key reason for the challenge of collectivization was suspicion from different groups within the community. Community discussions established the need to recognize the diverse perspectives held by the community regarding sex work. The varying perspectives included: (i) members who practice sex work and do not see this as wrong, (ii) those who do not practice sex work and are not against it, (iii) those who do not practice sex work and are against women entering this profession, (iv) and those who are involved in sex work and view it as wrong – of those some who wish to exit the profession while some wish to remain in the profession. Regardless of their perspectives, each identity viewed collectivization either as a threat or with suspicion.

Through discussions with various community members, it became clear that the suspicion of any external interventions stemmed from the community's experience with anti-trafficking interventions. As shared by one facilitator of an action research group,

> in Ram Nagar, the brush with law is very frequent and disruptive. Frequent police raids citing different sections of the Immoral Trafficking Prevention Act end up in women getting picked up and detained by the police, regardless of whether they are engaged in sex work and not. In fact, in the duration of this study, 14 women were detained by the police after a raid.

As one of the facilitators from Araria, Bihar shared, the community members were afraid of being targeted because of their association with any collective. However, during the project, there was a raid and the facilitators provided continued support to those who were detained. This helped gain trust from some community members and a few re-joined the collective. These raids also have a dire impact on the financial condition of these families, as they are forced to arrange money for court cases and bribes to keep the police away or stop the "rescue" of their women.

Away from their families, those young women who managed to pursue higher education at Patna City remarked that this kind of indiscriminatory action by the police made it very difficult even for those not engaged in sex work. Irrespective of the fact that they had moved away and were pursuing higher education, they were targeted by the police and often brought under the official scrutiny. Even in Patna city, these young girls from the Nat community were worried about people finding out their community identity,

> most of us do not share too many details about our names (as their surname would reveal their caste) or where we come from, if people find out our caste we are treated differently and we are constantly afraid of being falsely implicated by the police.

In another attempt to engage with the youth from these communities and build a community-led approach to research, Praxis organized a fellowship for eight youth from the Nat and Bediya community on conducting research with their own community. The youth underwent a five-day residential workshop with sessions on participatory research, gender, law, and basic video making. It was followed by the fellows going back and collecting data and conducting interviews with members of their communities. The research, which was conducted on themes selected by the fellows, was later drafted into research papers by them and presented at a conference in Delhi University. Focused on caste, education and livelihood, the research conducted by the fellows helped identify further challenges and coping mechanisms used by their community members. A key finding was that for most young girls from the Nat and Bediya community, early marriage was seen as a choice by them to avoid entering sex work. Another coping mechanism by some young women involved changing their surnames. Many families from the community in Mumbai change their surname and are engaged in different jobs. One community fellow found that one entire village of the Nat community had collectively decided to change their caste surname. It was learnt that none of the women from this village were engaged in sex work and that most of the men migrated as agricultural labor or daily wage labor to Punjab and other cities (Khatoon & Kumar, 2023).

## Conclusion

The current punitive anti-trafficking efforts often lead to re-criminalizing communities, as is the case with Nat and Bediya. The anti-trafficking bills tabled in India, including the most recent one in 2021,[3] have all embraced a disproportionately punitive strategy toward combating trafficking. The focus remains on rescue, raid, and rehabilitation. The sex workers "rescued" by the police are sent to shelter homes where they must stay, especially until they are witnesses in their court cases against the accused brothel manager/pimps/traffickers. Several reports reveal the dilapidated condition of these shelter homes and the abuse, exploitation, and harm that the sex workers endure in these homes (Majumdar, 2018). On the other hand, development efforts, which are frequently focused on preventive aspects such as education or livelihood, tend to put moral pressure on these communities by falsely portraying them as unwilling to look for alternative employment or casting NGOs as saviors. Failing to acknowledge the deep-rooted socio-economic inequity, these strategies have fallen short in supporting sex workers, underscoring the need for a comprehensive and multi-faceted approach that puts community-led knowledge at the core.

The lack of a multidimensional approach and nuanced understanding of the caste-based social context and concomitant economic structure when conceptualizing and planning anti-trafficking interventions not only causes interventions to get grounded in a moralistic frame, blurring the lines between sex work and trafficking, and more importantly creates resentment and hostility in these targeted communities. Frankly, the very terminology "anti-human trafficking" or "anti-sex trafficking" has become a taboo for most service providers that are still allowed into these communities.

One way of combating trafficking is by creating space for conversations between community members and exploring community needs and problems while accessing livelihood options or other practical solutions. To do this, the identity of the sex worker or the sex work industry cannot be linked purely to their occupation but will need to delve deeper and address the multitude of identities that affect their lives, particularly their caste (Naryanan et al., 2020).

A key learning outcome from Praxis' attempts at collectivization was to identify the instrumental role caste plays in the lives of these communities. The challenges posed by the groups point to the all-encompassing nature of caste. While some women from the Nat or Bediya community chose sex work, many do not want to engage in the sex trade but are compelled to do so for several reasons, including, but not limited to, the discrimination they face because of the traditional caste-based occupation (Jolly, 2013). Finding new livelihood options is limited because of the caste stigmatization in Indian society, which forces them to move away from the source area with the hope of hiding their identity and living an "anonymous" life in the bigger city, where anonymity (or the widespread use of pseudo-names) in urban settings would help conceal a lower caste's identity. "No one will give us a job. For many of us, even if we possess the skills required for the job, based on our caste or our past work, we are not given an opportunity" remarked a community member who was part of a study conducted by Praxis during the pandemic.[4] These women move away from their homes to find alternative livelihoods, which, in fact, further puts them at risk of being trafficked into the sex trade.

[3] Trafficking In Persons (Prevention, Care and Rehabilitation) Bill, 2021.

[4] This study by Praxis – Institute for Participatory Practices was conducted in 2020. As part of the 4th report in the Nomad Post series, it was titled "Supplementary not alternative livelihoods: Pandemic-induced impediments to livelihoods of bar dancers and sex workers".

Social interventions that are targeted at these communities have largely been "rescue-based" or HIV-focused; however, they often failed because they received minimal community support, especially when the community itself is entrenched in sex work and believes the work as "traditional" and legitimate. Additionally, such interventions do not address the core issues of caste-based deprivations. While the approach of such interventions are framed within a human rights context, of access to rehabilitation and "rescue," they are often shrouded in a mainstream moralistic framework.

In conclusion, to steer clear of moralistic or paternalistic perspectives seeping into interventions, there is a need for future anti-trafficking interventions to prioritize community engagement and address the deeper systemic issues that perpetuate vulnerability and exploitation.

## Disclosure statement

No potential conflict of interest was reported by the author(s).

## References

Ahmed, A., & Seshu, M. (2012). "We have the right not to be 'rescued'...": When anti-trafficking programmes undermine the health and well-being of sex workers. *Anti-Trafficking Review*, (1), 149–168. https://doi.org/10.14197/atr.201219

Bokil, M. (2002). De-notified and nomadic tribes: A perspective. *Economic and Political Weekly*, *37*(2), 148–154.

Dandekar, A. (2014). Invisible people, inaudible voices: The denotified tribes of India. *India International Centre Quarterly*, *41*(2), 90–96. http://www.jstor.org/stable/24390752

Doezema, J. (2010). *Sex slaves and discourse masters: The construction of trafficking*. Zed Books.

Editorial, E. P. W. (2008, October 4). Branded for life. *Economic & Political Weekly*, *43*(40), 6–7. https://www.jstor.org/stable/40278016?searchText=branded%20for%20life&searchUri=%2Faction%2FdoBasicSearch%3FQuery%3Dbranded%2Bfor%2Blife&ab_segments=0%2Fbasic_search_gsv2%2Fcontrol&refreqid=fastly-default%3Afb5bf629622d8f4964c8dd075a4f9b52.

Jolly, A. (2013). Sex as trade and tradition: For Bedia families, sex is a family business where young girls engage in prostitution with the consent of the community. India Today. Retrieved May 22, 2023, from https://www.indiatoday.in/magazine/society-and-the-arts/story/20131028-sex-trade-and-tradition-family-business-bedia-families-768084-1999-11-29

Khatoon, S., & Kumar, N. K. (2023). Ethical challenges for a community-based researcher: A case study from Bihar, India. *Community Development Journal*, *58*(1), 96–101. https://doi.org/10.1093/cdj/bsac042

Majumdar, U. (2018). Rape, drugs, assault: The rot in shelter homes goes far beyond. *Outlook India*. https://www.outlookindia.com/magazine/story/rape-drugs-assault-the-rot-in-shelter-homes-goes-far-beyond/300519

Miranda, W. (2011). Sex trafficking or sex work? Conceptions of trafficking among anti-trafficking organizations in Nepal. *Refugee Survey Quarterly*, *30*(3), 87–106. https://doi.org/10.1093/rsq/hdr007

Naryanan, P., Dheeraj D., Sinha, M., & Bharadwaj, S. (2020). Participation, social accountability and intersecting inequalities: Challenges for interventions to build collective identity with De-notified, Nomadic and semi-nomadic tribal communities in India. *Community Development Journal*, *55*(1), 64–82. https://doi.org/10.1093/cdj/bsz034

Pai, A., Seshu, M., & Murthy, L. (2018). Raided: How anti-trafficking strategies increase sex workers' vulnerability to exploitative practices. Sampada Grameen Mahila Sanstha. https://www.sangram.org/resources/RAIDED-E-Book.pdf

Praxis – Institute for Participatory Practices. (2018). *Towards community-led action research with Nat and Nat-Bediya community representatives to understand challenges associated with collectivisation of community members: An experiential account*.

Renke, B. (2008). The national commission for denotified, nomadic and seminomadic tribes. ministry of social justice and empowerment, government of India. *Report Vol: New Delhi*. Retrieved June 6, 2014, from, http://socialjustice.nic.in/pdf/NCDNT2008-v1.pdf

Sanders, T., & Campbell, R. (2014). Criminalization, protection and rights: Global tensions in the governance of commercial sex. *Criminology & Criminal Justice*, *14*(5), 535–548. https://doi.org/10.1177/1748895814543536

# Climate Change, Forced Migration and Trafficking in Persons: Risk of Young Women in Rural Cambodia

Puthborey Phon and Rumi Kato Price

**ABSTRACT**
Cambodia, a low-income country in the Mekong Delta region, potentially faces devastating impacts of climate change and associated natural and manmade disasters. Although anti-trafficking efforts in Cambodia have improved substantially, Cambodia remains a country of source, transit, and destination of trafficking in persons (TIP). Utilizing our preliminary research on young women in rural Cambodia as a case study, we discuss available, though fragmented, suggestive evidence to link climate change/disaster crisis and forced migration to TIP increases. Based on our and others' conceptual models, we further suggest that evidence-based anti-TIP mitigation measures in climate-impacted areas need to be culturally and migration-stage-specific to be successful.

## Introduction

Long before climate scientists' stark warnings (e.g., Intergovernmental Panel on Climate Change [IPCC], 2023) became part of popular discourse, experts on vulnerable immigrant populations and trafficking-in-persons (TIP) suspected a causal link between climate change/extreme weather and TIP victimization (Perch-Nielsen et al., 2008, Abubakar, et al., 2018). Climate change and extreme weather destabilize the local economy and geopolitical dynamics, increasing the magnitude of forced migration and TIP vulnerability, which increases the TIP victimization rate (Bharadwaj et al., 2021). This logic appears sound, particularly in the context of low-resource countries. Indeed, the association of climate change with poverty, political instability, gender inequality, and migration, potentially increasing TIP vulnerability, is well documented (Sheu et al., 2021). However, empirical studies substantiating this chain of logic are rarely conducted; where TIP cases are documented, the link tends to be anecdotal (see exceptional work by Bharadwaj et al., 2022). Nonetheless, this theory is consistent with the notion that climate change and extreme weather exacerbate systemic inequalities. A parallel between the COVID-19 pandemic (Todres & Diaz, 2021) and climate change/extreme weather can be seen. Both amplify structural inequalities in the global North–South dichotomy and within the country.

The Kingdom of Cambodia provides a case study to unpack the above theory because the country is a low-income country located in a region surrounding Tonlé Sap Lake, the largest freshwater lake in Southeast Asia. This essay will discuss the available and suggestive evidence linking climate change and extreme weather, forced migration, and TIP vulnerability, focusing on young women in rural Cambodia, and will suggest that human trafficking mitigation measures for this population need to be culturally and migration-stage specific, to be successful. Cambodia has a stable government; therefore, this essay does not discuss the situation of forced displacement due to armed conflict.

## Current State of Trafficking in Persons (TIP) in Cambodia

Cambodia is still struggling to fight against the transnational crime of human trafficking and remains a source, transit, and destination country. The trafficking of women and girls in Cambodia occurs in various forms, such as sexual exploitation, forced labor, especially in domestic servitude in Malaysia, forced marriage in China (Chhun et al., 2022), forced domestic work, begging, or street vending in Thailand and Vietnam (Office to Monitor and Combat Trafficking in Persons, 2022), among others. In addition, more women are serving as illegal surrogates for Chinese or Western families (Beech, 2022).

Cambodia's TIP situation turned grimmer during the COVID-19 pandemic, exacerbating the already emerging trends of increasing recruitment to force Cambodians into scam operations for labor exploitation (Kennedy & Southern, 2022), growing indebtedness to recruitment agencies, and passport confiscation among migrants (Office to Monitor and Combat Trafficking in Persons, 2022). Despite remarkable success in coping with the COVID-19 pandemic (Li, 2022), social and economic fallout from the pandemic could push an estimated 1.3 million more Cambodians under the poverty level (United Nations Development Programme [UNDP], 2020). The pandemic has weakened Cambodia's leading engines of economic growth (e.g., garments and manufacturing, tourism, and construction activities). An estimated 1.35 million Cambodian workers have lost their jobs, 58% of whom were female (Keo et al., 2022). Furthermore, female migrants (38% of Cambodian out-migrants) repatriated (National Committee for Counter Trafficking [NCCT], 2021) due to pandemic-related loss of livelihood, lack of employment opportunities, and reduced working hours (Oeur et al., 2022). They faced increased abuse and risk of domestic violence with little access to supportive services (United Nations Women, 2020). These repercussions could result in Cambodia's TIP situation being worse than that in pre-pandemic time.

Notwithstanding the devastating economic impact of the pandemic, the long-term potential growth of the Cambodian economy is promising. Although some remnant of the Khmer Rouge's legacy from 1975 to 1979 is still present (e.g., poverty, intergenerational trauma), the country experienced a period of high economic growth, and poverty reduction has been one of the fastest in the world (World Bank Group, 2023), suggesting the implementation of TIP countermeasures could lead to a high rate of investment returns.

### *Natural Disasters and Climate Change in Cambodia*

Approximately 46% of the 181,035 km$^2$ of Cambodia's land area is covered with tropical forests. The land is primarily low-lying, with the Central Plain occupying an extensive part of the area. The Plain features the basin of the Tonlé Sap Lake, the Bassac River plain, and the floodplains of the lowest Mekong River. Cambodia has two seasons – a dry season from November to April, followed by a monsoon season, which brings 80% of the annual rainfall. Between dry and monsoon seasons, the lake's surface area increases by up to 600%, with water levels fluctuating by 7–8 meters (United Nations Office for Disaster Risk Reduction [UNDRR], 2019). This process creates the country's most agriculturally productive ecosystems in the flood plains, which are central to the domestic food supply.

On the other hand, Cambodia is considered one of the world's most disaster-prone countries, ranked 16$^{th}$ out of 181 by the World Risk Index for 2020 (Behlert et al., 2020). Nearly annually, the country encounters droughts, floods, typhoons, storms, and sea-level rise that disrupt the livelihoods of Cambodians, especially in rural areas where 80% of the population relies on subsistence agriculture (Ministry of Health [MoH], 2020). For the past 10 years, an estimated average of 95,000 households have been affected by natural disasters yearly. For example, the 2022 floods affected 85,482 households with 4,498 households evacuated and 15 casualties. Hundreds of thousands of hectares of agricultural land and public infrastructures were largely damaged (Humanitarian Response Forum [HRF], 2022). The provinces around Tonlé Sap Lake are especially prone to flooding and drought (Lovgren, 2020).

Climate change impact is evident in Cambodia. Changes in temperature and rainfall had already started in the second half of the twentieth century (Ministry of Health, National Climinate Change

Committee [NCCC], 2013). The annual temperature has increased by 0.8°C since 1960 and will continue to rise in the twenty-first century, resulting in all areas of the country experiencing further temperature increases by an estimated 0.7 to 2.7°C by the 2060s. The average annual rainfall is expected to increase, with shorter, more intense wet seasons but longer, drier dry seasons (MoH, 2019). Anecdotal evidence from the fishing and agrarian communities living along Tonlé Sap Lake show that climate changes are already affecting their villages, including 1) an increased frequency of extreme weather events; 2) a shift in the duration and timing of the dry season to a dryer and more extended season; 3) a shift in the rainfall pattern to one of more significant variability and less predictability; and, 4) a significant increase in temperature and heat (Oudry et al., 2016).

### *Gender Inequality in the Climate Change and Trafficking-In-Persons Link*

Natural disasters and climate change are not gender-blind; women and girls are affected more than their male counterparts, even if they live under the same roof (Erman et al., 2021). A 20-year global study on natural disasters shows that the female death toll is higher than that of men when socio-economic gender inequality in that society is substantial (Asian Development Bank, 2014). Gender roles make women more vulnerable and less capable of adapting to climate change. Consequences for women are disproportionate (e.g., an increase in gender-based violence during and after a disaster, an increase in unpaid care work, marginalization in the labor market, girls dropping out of school, and an increase in unplanned migration and trafficking of women and girls) (National Committee of Disaster Management, 2013). A report indicates that the drought-afflicted communities in Cambodia use migration as a natural-disaster coping strategy (United States Agency for International Development [USAID], 2016). This is not to downplay the significance of the well-documented trafficking victimization among Cambodian men and boys (Cordisco Tsai et al., 2020); however, an effort to improve the unique gender-based services in Cambodia is needed for successful countermeasures of climate change-induced TIP vulnerability.

As of this writing, Cambodia does not have intervention plans to curb human trafficking before, during, or after a natural disaster. Climate change mitigation and adaptation strategies neither explicitly consider trafficking dynamics nor systematically incorporate poverty reduction or livelihood diversification schemes. Women are actively involved in agricultural activities, animal husbandry, and other rural economic activities, making them vulnerable to the negative impact of natural disasters and climate change. Such active economic involvement by women also provides opportunities for an economic development intervention.

## Public Health Mitigation Models in the Context of Climate Change and Natural Disasters

Public health-oriented approaches to TIP reduction, including survivor-centeredness, evidence-based effectiveness, and strategic partnerships, have become accepted as more effective, workable, and sustainable for solving the root causes of human trafficking (USAID, 2021). Human trafficking is a complex phenomenon that requires a deep understanding of the social, economic, and policy factors, among others, interacting at multiple levels. The traditional medical paradigm of intervention research, such as a randomized control study (RCT) for drug development, does not fit an intervention model for human trafficking without adequate preparatory phases (Skivington et al., 2021) because contextual understanding is of paramount importance in identifying workable and sustainable intervention models.

TIP victimization is a highly exploitative experience, and migration increases the risk of such victimization. Two recent well-designed studies illuminate the importance of contextual factors affecting multiple migration pathways. First, a USAID-funded intervention program evaluated the effectiveness of two treatments, an internet-based job-seeking platform and commune-specific needs-based technical assistance, targeted to Cambodia low-skilled migrants at risk for labor trafficking (Ahn et al., 2020). Among others, results showed that the knowledge of the risk of human trafficking did not translate to changes in attitude toward migration. Additionally, the program had trouble identifying male age groups who met the criteria for the study – finding that nearly three-quarters of the target sample were female. Second, an evaluation study of knowledge-based empowerment theory implementation tested among female migrants from Nepal, India, and Bangladesh indicated that the intervention was not effective (Zimmerman et al., 2021). Future research will need to incorporate contextual factors, such as destination, migration context, and intervention delivery processes for knowledge-based empowerment programs to reduce the risk of TIP. Authors noted that important contexts may be locally and population specific. In the case of Cambodia (not part of this study), geopolitically affected recruiting practices, local gender norms, and risk tolerance (Zimmerman et al., 2021) may all be important locally specific factors that impact young women's decision to migrate and further risk a TIP-vulnerable condition.

The complex contextualized system needs unpacking to fully understand the impact of climate change/extreme weather on young women in rural Cambodia. Several reports systematize the dynamic relationships between climate change/natural disasters and migration decisions. For example, floods in Cambodia are considered to have both direct and indirect effects; these effects shift the level of migration likelihood. In this context, migration decision is considered an adaptive mechanism for those affected by flooding. Another report considers three factors: pull factors coming from the country of destination, push factors coming from the country of origin, and intervening factors that depend on the push and pull factors of the country and destination (Oudry et al., 2016). Produced as part of the 27th UN Climate Change Conference of the Parties (COP27), IOM's (International Organization for Migration) call to action recommends the implementation of climate-resilient development plans separately for those planning to move, those on the move, and those who choose to stay (IOM, 2022).

A possible intervention development plan is proposed here to illustrate how elements across the migration cycle (see Figure 1) may overlap: employment needs are prominent in most stages. While in the pre-migration stage, information awareness and risk assessment training may be more important, at the immigration stage, a harm-reduction approach, as discussed by Hickle and Hallett (2016), may be more critical to reducing potential negative consequences. Such an intervention approach contradicts a "one-size-fits-all" intervention model that can be more easily implemented within a conventional RCT methodology. This stage-specific intervention model, nonetheless, can be used to identify what intervention works for whom and when before scaling up to an RCT-type efficacy study. A different efficacy assessment methodology may be needed if, in fact, multiple elements of intervention are necessary at different time periods to show sufficient effectiveness (see, for example, Shaffer et al., 2018; however, alternative trial methods have their drawbacks).

## Discussion

This brief essay attempts to highlight the current lack of research on how climate change/extreme weather may lead to forced migration and subsequently increase TIP vulnerability among young women in rural Cambodia. As with findings from other countries similarly situated to Cambodia, accumulating documentation supports the assessment of negative impacts of climate change and natural disasters on stable economic activities. It is also clearly documented that women are disproportionately affected by climate change and natural disasters. Country-specific reports from Cambodia and other countries in South-East Asia suggest that climate change does correlate with increased migration, although direct link between climate change and increased human trafficking incidents still requires empirical substantiation. Conceptually, we can accept that climate change disrupts traditional livelihood and alters local economy. Assuming the climate-TIP linkage, we advocate for a public health-oriented intervention model and provide an illustrative example of intervention elements that could be suitable for young women in rural Cambodia.

It is still a new area in the anti-trafficking research community to link climate change to increased vulnerability to TIP victimization. Cambodia presents a unique case where such research can greatly

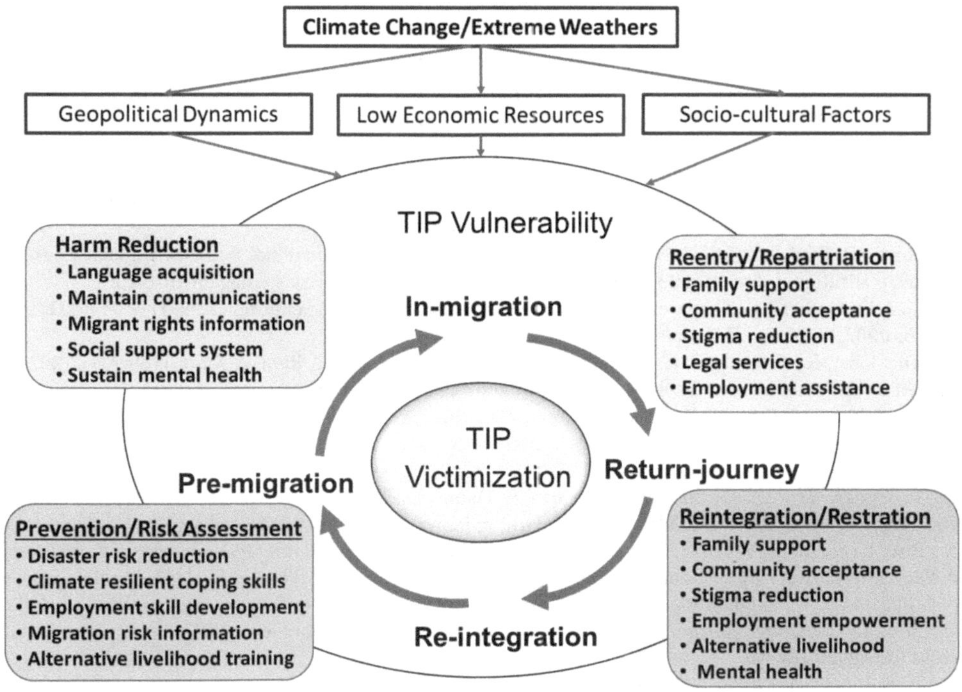


**Figure 1.** An illustrative intervention development conceptual model and migration stage-specific elements of the intervention plan.

enhance our understanding of the impact of climate change on the disruption of the local economy and forced migration. The challenge is for activists and researchers interested in mitigating climate change's impact on TIP victimization to develop measurable indicators and devise interventions for rigorous empirical tests. Establishing such evidence should be a means to develop a workable and sustainable intervention model through identifying modifiable causal paths connecting climate change and TIP victimization.

## Acknowledgments

Kneath Heard (Chab Dai Coalition), Thak Socheat (Cambodia Women's Crisis Center), and Robin Mauney contributed to the intervention development plan. Sheldon Zhang assisted in conceptualization of our intervention development model. Whitney Howland assisted in reviewing risk and protective factors for TIP vulnerability applicable to young women in Cambodia.

## Disclosure statement

No potential conflict of interest was reported by the author(s).

## Funding

Preparation of this essay was made possible in part through support provided by a Fulbright Scholar Program fellowship to the first author. The opinions expressed herein are those of the authors and do not necessarily reflect the views of the U.S. Department of State Bureau of Educational and Cultural Affairs.

## References

Abubakar, I., Aldrudge, R. W., Devakumar, D., Orcutt, M., Burns, R., Barreto, M. L., Dhavan, P., Fouad, F. M., Groce, N., Guo, Y., Hargreaves, S., Knipper, M., Miranda, J. J., Madise, N., Kumar, B., Mosca, D., McGovern, T. ... Zimmerman, C. (2018). On Behalf of the UCL–Lancet Commission on Migration and Health. *Lancet, 392*(10164), 2606–2654. https://dx.doi.org/10.1016/S0140-6736(18)32114-7

Ahn, R., Protik, A., Kirchhoff, B., & Bui, P. (2020). *Impact evaluation USAID/Cambodia countering trafficking in person (CTIP) program: Final report.* USAID. Democracy, Human Rights, and Governance Learning, Evaluation, and Research (DRG-LER) Activity. https://pdf.usaid.gov/pdf_docs/PA00X25V.pdf

Asian Development Bank. (2014). *Gender-inclusive disaster risk management tip sheet.* https://www.adb.org/sites/default/files/institutional-document/34130/files/gender-inclusive-disaster-risk-management-0.pdf

Beech, H. (2022, December 14). They were surrogates. Now they must raise the children. *New York Times.* https://www.nytimes.com/2022/11/26/world/asia/surrogacy-cambodia.html

Behlert, B., Diekjobst, R., Felgentreff, C., Manandhar, T., Mucke, P., Pries, L., Radtke, K., & Weller, D. (2020). World Risk Report 2020 Focus: Forced displacement and migration. Bundnis Entwicklung.

Bharadwaj, R., Bishop, D., Hazra, S., Pufaa, E., & Annan, J. K. (2021, September). *Climate-induced migration and modern slavery. A toolkit for policy-makers.* IIED. https://www.antislavery.org/wp-content/uploads/2021/09/ClimateMigrationReportSep2021_low_res.pdf

Bharadwaj, R., Chakravarti, D., Karthikeyan, N., Hazra, S., Daniel, U., Topno, S., & Abhilash, R. (2022). Climate change, migration and vulnerability to trafficking. IIED Working Paper, *IIED*, http://pubs.iied.org/20936IIED

Chhun, V., Bird, L., & Hoang, T. (2022). *Cambodia's Trafficked Brides: The Escalating Phenomenon of Forced Marriage in China.* Global Initiative. https://globalinitiative.net/analysis/cambodia-trafficked-brides-forced-marriage-in-china/

Cordisco Tsai, L., Lim, V., & Nhanh, C. (2020). Perspectives of boys on their experiences in human trafficking shelter programming in Cambodia. *Journal of Human Behavior in the Social Environment, 32*(1), 17–32. https://doi.org/10.1080/10911359.2020.1845902

Erman, A. E., Robbé, S. A. D.-V., Thies, S. F., Kabir, K., & Maruo, M. (2021). *Gender dimensions of disaster risk and resilience: Existing evidence.* the world bank group and the global facility for disaster reduction and recovery (GFDRR). https://documents.worldbank.org/en/publication/documents-reports/documentdetail/926731614372544454/gender-dimensions-of-disaster-risk-and-resilience-existing-evidence

Hickle, K., & Hallett, S. (2016). Mitigating harm: Considering harm reduction principles in work with sexually exploited young people. *Children & Society, 30*(4), 302–313. https://doi.org/10.1111/chso.12145

Humanitarian Response Forum (HRF). (2022, October). Situation report No. 2 – floods in Cambodia (2022). https://reliefweb.int/report/cambodia/floods-cambodia-2022-situation-report-sitrep-no-2-12-october-2022-humanitarian-response-forum-hrf

Intergovernmental Panel on Climate Change (IPCC). (2023). *Synthesis Report of the IPCC Sixth Assessment Report (AR6). Longer Report.*https://www.ipcc.ch/report/ar6/syr/downloads/report/IPCC_AR6_SYR_LongerReport.pdf

International Organization for Migration (IOM). (2022). *People on the move in a changing climate – linking Policy, evidence and action.* IOM. https://publications.iom.int/books/people-move-changing-climate-linking-policy-evidence-and-action

Kennedy, L., & Southern, N. P. (2022). *Modern slavery in the mekong's casinos.* Global Initiative. https://globalinitiative.net/analysis/modern-slavery-mekong-casinos/

Keo, B., Abdelhamid, A., & Kasper, E. (2022). June). *The Impact of COVID-19 Response Policies on Vulnerable Migrant Workers and Victims of Trafficking in Cambodia*, 1–44. https://doi.org/10.19088/CC.2022.002

Li, G. (2022, July 8). Cambodia, Vietnam top COVID recovery index as Asia fears new waves. *Nikkei Asia.* https://asia.nikkei.com/Spotlight/Coronavirus/COVID-19-Recovery-Index/Cambodia-Vietnam-top-COVID-recovery-index-as-Asia-fears-new-waves

Lovgren, V. (2020, August 17). "Cambodia's biggest lake is running dry, taking forests with it," *National Geographic.* https://www.nationalgeographic.com/science/article/cambodia-tonle-sap-lake-running-dry-taking-flooded-forest-fish.

Ministry of Health. (2020). *National strategic plan on disaster risk management for health 2020-2024.* Ministry of Health.

Ministry of Health (MoH). (2019). *National climate change action plan for public health 2019-2023.* Ministry of Health.

Ministry of Health, National Climinate Change Committee (NCCC). (2013). *Cambodia climate change strategic plan 2014– 2023.* Ministry of Health.

National Committee for Counter Trafficking (NCCT). (2021). *NCCT Annual Report 2021.*

National Committee of Disaster Management. (2013, November). *National Action Plan for Disaster Risk Reduction (NAP-DRR) 2014-2018*, pp.15. http://www.rcrc-resilience-southeastasia.org/wp-content/uploads/2017/12/2014_national_action_plan_for_disaster_risk_reduction__nap-drr__2014-2018_english.pdf

Oeur, I., Hak, S., Cham, S., & Nil, D. (2022, June). Exploring the nexus of Covid-19, precarious migration and child labour on the Cambodian-Thai border. Institute of Development Studies. https://doi.org/10.19088/IDS.2022.035

Office to Monitor and Combat Trafficking in Persons. (2022). *2022 trafficking in persons report.* U.S. Department of State, pp. 159.

Oudry, G., Pak, K., & Chea, C. (2016). *Assessing vulnerabilities and responses to environmental changes in Cambodia*. Eds. International Organization for Migration, Phonm Penh. https://environmentalmigration.iom.int/sites/g/files/tmzbdl1411/files/documents/MECC_Cambodia%20report.pdf

Perch-Nielsen, S. L., Baettig, M. B., & Imboden, D. M. (2008). Exploring the link between climate change and migration. *Climatic Change*, *91*(3–4), 375–393. https://doi.org/10.1007/s10584-008-9416-y

Shaffer, J. A., Kronish, I. M., Falzon, L., Cheung, Y. K., & Davidson, K. W. (2018). N-of-1 randomized intervention trials in health psychology: A systematic review and methodology critique. *Annals of Behavioral Medicine*, *52*(9), 731–742. https://doi.org/10.1093/abm/kax026

Sheu, J. C., Torres, M. I., Gordon, M. R., Nguyen, P. T., & Coverdale, J. H. (2021). Potential impact of climate change on human trafficking. A narrative review. *Journal of Nervous and Mental Disease*, *209*(5), 324–9. https://doi.org/10.1097/NMD.0000000000001312

Skivington, K., Matthews, L., Simpson, S. A., Crag, P., Baird, J., Blazeby, J. M., Boyd, K. A., Craig, N., French, D. P., McIntosh, E., Petticrew, M., Rycroft-Malone, J., White, M., & Moore, L. (2021). A new framework for developing and evaluating complex interventions: Update of medical research council guidance. *BMJ*, *374*, n2061. https://doi.org/10.1136/bmj.n2061

Todres, J., & Diaz, A. (2021). Covid-19 and human trafficking - the amplified impact on vulnerable populations. *JAMA Pediatrics*, *175*(2), 123–124. https://doi.org/10.1001/jamapediatrics.2020.3610

United Nations Development Programme (UNDP). (2020). Covid-19 Economic and social impact assessment in Cambodia. *UNDP Policy Brief*, (1). https://www.undp.org/cambodia/publications/covid-19-economic-and-social-impact-assessment-cambodia

United Nations Office for Disaster Risk Reduction (UNDRR). (2019). *Disaster Risk Reduction in Cambodia: Status Report 2019*. https://www.preventionweb.net/files/68249_682301cambodiaupdaed16oct2019.pdf

United Nations Women. (2020). *GUIDANCE: Addressing Emerging Human Trafficking Trends and Consequences of the COVID-19 Pandemic* . https://www.unwomen.org/sites/default/files/Headquarters/Attachments/Sections/Library/Publications/2020/Guidance-Addressing-emerging-human-trafficking-trends-and-consequences-of-the-COVID-19-pandemic-en.pdf

U.S. Agency for International Development (USAID). (2016, September). *Economic Targeting for Employment: A Study on the Drivers Behind International Migration from Cambodia and the Domestic Labor Market*. http://pdf.usaid.gov/pdf_docs/PA00MB44.pdf

U.S. Agency for International Development (USAID). (2021, December). *US Agency for International Development Policy on Countering Trafficking in Persons*. https://www.usaid.gov/sites/default/files/2022-05/December-2021_Revised-C-TIP-Policy.pdf

World Bank Group. (2023). *Cambodia - country partnership framework for the period of FY2019-2023*. World Bank Group.

Zimmerman, C., Mak, J., Pocock, N. S., & Kiss, L. (2021). Human trafficking: Results of a 5-year theory-based evaluation of interventions to prevent trafficking of women from South Asia. *Frontiers in Public Health*, *9*, 645059. https://doi.org/10.3389/fpubh.2021.645059

# Primary Prevention of Sex Trafficking: Time to Move the Needle on Demand Reduction

Marcel van der Watt

**ABSTRACT**
Consumer-level demand reduction is positioned as the primary prevention of sex trafficking, and researchers and practitioners are implored to expand the focus on consumer-level demand in scholarship and practice. Evidence of consumer-level demand is an ever-present piece of the physical, psychological, and sexual violence that stems from the overlapping systems of prostitution and sex trafficking. While multilateral legal obligations and political commitments geared toward discouraging the demand that fosters sex trafficking exist, actions that hold sex buyers accountable have been slow-moving. Research, too, frequently ignores the glaring role of sex buyers in ringfencing sex trafficking crimes, shrouding traffickers, and obscuring victims. This commentary is informed by the author's interspersing law enforcement and operational fieldwork dating back to 2002 and a recent study sponsored by the National Institute of Justice and completed by the National Center on Sexual Exploitation's Research Institute.

## Introduction

Almost 20 years have passed since Professor Donna Hughes brought the demand side of sex trafficking into sharper focus. She provided an insightful overview of a range of approaches that had been implemented and described laws, policies, and programs aimed at reducing the demand for prostitution in communities and countries. Her succinct description of "What is Demand?" (Hughes, 2004) poignantly accorded with my observations and experiences as a South African law enforcement officer and sex trafficking investigator in the years leading up to the country's hosting of the 2010 FIFA Soccer World Cup. The indelible demand factor and evidence of the overlapping systems of prostitution and sex trafficking were ubiquitous in police investigations and court testimonies that were widely covered in the media during this period (Hayward, 2008; Innocence for Sale, 2001; Mphande, 2010; Operation Priscilla, 2005; Roberts, 2009). At the same time, efforts to fully decriminalize South Africa's sex trade were relentless. Lobbyists and some researchers' placation of sex trafficking concerns as a "moral panic" and minimizing the role of sex buyers in fueling the demand that fosters sex trafficking was commonplace. For me, one of the conclusions reached by Prof Hughes, namely that "it is not possible to distinguish between men's demand for victims of sex trafficking from men's demand for commercial sex acts" (Hughes, 2004, p. 4), was not only spot on, but illuminated the dilemma at the nucleus of full decriminalization lobbying efforts.

At the time, one prominent study in Cape Town became a cornerstone in national efforts to fully decriminalize the sex trade. While survivors and anti-trafficking practitioners were not included in the research, managers and owners of all types of brothels were key contributors to a study that found "little evidence of trafficking for the purposes of prostitution" (Gould & Fick, 2008, p. xiii). Findings also included that few sex buyers seek to "employ the services" of "very young sex workers" (Gould & Fick, 2008, p. xiii) and that it is "most unlikely that client demand is fueling trafficking since demand is being adequately met" (p. 81). These findings were not only dislodged from the real-world experiences of sex trade survivors and anti-trafficking law enforcement officers, social workers, prosecutors, and service providers but were also incongruent with several research studies dating back to the mid-1990s that graphically describe excessive violence inflicted on women, and children as young as eight years old by sex buyers, brothel owners, and traffickers (Bermudez, 2008; Martens et al., 2003; Molo Songololo, 2000; O'Connell Davidson & Sanchez Taylor, 1996). Sex trafficking definitional truncation and the undercounting of sex trafficking prevalence in the research by Gould and Fick (2008) were subsequently pointed out by scholars and practitioners (see Dempsey, 2017; Swanepoel, 2018; Van der Watt, 2020).

Much work has since been invested in the problematization of consumer-level demand. What has crystallized over the past two decades is that consumer-level demand is an undeniable driver of online and offline prostitution and the same force that feeds domestic and international sex trafficking (Shapiro & Hughes, 2017; Shively et al., 2012, 2023; Thompson, 2017; Van der Watt, 2022, 2023). Yet, actions geared toward holding sex buyers accountable for the physical, psychological, and sexual violence endemic to prostitution and sex trafficking have been slow-moving, and casting demand as the propellant for an exploding global sex trade has been a source of some tension among scholars, and the impetus for much agitation by proponents of the full decriminalization of prostitution.

## International Calls to Combat Demand

Multilateral legal obligations and political commitments geared toward discouraging the demand that fosters sex trafficking are in existence and mandate action from participating countries. For example, Article 9(5) of the Protocol to Prevent, Suppress and Punish Trafficking in Persons Especially Women and Children, supplementing the United Nations Convention Against Transnational Organized Crime (United Nations, 2000) (hereafter Palermo Protocol) adopted by the UN in November 2000 mandates the strengthening of legislative and other measures such as "educational, social or cultural measures" that seek to "discourage the demand that fosters all forms of exploitation of persons, especially women and children, that leads to trafficking."

On December 15, 2022, United Nations resolution 77/194 (Trafficking in Women and Girls: United Nations, 2022) was adopted by the General Assembly and reiterated the need to eliminate the demand that fosters sex trafficking. It calls upon governments to:

> ... intensify their efforts to prevent and address, with a view to eliminating, the demand that fosters the trafficking of women and girls for all forms of exploitation and in this regard to put in place or to enhance preventive measures, including legislative and punitive measures to deter exploiters of trafficked persons, as well as ensure their accountability.

A comprehensive discussion of the need to combat demand was offered by Organization for Security and Co-operation in Europe (OSCE 2021) in a report which includes an analysis of Article 9(5) of the Palermo Protocol. It concludes that "the subsection does not target only the 'demand for trafficking' or the 'demand for sexual exploitation,' but rather demand that encourages exploitation that in turn leads to trafficking." Demand that is causally connected to exploitation (i.e., "fosters" the exploitation) thus merits a demand reduction response and, as they explain further:

> ... does not have to be designed or intended to increase exploitation or trafficking. This is a more expansive view of demand than simply the demand 'for' trafficking. In the context of trafficking for the purpose of exploitation of the prostitution of others, for example, this analysis extends the concept of demand to buyers or users whose conduct unintentionally or unknowingly motivates third parties to exploit prostitution. (p. 26–27)

The recognition of consumer-level demand as a stimulant for sex trafficking, and the accompanying calls to discourage it, are, therefore, well established.

### Demand and the System-Wide Transmission of Harm

Several reports and studies from the past five years provide insights into the nature of consumer-level demand in both the offline and online ecosystem and its nexus with sex trafficking in both liberalized and criminalized prostitution systems. Sometimes explicit but manifestly implicit, the residue of consumer-level demand is an ever-present piece of the physical, psychological, and sexual harms that stem from the overlapping systems of prostitution and sex trafficking. New Zealand's 2022 downgrade to Tier 2 for the second consecutive year in the annual State Department Trafficking in Persons Ranking List (U.S. State Department 2022) makes for an insightful case study of a country whose Prostitution Reform Act serves as the North Star for full decriminalization of prostitution and the removal of laws that target sex buyers. While it is no surprise that the government of New Zealand did not make efforts to reduce the demand for prostitution, several shortfalls in the government's response to sex trafficking raise serious questions. The government has "never certified a foreign victim of sex trafficking" (p. 413), and despite evidence of sex trafficking, neither has it "[n]ever identified an adult New Zealander as a victim of sex trafficking" (p. 413). New Zealand police are constrained by legal limitations on their ability to proactively screen for sex trafficking victims "within the legal commercial sex industry" (p. 413), including regulations prohibiting police from inspecting legal brothels without a complaint. The report concludes with experts who note that the prevalence of sex trafficking "among New Zealand women is significantly under-reported and under-detected" (p. 414). No mention is made of consumer-level demand or the seminal role of sex buyers as financiers and active participants in the exploitation equation. Instead, blameworthiness is apportioned to "traffickers [who] continue to target vulnerable populations, such as children, migrants, and adult victims of domestic and family violence for exploitation in sex trafficking" (p. 414). Yet, the glaring role of sex buyers in ringfencing sex trafficking crimes, shrouding traffickers, obscuring victims, and obfuscating harms must not be ignored. As a recent study of German sex buyers found, 55% admitted to having observed or paid a pimp or trafficker and "very rarely" reported trafficking to the authorities. Despite acknowledging having witnessed sex trafficking, only 1% of 96 German sex buyers had reported the suspicion of sex trafficking to authorities (Farley et al., 2022).

The South African Government has set in motion its ambitions to follow New Zealand's lead in fully decriminalizing the South African sex trade and removing all laws on sex buying, pimping, and brothel keeping. Present-day lobbying for full decriminalization of prostitution now has academics not only calling for sex buying to become legal but earmarks sex buyers as potential "peer educators [who] could instill and reinforce positive norms among clients" (Richter & Huysamen, 2023) and brothel owners to form "part of the social accountability network" that would "police" those who traffick women and children (Stoltz, 2023). What remains unsaid is that sex buyers have always flourished as *de facto* decriminalized because creating accountability for their crimes has never been a priority for the government.

The results are tragic. A technical report (Van der Watt, 2022) included a content analysis of 36 successfully prosecuted sex trafficking cases in which potentially thousands of male sex buyers were never held accountable. By implication, many rape cases have never been recorded, nor will they ever be solved. Brothels as cocoons for sex trafficking operations are deeply embedded in South African communities and operate with intractable impunity over protracted periods – sometimes years. The online sexual exploitation marketplace is also flourishing, with some of the top online adult websites, some advertising on public roadways and close to schools, implicated in successfully prosecuted sex trafficking cases. In one case *(State v Seleso)*, the child victim was exploited through the use of a live-streaming platform employed by her traffickers. The child victim's profile had over 6,000 log-ins over two years from sex buyers who spanned the globe. The dire South African consumer-level demand situation is arguably best summarized in the words of Magistrate John Montgomery in a case of sex trafficking and exploitation of mentally disabled children in a brothel *(State vs Matini & Another)*. He noted: "People's lives are worth what the next person pays for. It is a 'dog eats dog' world" (see Van der Watt, 2022).

In the U.S., the conduct of individuals (mostly men) who buy sexual access to people in prostitution and sex trafficking is proscribed by various state and federal laws (National Center on Sexual Exploitation, 2021; National Conference of State Legislatures, 2020), while persons under the age of 18 who are sexually exploited in prostitution are considered victims of child sex trafficking. Despite commendable efforts by law enforcement agencies and non-state actors in the United States to discourage the demand that fosters sex trafficking, consumer-level demand is relentless and particularly apparent in the online environment.

As part of a study that was sponsored by the National Institute of Justice, the National Center on Sexual Exploitation has documented 15 tactics that have been used in more than 2650 U.S. cities and counties to deter sex buyers from engaging in prostitution and sex trafficking systems (Shively et al., 2023). The study updated Demand Forum, a comprehensive online resource that includes city and county-level case studies of sex buyer activities (Demand Forum, 2023). In addition to adult and child sex trafficking, many harms were documented. These include the overlap of consumer-level demand with prostitution-related homicides, child sexual abuse material, child endangerment, serial rape, community complaints and community-level violence and harm.

Roe-Sepowitz (2019) explored the behavior and characteristics of a national cross-sectional sample of sex traffickers arrested for the sex trafficking of minors in the United States. A total of 1416 sex traffickers were identified in a six year period from 2010 to 2015. The number of arrests and the use of technology by sex traffickers progressively increased annually during this period. Online ads were used in nearly two-thirds of the cases ($n = 889$, 63.5%). A disturbing finding from this study was that such a significant commercial market exists for sex with minors. Roe-Sepowitz notes:

> While the demand for sex is significant, the demand for sex with minors is especially important to note. Sex traffickers of minors are intentionally offering children for sex, and adults are intentionally engaging in sex with children with no compunction or inhibition. (p. 627)

Finally, insights into the nature and scope of consumer-level demand in the online sexual exploitation marketplace are also evident from non-state actors (Epik and Street Grace) who collaborate with law enforcement to use artificial intelligence to discourage the demand that fosters sex trafficking (Van der Watt, 2023). Epik addresses consumer-level demand at the point of purchase by using a powerful stack of technologies. Over approximately 10 years, more than 250,000 attempts by an estimated 125,000 men intent on buying sexual access to another person have been logged by Epik. Gracie, an artificial intelligence chatbot launched by Street Grace, intercepts men who are looking to purchase sexual access to prostituted persons or sex-trafficked children. Gracie then sends these men deterrence messages that communicate the risks and consequences of their behavior. In a mere 5-month period, Gracie has:

- reached 25 States and 78 Cities
- exchanged more than 54,000 messages with people intent on purchasing sexual access to adults and children alike, and
- reported more than 6000 would-be predators to law enforcement agencies.

The potential of these technologies to both compute the scale of demand and deter sex buyers at the point of sale significantly eclipses those of human actors and also augments research insights concerning the system-wide transmission of demand-related harms.

## Research Gaps and Strategic Opportunities

Many law enforcement agencies across the United States have concluded that their efforts to reduce sex trafficking and other forms of commercial sexual exploitation must transcend the mere apprehension of sex traffickers and identifying victims. Their answer lies in addressing consumer-level demand and disrupting the revenue provided by sex buyers. Our research found that demand reduction tactics have been implemented for over 50 years and have proven feasible and effective (Shively et al., 2023). Moreover, the overlap of consumer-level demand with prostitution and sex trafficking systems is far from over-researched, nor has it garnered the prioritization in policy and practice it deserves. More can and should be done. To borrow from the "diamond" metaphor applied to human trafficking by Moloney (2015), consumer-level demand – like a diamond – should be picked up, analyzed, flipped over, turned around, and rotated to "reveal and inspect a new facet" (p. 28). The emic perspectives of sex trade survivors and frontline practitioners are critical to this endeavor. Researchers and policy makers must grapple with empirical evidence and knowledge wellsprings that intuitively, theoretically, and pragmatically point to consumer-level demand as enabler and perpetuater of sex trafficking. Moreover, research that obscures the role of sex buyers and that minimize the amount of abuse and coercion in the sex trade in furtherance of policies to fully decriminalize prostitution, must be challenged. Plenteous opportunities exist for further research and the discovery of hidden transcripts concerning the nature and scope of consumer-level demand, while the theory and practice of demand reduction – if fully embraced by state and non-state actors–can result in meaningful change and revenue streams for survivor support services. Artificial intelligence and emerging technologies provide copious opportunities to scale demand reduction at the national level and open new frontiers in efforts to map and measure the online sexual exploitation marketplace. The time for strategic (un) ambiguity, honest research, and targeted actions geared toward holding sex buyers accountable is now. Consumer-level demand reduction is *primary* prevention (Shively et al., 2023) and must be positioned at the front end of any prevention strategy.

## Disclosure statement

No potential conflict of interest was reported by the author(s).

## ORCID

Marcel van der Watt http://orcid.org/0000-0002-5556-8360

## References

Bermudez, L. G. (2008). "No experience necessary": The internal trafficking of persons in South Africa. Regional Office for Southern Africa, International Organization for Migration (IOM). https://pdf.usaid.gov/pdf_docs/PNADO562.pdf.

Demand Forum. (2023). https://demand-forum.org

Dempsey, M. M. (2017). What counts as trafficking for sexual exploitation? How legal methods can improve empirical research. *Journal of Human Trafficking, 3*(1), 61–80. https://doi.org/10.1080/23322705.2017.1280325

Farley, M., Kleine, I., Neuhaus, K., McDowell, Y., Schulz, S., & Nitschmann, S. (2022, November). *Men who pay for sex in Germany and what they teach Us about the failure of legal prostitution: A 6-Country report on the sex trade from the perspective of the socially invisible 'Freiers'.* Prostitution Research & Education. https://prostitutionresearch.com

Gould, C., & Fick, N. (2008). *Selling sex in Cape Town: Sex work and human trafficking in a South African City.* Institute for Security Studies. Retrieved from: https://www.issafrica.org/uploads/Book2008SellingSexInCT.pdf

Hayward, Y. (2008, September 5). Bay cop cracks human trafficking syndicate. *The Herald,* 1.

Hughes, D. M. (2004, August). *Best practices to address the demand side of sex trafficking.* University of Rhode Island Women's Studies Program. https://www.popcenter.org/sites/default/files/problems/trafficked_women/PDFs/Hughes_2004a.pdf

Innocence for sale. (2001). *Journeyman Pictures.* https://www.youtube.com/watch?v=kv35JG8g6vo.

Martens, J., Pieczkowski, M., & Van Vuuren-Smyth, B. (2003). *Seduction, sale & slavery: Trafficking in women & children for sexual exploitation in Southern Africa*. International Organization for Migration (IOM).
Moloney, C. J. (2015). Sociology of human trafficking. In M. J. Palmiotto (Eds.), *Combating human trafficking: A multidisciplinary approach* (pp. 27–45). CRC Press.
Molo Songololo. (2000). *The trafficking of children for purposes of sexual exploitation – South Africa.*
Mphande, H. (2010). Girls as young as 13 made to be prostitutes. *The Herald*, 6.
National Center on Sexual Exploitation. (2021, September 10). An overview of prostitution and solicitation laws in the United States. Demand Forum. https://demand-forum.org/wp-content/uploads/2022/06/USA_Overview-of-Prostitution-and-Solicitation-Laws-in-the-United-States.pdf
National Conference of State Legislatures. (2020, August 12). Human trafficking state laws. https://www.ncsl.org/civil-and-criminal-justice/human-trafficking-state-laws
O'Connell Davidson, J., & Sanchez Taylor, J. (1996). *Child prostitution and sex tourism: South Africa*. ECPAT International.
Operation Priscilla. (2005). *Journeyman Pictures*. https://www.youtube.com/watch?v=syhT3nTWFdI.
Organization for Security and Co-operation in Europe. (2021, June 10). Discouraging the demand that fosters trafficking for the purpose of sexual exploitation. https://www.osce.org/cthb/489388
Richter, M., & Huysamen, M. (2023, March 1). Sex work in South Africa: Why both buying and selling sex should be legal. *The Conversation*. https://theconversation.com/sex-work-in-south-africa-why-both-buying-and-selling-should-be-legal-198742
Roberts, R. (2009, August 13). *Mensehandel 'moeilike euwel om te bekamp'*. Die Burger.
Roe-Sepowitz, D. (2019, April 4). A six-year analysis of sex traffickers of minors: Exploring characteristics and sex trafficking patterns. *Journal of Human Behavior in the Social Environment, 29*(5), 608–629. https://doi.org/10.1080/10911359.2019.1575315
Shapiro, M., & Hughes, D. M. (2017). Decriminalized prostitution: impunity for violence and exploitation. *Wake Forest Law Review, 52*(2), 533–560.
Shively, M., Kliorys, K., Wheeler, K., & Hunt, D. (2012, April 30). *A national overview of prostitution and sex trafficking demand reduction efforts, final report*. Abt Associates. https://www.ojp.gov/pdffiles1/nij/grants/238796.pdf
Shively, M. Van der Watt, M. Thompson, L. Marshall, J. & Rousay, V.(2023). *National assessment of demand reduction efforts, part II: New developments in the primary prevention of sex trafficking*. National Institute of Justice Award #:2020-75-CX-0011. National Center on Sexual Exploitation, Washington, DC. https://www.ojp.gov/pdffiles1/nij/grants/308224.pdf
Stoltz, E. (2023, January 22). Anti-trafficking, human rights groups to reject amended sex trade bill. *Mail & Guardian*. https://mg.co.za/news/2023-01-22-anti-trafficking-human-rights-groups-to-reject-amended-sex-trade-bill/
Swanepoel, Z. (2018). Trafficking in persons (TIP): From a prosecutor's perspective [Paper presentation]. University of South Africa and Media Monitoring Africa TIP Talk Seminar, 21 August, University of South Africa, Muckleneuk, Pretoria.
Thompson, L. L. (2017). The global supply chain of sexual exploitation and the necessity of combating the demand for commercial sex. *Dignity: A Journal on Sexual Exploitation and Violence, 2*(3), 3. https://doi.org/10.23860/dignity.2017.02.03.08
United Nations. (2000). *Protocol to prevent, suppress and punish trafficking in persons, especially women and children, supplementing the united nations convention against transnational organized crime. General Assembly Resolution 55/25 Of 15 November 2000*: Retrieved from: https://www.ohchr.org/en/instruments-mechanisms/instruments/protocol-prevent-suppress-and-punish-trafficking-persons
United Nations. (2022). *Resolution 77/194: Trafficking in women and girls. Resolution Adopted by the General Assembly on 15 December 2022, Seventy-Seventh Session*. 2022. 2022: https://documents-dds-ny.un.org/doc/UNDOC/GEN/N22/759/64/PDF/N2275964.pdf?OpenElement
US State Department (2022). Trafficking in persons report. Office to monitor and combat trafficking in Persons. https://www.state.gov/reports/2022-trafficking-in-persons-report/
Van der Watt, M. (2020). Child trafficking and children in South Africa's sex trade: Evidence, undercounting and obfuscations. *Child Abuse Research: A South African Journal, 21*(1), 58–82. https://hdl.handle.net/10520/EJC-1d47701005
Van der Watt, M. (2022, June 2). Research into the nature and scope of trafficking in persons in South Africa: Prevalence insights from the criminal justice system and relevant reporting mechanisms. United States Agency International Development (USAID). https://pdf.usaid.gov/pdf_docs/PA00ZGPC.pdf
Van der Watt, M. (2023). Discouraging the demand that fosters sex trafficking: Collaboration through augmented intelligence. *Societies, 13*(4), 4. https://doi.org/10.3390/soc13040094

# Hot Soup and a Blanket Don't Mean You're Safe from Human Trafficking – Gaps in the System of Receiving and Supporting Women from Ukraine in Poland After the Russian Invasion

Zbigniew Lasocik

**ABSTRACT**

The profound effect of military conflicts on exposure and vulnerability to human trafficking is well understood but rarely studied. The war in the Ukraine has caused a mass displacement of the country's population, primarily women and children, who escape to stay alive. In a humanitarian response, the Polish society created a vast system to welcome and support these war refugees. In March and April of 2022, researchers from the University of Warsaw conducted a field study to examine the adequacy of the Polish relief system in safeguarding these refugees from human trafficking activities. The team conducted 54 interviews, field observations and informal conversations with service providers and refugees. The findings suggest that, while the Polish relief effort was heroic, the massive humanitarian program has not been able to pay adequate attention to the risk of human trafficking. Recommendations for broader policy and programmatic adjustments are presented in response to Ukrainians' continued status as refugees due to the prolonged military conflict in their home country.

## Introduction

From 24 February 2022 to 1 March 2023, ten million Ukrainian citizens – mainly women and children – crossed the Ukrainian-Polish border after the Russian invasion. The average monthly arrivals were 700,000, peaking at more than 2,000,000 in March 2022 (Statista, 2023; UNICEF, 2023). There have been few instances throughout history when so many people moved from one country to another in such a short time, and there is no instance of two million people suddenly fleeing to a neighboring country that did not have to build refugee camps to house them (UNHCR, 2022). Most of those fleeing Ukraine have been women, children, and older adults since men of fighting age are not allowed to leave the country. Research suggests a connection between migration under vulnerable conditions (i.e., fleeing from war, irregular migration) and criminal forms of exploitation such as trafficking in human beings, forced labor and other forms of modern slavery (Zhang et al., 2014; David et al., 2019). Such vulnerability extends from the refugees' precarious legal status and disruptions to their livelihood. The sheer scale of displacement in the context of the war in Ukraine has only exacerbated the situation.

The war began in the winter, which made crossing the border difficult, especially on foot (Al-Jazeera, 2022; Sieradzka, 2022). Many waited hours on the Ukrainian side while the Polish Border Guard cut the paperwork to the bare minimum. Once inside Poland, the refugees were greeted by crowds of volunteers offering hot soup and blankets. Many Polish citizens opened their homes to accommodate the weary refugees (Wójcik, 2023). There was a "movement of warm hearts" in the first days of the war (Lasocik, 2022). Poles shuttled the newcomers throughout the country and even abroad. Because there was no mandatory registration system, no one knows exactly how many refugees arrived – or how many have fallen through the cracks in the system.

## Armed Conflict as a Source of Danger to Refugees

The fact that armed conflicts "create" human trafficking situations and other forms of gross rights abuses is well established (Rathgeber, 2002; Cockayne & Walker, 2016; Kosanovich, 2017; Nwadinobi, 2020), and the mechanisms by which this takes place are well documented. People forced to migrate are suddenly deprived of their natural social context, sources of strength, and optimism. Young women and girls become susceptible to sexual exploitation. UN experts referred to these mechanisms in a terse statement adopted in the shadow of the war in Ukraine on World Day Against Trafficking in Persons:

> Conflict situations greatly increase the risks of trafficking in persons. Women and girls, particularly those who are displaced, are disproportionately affected by trafficking for the purpose of sexual exploitation, often combined with other forms of exploitation, such as forced and child marriage, forced labor and domestic servitude. Trafficking in persons of all ages is often a tactic used by armed groups, contributing to continued instability, conflict and displacement, hindering processes of peace building, durable solutions to displacement, and transition to peace and security. (Office of the United Nations High Commissioner for Human Rights [OHCRH], 2022)

Russia's invasion of Ukraine has upended the lives of millions who suddenly found themselves dependent on others for survival and thus vulnerable to exploitation and human trafficking. There have been several attempts to understand this war-induced trafficking phenomenon. One such study in March 2022 by Human Rights Watch (Human Rights Watch, 2022) interviewed women fleeing Ukraine and Poles involved in humanitarian aid. The study found that four out of 20 (20%) people interviewed had met with suspicious offers and one with an attempt at exploitation. Another study by La Strada International in May 2022 attempted to estimate the extent of the risk and pointed out gaps in the institutional response to the situation in Ukraine. The report found that there have been cases of human trafficking, and the risk of further cases is very high (Hoff & de Volder, 2022). These threats prompted Europol to announce (though not until 27 March 2022) an Early Warning Notification to alert Member States that there was a risk of human trafficking and exploitation of people fleeing Ukraine (Europol, 2022).

The primary objective of this study was to shed some light on how the characteristics of Poland's humanitarian system should be expanded to safeguard Ukrainian women and children from falling victim to human trafficking.

## Methodology

In mid-March 2022, members of the Team of the Human Trafficking Study Center at the University of Warsaw researched the system for receiving refugees and its effectiveness at controlling and preventing crime – mainly sexual crimes and human trafficking. Data collection took place at four border crossings between Ukraine and Poland and at two nearby reception points and four local shelters. The research team conducted interviews with 54 individuals who provided services to refugees from Ukraine. We refer to these individuals as officers of what we will call the "reception and support system" for Ukrainians in Poland. The research sample was a mixture of purposeful and convenient selection. Simple random sampling was not possible due to the circumstances at the border, e.g., crowds of people, pressing problems to solve, and cold weather. For the same reasons, we limited data collection on socio-demographic characteristics to a minimum, as shown in Table 1 below. The sample included about the same number of women and men. Most respondents were between 30 and 50, with an average age of 36, with an age range of 17–70. Most respondents held a bachelor's or master's degree.

**Table 1.** Demographics of the Respondents.

| | Frequency | Percent |
|---|---|---|
| Sex | | |
| Male | 28 | 52 |
| Female | 26 | 48 |
| Age | | |
| 17–30 | 13 | 24 |
| 31–50 | 34 | 63 |
| 51 + | 6 | 11 |
| No data | 1 | 2 |
| Education | | |
| Vocational | 1 | 2 |
| High school | 14 | 26 |
| College (bachelor/masters degrees) | 33 | 61 |
| Student | 5 | 9 |
| No data | 1 | 2 |
| Occupation (when known) | | |
| Local and state administration | 11 | 20 |
| NGOs | 8 | 15 |
| Law enforcement | 7 | 13 |
| Army | 5 | 9 |
| Telecommunication company | 2 | 4 |
| Unknown | 21 | 39 |
| *Total* | *54* | *100* |

Some interviewees were civilian volunteers from various institutions and non-governmental organizations; others were members of the Police, Border Guard, Customs Service, Fire Brigade, Territorial Defense Forces soldiers, or scouts. The research team also spoke with paramedics, state and local government officials, phone card distributors, kindergarten teachers, court secretaries, and dieticians. The sample also included four people from Ukraine, two current refugees helping their compatriots, and two Ukrainians who lived in Poland for many years. Several respondents said they knew very little or gave the impression that they were afraid to speak.

All the interviews were carried out with the respondents' consent, individually, based on an interview guide, and under conditions that guaranteed confidentiality and freedom of expression. Two Ukrainians, war refugees themselves who engaged in serving their compatriots, were interviewed in Russian by the team leader. The rest of the interviews were in Polish, as over 90% of the respondents spoke Polish. Due to time pressure and field conditions, the average interview time was 15–20 minutes. It must be noted that the research team could not review any actual cases of human trafficking (e.g., from the police or border guard) because of the circumstances of war and for data protection reasons.

## Results

All the respondents reported that the Poles went to great lengths to ensure adequate sustenance such as hot drinks, food, shelter, or clothing (Baszczak et al., 2022; Rabij, 2022). An example of a measure of the quality of the "service" offered, according to the respondents, was that the women received feminine hygiene items, and the children were given toys. But that was a kind of "first aid." The real challenge was to find answers to the questions: What next? Where can they go? And here, the respondents said with one voice: no one was left without a roof over their heads. The *New York Times* commented: "This huge, sudden influx of refugees has given rise to an enormous grassroots movement across Polish society, as private individuals have mobilized to raise funds and offer free accommodation and transport to the refugees" (Petriczko, 2022).

The situation was slightly different when the respondents were asked whether Poland ensured that women and children from Ukraine were safe, especially from crime, such as sexual crimes or human trafficking, as shown in Table 2. Many respondents admitted that they had never considered the risk of

**Table 2.** Safety of Ukrainians in Poland.

| Are Ukrainian women fleeing the war safe in Poland? | Frequency | Percent |
|---|---|---|
| Yes | 18 | 33 |
| No, "We cannot protect them well" | 6 | 11 |
| "Yes and no" | 8 | 15 |
| "Difficult to say," "We do our best" | 3 | 6 |
| No opinion | 11 | 20 |
| No answer | 8 | 15 |
| *Total* | *54* | *100* |

being victimized, especially human trafficking. But they acknowledged that the massive influx of women and a lack of control could lead to various forms of enslavement and exploitation.

Although the respondents' opinions on the safety of refugees in Poland were ambiguous, they all agreed on two issues. First, regarding the risk of becoming a victim of a crime, respondents saw a difference between the level of safety for women and children when crossing the border and the places where they were being transported. Second, the dominant view among the interviewees was that their main task was to help. One of the respondents put it this way: "We do what we can to meet basic needs," and it is the responsibility of the government to control the risk of crime, including human trafficking. Three suggestions emerged from these respondents on increasing safety for Ukrainian women in Poland. First, government agencies, particularly the police, should improve the flow of information, such as tips on safety concerns, because two foreign men were seen in the vicinity of one of the reception centers and were using binoculars to observe the reception center activities. The police questioned these two men, but no information about the incident was passed on to the volunteers. Second, there should be increased coordination between reception centers and regular government agencies. Respondents felt that refugee women and children should always be placed under the care of government service agencies. Third, there should be more training for all stakeholders who come in contact with refugees to learn about human trafficking. Apart from police officers and border guards, none of the respondents had training in human trafficking or forced labor.

It was assumed that the best way to control or manage the risk of exposure to human trafficking is through the system established to look after these refugees. It was essential to check whether the officers of this system were aware of its existence. At the time of the research, the refugee reception system had been in place only for a short period of time, after 24 February.

The research team assumed that some respondents may not be aware that a refugee reception system already existed. This assumption was confirmed, as shown in Table 3. Half of the respondents were unaware of the refugee reception system of which s/he was already a part.

Although a small sample and mostly anecdotal data, the results should be viewed in the context of the objective of this paper and the circumstances at the time of the study. The people with whom we spoke focused solely on meeting people's needs and did not have the time and energy to examine the risk of victimization posed to these refugee women and children, including human trafficking. Those who were more reflective and critical had seen weaknesses (i.e., gaps) in the system, such as a lack of registration during the first few days after the war began. When the registration system did come into existence, it was criticized as being "leaky" because registration as such was not mandatory and was carried out in a very simplistic way –

**Table 3.** Perception of the System's Existence.

| Does a reception and support system exist in Poland? | Frequency | Percent |
|---|---|---|
| Yes | 27 | 50 |
| No | 12 | 22 |
| "I am not aware" | 13 | 24 |
| Ambiguous answer | 2 | 4 |
| *Total* | *54* | *100* |

"on paper." Thus, it was difficult to verify the destinations to which women and children from Ukraine were sent. In other words, the reception and support system were created spontaneously by members of the Polish society in response to a crisis. Around one-third of these respondents, i.e., "officers" of the reception system, admitted that the interview was the first time they had really been asked to consider the subject and risk of victimization and human trafficking.

A sizable number of these respondents, 13%, stated they did not know how to answer the question. Later, some of them added that "some institutions," perhaps the police or the state in general, was probably responsible – but the first answer, given without reflection, was most telling. The same (13%) respondents also said that the safety of Ukrainians was everyone's responsibility.

For most of our respondents, it was the national government and its agencies – mainly the police and border guards – that were responsible for these refugees' safety. More specifically, 85% of the respondents mentioned government agencies, most frequently "the police" (18 times), "the national government" (nine times), and "local government" (seven times). Other answers included "uniformed law enforcement," "all state institutions," and "local government." Interestingly, two people thought that women should care for their safety. One stated that it was the volunteers' job, and another responded that it was Ukraine's responsibility. One respondent did not answer the question at all.

## Discussion/Comments

In the first days of the war, concerns about the safety of Ukrainian women and children coming to Poland were utterly absent from the agenda of the reception and support system. Obviously, people's survival was the top priority, yet the experience of the European migration crisis of 2015/2016 shows that refugees' security is equally essential (Kilchling, 2016; Risk Analysis for 2016). After a few days of operation, law enforcement agencies were included, and the system was enhanced with various forms of "precautionary" and security measures, such as simple registration of Ukrainians, constant police presence at the reception points and in the shelters, and the police verifying the identity of drivers offering to drive victims to another destination.

Since most would agree that mass displacement of people may lead to human trafficking victimization, five factors deserve consideration in analyzing the human trafficking situation in the Polish refugee context. The first and most obvious element is the *war* in Ukraine. The second is the *movement* of many women, children, and senior citizens across the border. The third element is *weather* – the influx of people began in the late winter, with cold, snowy days in late February and early March. The fourth is the *scale* – with tens of thousands of people crossing the border daily. And finally, the *dynamics of the border crossing* itself – which was often tricky on the Ukrainian side, but relatively easy and simplified on the Polish side, where people were often allowed to cross without a proper identity document.

For this article, it makes sense to map (Ratcliffe, 2010; Pedersen; Budtz et al., 2020) the different scenarios that female refugees crossing into Poland may go through. Three factors assert themselves: 1) the way the person crosses the border; 2) whether someone is waiting for her in Poland or not; and 3) whether she benefits from the services offered by the reception and support system. If a Ukrainian woman, children, and seniors crossed the border in their car and came to stay with relatives or friends, their situation was less risky. But for those who crossed the border on foot, had no one waiting for them in Poland, and who did not engage the system for any reason, the risk of becoming a victim of a crime, including human trafficking, obviously increased.

While hot soup and a blanket can be provided at the border, the state must consider continued protection against crime and human trafficking victimization (van Kempen, 2013; UNODC, n.d.). This is because the state has the resources and knowledge to control the knowledge, such as information on the risks and threats that Ukrainian refugees face. But thus far in this crisis, no such control has been exercised, which was the most significant gap in the reception and support system, a gap that could lead to crime and human trafficking.

From the research team's observations, the reception centers were not protected in the early days of the war. Any person could offer transport to any destination – at best, free of charge, in good faith, and at worst – for criminal purposes. There were also cases of people offering services for a fee. The transport registration and verification system introduced after several days quickly eliminated such practices.

Registration was mandatory in shelters near Warsaw and other cities throughout Poland. While staying in a shelter or hostel was a safe option, traveling abroad could be risky, especially for young women with little experience and no language skills. These are obvious factors of vulnerability to human trafficking. The risks could be mitigated if the reception system in the host country functioned adequately and there was direct communication between the receiving destination and the Polish shelter.

Staying in a shelter "permanently" did not eliminate the risk, though. Young women may explore the area, contact local people, and look for jobs. As a result, some of them encountered "harassment" on the streets or on public transport. However, no evidence exists that such incidents were explicitly related to the women's refugees.

## Reflections on the Gaps in the Response System

The war in Ukraine created a problematic situation for Polish law enforcement, border security, and social services. There is a need to study the threat of crimes committed on either side of the border by domestic and international criminal groups (A Common Anti-Trafficking Plan to Address the Risks of Trafficking in Human Beings and Support Potential Victims Among Those Fleeing the War in Ukraine. (2022a). Within a short time after the outbreak of the war, three international institutions published documents that made basic recommendations to the authorities of member countries on how to best meet the needs of victims remaining in or fleeing from the war zone in Ukraine and to minimize the risk of human trafficking and other crimes.

The first institution to react was the Organization for Security and Co-operation in Europe (OSCE), which, on 9 March 2022, published *Recommendations of the OSCE Special Representative and Coordinator for Combating Trafficking in Human Beings (SR/CTHB) on the need to enhance anti-trafficking prevention amid mass migration flows* (OSCE, 2022). Three weeks later, on 29 March, several European Union entities, including the Home Affairs Council, jointly adopted a document referred to as the *10-point plan for stronger European coordination on welcoming those fleeing Ukraine* (Long, 2022), and on 4 May 2022, The Council of Europe Expert Group GRETA proposed the *Guidance Note on addressing the risks of trafficking in human beings related to the war in Ukraine and the ensuing humanitarian crisis* (GRETA Issues Guidance Note on Addressing the Risks of Trafficking in Human Beings Related to the War in Ukraine and the Ensuing Humanitarian Crisis (2022c).

Following the documents' recommendations should ensure that people fleeing the war find safe refuge and that state authorities maintain control over the inflow. The recommendations provide institutional, organizational, and legal solutions for creating a more effective refugee reception and support system and offer a benchmark for assessing the solutions adopted in a particular country.

A critical remark must be made on these policy documents because they were created several weeks to a few months after the war broke out. So, there is reason to believe that none of the institutions had a relevant draft prepared before the start of the conflict.[1] Yet more importantly, the compatibility of the reception and support system in Poland with the above recommendations could only be an *ex-post* evaluation because that system was created spontaneously – and, of course, after the fighting began. Only now is it possible to examine the extent to which the spontaneous measures taken by the Polish society were in line with the standards proposed by key international institutions – certainly a subject worthy of further research.

[1]The European Union delegation in Kiev was evacuated two weeks before the outbreak of the war.

There is a consensus among the authors of the reports that people fleeing the conflict zone should be registered. We know from the interviews that the system established in Poland did not meet this requirement – certainly for the first few days or even up to a week in many places. And when registration did take place, it was done very crudely – usually on paper.

Again, referring to the interviews, despite being encouraged to register, most Ukrainians showed no interest in doing so – because they didn't understand why it was necessary or, as mentioned above, feared that it might complicate their legal situation. As a result, many women and children (we don't know how many) failed to register. They disappeared from the system's radar if they chose not to go to a larger shelter (with mandatory registration).

The reports also point to verifying the credentials of volunteers and those offering transport and accommodation. In the case at hand, this was simply impossible. First, because the volunteers were urgently needed. It was impossible to ask the refugees: "Who are you, and why did you come here?" Second, with thousands of refugees, the transport needs were enormous, and anyone who wanted to help was treated as a savior, primarily because of the weather conditions. Third, volunteers who gave themselves specific roles (e.g., soup ladler, guide, or cook) did not have the requisite knowledge to judge others' intentions. Fourth, without a strong state authority, there was no way to check drivers or destinations hundreds of kilometers from the border. Respondents stressed that they were focused entirely on meeting the needs of thousands of refugees and had no time to think about anyone with bad intentions and a plan to enslave and exploit refugees.

In such situations, children, especially those traveling unaccompanied by guardians, deserve special attention. For obvious reasons, compulsory schooling and psychological support are essential for children who have experienced trauma (Ayalon, 1998; Barenbaum et al., 2004). The international institutions agree that gathering information about refugees and their needs is vital to successful aid planning. War refugees should be adequately informed about the dangers they may face and the opportunities and privileges the state grants them. The competence of those working directly with victims of war should be improved, as should citizens' knowledge and awareness.

Finally, the reports emphasize that Member States must allocate adequate funds to deal with the crisis. Obviously, direct aid costs money. However, so does adapting social infrastructure to refugees' needs or training officials of various public institutions.

At its creation, the reception and support system intuitively created by the Polish public after 24 February 2022 did not meet many of the parameters outlined in the above documents. Of course, one can argue that all three reports were created well after the start of the war, which means that they considered the weaknesses and adverse experiences of the systems created in Ukraine's neighboring countries. But it must be recognized that the standards of conduct the reports propose are also based on experience accumulated over the years by the international community. Significantly, the mandate of all three documents is placed on the state, not society in general.[2]

## Summary

The war in Ukraine represents a unique opportunity to examine how a refugee situation, when "poorly" handled, can lead to human trafficking activities. Based on the interviews and a review of the main initiatives made at the national, European, and international levels, several gaps were identified in the Polish "reception and support system." Even before 24 February 2022, when the outbreak of war was almost inevitable, the state authorities did not adequately prepare to receive a massive influx of refugees and guarantee their safety. A spontaneous mass social movement arose in society to meet the basic needs of those entering the country, but there were severe security gaps that the state should have filled. Not all refugees were registered, and the system for verifying how and where refugees were

[2]According to recent data, when considering bilateral aid in terms of percentage of GDP, Poland ranked 7$^{th}$, with countries like Estonia, Latvia and Lithuania being at the top (see Armstrong, 2023).

going was inefficient. Improvements were only made after the system had been in place for several days. Another gap was the lack of attention paid to raising refugees' awareness of the risks they might face. NGOs and academia have since done a lot in this respect, but their results remain modest without state support.

## Disclosure statement

No potential conflict of interest was reported by the author(s).

## References


*A Common Anti-Trafficking Plan to Address the Risks of Trafficking in Human Beings and Support Potential Victims Among Those Fleeing the War in Ukraine.* (2022a). Retrieved April 03, 2023, https://home-affairs.ec.europa.eu/system/files/2022-05/Anti-Trafficking%20Plan_en.pdf.

Al-Jazeera. (2022). *Photos: Ukrainians Flee to Borders En Masse.* Retrieved July 19, 2023, https://www.aljazeera.com/gallery/2022/2/26/photos-ukrainians-fleeing-to-the-border-seek-refuge.

Armstrong, M. (2023). *The Countries Committing the Most Aid to Ukraine.* Retrieved July 11, 2023, https://www.statista.com/chart/28489/ukrainian-military-humanitarian-and-financial-aid-donors/.

Ayalon, O. (1998). Community healing for children traumatized by war. *International Review of Psychiatry, 10*(3), 224–233. https://doi.org/10.1080/09540269874817

Barenbaum, J., Ruchkin, V., & Schwab-Stone, M. (2004). The psychosocial aspects of children exposed to war: Practice and policy initiatives. *Journal of Child Psychology and Psychiatry, 45*(1), 41–62. https://doi.org/10.1046/j.0021-9630.2003.00304.x

Baszczak, Ł., Kiełczewska, A., Kukołowicz, P., Wincewicz, A., & Zyzik, R. (2022). *Pomoc polskiego społeczeństwa dla uchodźców z ukrainy. (help of the Polish society for refugees from Ukraine) polski instytut ekonomiczny.* Polish Economic Institute.

Budtz, P., Grønvad, D. F., & Hvidtfeldt, J. (2020). Methods for mapping the impact of social sciences and humanities – a literature review. *Research Evaluation, 29*(1), 4–21. https://doi.org/10.1093/reseval/rvz033

Cockayne, J., & Walker, S. (2016). *Fighting human trafficking in conflict. 10 ideas for action by the united nations security council.* United Nations University.

David, F., Bryant, K., & Larsen, J. J. (2019). *Migrants and their vulnerability to human trafficking, modern slavery and forced labour.* International Organization for Migration.

Europol. (2022). War in Ukraine – refugees arriving to the EU from Ukraine at risk of exploitation as part of THB. Retrieved March 28, 2023, https://www.europol.europa.eu/publications-events/publications/early-warning-notification-war-in-ukraine-refugees-arriving-to-eu-ukraine-risk-of-exploitation-part-of-thb#downloads.

*GRETA Issues Guidance Note on Addressing the Risks of Trafficking in Human Beings Related to the War in Ukraine and the Ensuing Humanitarian Crisis.* (2022c). Retrieved April 03, 2023, https://www.coe.int/en/web/anti-human-trafficking/-/greta-issues-guidance-note-on-addressing-the-risks-of-trafficking-in-human-beings-related-to-the-war-in-ukraine-and-the-ensuing-humanitarian-crisis.

Hoff, S., & de Volder, E. (2022). *Preventing Human Trafficking of Refugees from Ukraine: A Rapid Assessment of Risks and Gaps in the Anti-Trafficking response.La Strada International.* p. 2. Retrieved March 28, 2023, https://www.europol.europa.eu/publications-events/publications/early-warning-notification-war-in-ukraine-refugees-arriving-to-eu-ukraine-risk-of-exploitation-part-of-thb.

Human Rights Watch. (2022). *Poland: Trafficking, Exploitation Risks for Refugees.* Retrieved March 28, 2023, https://www.hrw.org/news/2022/04/29/poland-trafficking-exploitation-risks-refugees.

Kilchling, M. 2016. Migrants as victims – victimological perspectives of human smuggling and human trafficking. *Freedom from Fear. 12.* Retrieved June 30, 2023, https://f3magazine.unicri.it/?p=1298

Kosanovich, K. (2017). Connecting human trafficking and conflict Global initiative against organized crime. Retrieved June 30, 2023, https://globalinitiative.net/analysis/human-trafficking-conflict/.

Lasocik, Z. (2022). Jak ocalić kobiety z Ukrainy przed handlarzami ludźmi? [How to save Ukrainian women from human traffickers?], *Gazeta Wyborcza* Daily. Retrieved March 28, 2023, https://wyborcza.pl/7,75968,28367081,jak-ocalic-kobiety-z-ukrainy-przed-handlarzami-ludzmi.html.

Long, O. (2022). *10-Point Plan for Stronger European Coordination on Welcoming Those Fleeing Ukraine.* Retrieved April 03, 2023, https://ec.europa.eu/migrant-integration/news/10-point-plan-stronger-european-coordination-welcoming-those-fleeing-ukraine_en.

Nwadinobi, E. A. (2020). Trafficking and the boko haram conflict: The not so good, the bad, and the outright ugly. In J. Winterdyk & J. Jones (Eds.), *The Palgrave international handbook of human trafficking* (pp. 419–236). Palgrave Macmillan.

OHCHR. (2022). *Joint Statement. World Day Against Trafficking in Persons: The International Community Must Strengthen Prevention and Accountability for Trafficking in Persons in Conflict Situations*. Retrieved March 29, 2023, https://www.ohchr.org/sites/default/files/documents/issues/trafficking/statements/2022-07-29/2022-7-29-2022-World-day-against-trafficking-final-joint-statement.pdf.

OSCE. (2022). *Recommendations of the OSCE Special Representative and Co-Ordinator for Combating Trafficking in Human Beings on the Need to Enhance Anti-Trafficking Prevention Amid Mass Migration Flows*. Retrieved March 28, 2023, https://www.osce.org/cthb/513784.

Petriczko, A. (2022). For this border crisis, poles extend a warm welcome, unlike last time. *New York Times*. Retrieved June 29, 2023, https://cis.mit.edu/publications/analysis-opinion/2022/border-crisis-poles-extend-warm-welcome-unlike-last-time.

Rabij, M. (2022). Granice wytrzymałości. Jak Polacy pomagają Ukraińcom [Endurance Limits. How Poles Help Ukrainians] *Tygodnik Powszechny* Weekly. Retrieved June 29, 2023, https://www.tygodnikpowszechny.pl/granice-wytrzymalosci-jak-polacy-pomagaja-ukraincom-172022.

Ratcliffe, J. (2010). Crime mapping: Spatial and temporal challenges. In A. Piquero & D. Weisburd (Eds.), *Handbook of quantitative criminology* (pp. 5–24). Springer.

Rathgeber, C. (2002). The victimization of women through human trafficking – an aftermath of war. *European Journal of Crime, Criminal Law and Criminal Justice*, *10*(2), 152–163.

*Risk Analysis for 2016*. (2016). Warsaw: Frontex. Retrieved June 29, 2023, https://frontex.europa.eu/assets/Publications/Risk_Analysis/Annula_Risk_Analysis_2016.pdf.

Sieradzka, M. (2022). *Thousands of Ukrainians Cross Polish Border*. Retrieved March 19, 2023, https://www.dw.com/en/eyewitness-thousands-of-ukrainians-flood-polish-border/a-60937731.

Statista. (2023). Number of border crossings between Ukraine and central and eastern European (cee) countries after russia's invasion of Ukraine from 24 February to 26 June, 2023, by selected country. Retrieved July 11, 2023, https://www.statista.com/statistics/1293403/cee-ukrainian-refugees-by-country/.

UNHCR. (2022). *Poland Welcomes More Than Two Million Refugees from Ukraine*. Retrieved March 27, 2023, https://www.unhcr.org/news/press/2022/3/623481 1a4/poland-welcomes-million-refugees-ukraine.html.

UNICEF. (2023). Ukraine Refugee Response Humanitarian Situation Report (Full-Year): 24 February 2023. Retrieved July 11, 2023, https://reliefweb.int/report/ukraine/unicef-ukraine-refugee-response-humanitarian-situation-report-full-year-24-february-2023.

UNODC. (n.d.). *Positive and Negative Obligations of the State*. Retrieved March 29, 2023, https://www.unodc.org/e4j/zh/tip-and-som/module-2/key-issues/positive-and-negative-obligations-of-the-state.html.

van Kempen, P. H. (2013). Four concepts of security – a human rights perspective. *Human Rights Law Review*, *13*(1), 1–23. https://doi.org/10.1093/hrlr/ngs037

Wójcik, K. (2023). Polacy otworzyli domy i portfele dla uchodźców. Niemal 2 mln uchodźców skorzystało z gościny w polskich domach i w miejscach zbiorowego zakwaterowania [Poles opened their homes and wallets to refugees. Nearly 2 million refugees were put up in Polish homes and places of collective accommodation]. *Rzeczpospolita Daily*, *02*(24), Retrieved March 28, 2023, https://www.rp.pl/cudzoziemcy/art38015911-polacy-otworzyli-domy-i-portfele-dla-uchodzcow.

Zhang, S. X., Spiller, M. W., Finch, B. K., & Qin, Y. (2014). Estimating labor trafficking among unauthorized migrant workers in San Diego. *The Annals of the American Academy of Political and Social Science*, *653*(1), 65–86. https://doi.org/10.1177/0002716213519237

# Criminalizing Human Trafficking Has Not Made a Difference: A Law Enforcement Failure

Yvon Dandurand

**ABSTRACT**
Law enforcement efforts of the past 20 years have failed to curb human trafficking and migrant smuggling. There are many reasons for the failure of the present anti-human trafficking regime. If law enforcement and prosecution efforts against human trafficking have proved inept, it may be due less to weak international or national legal frameworks than to a general law enforcement negligence to address the problem effectively. Added to that is the progressive disinvestment from international law enforcement cooperation, which has led law enforcement agencies to ignore the transnational nature of human trafficking and redefine it as a primarily domestic problem. Enforcement agencies must move beyond reactive responses and adopt strategic and proactive approaches to investigating and prosecuting organized crime and human trafficking. Ideas are offered on how to reverse the blatant lack of law enforcement attention to human trafficking, especially labor trafficking.

Twenty-three years ago, the international community specifically criminalized human trafficking as distinct from migrant smuggling. The United Nations Convention Against Transnational Organized Crime (the UNTOC Convention) and its related protocols on trafficking in persons and migrant smuggling were designed to facilitate a law enforcement response and strengthen international cooperation in detecting, investigating, and prosecuting these crimes. Since then, the number of reported victims of human trafficking has increased every year, except perhaps for obvious reasons during the COVID-19 pandemic (UNODC, 2022). Human traffickers have become more sophisticated and, with the help of new technologies, much better at avoiding detection.

One finds it difficult to argue that our current approach to preventing and eliminating human trafficking has achieved results of any significance. On the contrary, all evidence points to the opposite conclusion, including the ever-growing prevalence of human trafficking and the lack of effective prosecution of that crime (Jahn & Dandurand, 2019). It is also easy to observe the galloping growth of the migrant smuggling industry and the untold numbers of human trafficking victims that it dissimulates. There is no sign that the current approach has effectively curbed the related problems of human trafficking and migrant smuggling.

There are undoubtedly many reasons for the failure of the present anti-human trafficking regime. One is the failure of the international legal framework introduced by these international legal instruments (Dandurand & Jahn, 2019). Another reason is the weak and lackadaisical implementation of the international framework (Dandurand & Chin, 2015).

Few countries have managed to bridge the chasm between adopting new laws and policies to counter human trafficking and their implementation. Despite the promises of laws that promote the detection, investigation, and prosecution of human trafficking crimes, successful prosecutions remain relatively rare (Farrel & Kane, 2019). Many countries lack the will or the capacity to take effective action (Blanton et al, 2019). Despite some evidence of raised awareness and increased funding levels, organizations are still struggling to demonstrate impact and discern what works to combat human trafficking (Bryant & Landman, 2020).

Labor trafficking, or trafficking for the purposes of labor exploitation, still does not receive the attention it deserves. The policy discourse is dominated by a concern for trafficking for the purpose of sexual exploitation, and that has been reflected in law enforcement priorities. Yet, despite the priority officially accorded to control labor trafficking and forced labor, few cases are identified and prosecuted. Labor trafficking is under-identified and rarely investigated (Farrell & Pfeffer, 2014).

The primary interest behind the international legal framework is to promote international cooperation (Article 1 of the UNTOC Convention, Article 2 of the Palermo protocol). Yet, international cooperation in detecting, investigating, and prosecuting human trafficking remains as problematic as ever (Boister, 2016; Dandurand, 2012). By most accounts, the international criminal justice cooperation regime remains weak, fragmented, and inconsistent. It has become profusely clear that current international cooperation legacy mechanisms, such as the UNTOC convention and the Palermo Protocol, are largely inefficient considering the new technologies, the constant shifts in criminal patterns, and the paralyzing politicization of international cooperation in criminal matters.

Big but still uncertain geopolitical changes and the decline of the rule-based liberal order have seemingly led to a gradual retreat from the rule of law and shrunk states' commitment to implementing a comprehensive rule-based international criminal justice cooperation regime (Dandurand & Jahn, 2022). More specifically, progressive disinvestment from international law enforcement cooperation has led law enforcement agencies to ignore the transnational nature of human trafficking and redefine it as a primarily domestic problem.

At the same time, the enforcement of migrant smuggling laws is narrowly conducted and willfully ignores the fact that smuggling activities are often but the visible tip of human trafficking schemes. The distinction between human trafficking and migrant smuggling, which is never clear-cut, is blurred further by the dominant focus on immigration control and border protection. Irregular migratory flows are not comprised of clear-cut categories of migrants. The law may posit a distinction between illegal migrants, victims of human trafficking, and refugees, but in practice, migrant smuggling, facilitating the movement of refugees, and trafficking in persons often overlap. Given the clandestine nature of these activities and the complexities of migration flows, it is difficult to determine to what degree certain smuggling and trafficking organizations overlap and merge their operations.

One cannot trust the official discourse on the success of the current approach. With few exceptions, the polite and self-congratulating speeches by State parties' representatives often betrayed that little effective action has occurred in the 23 years since adopting these international instruments. The recent week-long Eleventh Session of the Conference of Parties (COP) to the UNTOC Convention, which focused on implementing the Palermo Protocol, was very revealing. The resolution adopted by the COP at the end of that session refers to the need to proceed further with the implementation of the various measures included in the Protocol, with an additional focus on the role of technology and the need for State parties to effectively address the challenges presented by the misuse and abuse of information and communications technologies by human traffickers. However, there was no mention of the total inadequacies of those measures and the failure of law enforcement agencies to confront the ever-growing problem of human trafficking. A recent review of the TOC Convention and the Palermo Protocol implementation in Canada also revealed disappointing results (Jahn & Dandurand, 2022).

However, as depressing as the above stock-taking exercise may be, it is too easy to blame the international legal framework. If law enforcement and prosecution efforts against human trafficking have declined worldwide in recent years, it may be due less to weak international or national legal frameworks than to a general law enforcement negligence to take the problem seriously.

If law enforcement agencies took the problem of human trafficking as seriously as they do other illicit markets and dangerous criminal networks, they would invest more in understanding human trafficking patterns, developing the strategic and tactical intelligence they need to disrupt and dismantle the criminal networks, and engage in effective international law enforcement cooperation. They have not, at least not in a manner comparable to their efforts in areas that they consider real priorities.

Because of the dynamic nature of organized crime, police and prosecution services must constantly refine and perfect their strategies. They must consider how criminals behave strategically to avoid detection and prosecution. Enforcement agencies must move beyond reactive responses and adopt strategic and proactive approaches to investigating and prosecuting organized crime, especially human trafficking.

Criminal organizations involved in various illicit markets, including human trafficking, have benefited from the increasingly open global economy, and developed powerful tools, techniques and relationships to thwart government attempts to detect, investigate, and sanction their activities. As a result, human traffickers continue their activities and collect their profits with relative impunity. The fact that in recent years, very few investigations have led to the neutralization or dismantlement of the very active migrant smuggling and human trafficking networks suggests that there is a need to reconsider present law enforcement methods and strategies and build more effective ones.

It is as if law enforcement agencies have abandoned the fight. Why insist on criminalizing human trafficking if there is no simultaneous determination to investigate and prosecute it as a serious crime? Yet, in most countries, the investigation of human trafficking is still very weak compared to the investigation of other types of trafficking.

There are many reasons for this, including the fact that, as previous research indicates: (1) victims of human trafficking are hesitant to report their victimization to the authorities, especially survivors of labor trafficking; (2) proactive investigations require long-term investments which few law enforcement agencies are prepared to make; (3) the laws relating to human trafficking are complex and impose evidentiary requirements that are hard for law enforcement to satisfy; (4) the collection, analysis and sharing of criminal intelligence relating to human trafficking are fragile; and, (5) international cooperation in transnational cases is uncertain, complex and costly.

What can one propose to reverse the blatant lack of law enforcement attention to human trafficking, especially labor trafficking?. Below are some possible suggestions:

- As law enforcement officials have been advocating, there is a need for national legislators to review the legal definitions of trafficking in persons to simplify the evidentiary requirements that must be satisfied in order to lead to a conviction.
- There is also a need to reconsider the reward structures within law enforcement. It is indeed more immediately rewarding for the police to proceed with a drug trafficking investigation and demonstrate results in the form of a few kilos of drugs and a few firearms on a table, ready for a photo opportunity than to proactively investigate and dismantle a network of human traffickers operating across borders. Protecting the border is also more visible and more likely to be publicly praised than protecting foreigners and other vulnerable groups coerced or deceived into exploitative situations.
- Law enforcement priorities must be reconsidered. The detection and investigation of human trafficking cases are typically not given a very high priority. Criminal gangs and criminal networks are often blamed for human trafficking, yet anti-gang initiatives and organized crime investigations rarely include a specific focus on criminal organizations involved in human trafficking. The official priorities identified by specialized organized crime or anti-gang agencies rarely include human trafficking, which usually falls into the "and other serious crimes" category. Rarely does fighting human trafficking get that kind of attention, and fighting labor trafficking hardly gets any attention. This raises multiple issues of police governance in the setting of law enforcement priorities (Dandurand, 2017).
- For law enforcement agencies, in most instances, the main determining factor for priority setting is the budgetary process, during which the need for sustained and intensive law enforcement

efforts is often sacrificed to balance a budget or produce immediate results. However, other factors affect those decisions, including the perceived likelihood of success of an investigation or prosecution, media and other public pressures on law enforcement, local law enforcement priorities as perceived by the population or revealed through surveys, etc.

- Countering human trafficking requires establishing effective police governance and accountability mechanisms. Governance includes key management issues such as policy formation and implementation, determining priorities and strategies, the allocation of resources, deployment strategies and decisions, implementing standards, preventing corruption internally, and maintaining internal discipline (Dandurand, 2020). Weak governance can undermine the effectiveness of police actions against organized crime, including human trafficking and migrant smuggling.
- Related to issues of effective governance, there are also questions of accountability for results. Unless they are overseen and held accountable for results, law enforcement agencies are not likely to devote resources to the proactive prosecution of human trafficking. In fact, most countries struggle to balance preserving some level of law enforcement independence to protect it against undue political interference and the need for deeper accountability for police practices, conducts, use of resources, and results.
- There are always law enforcement capacity issues, but these issues are too often used as excuses for inaction. Some consistent law enforcement patterns suggest that there remain misconceptions and generalizations regarding human trafficking and the victims and traffickers (Cunha et al., 2022), and their narrow focus does not include labor trafficking (Barrick et al., 2014). Law enforcement training has lagged, but perhaps more importantly, how human trafficking is investigated and prosecuted should be reimagined (Binder, 2022).
- Law enforcement strategies are also in need of further examination. Most law enforcement agencies rely on reactive strategies dependent on human trafficking victims coming forward. One way to justify inaction is to blame victims for not reporting the offense. Yet, when the same law enforcement agencies focus on other major illicit markets or respond to victimless offenses, they find ways to act without a rebuke by a victim. Modern thinking about weakening criminal networks and controlling illicit markets through law enforcement is rarely applied to control human trafficking.
- There is a growing body of literature on the challenges law enforcement encounters in preventing and responding to human trafficking. However, there is much less written about how to successfully face these challenges. In fact, research on human trafficking has not sufficiently examined the factors that explain why some police agencies are more successful than others at developing organizational responses to human trafficking crimes (Farrell, 2014). As Farrell and Pfeffer (2014) explain, there is much the police can do to improve their response to human trafficking, but real change requires a commitment beyond raising awareness and allocating resources. Farrell (2012) makes several recommendations to improve responses to human trafficking, including increasing law enforcement leadership buy-in, enhancing the ability of frontline officers to recognize human trafficking incidents, developing specialized and proactive investigations, including the training of specialized investigators, and utilizing multi-agency approaches to ensure more prosecutions and to restore victims.
- Human trafficking is economically motivated. Criminal networks create structural systems of individuals that connect traffickers to other traffickers and their victims. Moreover, human trafficking (whether local or transnational) is increasingly facilitated by communication technologies and the Internet. This presents new challenges for law enforcement, as the use of these technologies by human traffickers and migrant smugglers often seems to grow more quickly when compared to the development of investigative techniques, means and methods.

Law enforcement officials sometimes try to deflect criticisms by opposing human trafficking prevention programs to interdiction activities. They suggest that they are dealing with a failure of prevention efforts. Yet, the best way to prevent human trafficking is to go after those who facilitate it and take the profit out of it. Human traffickers, like migrant smugglers, are in it for the money. Awareness-raising activities and innovative public education programs cannot significantly reduce human trafficking unless they complement robust law enforcement initiatives.

## Disclosure statement

No potential conflict of interest was reported by the author(s).

## References

Barrick, K., Lattimore, P. K., Pitts, W. J., & Zhang, S. X. (2014). When farmworkers and advocates see trafficking but law enforcement does not: Challenges in identifying labor trafficking in North Carolina. *Crime, Law and Social Change, 61*(2), 205–214. https://doi.org/10.1007/s10611-013-9509-z

Binder, E. (2022). Getting out of traffic: Applying white collar investigative tactics to increase detection of sex trafficking cases. *Journal of Criminal Law and Criminology, 112*(3), 631–664. https://doi.org/10.21428/cb6ab371.a4770806

Blanton, R. G., Blanton, S. L., & Peksen, D. (2019). Confronting human trafficking: The role of state capacity. *Conflict Management and Peace Science, 37*(4), 471–489. https://doi.org/10.1177/0738894218789875

Boister, N. (2016). The cooperation provisions of the un convention against transnational organised crime: A 'toolbox' rarely used? *International Criminal Law Review, 16*(1), 39–70. https://doi.org/10.1163/15718123-01601008

Bryant, K., & Landman, T. (2020). Combatting human trafficking since Palermo: What do we know about what works? *Journal of Human Trafficking, 6*(2), 119–140. https://doi.org/10.1080/23322705.2020.1690097

Cunha, A., Gonçalves, M., & Matos, M. (2022). Exploring perceptions of Portuguese police about human trafficking victims and perpetrators. *Crime, Law and Social Change, 77*(3), 253–273. https://doi.org/10.1007/s10611-021-09991-w

Dandurand, Y. (2012). International cooperation. In J. Winterdyk, B. Perrin, & P. Reichel (Eds.), *Human trafficking: Exploring the international nature, concerns, and complexities* (pp. 207–232). CRC Press.

Dandurand, Y. (2017). Human trafficking and police governance. *Police Practice & Research, 18*(3), 322–336. https://doi.org/10.1080/15614263.2017.1291599

Dandurand, Y. (2020). *Organized crime, illegal markets, and police governance.* ICCLR.

Dandurand, Y., & Chin, V. (2015). Implementation of transnational criminal law: Issues and challenges. In N. Boister & R. Currie (Eds.), *The Routledge handbook of transnational criminal law* (pp. 437–441). Routledge.

Dandurand, Y., & Jahn, J. (2019). The failing international legal framework on migrant smuggling and human trafficking. In J. Winterdyk & J. Jones (Eds.), *The Palgrave international handbook of human trafficking* (pp. 783–800). Palgrave Macmillan, Sham. https://doi.org/10.1007/978-3-319-63192-9_47-1

Dandurand, Y., & Jahn, J. (2022). The future of international criminal justice cooperation: A retreat from the rule of law? In S. Redo (Ed.), *The rule of law in retreat* (pp. 209–244). Lexington Books.

Farrel, A., & Kane, B. (2019). Criminal justice system responses to human trafficking. In J. Winterdyk & J. Jones (Eds.), *The Palgrave international handbook of human trafficking* (pp. 641–657). Palgrave Macmillan, Sham.

Farrell, A. (2014). Environmental and institutional influences on police agency responses to human trafficking. *Police Quarterly, 17*(1), 3–29. https://doi.org/10.1177/1098611113495050

Farrell, A., & Pfeffer, R. (2014). Policing human trafficking: Cultural blinders and organizational barriers. *The Annals of the American Academy of Political and Social Science, 653*(1), 46–64. https://doi.org/10.1177/0002716213515835

Farrell, A. (2012). Improving law enforcement identification and response to human trafficking. In Winterdyck, J., Perrin, B., & Reichel, P. (Eds.), *Human trafficking: Exploring the international nature, concerns and complexities* (pp. 182–206). CRC Press.

Jahn, J., & Dandurand, Y. (2019). Any progress yet? The role of civil society in monitoring anti-human trafficking efforts. *Justice Report, 34*(3), 21–24.

Jahn, J., & Dandurand, Y. (2022). *The implementation and impact in Canada of the united nations convention against transnational organized crime and its protocols.* ICCLR.

UNODC. (2022). *Global Report on Trafficking in Persons - 2022.* United Nations Office on Drugs and Crime. https://www.unodc.org/documents/data-and-analysis/glotip/2022/GLOTiP_2022_web.pdf

# The Canada Declaration for a Human Trafficking and Slavery Free Canada: Justice or Just Words?

Holly Wood

**ABSTRACT**
In April 2023, The Canada Declaration for a Human Trafficking and Slavery Free Canada was unveiled and signed by select members of Canada's anti-human trafficking movement at the Human Rights Museum in Winnipeg, Manitoba. The Declaration sets out several items for Canada's attention, hoping to end all forms of modern slavery in Canada in the coming years. While the Declaration has good intentions behind it, this critique sets out to identify and discuss some of the critical issues within it and offers suggestions on how organizers, politicians, and Canada's leading anti-human trafficking organizations can turn performative rhetoric into real change.

The Canada Declaration for a Human Trafficking and Slavery Free Canada ("The Declaration") (see "The Canada declaration for a human trafficking and slavery free Canada, 2023") is a step forward in the fight against human trafficking in Canada. The Declaration was introduced at the Beyond Net Zero: The Canada Declaration to End Human Trafficking Symposium, hosted by the Rotary Action Group Against Slavery ("RAGAS"), Not In My City, International Justice Mission and The Mekong Club in Winnipeg, Manitoba, Canada on April 2nd and 3rd, 2023. The Symposium, which was attended by select members of Parliament, senators, survivors of human trafficking, anti-human trafficking organizations and service providers, recognizing that human trafficking is an inherent violation of an individual's human rights, freedoms, dignity, and humanity. It highlights those most affected by human trafficking in Canada – young women and girls, with particular attention to Indigenous women and girls and LGBTQ2+ youth. It is a commendable Declaration for emphasizing the complexity of the crime and the need for more awareness. However, The Declaration has a few issues.

It is important to note that while many leaders in the field (namely, members of the organizing committee and three survivors of human trafficking) were asked to consult on the Declaration, there was a call for more representation of Indigenous survivors and communities, service providers, and those who are knowledgeable in the field to provide insight before its signing. There were limited attendees in the healthcare, housing, prevention education, border security and technology sectors, which lends itself to issues if The Declaration is to end human trafficking in Canada full stop.

The Declaration calls on Canadians to support efforts against human trafficking by making confirmed "slavery-free" choices. While I agree with this, the reality is that fast fashion and unethically sourced clothing are everywhere. The Declaration and subsequent organizations supporting it should provide a list of unethical clothing companies to avoid and provide resources on the reality of labor trafficking to the public.

The Declaration sets forth an action item asking Canadians to learn more about human trafficking. The Declaration must go beyond simply telling Canadians to take action, it must tell them *how* to take action. This can include providing more funding for anti-human trafficking organizations that provide professional development and prevention education programming for children and adults. This education should be mandated in schools across the country and should be culturally relevant, age-appropriate, and available in both official languages (English and French), as well as Spanish, Indigenous languages, and others, as required.

The Declaration should also endeavor to provide a list of organizations that support survivors and make this available to the public. This would increase knowledge-sharing and community efforts. Finally, training on the "do no harm" approach should be provided publicly to support the implementation of The Declaration.

The Declaration calls on the Federal Government to take action to prevent and eradicate human trafficking. First, The Declaration calls on the Government to center survivor voices by launching the National Survivor Advisory Committee (NSAC). The Survivor-led Advisory Committee on Human Trafficking was established in 2019 but has yet to have a committee appointed to it. The Declaration should call for the appointment of a leadership role and panel for the Survivor-led Advisory Committee on Human Trafficking and build a network of survivors and people educated on human trafficking to staff the committee as soon as possible if it wishes to fulfill the related calls to action.

The Declaration calls for the Government to shield survivors from criminality incurred during trafficking. It should call for the immediate drafting and subsequent enactment of legislation that provides amnesty for survivors of human trafficking who were criminalized while under the control of their traffickers.

The Declaration calls on the Government to increase specialized services and shelters available to survivors. While there is a lack of resources available for survivors, especially in provinces like Saskatchewan and the Northwest Territories, the Government cannot just increase the number of services available without the important funding mechanisms for those providers to maintain adequate, culturally appropriate and personalized services. This would require increasing federal and provincial funding, renewing funding promptly, and setting these organizations up for success through additional funding opportunities.

The Declaration's recommendation for increasing training available for prosecutors and judges should expand to training for law enforcement and court staff and should seek to mandate this across all levels of courts in Canada. However, current research shows that introducing such training is not always effective and often leaves victim-survivors with a sense of false hope.

The Declaration's call to require all federally regulated industries and workplaces to provide training to employees who may interact with a victim of human trafficking is a great idea. However, the Declaration should call on provincial governments to expand this to every jurisdiction and every workplace in the following areas: manufacturing, hospitality, transportation, massage parlors, adult entertainment, health care, and retail.

The Declaration calls on the government to implement measures to aid in the fight against labor trafficking by requiring reporting from Canadian companies. The Declaration should take this one step further and call for supply chain companies to submit an annual report, partake in a workplace inspection completed by a third party, and implement hefty fines for noncompliance. Enforcement is critical in this regard.

Finally, The Declaration suggests that the government maintain a national Human Trafficking Strategy with measurables and annual reporting. This strategy is currently released every five years. The Declaration should suggest that the measurables and annual reporting take effect at the beginning of the following year, 2024. Timelines should be discussed with service providers, leaders and survivors as soon as possible to determine how long each measurable item would take, and a deadline should be set and enforced. The government should also be required to hire a third-party agency that will maintain a list of measurables and hold the government accountable for completing said measurables in a reasonable amount of time, not an open-ended amount of time.

Another critical issue is that The Declaration is unlikely to successfully end or prevent human trafficking. Without all voices and nationwide participation from all communities, governments, and sectors, The Declaration, much like any international law Convention or Protocol, has no enforcement behind it. While citizens, organizations, and governments can agree to do their part by honoring the recommendations within The Declaration, without an enforcement mechanism, The Declaration falls into the bracket of performative action instead of meaningful, sustainable action. This begs the questions, "what sets The Declaration apart from the other international legal tools that already exist, such as The Palermo Protocol?" If similar international conventions already exist (and are not solving the issue of human trafficking), what difference will The Declaration make? How effective will it be considering the sensitive and controversial nature of the crime? The Declaration is not legally binding and leaves a lack of accountability in its midst, while making the organizers look suitable for proposing such an endeavor.

At the signing of the Declaration, organizers called on all attendees to return in one year to discuss next steps. The Declaration should have outlined a definitive action plan so that steps have already been taken when everyone meets in 365 days. Moral statements are great, but words are not helping victims and survivors of human trafficking. Without tangible action and adequate enforcement, this Declaration will become another example of performative rhetoric.

## Disclosure statement

No potential conflict of interest was reported by the author(s).

## Reference

The Rotary Action Group Against Slavery, International Justice Mission Canada, The Mekong Club, Not In My City. (2023). *The Canada declaration for a human trafficking and slavery free Canada*. https://www.canadadeclaration.ca/read-the-declaration

# The Capacity of the International Criminal Court to Fight Human Trafficking

Filip Vojta

**ABSTRACT**
The ongoing war in Ukraine has again highlighted the link between conflict and trafficking in persons, especially refugees. Despite the understanding that trafficking in human beings in the context of armed conflict (and sometimes even outside of it) can amount to an international crime, both research and anti-trafficking policies tend to view trafficking as a (trans)national phenomenon. As a result, the potential of the International Criminal Court (ICC), a permanent international criminal tribunal tasked with adjudicating perpetrators of international crimes, to contribute to the fight against human trafficking remains largely neglected in current discourses. To fill this gap and, at the same time, facilitate efforts to build an effective and sustainable capacity to combat human trafficking at the (trans)national and international levels (UN Sustainable Development Goal 16), this article has two objectives. First, it examines the ICC's procedural capacity to combat human trafficking, focusing on its support for domestic investigations and prosecutions and the requirements for effectively transferring prosecutions to the international level. Second, it analyzes the substantive requirements for qualifying human trafficking as an international crime for purposes of effective prosecution at the ICC in light of recent jurisprudence, especially the *Ongwen* case.

## Introduction

With renewed acts of aggression since February 2022, the Russian Federation has escalated the latent armed conflict in Ukraine into a full-blown war. The masses of refugees fleeing the conflict in the months since have prompted an immediate response from various organizations warning of an increased risk of trafficking of vulnerable groups, such as unaccompanied children, internally-displaced persons and those without access to temporary protection (see e.g. Group of Experts on Action against Trafficking in Human Beings [GRETA], 2022; International Organization for Migration [IOM], 2022; Organization for Security and Co-operation in Europe [OSCE], 2022; United Nations International Children's Emergency Fund [UNICEF], 2022; United Nations Office on Drugs and Crime [UNODC], 2022a). Due to the protracted nature of the conflict and the sensitive nature of human trafficking, it remains challenging to quantify the scale of the problem (see Cockbain & Sidebottom, 2022; Hoff & de Volder, 2022). For example, a survey by the European Union Agency for Fundamental Rights (FRA) of 14,685 persons who had fled Ukraine in the period after 24 February 2022 found that 63% of the participants had experienced conflict-related violence in Ukraine and 39% had experienced severe hardship while fleeing Ukraine (FRA, 2023). The authors caution against taking the results at face value due to the highly personal and often disturbing nature of the experiences, particularly among female participants, who make up the majority of the sample (91%) and who may be less inclined to report the true nature and extent of the experienced incidents (FRA, 2023). Concerns about the discrepancy between reported and actual crime – the latter possibly also including trafficking-related victimization – echo those raised in previous reports about the relatively low number of trafficking cases prosecuted in EU member states since the renewal of the conflict (see FRA, 2022; UNODC, 2022a). More specifically, while the low number may be due to the anti-trafficking measures applied, the possibility that many cases have not yet come to the attention of law enforcement is taken seriously.

Despite the reaffirmed understanding in the above gray literature that armed conflict exacerbates the risk of human trafficking (see also UN Special Rapporteur, 2017; UNODC, 2018), academic research on the link between the phenomena remains scarce. In a recent literature review, Cockbain and Sidebottom (2022) emphasized that the analytical lens for human trafficking – even in conflict and post-conflict settings – remains that of transnational organized crime. Similarly, evaluations of the "3Ps" facets of anti-trafficking policies (i.e. protection, prevention and prosecution) typically relate to monitoring how effectively government agencies translate transnational instruments and standards into legislation and policy at the national level (Bryant & Landman, 2020). As a result, the fact that human trafficking, as a transnational and national crime, can also amount to an international crime in the context of armed conflict (and sometimes even outside of it) remains largely neglected in the current discourse. Accordingly, the role of international criminal tribunals in combating human trafficking has only marginally been analyzed.[1]

Following the closure of the UN *ad hoc* international criminal tribunals for the former Yugoslavia (International Criminal Tribunal for the former Yugoslavia [ICTY]) and Rwanda (International Criminal Tribunal for Rwanda [ICTR]), the International Criminal Court (the ICC or the Court) remains the sole international criminal tribunal to adjudicate perpetrators of international crimes (i.e. war crimes, crimes against humanity, genocide and the crime of aggression). In 2022, the ICC received unprecedented support from its Member States to open an investigation into international crimes committed in Ukraine (Office of the Prosecutor, 2022e). On 17 March 2023, the investigation resulted in an arrest warrant for Vladimir Vladimirovich Putin, President of the Russian Federation, and Maria Alekseyeva Lvova-Belova, Commissioner for Children's Rights within Putin's Office, on suspicion of committing war crimes of unlawful deportation and transfer of children from occupied territories in Ukraine to Russia (ICC, 2023a). The possibility that the alleged crimes include *de facto* cases of human trafficking should not be excluded, especially given the involvement of children as "spoils of war" (Vasiliev, 2023) and their unlawful transportation to another country using coercive means. These recent developments raise the question of how exactly the ICC can contribute to the fight against human trafficking, including overcoming persistent challenges to building an effective and sustainable capacity, such as the provision of reliable facts and evidence of human trafficking and its effective prosecution at the national and international levels (see e.g., Winterdyk, 2018, 2019). In the first part of this article, I examine the ICC's "procedural" capacity to combat human trafficking, focusing on its support for domestic investigations and prosecutions and the procedural requirements for effectively transferring prosecutions to the international level. In the second part, I discuss the substantive requirements for qualifying human trafficking as an international crime for the purpose of effective prosecution at the ICC. The analysis is based on a document review, including academic and gray literature, the ICC legislation and jurisprudence, *ad hoc* and hybrid tribunals' jurisprudence, media reports and policy briefs.

[1]Exceptions include, for example (Alhadi, 2020; Aston, 2016; Bradfield, 2020a, 2020b; Kim, 2011; Knust & Lingenfelter, 2019; Moran, 2014; Siller, 2016; Tavakoli, 2009; van der Wilt, 2014 and Pocar, 2007). Given that existing research is conducted in international (criminal) law, it seems to be largely neglected in discourses on trafficking at the (trans-)national level.

## The ICC's Procedural Capacity to Fight Human Trafficking

As a treaty-based international criminal tribunal, the ICC has the prerogative to adjudicate perpetrators of international crimes committed on the territory of states accepting its jurisdiction or by their citizens (the ICC Statute, Art. 12). Pursuant to a specific agreement or a UN Security Council (UNSC) referral, it can also extend its jurisdiction to the territory of any other state (Art. 12(3) and 13(b)). However, the actual exercise of the ICC's jurisdiction is not automatic as every state has to exercise its own criminal jurisdiction over those responsible for international crimes (the ICC Statute, Preamble, para. 6). It is only when a state fails to do so, or is unwilling or unable to carry out proceedings genuinely, that a case becomes admissible before the ICC (Art. 17). In essence, this jurisdictional complementarity gives primacy to domestic investigations and prosecutions.

### *Support to Domestic Investigations and Prosecutions: Positive Complementarity*

While the ICC's Office of the Prosecutor (OTP) relies on the assistance of national authorities in its own investigations (e.g., in obtaining access to crime scenes, taking evidence or tracing assets), national authorities can also benefit from the Court's 20 years of experience in prosecuting international crimes. In fact, the OTP has repeatedly emphasized the need to support national efforts to prosecute international crimes and related criminal conduct, e.g., by sharing information and knowledge about case-building and evidence databases (see OTP, 2010, 2015, 2019). The use of technology to preserve and access vast amounts of evidence (e.g., video and audio data, multilingual testimonies, and medical reports) is critical to the successful prosecution of complex forms of crime, such as human trafficking, which often take place over long periods of time, involve multiple perpetrators and victims, and have cross-border, chain-of-command operational structures (see, e.g., Bales, 2016; Winterdyk, 2019). Many states, especially those directly impacted by a conflict, may lack such resources, so their cooperation with the ICC is necessary. The OTP has emphasized an increased reliance on state-of-the-art technology in its work, such as using artificial intelligence, machine-learning tools and digital translation platforms to make obtained data more malleable and more accessible to investigators and analysts (OTP, 2022a). Consequently, this should also enable law enforcement authorities across different states to present, where relevant and necessary, such data as evidence to a court of law.

Recent practice supports this development and illustrates how the ICC's investigation of international crimes can simultaneously facilitate national investigations of related serious crimes. Since 2011, the ICC has been conducting investigations into alleged international crimes committed in Libya.[2] As a significant part of the investigative policy, the OTP has been focusing on crimes against vulnerable groups, i.e. women, children, migrants and refugees, which, according to the statement of the ICC Prosecutor, may also constitute war crimes and crimes against humanity (OTP, 2022a; 2022c). During the investigation, the OTP has received ample evidence that migrants and refugees in Libya have been subject to various crimes, including arbitrary detention, enforced disappearance, sexual and gender-based violence, extortion and forced labor (OTP, 2022d). Many of these crimes, in addition to potentially constituting international crimes in their own right, may also constitute cases of trafficking in persons. Through cooperation with law enforcement authorities in Ethiopia, Italy, the Netherlands, the United Kingdom and Spain, including the sharing of information and evidence and through joint witness interviews, the OTP has actively assisted in the investigation and arrest of two key suspects of human trafficking in Libya (OTP, 2022c). The suspects, who allegedly trafficked migrants from Africa to Europe and subjected them to brutal violence along the way, including in camps located in Libya, were arrested in Ethiopia and extradited to Italy and the Netherlands for prosecution.

The case described above illustrates the so-called positive approach to complementarity, whereby national responsibility for the investigation and prosecution of conduct that constitutes or may constitute international crimes is enhanced through cooperation with the ICC. By enabling domestic

[2]See the ICC web page, *Situation in Libya* (ICC-01/11), https://www.icc-cp .int/libya.

proceedings, the ICC indirectly contributes to reaffirming the rule of law at the global level and preventing serious crimes. Consequently, in terms of *realpolitik*, national proceedings reduce both the excessive use of the ICC's resources and the need for the ICC to violate state sovereignty, albeit legitimately, by prosecuting such cases at the international level. In the context of the Ukrainian conflict, it is conceivable that the ICC's investigations, such as the one against Putin and Lvova-Belova, may generate a body of evidence that will be accessible to national authorities and thus useful in facilitating domestic prosecutions of many other serious crimes, including conflict-related trafficking cases. Various frameworks for such cooperation are already in place, including the OTP's participation with other European States, under the auspices of the European Union Agency for Criminal Justice Cooperation (Eurojust), in a Joint Investigation Team (JIT) for crimes committed in Ukraine and the establishment of an ICC country office in Ukraine (see Bosco, 2022; ICC, 2023b; OTP, 2022b).

### *International Investigations and Prosecutions*

Notwithstanding the ICC Prosecutor's preference to view the Court as "a hub" for domestic law enforcement cooperation rather than "an apex criminal court" (OTP, 2022a), it is precisely the Court's power to override state sovereignty when national authorities are genuinely unwilling or unable to investigate or prosecute criminal conduct that is the distinguishing (and arguably most important) feature of its mandate. For this purpose, it is irrelevant how the conduct is incriminated at the national level as long as it meets the elements of the international crimes codified in the ICC Statute (see Arts. 6, 7, 8, 8 *bis*; also the ICC Elements of Crimes) and is sufficiently severe to warrant the involvement of the Court (the ICC Statute, Arts. 17(1)(d) and 53). This is a practical caveat, as many states may not have harmonized their criminal codes with the ICC Statute. Also, given that the 2000 UN Trafficking Protocol leaves the charge of trafficking to domestic law, definitions of the crime tend to vary according to national legislation (Alhadi, 2020; Knust & Lingenfelter, 2019; van der Wilt, 2014). The quality of the conduct counts, not its nomenclature, and it would have been a major obstacle to the ICC's mandate if the Court's prosecutions had depended on harmonization with often disparate national criminal laws. Thus, for human trafficking to be prosecuted by the ICC, it is relevant whether the conduct can be subsumed under the crimes listed in the Statute and whether it is sufficiently serious.

The criterion of sufficient seriousness, or "gravity," is a procedural rather than a substantive factor, as all crimes within the Court's jurisdiction threaten "international peace, security and well-being of the world" (the ICC Statute, Preamble, para. 3) and are therefore sufficiently severe enough to warrant the involvement of the Court. Since this is virtually impossible given the Court's resources, the criterion is used to prioritize cases and exclude from international prosecution those that, even though technically falling under the Court's jurisdiction, are of marginal gravity. In 2020, the ICC Appeals Chamber in *The Prosecutor v. Al Hassan* established that the gravity assessment must be made on a case-by-case basis, involving "a holistic evaluation of all relevant qualitative and quantitative criteria" (para. 127(iii)).[3] It further stipulated that even though some quantitative criteria, such as the number of victims, are certainly relevant, they are not, in themselves, determinative of the case's gravity (paras. 97 and 127(iii) and (vi)). In light of the jurisprudence, it is reasonable to conclude that not all cases of human trafficking, even if they constitute an international crime, will be eligible for prosecution by the ICC on the basis of the gravity criterion.

The final criterion for the admissibility of human trafficking before the ICC is the unwillingness or inability of national authorities to genuinely investigate or prosecute the case. In assessing the unwillingness, the Court will examine whether national proceedings

> are being carried out to shield a person from individual criminal responsibility, whether there have been unjustified delays in the proceedings, whether a lack of independence or impartiality can be observed, or whether

---

[3]Such criteria may include, for example, the extent of the damage caused, the nature and circumstances of the crime, the degree of participation, the intent and motive of the accused person, and the number of victims (The Prosecutor v. Al Hassan, 2020, para. 89).

the proceedings are in any other way inconsistent with an intent to bring a defendant to justice (Knust & Lingenfelter, 2019, p. 1771–1772; see the ICC Statute, Art. 17(2)).

The determination of inability, on the other hand, is dependent on whether, due to a collapse or unavailability of its justice system, the state is unable to obtain the accused or the relevant evidence and testimony or is otherwise unable to carry out its proceedings (the ICC Statute, Art. 17(3)).

## The ICC's Substantive Capacity to Fight Human Trafficking

The discussion of trafficking in persons as an international crime under the ICC Statute revolves primarily around a single offense, the crime against humanity of enslavement, as codified in Art. 7(1)(c) (see, e.g. Alhadi, 2020; Aston, 2016; Kim, 2011; Knust & Lingenfelter, 2019; Moran, 2014; Siller, 2016; van der Wilt, 2014) This focus is understandable. On one hand, crimes against humanity can be committed in peacetime and during armed conflict, allowing the Court to exercise jurisdiction over criminal conduct that is not exclusively conflict-related. Given the pervasiveness of trafficking outside of conflict zones,[4] this is a welcome addition to the arsenal of global anti-trafficking measures. On the other hand, the focus on the crime against humanity of enslavement is obvious in that the provisions of the ICC Statute (Art. 7(2)(c)) and the ICC Elements of Crimes (Footnote. 11) explicitly include trafficking in persons, especially women and children, within the material elements of the offense. However, other international crimes in the ICC Statute, such as sexual slavery as both a crime against humanity and a war crime, also include human trafficking in their material elements, yet they remain somewhat neglected in the discussion.

The 1998 ICC Statute included human trafficking in its provisions before the 2000 UN Trafficking Protocol provided its definition. In response, some commentators have lamented the lack of definitional clarity in the ICC Statute and expressed uncertainty about how trafficking in persons should be interpreted in the ICC Statute in light of both the 1926 Slavery Convention and the 2000 UN Trafficking Protocol (see, e.g., Kim, 2011; Siller, 2016; van der Wilt, 2014).[5] It was only after the ICC handed down judgments in several cases explicitly dealing with enslavement and sexual slavery (The Prosecutor *v.* Dominic Ongwen, 2021; The Prosecutor v. Bosco Ntaganda, 2019; The Prosecutor v. Germain Katanga, 2014) that the material relationship between human trafficking, enslavement, and sexual slavery could be more clearly discerned. The following subsections discuss these developments in order to clarify under what circumstances trafficking in persons may constitute an international crime and thus be prosecuted directly by the ICC. The subsections are as follows: first, the contextual elements of each crime that includes human trafficking are discussed as they give the crime an "international dimension" (Cryer et al., 2021, p. 230); second, the jurisprudential interpretation of the substantive elements of each crime is discussed in order to clarify the ICC judges' view of the relationship between human trafficking, enslavement, and sexual slavery as international crimes.

### *Enslavement and Sexual Slavery as Crimes Against Humanity*

#### *Contextual Elements*

Based on the ICC Statute, for conduct to constitute a crime against humanity, both the contextual and material elements of the crime must be satisfied. More specifically, if considering human trafficking, it would have to be committed "as part of a widespread or systematic attack directed against any civilian population, with [perpetrator's] knowledge of the attack" (the ICC Statute, Art. 7(1)). These contextual elements must be proven in sequence: first, that an attack consisting of multiple commissions of acts

[4]The 2022 Global Report on Trafficking in Persons shows an increase in the number of detected trafficking victims in the Global North, as opposed to countries in the Global South, which are more often associated with armed conflict (UNODC, 2022b).

[5]This is just one part of an ongoing discussion about the pros and cons of conflating slavery with enslavement and human trafficking in international law and policy (see also Allain, 2013; Atak & Simeon, 2015; Chuang, 2014; Gallagher, 2010; Palacios-Arapiles, 2022; Pocar, 2007; Scarpa, 2008; Tavakoli, 2009).

incriminated as crimes against humanity was perpetrated against a civilian population "in furtherance of a State or organizational policy" (Art. 7(2)(a)); second, that it was widespread or systematic; and third, that the perpetrator knew or intended that the crime (i.e., trafficking) was part of the attack. Until recently, a significant part of the discussion has been devoted to the question of whether trafficking in persons can actually satisfy these contextual elements to qualify as an international crime (see, e.g., Alhadi, 2020; Kim, 2011; Knust & Lingenfelter, 2019; Obokata, 2005; Siller, 2016; van der Wilt, 2014). The crux of the matter is the nexus between individual acts of trafficking and the broader context of an attack against civilians. In considering whether individual conduct constitutes a "part" of the attack, its relationship to both the "attack as a whole" and its "various components," such as the pattern of crimes or the type of victims, is analyzed so that "isolated acts that clearly defer in their nature, aims and consequences" will not be considered a part of the attack (The Prosecutor v. Germain Katanga, 2014, para. 1124).

In practice, trafficking by *members* or *close associates* of criminal organizations responsible for a widespread or systematic attack against civilians, such as Los Zetas-type drug cartels, ISIS-type terrorist groups, or LRA-type paramilitaries, would clearly fall within the scope of this interpretation, as they would not be able to deny their knowledge of the attack (see The Prosecutor v. Dominic Ongwen, 2021, para. 2805). Perpetrators of state-sponsored peacetime trafficking occurring widely and systematically, such as forced prison labor in certain states, would also fit this interpretation. Forced labor during a lawful sentence imposed by the state is not customarily prohibited (Article 8(3)(c)(i) of the 1966 International Covenant on Civil and Political Rights [ICCPR]), but it may be prohibited if, by its nature and circumstances, it amounts to cruel, inhuman or degrading treatment or punishment (ICCPR, Art. 7). The mistreatment of prisoners in U.S. prisons who are forced, often with threats of violence, into work arrangements with unsafe working conditions, dilapidated living facilities, and without compensation may amount not only to human trafficking but also to crimes against humanity because such mistreatment is sanctioned as official state policy by the 13th Amendment[6] to the U.S. Constitution, is widespread and systematic in nature, and involves officials at the local, state and federal levels, thus satisfying the contextual elements of enslavement as a crime against humanity under the ICC Statute (see ACLU & GHRC, 2022; Alhadi, 2020).[7]

In such cases where the perpetrators are *not directly affiliated* with criminal organizations or the state and may have only vague knowledge of the attack, establishing the nexus between individual acts of trafficking and the broader context of the attack would arguably be more challenging. For example, isolated cases of trafficking of refugees from Ukraine in EU member states would most likely fall outside ICC's jurisdiction because their objective contribution to the ongoing attack against Ukrainian civilians would be considered marginal, even though the perpetrators knew they were trafficking in targeted civilians. On the other hand, there may be traffickers unaffiliated with Putin's regime, but who are nevertheless opportunistically focused on exploiting and prolonging the misery of many Ukrainian refugees, thus contributing significantly to the overall attack on Ukrainian civilians (see the "nature, aims and consequences" criteria in *Katanga* above). In the absence of prosecution at the national level, such a case, if deemed serious enough, could hypothetically be prosecuted at the ICC as a crime against humanity of enslavement or sexual slavery. Consequently, it can be argued that many, though certainly not all, cases of human trafficking could indeed satisfy the contextual elements of crimes against humanity and thus be prosecuted by the ICC (cf. van der Wilt, 2014). The Court's evolving interpretation of the contextual elements will be necessary in determining how strong the link between individual conduct and the overall attack against the civilian population must be for such conduct to qualify as a crime against humanity (similarly, Knust & Lingenfelter, 2019). Finally, in addition to the

[6]Section 1.: Neither slavery nor involuntary servitude,except as a punishment for crime whereof the party shall have beenduly convicted, shall exist within the United States, or any placesubject to their jurisdiction.

[7]The challenge to prosecuting such cases at the ICC is not only the potential lack of jurisdiction of the Court due to the non-ratification of the ICC Statute in those states where state-sponsored crimes may be rampant, but also the fact that some of these states, such as the U.S., Russia and China, have a permanent seat on UNSC, which allows them to effectively block any attempts to adjudicate cases in which their government may be implicated on the basis of a UNSC referral to ICC.

contextual elements, trafficking in persons must meet the material elements of enslavement or sexual slavery to qualify as a crime against humanity under the ICC Statute.

### *Material Elements*

As noted above, the ICC Statute includes human trafficking in enslavement and sexual slavery as crimes against humanity. Art. 7(2)(c) defines enslavement as "the exercise of any or all of the powers attaching to the right of ownership over a person and *includes the exercise of such power in the course of trafficking in persons, in particular women and children*". Some authors have questioned what material impact this inclusion of trafficking in persons may have on the scope of the definition of enslavement in the ICC Statute, which otherwise closely resembles the definition of slavery as provided in the 1926 Slavery Convention.[8] Siller (2016, p. 414), for example, argues that "a plain reading" of the definition would only permit the "prosecution of those traffickers who also enslave." To the extent that such an interpretation favors the traditional dichotomy between trafficking and slavery, i.e., where trafficking "criminalizes the process of acquiring persons for their exploitation" and slavery criminalizes "the treatment imposed on a person" it is not considered problematic because it does not appear to change the definition of slavery in any substantive way (Siller, 2016, pp. 407, 414–415). Interestingly, the ICC Elements of Crime, an official interpretive instrument of the ICC Statute, turns this interpretation on its head by stating in paragraph 1 that in addition to "buying, selling, hiring, and bartering" people can also be enslaved by imposing on them a deprivation of liberty *similar* to the exercise of powers associated with ownership. More specifically, Footnote 11 instructs that such conduct "includes trafficking in persons, in particular women and children." Thus, the Elements merged the concepts rather than maintaining the dichotomy, *subsuming* trafficking under enslavement. Notably, the judges in the *Ongwen* case, the first ICC case tackling the charges of enslavement, emphasized this subsumption by providing a non-exhaustive list of factors indicating the existence of enslavement (para. 2712). Many of these factors reflect the "conduct" (e.g., control of movement, the physical environment and measures preventing escape), "means" (e.g. force, the threat of force or coercion, subjection to cruel treatment and abuse, psychological control or pressure, the abuse of the victim's vulnerability) and "purpose" (e.g., control of sexuality, forced labor and subjecting the person to servile status) elements of trafficking in persons according to the UN Trafficking Protocol.[9] The fact that the judges relied not only on the previous jurisprudence of the ICC (the *Ntaganda* case, para. 952; the *Katanga* case, para. 976), but also on that of the *ad hoc* and hybrid tribunals, i.e., the ICTY (Prosecutor v. Kunarac et al., 2002, para. 119), the Special Court for Sierra Leone (Prosecutor v. Charles Ghankay Taylor, 2012, para. 447), and the Extraordinary Chambers in the Courts of Cambodia (Prosecutor v. Duch, 2010, para. 342), in explaining the factors is praised by some authors as indicative of a new authoritative approach to the interpretation of slavery (Palacios-Arapiles, 2022, p. 455). To the extent that the judges in the *Ongwen* case focused significantly on the *process* of acquiring victims (e.g., abduction) and reduced the relevance of other factors traditionally associated with slavery, such as a minimum duration, commercial transaction, or legal ownership, this interpretation of enslavement seems more appropriate to grasp the contemporary "mutations" of the phenomenon; including human trafficking.

Sexual slavery as a crime against humanity (ICC Statute, Art. 7(1)(g)-2), is a specific form of enslavement characterized by an additional material element, i.e. that the perpetrator, in addition to violating personal liberty (enslavement), also restricted sexual autonomy by forcing the victim to perform at least one act of a sexual nature (sexual slavery). Since sexual slavery includes all elements of

[8]Art 1(1): "Slavery is the status or condition of a person over whom any or all of the powers attaching to the right of ownership are exercised".

[9]Art. 3(a) of the 2000 UN Trafficking Protocol criminalizes certain acts (i.e. recruitment, transportation, transfer, harboring or receipt of persons) done by certain means (i.e. "the threat or use of force or other forms of coercion, of abduction, of fraud, of deception, of the abuse of power or of a position of vulnerability or of the giving or receiving of payments or benefits to achieve the consent of a person having control over another person") for the purpose of exploitation (e.g. prostitution of others or other forms of sexual exploitation, forced labor or services, slavery or practices similar to slavery, servitude or the removal of organs) as "trafficking in persons".

enslavement, it is understood that it may also include those trafficking cases where sexual abuse of various kinds may be present (the ICC Elements of Crimes, Footnote 18). However, as the judges in the *Ongwen* case emphasized, the concurrence of these two crimes is not allowed, i.e., to the extent that all the elements of sexual slavery are met, the same facts are not further considered as enslavement (paras. 3051 and 3086). This could be seen as an indication of the special gravity of sexual slavery as opposed to "ordinary" enslavement. In the *Ongwen* case, the first ICC case to convict for both enslavement and sexual slavery, the judges somewhat controversially also considered the perpetrator's conduct and the victim's experience outside the scope of the charges to determine the gravity of the crime of enslavement (The Prosecutor V. Dominic Ongwen, Sentence, 2021, paras. 312, 313, 354). Specifically, even though some enslaved victims were not raped during the period charged, the fact that they were raped afterward was considered a "natural consequence" of their slavery and thus significantly influenced the judges' determination of the severity of the enslavement, resulting in the same sentence (20 years) as for the sexual slavery crimes. (paras. 308, 314, 355). It can be tentatively concluded that the sentence for enslavement might have been lower had it not been for the controversial determination of the gravity of the crime. In fact, in cases where the victims were abducted and subjected to forced labor within the period charged, but there were no findings of sexual abuse within or beyond the period charged, the sentences for enslavement were significantly lower. (14 years; paras. 168, 200, 237, 272).

### *Sexual Slavery as a War Crime*

Trafficking may also be prosecuted by the ICC as a war crime of sexual slavery. Similar to the crimes against humanity above, the conduct must meet certain contextual elements to qualify as a war crime. Specifically, the ICC Elements of Crime require that the conduct be committed "in the context of" and "associated with" an armed conflict, whether international (Art. 8(2)(b)(xxii)-2) or non-international (Art. 8(2)(e)(vi)-2) in character. The perpetrator must be aware of the factual circumstances that established the existence of such a conflict. Again, the interpretation of these contextual elements, i.e. the nexus between the conduct and the armed conflict, will determine the scope of trafficking cases that may amount to war crimes.

Technically, the ICC may have jurisdiction over war crimes committed outside the conflict zone (e.g., in neighboring states) as long as the jurisdictional requirements are met and the nexus to an armed conflict is established (see e.g. Situation in the Islamic Republic of Afghanistan, 2020, para. 79; Situation in the Republic of Burundi, 2017, paras. 193, 194). For example, whether the trafficking of Ukrainian refugees in other European states constitutes a war crime of sexual slavery will depend on whether the perpetrators are nationals of an ICC State Party and whether there is a sufficiently close connection to the armed conflict in Ukraine. International jurisprudence has been fairly consistent in arguing that crimes that are temporally or geographically remote from the actual conflict may nevertheless constitute war crimes (see the *Ongwen* case, para. 2689; The Prosecutor v. Jean-Pierre Bemba Gombo, 2016, para. 144; the *Kunarac et al.* case, para. 57). Further, while the conflict must have influenced the perpetrator's decision, ability, or manner of committing the crime, the perpetrator need not be a member of a party to the conflict (e.g. the *Bemba Gombo* case, para. 143; the *Katanga* case, para. 1176.). For example, to the extent that refugees fleeing a conflict to a neighboring country may be seen as a lucrative opportunity (decision) to be seized by falsely luring them to "safety" whereupon they are confined, coerced into obedience, and sexually assaulted (ability/manner), civilian traffickers outside the conflict zone could also be found guilty of the war crime of sexual slavery. Regarding the element of awareness, it could plausibly be argued that the perpetrators were aware of the conflict insofar as it influenced their decision, ability and manner to commit the crime (for a similar argument in support of such a construction of the "nexus requirement" for trafficking as a war crime, see Bradfield, 2020b). The material elements of trafficking would also have to mirror those of sexual slavery as a crime against humanity (see above).

Although there is no general offense of enslavement as a war crime in the ICC Statute, trafficking in persons could potentially also meet the elements of other war crimes, such as unlawful deportation, transfer or confinement, conscription and enlistment of child soldiers, or enforced prostitution. Some authors similarly argue that different aspects of the trafficking phenomena could technically also be charged under other war crimes or crimes against humanity, such as torture, inhuman treatment or rape (see Knust & Lingenfelter, 2019). To the extent that trafficking in persons may simultaneously satisfy the elements of both war crimes and crimes against humanity, the list of offenses in the ICC Statute seems more than adequate to effectively address the various dimensions of the phenomenon, provided that the cases are serious enough.

## Conclusion

Contrary to some views that bemoan the lack of trafficking cases prosecuted by the ICC (e.g., Alhadi, 2020; Bradfield, 2020a) this article argues that both the legal framework and jurisprudence show that the ICC's capacity to address trafficking in persons – either by assisting domestic investigations and prosecutions or by trying trafficking cases itself under a different banner – is alive and well. This is not to deny the existence of practical challenges to using this capacity, which often revolve around the (un) willingness of states, especially those supporting the crimes themselves, to cooperate with the ICC. Nevertheless, as recent practice shows, there are tangible improvements in this regard, and it is hoped that the acceptance of technological advances in the collection, preservation and accessibility of evidence will not only make the ICC a desirable partner in (trans)national efforts to combat human trafficking, but also enable the Court to effectively prosecute such cases itself, if necessary. The Court's seminal interpretation of enslavement in the *Ongwen* case, which drew on many essential elements of the UN definition of trafficking in persons, emphasized the commonality of the phenomena and the need to interpret slavery in accordance with contemporary circumstances and its evolving phenomenology. Consequently, it remains to be seen whether and how such an interpretation might influence the harmonization of national criminal legislation with the ICC Statute and whether it will also affect the interpretation of these crimes at the national level.

## Disclosure statement

No potential conflict of interest was reported by the author.

## ORCID

Filip Vojta http://orcid.org/0000-0002-4786-2463

## References

ACLU & GHRC. (2022). Captive labor. Exploitation of incarcerated workers. Research Report [in italics]. American Civil Liberties Union (ACLU) and the University of Chicago Law School Global Human Rights Clinic (GHRC). https://www.aclu.org/report/captive-labor-exploitation-incarcerated-workers

Alhadi, N. (2020). Increasing case traffic: Expanding the International Criminal Court's focus on human trafficking cases. *Michigan Journal of International Law*, *41*(3), 541–580. https://doi.org/10.36642/mjil.41.3.increasing

Allain, J. (2013). *Slavery in international law: Of human exploitation and trafficking*. Martinus Nijhoff Publishers.

Aston, J. N. (2016). *Trafficking of women and children: Article 7 of the Rome statute*. Oxford University Press.

Atak, I., & Simeon, J. C. (2015). Human trafficking: Mapping the legal boundaries of international refugee law and criminal justice. *Journal of International Criminal Justice*, *12*(5), 1019–1038. https://doi.org/10.1093/jicj/mqu093

Bales, K. (2016). *Blood and earth: Modern slavery, ecocide, and the secret to saving the world*. Random House.

Bosco, D. (2022, October 27). *The ICC's impact in Ukraine*. Lawfare. https://www.lawfareblog.com/iccs-impact-ukraine

Bradfield, P. (2020a, October 29). *Trafficking in persons – the forgotten international crime? – part 1*. Opinio Juris. http://opiniojuris.org/2020/10/29/trafficking-in-persons-the-forgotten-international-crime-part-1/

Bradfield, P. (2020b, October 29). *Trafficking in persons – the forgotten international crime? – part II*. Opinio Juris. http://opiniojuris.org/2020/10/29/trafficking-in-persons-the-forgotten-international-crime-part-ii/

Bryant, K., & Landman, T. (2020). Combatting human trafficking since Palermo: What do we know about what works? *Journal of Human Trafficking*, *6*(2), 119–140. https://doi.org/10.1080/23322705.2020.1690097

Chuang, J. A. (2014). Exploitation creep and the unmaking of human trafficking law. *The American Journal of International Law*, *108*(4), 609–649. https://doi.org/10.5305/amerjintelaw.108.4.0609

Cockbain, E., & Sidebottom, A. (2022). War, displacement, and human trafficking, and exploitation: Findings from an evidence-gathering roundtable in response to the war in Ukraine. *Journal of Human Trafficking*, 1–29. https://doi.org/10.1080/23322705.2022.2128242

Cryer, R., Robinson, D., & Vasiliev, S. (2021). *An introduction to international criminal law and procedure* (4th ed.). Cambridge University Press.

FRA. (2022). *The Russian war of aggression against Ukraine – the broad fundamental rights impact in the EU. Bulletin #2*. European Union Agency for Fundamental Rights (FRA). https://fra.europa.eu/sites/default/files/fra_uploads/fra-2022-ukraine-bulletin-2_en.pdf

FRA. (2023). *Fleeing Ukraine: Displaced People's experiences in the EU. Ukrainian survey 2022*. European Union Agency for Fundamental Rights (FRA). https://fra.europa.eu/sites/default/files/fra_uploads/fra-2023-ukraine-survey_en.pdf

Gallagher, E. T. (2010). *The international law of human trafficking*. Cambridge University Press.

GRETA. (2022, March 17). *Human trafficking experts: States must urgently protect refugees fleeing Ukraine*. Council of Europe. https://www.coe.int/en/web/portal/-/human-trafficking-experts-states-must-urgently-protect-refugees-fleeing-ukraine

Hoff, S., & de Volder, E. (2022). *Preventing human trafficking of refugees from Ukraine: A rapid assessment of risks and gaps in the anti-trafficking response*. La Strada International.

ICC. (2023a, March 17). *Situation in Ukraine: ICC judges issue arrest warrants against Vladimir Vladimirovich Putin and Maria Alekseyevna Lvova-Belova*. International Criminal Court, Press Release. https://www.icc-cpi.int/news/situation-ukraine-icc-judges-issue-arrest-warrants-against-vladimir-vladimirovich-putin-and

ICC. (2023b, March 23). *Ukraine and International Criminal Court sign an agreement on the establishment of a country office*. International Criminal Court, Press Release. https://www.icc-cpi.int/news/ukraine-and-international-criminal-court-sign-agreement-establishment-country-office.

IOM. (2022, March 16). *IOM warns of increased risk of trafficking in persons for people fleeing Ukraine*. International Organization for Migration. https://www.iom.int/news/iom-warns-increased-risk-trafficking-persons-people-fleeing-ukraine

Kim, J. (2011). *Prosecuting human trafficking as a crime against humanity under the Rome statute*. Columbia Law School Gender and Sexuality Online (GSL Online). https://ssrn.com/abstract=1779263

Knust, N., & Lingenfelter, K. (2019). Individual criminal responsibility beyond the state: Human trafficking as both a transnational and an international crime. In J. Winterdyk & J. Jones (Eds.), *The Palgrave international handbook on human trafficking* (pp. 1765–1782). Palgrave Macmillan.

Moran, C. F. (2014). Human trafficking and the Rome statute of the international criminal court. *The Age of Human Rights Journal*, *3*, 32–45.

Obokata, T. (2005). Trafficking of human beings as a crime against humanity: Some implications for the international legal system. *The International and Comparative Law Quarterly*, *54*(2), 445–457. https://doi.org/10.1093/iclq/lei005

Office of the Prosecutor. (2010, February 01). *Prosecutorial Strategy 2009-2012*. International Criminal Court. https://www.icc-cpi.int/sites/default/files/NR/rdonlyres/66A8DCDC-3650-4514-AA62-D229D1128F65/281506/OTPProsecutorialStrategy20092013.pdf

Office of the Prosecutor. (2015, July 06). *Strategic Plan 2016-2018*. International Criminal Court. https://www.legal-tools.org/doc/7ae957/pdf/

Office of the Prosecutor. (2019, July 17). *Strategic plan 2019-2021*. International Criminal Court. https://www.icc-cpi.int/sites/default/files/itemsDocuments/20190726-strategic-plan-eng.pdf

Office of the Prosecutor. (2022a, April 29). *ICC prosecutor, Karim A.A. Khan QC, outlines renewed approach to investigations in the situation in Libya to the United Nations Security Council*. International Criminal Court. https://www.icc-cpi.int/news/icc-prosecutor-karim-aa-khan-qc-outlines-renewed-approach-investigations-situation-libya

Office of the Prosecutor. (2022b, April 25). *Statement by ICC Prosecutor, Karim A.A. Khan QC: Office of the prosecutor joins national authorities in Joint Investigation Team on international crimes committed in Ukraine*. International Criminal Court. https://www.icc-cpi.int/news/statement-icc-prosecutor-karim-aa-khan-qc-office-prosecutor-joins-national-authorities-joint

Office of the Prosecutor. (2022c, October 21). *Statement of ICC Prosecutor Karim A.A. Khan KC on arrest and extradition of suspects in relation to crimes against victims of trafficking in Libya*. International Criminal Court. https://www.icc-cpi.int/news/statement-icc-prosecutor-karim-aa-khan-kc-arrest-and-extradition-suspects-relation-crimes.

Office of the Prosecutor. (2022d, September 07). *Statement of ICC Prosecutor, Karim A.A. Khan QC: Office of the Prosecutor joins national authorities in Joint Team on crimes against migrants in Libya*. International Criminal Court. https://www.icc-cpi.int/news/statement-icc-prosecutor-karim-aa-khan-qc-office-prosecutor-joins-national-authorities-joint-0

Office of the Prosecutor. (2022e, March 02). *Statement of ICC Prosecutor, Karim A.A. Khan QC, on the situation in Ukraine: Receipt of referrals from 39 states parties and the opening of an investigation*. International Criminal Court. https://www.icc-cpi.int/news/statement-icc-prosecutor-karim-aa-khan-qc-situation-ukraine-receipt-referrals-39-states

OSCE. (2022, April 22). *Recommendations on enhancing efforts to identify and mitigate risks of trafficking in human beings online as a result of the humanitarian crisis in Ukraine*. Organization for Security and Co-operation in Europe (OSCE). https://www.osce.org/files/f/documents/4/c/516423_0.pdf

Palacios-Arapiles, S. (2022). The interpretation of slavery before the International Criminal Court: Reconciling legal borders? *Max Planck Yearbook of United Nations Law Online*, *25*(1), 416–456. https://doi.org/10.1163/18757413_02501023

Pocar, F. (2007). Human trafficking: A crime against humanity. In E. U. Savona & S. Stefanizzi (Eds.), *Measuring human trafficking: Complexities and pitfalls* (pp. 5–12). Springer.

The Prosecutor v. Al Hassan Ag Abdoul Aziz Ag Mohamed Ag Mahmoud. (2020a). *Judgment on the appeal of Mr Al Hassan against the decision of Pre-Trial Chamber I entitled 'Décision relative à l'exeption d'irrecevabilité pour insufficance de gravité de l'affaire soulevée par la défense'*. No.: ICC-01/12-01/18 OA. https://www.icc-cpi.int/sites/default/files/CourtRecords/CR2020_00536.PDF

The Prosecutor v. Bosco Ntaganda, Judgment. (2019). No.: ICC-01/04-02/06. https://www.legal-tools.org/doc/80578a/pdf

Prosecutor v. Charles Ghunkay Taylor. (2012). *Trial judgement, case no.: scsl-03-01-t*. https://www.legal-tools.org/doc/8075e7/pdf

The Prosecutor v. Dominic Ongwen, Sentence. (2021). No.: ICC-02/04-01/15. https://www.icc-cpi.int/sites/default/files/CourtRecords/CR2021_04230.PDF

*The Prosecutor v. Dominic Ongwen, Trial Judgment*. (2021). *No.: ICC-02/04-01/15*. https://www.icc-cpi.int/sites/default/files/CourtRecords/CR2021_01026.PDF

Prosecutor v. Dragoljub Kunarac, Radomir Kovač and Zoran Vuković, Appeal Judgement. (2002). *Case No.: IT-96-23 & IT-96-23/1-A*. https://www.legal-tools.org/doc/029a09/pdf

The Prosecutor v. Germain Katanga. (2014). *Judgment pursuant to article 74 of the Statute, No.: ICC-01/04-01/07*. https://www.icc-cpi.int/sites/default/files/CourtRecords/CR2015_04025.PDF

The Prosecutor v. Jean-Pierre Bemba Gombo. (2016). *Judgment pursuant to Article 74 of the Statute, No.: ICC-01/05-01/08*. https://www.legal-tools.org/doc/edb0cf/pdf

Prosecutor v. Kaing Guek Eav Alias Duch. (2010). *Trial Judgement, Case File/Dossier No. 001/18-07-2007/ECCC/TC*. https://www.legal-tools.org/doc/dbdb62/pdf

Scarpa, S. (2008). *Trafficking in human beings: Modern slavery*. Oxford University Press.

Siller, N. (2016). 'Modern slavery': Does international law distinguish between slavery, enslavement and trafficking? *Journal of International Criminal Justice*, *14*(2), 405–428. https://doi.org/10.1093/jicj/mqv075

Situation in the Islamic Republic of Afghanistan. (2020b). *Judgment on the appeal against the decision on the authorisation of an investigation into the situation in the Islamic republic of Afghanistan*, No. ICC-02/17 OA4. https://www.legal-tools.org/doc/x7kl12/pdf

Situation in the Republic of Burundi. (2017 October, 25). P*ublic Redacted Version of "Decision Pursuant to Article 15 of the Rome Statute on the Authorization of an Investigation into the Situation in the Republic of Burundi", ICC-01/17-X-9-US-exp*. No. ICC-01/17-X (2017). https://www.legal-tools.org/doc/8f2373/pdf

Tavakoli, N. (2009). A crime that offends the conscience of humanity: A proposal to reclassify trafficking in women as an international crime. *International Criminal Law Review*, *9*(1), 77–98. https://doi.org/10.1163/157181209/398826

UNICEF. (2022, March 19). *Children fleeing war in Ukraine at heightened risk of trafficking and exploitation*. United Nations International Children's Emergency Fund (UNICEF). https://www.unicef.org/press-releases/children-fleeing-war-ukraine-heightened-risk-trafficking-and-exploitation

UNODC. (2018). *Global report on trafficking in persons 2018* (UNODC research). United Nations Office on Drugs and Crime. https://www.unodc.org/documents/data-and-analysis/glotip/2018/GLOTiP_2018_BOOK_web_small.pdf

UNODC. (2022a). *Conflict in Ukraine: Key evidence on risks of trafficking in persons and smuggling of migrants* (UNODC research update December 2022). United Nations Office on Drugs and Crime. https://www.unodc.org/documents/data-and-analysis/tip/Conflict_Ukraine_TIP_2022.pdf

UNODC. (2022b). *Global report on trafficking in persons 2022* (UNODC research). United Nations Office on Drugs and Crime. https://www.unodc.org/documents/data-and-analysis/glotip/2022/GLOTiP_2022_web.pdf

UN Special Rapporteur on Trafficking in Persons, Especially Women and Children. (2017). *Sale and sexual exploitation of children, including child prostitution, child pornography and other child sexual abuse material; and trafficking in persons, especially women and children (A/72/164).* UN General Assembly. https://documents-dds-ny.un.org/doc/UNDOC/GEN/N17/218/83/PDF/N1721883.pdf?OpenElement

van der Wilt, H. (2014). Trafficking in human beings, enslavement, crimes against humanity: Unraveling the concepts. *Chinese Journal of International Law, 13*(2), 297–334. https://doi.org/10.1093/chinesejil/jmu015

Vasiliev, S. (2023, March 20). *The international criminal court goes all-in: What now?* Ejil: Talk!, Blog of the European Journal of International Law. https://www.ejiltalk.org/the-international-criminal-court-goes-all-in-what-now/.

Winterdyk, J. (2018). Combating (child) human trafficking: Building capacity. *Oñati Socio-Legal Series, 8*(1), 106–129. online. https://doi.org/10.35295/osls.iisl/0000-0000-0000-0921

Winterdyk, J. (2019). Explaining human trafficking: Modern day slavery. In J. Winterdyk & J. Jones (Eds.), *The Palgrave international handbook on human trafficking* (pp. 1257–1274). Palgrave Macmillan.

# How Do Local Efforts Address a Global Issue? Communities Need Good Data

Annjanette R. Alejano-Steele, Amanda A. Finger, and Kara Napolitano

**ABSTRACT**

This essay offers reflections and lessons learned from one organization's efforts to contribute to and measure progress statewide within the United States. Through collecting inclusive data using community-based participatory methods, local efforts can be sustained by building upon locally tailored solid tools and longitudinally gathering statewide data to demonstrate gaps and progress. Inclusive data drive political and systems buy-in, increase responsible public awareness initiatives, help community members and professionals understand what human trafficking looks like in their communities, and help secure resources to respond. Over the last 10 years of data collection, we have seen progress as Colorado communities have initiated responses with local resources and political will. Among the lessons learned in creating comprehensive community responses, patient and mutually beneficial time is necessary to establish intersectional and interprofessional collaborations that are transparent and tailored to unique community geographies and demographics.

This essay offers reflections and lessons learned from one organization's efforts to contribute to and measure progress in our home state of Colorado. The Denver-based Laboratory to Combat Human Trafficking (LCHT) initiated its anti-trafficking efforts in 2005, the same year that federal grant monies poured into Colorado to establish coalitions to conduct law enforcement and service provider training and create protocols to support victims of human trafficking. LCHT was part of the burgeoning national anti-trafficking momentum to build local responses to the "new crime of human trafficking" heralded by the Presidents Bill Clinton and George W. Bush administrations as a successful outcome in a globalized world. As that momentum created successes and challenges over recent decades, we have written about the challenges of this top-down approach versus a locally driven social movement to address human trafficking in our communities (A. Miller et al., 2022). This essay elaborates upon the challenges and underscores the necessity of ensuring community voices stay squarely centered on these complex responses. Although the "case study" focuses on the LCHT program, the commentary and issues (based on our observations and research) are generalizable to many other NGOs.

## Laboratory to Combat Human Trafficking History and Positionality

In the United States, multisector responses to human trafficking began to take shape fervently in the years following the passage of the United Nations Protocol to Prevent, Suppress and Punish Trafficking in Persons, Especially Women and Children (2000) and the U.S. Trafficking Victims Protection Act (2000). Colorado was among many states to examine the state-level nuances of this global human rights abuse (A. Alejano-Steele et al., 2019). In these formative years, international and U.S. policies on human trafficking shaped state-level responses as funding from the U.S. Department of Justice catalyzed the creation of task forces around the U.S., prioritizing prosecution and protection for victims of human trafficking. Public awareness narratives then focused on human trafficking as a transnational organized crime or a gender violence issue primarily affecting foreign nationals. By 2006, Colorado legislation defined Trafficking in Adults, Trafficking in Children and Coercion of Involuntary Servitude.

Following the passage of state-level legislation, Colorado focused on training law enforcement agencies, serving foreign nationals or child victims of trafficking, and conducting outreach to "at-risk" populations (e.g., detainees, migrant farm workers, and unhoused youth). Colorado anti-trafficking coalitions developed response protocols to serve survivors of all forms of human trafficking and established cross-sector partnerships between law enforcement and community-based organizations. Several of these founding coalitions also invited grassroots organizers, and advocates from immigration rights, labor rights, and child welfare fields, and some coalitions enabled community members to step into response efforts. Including these different perspectives helped expand beyond a "professionalized response" and embed awareness of human trafficking in various communities around the State. However, like many states, federal funding fluctuations created challenges in sustaining Colorado's human trafficking responses as these funds were often the sole or major source of support for programs. As we have witnessed in our State, participation and momentum from community members and survivor leaders at the forefront, alongside frontline professionals, often reveal other essential priorities for addressing human trafficking beyond funded mandates. These tensions continue to play out across our State.

Due to prosecutorial challenges and complaints from law enforcement about the enforceability of the 2006 Colorado human trafficking laws, significant 2014 legislative improvements brought Colorado's definition of human trafficking in children and adults in line with most other states around the country. Colorado House Bill 14–1273 also established the Governor-appointed Colorado Human Trafficking Council (CHTC), signaling human trafficking as a State priority. The CHTC's membership structure followed the United Nations "4P" comprehensive framework cited in international and federal instruments. Council members included survivors and governmental and non-governmental stakeholders from around the State, widening the response field beyond prosecution and survivor protections to fold in prevention and partnership efforts. Additionally, anti-trafficking coalitions were sprouting around the State to shore up regional and sector-specific efforts (e.g., child welfare); currently, 18 citizen-led and professional partnership efforts throughout Colorado.

The Laboratory to Combat Human Trafficking (LCHT) has participated in Colorado's evolving statewide anti-trafficking efforts since 2005. In its early years, LCHT began its efforts as the Colorado initiative of a Washington, D.C.-based organization, affording a national perspective to the Colorado anti-trafficking landscape. After nearly five years, the need for Colorado-centered responses and commitment to providing community-based research led the Colorado coordinators to depart the national organization and create a separate nonprofit, the Laboratory to Combat Human Trafficking.

Over its 18-year history, LCHT has witnessed the steady rise of survivor leadership, the evolution of trauma-informed investigations and survivor-centered prosecution responses, the introduction of alternative forms of justice, and, importantly, the complexities of partnership. As a non-governmental organization (NGO), LCHT's participation in many Colorado partnerships has allowed it to work with federal and state "systems actors" and grassroots organizations. With its foundation in providing training and technical assistance, LCHT has learned from and alongside partners to understand the nuances of human trafficking in Colorado. We have observed the siloed nature of anti-trafficking efforts and the lack of a cohesive picture beyond prosecution counts; this is where research and the need for good data are considered.

## Communities Need Good Data

From a state-level perspective, 20 years since the passage of the Trafficking Victims Protection Act, Colorado, has been characterized as a "hotbed" of human trafficking because of its high number of investigations. This claim is not unique to Colorado, as anti-trafficking advocates and researchers seek an understanding of the scope of human trafficking across the United States. We must be cautious with such statements, as every State struggles to understand and comprehensively measure human trafficking within its borders. Like most states, Colorado has no central mechanism to measure or track the problem. LCHT's research endeavors have sought to learn *how*, and *which* organizations and agencies are responding to human trafficking around our State and have highlighted strengths and gaps in local response in the context of funding fluctuations, pandemic pivots, and adaptations over time.

While data on the prevalence of human trafficking remains insufficient in Colorado and worldwide, we have several ways to track reported cases in the state. And, as awareness of human trafficking grows, and a more nuanced understanding of the complexities of both labor and sex trafficking develops, we see the opportunities for data collection on incidences also increase. The CHTC is tasked with collecting and reporting on these data annually. Before the 2014 legislative update, Colorado had successfully prosecuted two of ten human trafficking cases where Colorado's statutes were used to charge someone with either labor or sex trafficking. Since 2015, post-legislative updates, there have been 267 unique human trafficking cases in the state, resulting in 200 human trafficking convictions (cases where the perpetrator was acquitted of human trafficking most commonly ended in a plea deal) (Colorado Division of Court Services, 2022). In subsequent years, Colorado has continued to improve and update human trafficking legislation. One significant bill that resulted in a new source of reporting and data was the Child Sex Trafficking as a form of the Child Abuse law of 2016. This law required mandatory reporters of child abuse to report child sex (and later also labor) trafficking. In the first year of collecting reports to the Colorado Child Abuse Hotline (2018), there were 325 reports. The number of reports has remained consistently over 300 since 2018. The Colorado Human Trafficking Hotline is another tool for data collection. Similar to the National Human Trafficking Hotline, this statewide tip and referral hotline collect data from callers and texters reporting cases of trafficking and seeking resources for support and/or a criminal justice response. In the early days of the hotline (2007–2013), it received 30–60 calls yearly. However, hotline calls have grown exponentially in the last 10 years. In 2022, the hotline received over 1,000 from more than 800 unique individuals. One additional source of data collected on incidences of human trafficking in Colorado is from our NGO collaborators across the State, some of whom received federal or state funding to support survivors. These data indicate hundreds of victims of trafficking each year in the state who reach out to the hotline or directly to service providers for support who do not report the crime to law enforcement (Colorado Department of Public Safety, 2022; Colorado Division of Court Services, 2022).

While country-level reporting is a crucial feature of the annual TIP report, we have a far better-nuanced understanding as one of the 50 states represented within the more extensive United States report. It calls for a broader question as to whether any states have accurate estimates given the challenges of data sharing and the lack of comprehensive databases that gather data into a single estimate that will better support community-level anti-trafficking responses. For now, gaps remain for ways that states can understand how we are progressing systematically and comprehensively to address human trafficking overall.

Community-level data require clearly defined geographic boundaries, inclusive definitions for what data include, and standards for good data. Data collection activities have historically fallen under the purview of funders, governments and research institutes within Research Intensive Universities. Funders hold significant power in determining who is deemed worthy of conducting research and what research questions are worth asking (INCITE!, & Incite! Women of Color Against Violence, 2007), and communities often push back on extractive data collection methods and reasonably question *who* gets counted in the data (Colorado Health Foundation, 2023; Dean-Coffey, 2018; Equitable Evaluation Initiative, 2018; Wilkerson, 2020). Our NGO position and history in the local movement allow us to build on well-established partnerships and conduct community-based participatory research to ensure community-centered and survivor-partnered research designs.

Like so many researchers and anti-trafficking organizations, we grapple with the larger question of how states know the problem(s) they are solving in their community responses to human trafficking. Our training, leadership, and hotline programs have afforded us the questions, strengths, and challenges in meeting community needs. For example, we hear about the struggles involved with data collection at the organizational level, the grant protections surrounding data sharing, and the lack of collective community databases that would paint a comprehensive picture of the collaborative efforts of task forces and coalitions. Community members implore us to critically examine response approaches beyond prosecution counts; we have heard how systems have failed the most vulnerable.

Our longevity in the field has allowed us to understand the complexities of what community members call "data" and the deafening call for counts of prosecutions as the measure of success. It is rare for cross-system data sharing to occur due to legal and grant restrictions; in the cases of prevention outreach and hotline endeavors, the key data outcomes are referral counts, underscoring the importance of providing access and connecting people to resources beyond cases. Beyond the data systems that track prosecutions, we widen the definition to encompass diverse efforts – survivor identification, service counts, centralized survivor experiences, anecdotes, and community narratives. With a collection of good qualitative and quantitative data, we can better convey an understanding of human trafficking within Colorado that does not resort to fear-based tactics or solely rely on the criminal justice system. Conducting community-based participatory research enabled us to bridge systems and grassroots efforts (A. Miller et al., 2023).

Despite these challenges, the data matter – we have observed numerous instances where good, inclusive data drive political and systems buy-in, including funding. Good data increase responsible public awareness initiatives, helping community members and professionals understand what human trafficking looks like in their communities (both urban and rural) and resources to respond. Good data increases victim identification, investigations and prosecutions, and long-term survivor services. Without good data, funders are reluctant to commit funds to anti-trafficking initiatives or operate under the misapprehension that they are uniquely separate from other forms of violence and exploitation. Without quality data, first responders miss or misidentify victims of this form of exploitation.

### Moving Beyond Assumptions and Best Guesses

The Colorado Project identifies promising practices and areas for improvement from survivors, practitioners, and researchers, gathering insights that can foster partnerships, shape policy, and identify critical opportunities for the anti-trafficking movement. The impetus for LCHT's Colorado Project (and we suspect the case is similar for many other NGOs) was to advance the movement beyond assumptions and best guesses by providing a baseline data measure to compare future efforts. LCHT has conducted three iterations of the Colorado Project (Laboratory to Combat Human Trafficking, 2013a, 2013b, 2019a, 2019b), with the resulting reports and Colorado Action Plans produced in 2013, 2019, and 2023. We began with the broad question of whether there was a problem in Colorado and, what it would take to end human trafficking, how we would capture responses comprehensively and not simply prosecutions. We gathered data on who provided prevention, protection, prosecution, and partnership efforts, but more importantly, how they were offered within our diverse Colorado communities. We also asked about the types of exploitation regions across the State were seeing and how they showed up for services.

Innovative efforts to change how questions are asked and shaped by community members have been underway in the name of equity and inclusion. One resonant reflection posed in community research states, "If evidence matters, we must care about how it gets made" (Chicago Beyond, 2023). The design of the Colorado Project has maintained its steadfast commitment to inclusion on multiple levels (reflected in social ecology and multidisciplinary collaboration), in the service of co-designing solutions instead of simply pointing out problems. LCHT has hosted various convenings and recorded community needs through the multisector creation of the supplemental Colorado Action Plans.

Doing so is not without its challenges. Accountability from the perspective of an NGO looks like advocacy to amplify statewide gaps and to continually engage other sectors to better understand the diversity of complex challenges across the 64 counties and 18 task forces and coalitions. Further, we explore the complexity of compounding variables from a community perspective; we cannot focus solely on numbers without context. Each Colorado community has created community responses through best-informed guesses, assumptions, and piecemeal approaches, often with limited resources and diverse community will. As the field builds better bases of evidence accounting for these numerous community variables, hope remains for sustaining the steady pace of social change.

### *Building a More Sustainable Movement*

LCHT has partnered with survivors and leaders in parallel movements like LGBTQI rights groups or Murdered and Missing Indigenous Relatives Task Forces, victim service providers, prevention educators, coalitions, and law enforcement, investing time in building relationships with system leaders. This work is rooted in both evidence and a deep respect for the lived experiences of the many marginalized communities that have historically been left out of anti-trafficking collaborations and efforts (Fehrenbacher et al., 2020; Laboratory to Combat Human Trafficking, 2013b; Lockyer, 2022; McKenzie, 2023; Survivor Alliance and the University of Nottingham Rights Lab, 2020). By showing up as allies and collaborators to learn from and with community members, deeply listening to their challenges, and readily supporting them when requested, LCHT has developed trusting and sustained relationships with survivors, practitioners, and systems and non-systems agencies across the State.

As one example, working alongside Native American communities in Colorado and expanding knowledge of how the crime of human trafficking and the epidemic of Murdered and Missing Indigenous Relatives intersect is a vital component of LCHT's goals of inclusivity in our work and a comprehensive and culturally appropriate response to the crime in Colorado. Historically, Native American communities in Colorado have been largely excluded from anti-human trafficking conversations, misidentified in investigations, and prohibited from accessing culturally appropriate resources due to this exclusion. As allies and accomplices, we have respectfully worked to earn and build trust with Native American community members in urban areas of Colorado (where many Indigenous people in the State reside) and in rural communities located in the southwest Four Corners area, including two reservations adjacent to the Navajo Nation. Building from natural introductions over the last decades, LCHT respectfully participated in community conversations and training led by tribal leaders, actively listened to and integrated their wisdom, and learned alongside communities. As indicators of our ongoing commitment to the region, in 2022, La Plata County and the Southern Ute Reservation were two of LCHT's ten most visited regions in the State. Through these reliable connections and exchanges, we continue to authentically work together toward expanding knowledge and resources inclusive of indigenous communities.

## Respect That Communities are Doing the Best They Can to Collaborate with the Tools They Have Available

LCHT's various vantage points within the Colorado movement have enabled us to hear one straightforward premise statewide: No matter when or how community leaders take up the mantle to initiate responses to human trafficking, they do the best they can with the tools they have available at the time.

Many of the current anti-trafficking task forces and community coalitions have sustained their work through global and national pivots, among them the COVID-19 pandemic and movements urgently calling for racial justice, trans justice, immigrant justice, and ending violence.

Intersectional and interprofessional collaborations are critical to comprehensive community responses that must be transparent and tailored to unique community geographies and demographics. *Intersectional* collaborations span sectors (e.g., criminal justice and human services) and disciplines (e.g., social work, international studies, and gender studies) (Foot, 2015), while the act of *interprofessional* collaboration bridges across organizational protocols, agency missions, and movements. Interprofessional efforts require deep and complex discussions, debates, and consensus about how partners work in complementary ways. Importantly, attention to intersectional *identities* ensures that survivors lived experiences and practitioners who are people of color and identify as LGBTQI (among many possible intersectional identities) are essential. LCHT, in its role as a community partner, has offered training, convenings, toolkits, and blogs to specifically support capacity; recent efforts have focused on supporting protocol development for partnerships and agencies working in targeted sectors. LCHT's programs have granted us access to community discussions where diverse partners often start with a shared understanding of exploitation and violence and the dedication to building safe communities.

As a result of sitting in the range of discussions with numerous stakeholders over the years, we are seeing an evolution in Colorado of how this type of inclusive collaboration allows for an exchange over the nature of violence and exploitation – of root causes – across our communities. We hope that inclusive and cross-issue partnerships will be one of the keys to sustaining anti-trafficking efforts.

## Next Steps on Horizon: Moving the Proverbial Needle

Human trafficking has long been a challenge and will continue to be so, as global estimates show that the number of trafficked individuals has increased in recent years (U.S. Department of State, 2020; International Labor Organization, Walk Free & International Organization for Migration, 2022). The evolving nature of this human rights abuse requires organizations and systems to remain ever-vigilant and adaptive to changes in knowledge and resources. In our experience, partnering allows us to more robustly understand the complexities of both responses (i.e., who falls through proverbial "cracks") and the root causes of violence and exploitation in communities. In 2017, LCHT launched a significant undertaking around our long-term organizational vision, outlining a 2035 vision and detailed monitoring, evaluation and learning plans geared toward impact evaluation. Reflecting on how we might address the conditions that enable exploitation to occur, we set out to consider global root causes like far-reaching poverty, political strife, public health emergencies, war, and terrorism that can lead to displaced individuals, families, and even communities, making more people vulnerable to trafficking. We also consider climate change, other environmental issues, economic migration, systems perpetuating inequality, and civil unrest that create geopolitical, social, and economic concerns. We define new goals and learning questions and create an impact framework to guide LCHT in addressing these root causes.

Colorado Project Action Plan 2023 aims to identify far fewer concrete recommendations that reflect the most pressing needs emerging from the Colorado Project focus groups, interviews, and survey data. We hope that this narrowed focus on concrete recommendations will improve momentum, political will, and partnership opportunities (Laboratory to Combat Human Trafficking, 2021), creating a guiding roadmap for filling some of the most critical gaps.

The work of comprehensively combating human trafficking is reflected in the name of our organization and the mission, vision, and values that drive LCHT's work. As we do our part in moving the proverbial needle to end human trafficking, we see clearly the complexities of anti-trafficking work that require honoring community strengths and ensuring a mix of diverse perspectives in this laboratory. We see what is possible in creatively innovating to comprehensively fill gaps, how critical thinking supported by evidence-based research can pave new pathways, and how pivots in times of uncertainty prevail with community leaders' resilience, tenacity, and wisdom.

## Disclosure statement

No potential conflict of interest was reported by the author(s).

## ORCID

Annjanette R. Alejano-Steele http://orcid.org/0009-0009-3563-9502

## References


Alejano-Steele, A., Finger, A., & Landerholm, M. (2019). Chapter 14: Service coordination: Building a multi-agency community-based coalition. In M. Burke (Ed.), *Working with the human trafficking survivor: What therapists, human service and health care providers need to know* (pp. 167–190). Routledge.

Chicago Beyond, (2023). https://chicagobeyond.org/researchequity/

Colorado Department of Public Safety. (2022). 2022 Colorado human trafficking council annual report. Retrieved from: https://cdpsdocs.state.co.us/ovp/Human_Trafficking/report/2022-Annual-Report-Full.pdf

Colorado Division of Court Services. (2022). Human trafficking cases reported/prosecuted within 22 judicial districts, 2015–2022 § 18-3-503 C.R.S., § 18-3-504 C.R.S., and § 18-3-504 (2) C.R.S.; Division of Court Services, State of Colorado: 2022.

Colorado Health Foundation. (2023). Colorado Collaboratory on Equitable Evaluation. https://coloradohealth.org/colorado-collaboratory-equitable-evaluation#:~:text=The%20Colorado%20Collaboratory%20will%20provide,and%20learn%20from%20one%20another.

Dean-Coffey, J. (2018). What's race got to do with it? Equity and philanthropic evaluation practice. *American Journal of Evaluation*, *39*(4), 527–542. https://doi.org/10.1177/1098214018778533

Equitable Evaluation Initiative. (2018). Shifting the evaluation paradigm: The equitable evaluation framework™ https://www.equitableeval.org/ Retrieved March 22, 2023.

Fehrenbacher, A. E., Musto, J., Hoefinger, H., Mai, N., Macioti, P. G., Giametta, C., & Bennachie, C. (2020). Transgender people and human trafficking: Intersectional exclusion of transgender migrants and people of color from anti-trafficking protection in the United States. *Journal of Human Trafficking*, *6*(2), 182–194. https://doi.org/10.1080/23322705.2020.1690116

Foot, K. (2015). *Collaborating against human trafficking: Cross-sector challenges and practices*. Rowman & Littlefield.

INCITE!, & Incite! Women of Color Against Violence. (2007) . *The revolution will not be funded: Beyond the nonprofit industrial complex*. INCITE!, & Incite! Women of Color Against Violence, South End Press.

International Labour Organization, Walk Free, and International Organization for Migration. (2022). Global estimates of modern slavery: Forced labour and forced marriage. In *International Labour Organization (ILO), Walk Free, and International Organization for migration(IOM)*. Geneva. https://www.Walkfree.org/reports/global-estimates-of-modern-slavery-2022/.

Laboratory to Combat Human Trafficking. (2013a). *Colorado Project National Survey Report*, https://combathumantrafficking.org/report-downloads/LCHT-ColoradoProject_NationalSurveyReport.pdf

Laboratory to Combat Human Trafficking. (2013b). *Colorado Project Statewide Data Report*. https://combathumantrafficking.org/report-downloads/LCHT-ColoradoProject_StatewideDataReport.pdf

Laboratory to Combat Human Trafficking. (2019a). *Colorado project to comprehensively combat human trafficking 2.0*. https://combathumantrafficking.org/wp-content/uploads/2020/11/Colorado_Project_2_0-by_LCHT.pdf

Laboratory to Combat Human Trafficking. (2019b). Colorado Action Plan 2.0. In *Laboratory to combat human trafficking*. CO. https://combathumantrafficking.org/report-downloads/Action_Plan_2_0-by_LCHT.pdf

Laboratory to Combat Human Trafficking. (2021). *Partnership Toolkit*. Available at https://combathumantrafficking.org/toolkit/

Lockyer, S. (2022). Beyond inclusion: Survivor-leader voice in anti-human trafficking organizations. *Journal of Human Trafficking*, *8*(2), 135–156. https://doi.org/10.1080/23322705.2020.1756122

McKenzie, S. (2023). Listen to black survivors. Blog. Polaris. Retrieved April 27, 2023 at https://polarisproject.org/blog/2023/02/listen-to-black-survivors/

Miller, A., Alejano-Steele, A. R., Finger, A., & Napolitano, K. (2022). The Colorado project to comprehensively combat human trafficking: Community-based participatory research in action. *Journal of Human Trafficking*, *8*(1), 59–81. https://doi.org/10.1080/23322705.2021.2019532

Miller, A., Laser, J., Alejano-Steele, A., Napolitano, K., George, N., Connot, N., & Finger, A. (2023). Lessons learned from the Colorado project to comprehensively combat human trafficking. *Societies*, *13*(3), 51. https://doi.org/10.3390/soc13030051

Survivor Alliance and the University of Nottingham Rights Lab. (2020). Nothing about us without us. Survivor Alliance and the University of Nottingham Rights Lab. Retrieved March 12, 2023 at https://static1.squarespace.com/static/5ee517995ce62276749898ed/t/5f215611a49b295221978a72/1596020247172/briefing_nothing_about_us_without_us.pdf

U.S. Department of State. (2020). *U.S. Department of State. Trafficking in Persons Report*: Accessed on 9/18/2022 at https://www.state.gov/humantrafficking-about-human-trafficking/#:~:text=With%20an%20estimated%2024.9%20million,them%20for%20their%20own%20profit.

Wilkerson, I. (2020). *Caste: The origins of our discontents.* Random House.

# Index

Note: Tables are indicated by **bold**.

FSC
www.fsc.org
MIX
Papier | Fördert gute Waldnutzung
FSC® C083411

Kolibri 360 GmbH
Ferdinand-Jühlke-Straße 7
99095 Erfurt, Deutschland
produktsicherheit@kolibri360.de